"A fascinating and evidence-packed book on how poverty cannot be viewed in isolation but must be considered in connection with overlapping and compounding crises – which often affect poor communities simultaneously. The author makes a compelling argument for integrating poverty reduction programs with, for example, disaster relief and conflict resolution programs."

Dr Christian Oldiges, Chief, Social Policy Section, Socio-economic Development Division, United Nations Economic Commission for Africa.

"In this incisive and timely work, Dr. Vidya Diwakar masterfully unpacks the complex interplay between poverty and multiple overlapping crises, offering a rich conceptual framework, grounded evidence from diverse country contexts, and urgently needed policy pathways to disrupt cycles of vulnerability. A must-read for researchers, practitioners, and policymakers alike."

Dr Orzala Nemat, Director, Development Research Group LTD, and former Director, Afghanistan Research and Evaluation Unit.

"Diwakar's excellent volume makes an important contribution to the literature by exploring the complex interrelationships between poverty and 'polycrisis' (related to the intersection of climate change, conflict and economic instability) drawing on multiple countries in the Global South and a range of research methods. It will be of great interest to scholars, policy-makers and practitioners, working on poverty and related issues."

Professor Paul Shaffer, Department of International Development Studies, Trent University.

Poverty in Polycrisis

We are living in a period of global volatility in which intersecting crises are combining with devastating impacts for people already living in and near poverty. This book carefully examines the dynamics of these crises and challenges us to find new ways forward for policies and programming that more effectively meet the needs of the world's most vulnerable populations.

The book highlights the lived experiences of those who are impacted most by poverty amidst intersecting crises—namely climate-related disasters, violent conflict and economic instability—drawing on the author's 15 years of experience in sub-Saharan Africa and South and Southeast Asia. It examines chronic poverty amidst intersecting crises, highlighting how new impoverishment may emerge, and even surprisingly how some people manage to escape or remain out of poverty in these contexts. It offers a multi-scalar, dynamic investigation of poverty and intersecting crises to identify ways forward for policies and programming.

It is an essential read for practitioners working on poverty and inequality reduction in low- and middle-income countries, as well as for researchers and students of global development, environmental and peace studies, and economics, public policy and sociology more broadly.

Vidya Diwakar is Deputy Director of the Chronic Poverty Advisory Network, and a Senior Research Fellow at the Institute of Development Studies, UK.

Rethinking Development

Foreign Aid and its Unintended Consequences
Dirk-Jan Koch

Reformers in International Development
Five Remarkable Lives
David M. de Ferranti

Young People in the Global South
Voice, Agency and Citizenship
Edited by Kate Pincock, Nicola Jones, Lorraine Van Blerk and Nyaradzayi Gumbonzvanda

Community-Led Development in Practice
We Power our Own Change
Edited by Elene Cloete and Gunjan Veda

Post-Development from the Global South
Radical Alternatives or Ambivalent Engagements?
Edited by Sally Matthews and Alba Castellsagué

Digital Inclusion in an Unequal World
An Emancipatory Manifesto
Tim Unwin

Poverty in Polycrisis
Dynamic Pathways for Lasting Change
Vidya Diwakar

The Decentralization Delusion
Challenging the Underlying Assumptions of Development
Ruby Dagher and Nana Afia Aku Ofori-Yentumi

For more information about this series, please visit: www.routledge.com/Rethinking-Development/book-series/RDVPT

Poverty in Polycrisis
Dynamic Pathways for Lasting Change

Vidya Diwakar

Routledge
Taylor & Francis Group
LONDON AND NEW YORK

Designed cover image: Cover artwork by Vidya Diwakar.

First published 2026
by Routledge
4 Park Square, Milton Park, Abingdon, Oxon OX14 4RN

and by Routledge
605 Third Avenue, New York, NY 10158

Routledge is an imprint of the Taylor & Francis Group, an informa business

British Library Cataloguing-in-Publication Data
A catalogue record for this book is available from the British Library

Library of Congress Cataloging-in-Publication Data
A catalog record has been requested for this book

ISBN: 978-1-032-82136-8 (hbk)
ISBN: 978-1-032-82134-4 (pbk)
ISBN: 978-1-003-50312-5 (ebk)

DOI: 10.4324/9781003503125

Typeset in Times New Roman
by Taylor & Francis Books

Contents

Figures

Tables

Boxes

Foreword

Vidya Diwakar has written a book for our times. There has been much discussion in the media and academia on polycrisis, or multiple, intersecting crises, across the world during recent years. Little of that has focused on the substantial effects of simultaneous or sequenced crises on poor and vulnerable people in the world's remaining high-poverty countries in Africa and Asia. *They* are used to managing their personal crises due to ill health preventing work, deaths of breadwinners and family breakdown including in gender and generational relationships, often with little assistance from the mechanisms wealthier people fall back on—insurance, enforced agreements about separation or divorce, protections for widows or the welfare state more generally. However, they face much greater challenges when they have to cope additionally with larger-scale crises such as conflict, drought, flood, food price inflation. Coping strategies which can limit the damage from a single crisis may not be up to the scope of these twenty-first-century challenges.

The objective of this book is to examine the research evidence on how poor and vulnerable people cope in such situations, to identify what external interventions are useful in supporting their strategies and helping them to avoid deeply damaging coping strategies, and to learn what approaches governments and other potential supporters of poor people and their livelihoods can best offer to prevent or mitigate the worst effects of polycrisis. Understanding how people survive such situations, and how some even prosper, is the foundation for the analysis.

It closes with suggestions for national and international decision-makers which are supported by or draw on the evidence about building resilience to individual and multiple crises and about putting an emphasis on recovery into all development as well as humanitarian programming, both of which actions go well beyond the current agendas in those fields. The book is an exhortation in these difficult times of financial resource constriction and loosening social contracts to innovate and think and act out of siloes to assist the world's poorest and most vulnerable face the crises we all have to face, if differentially.

The book is also well founded conceptually, with an equal focus on both equity and risk, two ideas which are rarely combined: disaster risk management and humanitarian actors tend to focus on managing risk; development specialists focus on equity as well as growth. Combining these perspectives is yet another attempt to bridge the humanitarian–development divide. This is timely, as the highest risk humanitarian situations are protracted crises, which have been starved of developmental investments because of the levels of risk, where humanitarian support, increasingly in the form of social cash transfers as well as food, medical and educational assistance, can provide a basis for development, but where people in those situations clearly want and need so much more. The solution to the protracted nature of the crises also requires new approaches to development, even while crises persist, to address the inequalities which underlie long-term conflict or vulnerability to other crises, as this can help open the way to peace and resilience.

The book offers critical perspectives, too, about the damage which inadequately assessed and mitigated policies can inflict on poor people. These include macroeconomic or public health management policies which are implemented for good reasons, but without the risk and equity perspectives and accompanying actions which could prevent harm.

This is a book for today's decision-makers in international and national development, for humanitarian actors at all levels and for the students who will be tomorrow's decision-makers. It merits translation into many languages.

Andrew Shepherd
Director, Chronic Poverty Advisory Network
Honorary Research Associate, Institute of Development Studies
Senior Research Associate, ODI, London

Acknowledgements

This book stems from my work within the Chronic Poverty Advisory Network (CPAN), where I have been collaborating for over a decade with exceptional qualitative, quantitative and mixed methods researchers based in the UK and in CPAN's 17 low- and middle-income partner countries to understand drivers of poverty dynamics. The book draws on existing CPAN country studies of poverty dynamics, builds on discussions within the network and newly re-analyses CPAN mixed methods data to draw out crisis intersections.

CPAN partners played an instrumental role in qualitative data collection for previous country studies of poverty dynamics across the 15 countries analysed in this book, for which I am hugely appreciative. I am also indebted to the people and communities who gave their time and openness to be interviewed in those country studies of poverty dynamics.

I am moreover hugely grateful to Lucia da Corta for a remarkably nuanced and thorough review of an earlier draft of the book, Andrew Shepherd for invaluable comments on Chapters 1, 2, 7 and 8 and Kate Bird for equally insightful comments on Chapters 3 to 6. In this process they drew on their extensive experience researching poverty dynamics, including by leading several of the poverty dynamics country studies on which my analysis builds. Andrew's intellectual and policy-driven leadership of CPAN has been a source of inspiration in this process.

Alongside this, I would like to sincerely thank Marta Eichsteller for her coding of pre-pandemic qualitative data across most countries presented in this book as part of mixed methods country studies of poverty dynamics, which meant that my re-analysis of the qualitative dataset was significantly streamlined. Cheryl Joseph provided exceptional research assistance, mapping projects and programmes that responded to polycrisis across the countries represented in this book, which formed much of the evidence base on which Chapter 7 draws.

Finally, my thanks go to the FCDO, particularly the DEEP programme, for financial support for part of this book's development and its Open Access costs. My views expressed in this publication do not necessarily reflect the views of the FCDO, and all errors remain my own.

Part I

Framing the polycrisis: theory, concepts and poverty linkages

1 Introduction

The world is experiencing a period of global volatility, characterised by the intersections of violent conflict, climate-related disasters, economic polarisation and the legacies of a global pandemic. While intersecting crises are not new (Morin and Kern, 1999), recent years have seen fundamental systemic shifts in global systems, norms and institutions that characterise and reinforce these crises. The increasing frequency and intensity of climate-related disasters is adding a new urgency to the issue. These interrelated crises in turn have devastating impacts on people in or near poverty, who often have limited ability to withstand their immediate effects and longer-term consequences.

Yet while scholars and practitioners recognise the presence of multiple crises, current approaches to conceptualise or respond to their intersections are inadequate. This is partly because such approaches fail to adopt a multi-scalar framing of crises dynamics and their intersections, do not sufficiently consider the lived experiences of those who are affected most, and without a temporal or longitudinal approach tend to focus on proximate drivers or conflate these with the root causes of crises. These omissions are important limitations especially given the widespread impoverishment that crises and their intersections generate, driving in turn the amplified and protracted nature of polycrisis. Perhaps as a result, poverty eradication policies remain focused on pushing people out of poverty and much less so on preventing people from falling into poverty. Consequently, failure to account for polycrisis at best leads to ineffective policies to eradicate poverty. At worst, it drives the creation or continuity of harmful policies that may amplify disadvantages of the most vulnerable people in society.

The purpose of this book is to explore the relationship between poverty and polycrisis to inform more coherent and responsive policy and programming—particularly interventions that prioritise prevention, resilience-building and recovery. To support this objective, the book draws on case studies of poverty dynamics amidst intersecting crises from 2010 to the present in sub-Saharan Africa and South and Southeast Asia. It examines chronic poverty amidst polycrisis, new impoverishment that may emerge and even, surprisingly, how some people manage to escape or remain out of poverty in these contexts through adaptation supported by pro-poor systems. If offers a multi-scalar

DOI: 10.4324/9781003503125-2

and dynamic investigation of poverty and polycrisis focused on learning from typical cases as well as outliers.

They book's key argument is that different strands of polycrisis—namely climate-related disasters, violent conflict and economic instability—can reinforce each other to drive, prolong and deepen poverty. These structural and increasingly frequent intersecting crises subvert state support, strain livelihoods, forcibly separate people and shatter assets and lives. Alongside their direct impacts, polycrisis interact with micro-level shocks and stressors and overwhelm multi-level coping systems, reinforcing negative feedback loops. The negative poverty dynamics in turn affect the legitimacy of the social contract, including how social factors like class, gender or race shape those state–citizen relationships. Negative poverty dynamics also affect the nature of sustainable growth from below. Together, these factors combine to produce or amplify polycrisis. This poverty–polycrisis trap constrains preventive and recovery-focused solutions.

These juxtapositions and feedback loops are important because they can help to understand the ways in which crises evolve, become crises, intersect and escalate—and how solutions are shaped in response. Drawing on multi-country evidence, this book calls on governments and donors to start treating poverty as an emergency requiring proportional responses that recognise its acute, protracted and dynamic dimensions. The latter necessitates moving beyond crisis-by-crisis responses to instead build a more equitable (i.e. fair and inclusive) risk-informed system that spans both resilience (systematically pre-crisis and during crisis) and recovery (post-crisis) phases.

Why focus on poverty dynamics amidst intersecting crises? First, this focus is critical to better reflect the current context of poverty eradication. As outlined in Chapter 2, macro-level crises are intersecting in unprecedented ways. Yet, there is limited recognition of the ways that different crises can intersect to differentially affect people's wellbeing and pathways out of poverty. This is discussed in Chapters 3 and 4 in terms of climate–economic crises and climate–conflict crises, respectively, and in Chapter 5 in relation to humanitarian contexts which are distinguished by the scale and intensity of complex, protracted crises often compounded by a breakdown of the rule of law. Second, there are also anticipated long-term effects of these crises, investigated through erosive coping mechanisms and forms of sustained impoverishment and intergenerational persistence of poverty, as discussed in Chapter 6, but also the ways in which some households are navigating these challenging contexts to escape or remain out of poverty. Finally, intersecting crises and their consequences for people in and near poverty have clear implications. Ways forward for policies and programming that can more effectively meet the needs of the most vulnerable populations in low- and middle-income countries are discussed in Chapters 7 and 8.

This chapter proceeds as follows. Section 1.1 overviews key themes explored in this book focusing on theories and concepts that underpin pathways into and out of poverty amidst crises. Section 1.2 then summarises the mixed methods evidence base underlying the analysis. Section 1.3 concludes, highlighting the contributions of the analysis.

1.1 Key terms

1.1.1 Poverty and its dynamics

There is a long history of work on understanding poverty. Pre-eminent amongst this is the recognition of poverty as an absolute concept, typically referring to a level of resources needed to sustain life and linked to a lack of basic needs. In this vein, poverty is commonly measured through a person's income or consumption falling below a national or international poverty line. Other conceptualisations acknowledge relative poverty where notions of participation in society and access to resources gain eminence, draw attention to human development and capabilities including links with multidimensional deprivations, or centre on issues linked to social exclusion and vulnerability. Critical perspectives further expand this view, framing poverty as rooted in structural and historical inequalities, shaped by intersecting identities such as gender, race and caste, and sustained through unequal social relations. Post-colonial and participatory approaches also call attention to locally grounded understandings, lived experiences and the role of power in defining and addressing poverty.

In this book, the analysis of poverty using household survey data relies on monetary definitions, primarily reliant on national poverty lines. Recognising, however, that this is a narrow conception of deprivation, we also expand this remit to capture participatory definitions of what it means to be living in poverty and the multiple deprivations and conditions of vulnerability this may generate—thus moving towards a more multidimensional perspective of poverty embedded in different forms of assets, capabilities and wellbeing. This starts from a universalist definition (see Annex Table B1) that has been adapted in different country contexts by people in and near poverty interviewed as part of the evidence base outlined in Section 1.2.

The focus of this book moreover goes beyond static measures of poverty to draw attention to its dynamics over time (see Box 1.1 for definitions). This builds on a history of work on poverty dynamics, most notably by the Chronic Poverty Research Centre (CPRC) in the 2000s and its successor, the Chronic Poverty Advisory Network (CPAN), in the 2010s and 2020s. CPAN has argued that getting to zero poverty requires not just tackling the chronicity or long-term persistence of poverty, but also preventing households from falling into poverty or becoming impoverished, and ensuring that escapes from poverty are sustained over time (Shepherd et al., 2014). This dynamic conception of poverty has clear implications, recognising that some of the types of policies to tackle chronic poverty (e.g. through agricultural market improvements or affirmative actions) may be notably different from policies meant to prevent impoverishment (e.g. disaster risk management or universal health coverage) or sustain poverty escapes (e.g. through land policy reforms enabling renting in and out) (Shepherd et al., 2014).

Box 1.1 Definitions of poverty trajectories used in this study

Chronic poverty is long-term poverty that persists over many years or even a lifetime and is often transmitted across generations (i.e. intergenerational poverty). The quantitative data refers to households consistently under the reference poverty lines across waves. In the qualitative data, it refers to households that have been living in poverty for five years or more.

Transient poverty in the quantitative analysis refers to the process whereby a person or household that is non-poor (above the reference poverty line or in the top three participatory wealth ranking (PWR) levels) at some point in the survey subsequently slips into poverty (under the poverty line or in bottom three PWR levels)—hence experiencing impoverishment, a transitory escape from poverty, or churning around the poverty line. We further disaggregate by these more detailed trajectories across the quantitative and qualitative analysis.

Resilience refers to individuals or households that either escape from or remain out of poverty over the long term (a sustained poverty escape or remaining never poor across survey waves of the quantitative data, or in the last five years or more in the qualitative data). Specific trajectories within these categories (e.g. sustained poverty escapes, never being poor) are delineated in the quantitative and qualitative analysis where relevant.

Source: adapted from Shepherd et al., 2014.

Given the acute dimensions of poverty in emergency contexts that stems from structural conditions generating both poverty and crises, this book argues that it is time to start treating poverty itself as an emergency. This would mean that we respond to poverty with the same urgency and scale as a humanitarian crisis. It also means that we need to integrate long-term poverty solutions into emergency responses systems. Indeed, treating poverty as an emergency that requires a crisis-level response leads us to a focus on balancing general capacity-strengthening to build resilience with policy responses during and post-crises that can rebuild people's lives and livelihoods.

1.1.2 Polycrisis

The premise of this book is that today's poverty and the context through which it is generated or amplified is increasingly marked by climate change, violence, economic crises and their intersections. In other words, we live in an era marked by crises. A crisis may be "a disruption that physically affects a system as a whole and threatens its basic assumptions, its subjective sense of self, and its existential core" (Pauchant and Mitroff, 1992 p. 15). However, this definition somewhat obscures the complexity inherent in crises, where starting points may be difficult to define as crises may instead slowly develop over time and become protracted (Williamson and Courtney, 2018; Boin et al., 2020; OECD, 2017). Indeed, many crises may become protracted and so there is a case for viewing "crisis as context", insofar as it becomes a constant feature rather than a one-off disruption (Vigh, 2008). In other words, crises often stop being temporary emergencies and instead become part of the everyday reality people live through.

Other common strands of studies of the multi-dimensional nature of crises draw attention to their structural dimensions and processual focus as well as the intersectionality of impacts and the window of opportunity these may offer to reset or strengthen resilience (Harvey, 2012; Klein, 2008; Sen, 1980; Nixon, 2011). We bring together these various components to view crises as: 1) multi-scalar disruptions with deep and society-wide impact, 2) often of a slow-burning or protracted nature with evolving dimensions rather than isolated events, and which are 3) socially constructed, shaped by structural conditions and lived experience. In other words, we use the term "crisis" to refer to both sudden-onset events (such as climate-related disasters, outbreaks of violence or financial crashes) as well as their underlying slower-moving or structural trends (like prolonged drought, persistent insecurity or chronic economic stress).

This book focuses on three types of crises, reflected in environmental, social and economic domains and embedded within varied governance structures and political challenges. These three crises are outlined below.

Environmental: the environmental crises domain within this book focuses on climate-related disasters, especially hydrological and geophysical hazards that generate these disasters. These disasters threaten the health of ecosystems and people. They may further be embedded in longer-term "slow-burning" factors, such as widespread pollution, biodiversity loss, deforestation or desertification, and the exploitation of natural resources. Unsustainable human activities and overconsumption by the rich can degrade or destroy the natural environment and make the effects of natural hazards particularly severe. Within our focus on climate-related disasters, Chapters 3–6 draw attention especially to floods and drought within these categories, though they also make reference to typhoons, storms, extreme temperatures and epidemics more broadly. In addition, the COVID-19 pandemic (biological hazard) is also reflected in the data analysis, but mainly in terms of the economic crisis it generated.

Economic: issues such as high inflation and debt may converge to create macro-level economic crises. The COVID-19 pandemic was also an economic crisis due to the impacts of lockdowns, job losses, disrupted supply chains, inflation, reduced remittances and pressure on basic goods and services. On top of this, policy responses partly related to the pandemic were overly harsh, poorly targeted or failed to cushion the impact on poor and vulnerable groups—such as inequalities in vaccine rollout, rapid devaluation without accompanying safety nets, subsidy removal or monetary tightening that exacerbated inequality. Finally, this was situated within a broader set of intersecting economic crises during the COVID-19 period, such as the Russia–Ukraine war (affecting fuel and food prices), global supply chain issues and domestic policy choices (e.g. removal of fuel subsidies), all of which compounded the pandemic's effects—especially for those already living in or near poverty. In our analysis, we focus especially on high rates of revenue loss and price hikes in key goods and services consumed by people in poverty as symptomatic of these crisis conditions. While these indicators may exaggerate the scale of economic crisis when viewed in isolation, they help reveal the deeper, structural drivers of crisis conditions, pushing us beyond an episodic understanding of economic shocks.

Social: our main focus in this domain is on violent conflict, as one of the most acute and destabilising forms of social crisis. We approach violent conflict as a social process given that it results from the "systematic breakdown of the social contract resulting from and/or leading to changes in social norms, which involves mass violence instigated through collective action" (Justino et al., 2013). Such conflict often stems from a failure to protect survival, basic needs, freedoms and opportunities for prosperity, especially for certain demographic groups liable to take up arms and excluded or disadvantaged political groups. There are however variations that characterise these interactions, depending for example on the intensity and locality of violence, histories of conflict, types of violence (e.g. inter-state wars, armed insurrections or other forms of organised violence) and ideologies of armed groups. Alongside this, we also consider other forms of insecurity such as theft, kidnapping or assault that also reflect a breakdown in the social contract.

When multiple crises emerge, they may invariably intersect, not least given the often-underlying systemic failures that drive chronic crises. For example, weak environmental regulation can lead to underfunding climate adaptation that in turn drives inadequate disaster preparedness. Similarly, unequal access to resources can render people in poverty disproportionately affected by climate change and drive social unrest and conflict. Indeed, this recognition of polycrisis refers to the "complex intersolidarity of problems, antagonisms, crises, uncontrolled processes, and the general crisis of the planet" (Morin and Kern, 1999, p. 74). In today's era, defined as one of polycrisis, scholars draw attention to the difficulty in separating out these crises and their role moreover in generating feedback loops that reinforce the crises (Tooze, 2022; Davies and Hobson, 2023). Other strands of the polycrisis literature in low- and middle-income countries variably focus on public administration responses to crises, the need for poverty reduction to be achieved without high costs to the environment, challenges and opportunities in the Global South pointing to technological advancements and regional cooperation, and how to meet challenges in global futures, to name a few (Moloney et al., 2025; Adam and Rena, 2025; World Bank, 2024; Albert, 2024).

There are equally critiques of the term "polycrisis". These are linked to its ambiguity, lack of novelty given interconnected crises historically linked to capitalism and colonialism in the Global South, and its potential sidelining of the political root causes of crises (Fraser and Vogel, 2017; Tooze, 2022). Its implications in turn may drive "crisis fatigue" or institutional paralysis given the inherent complexity and salience of intersecting crises. Moreover, crises are often only recognised "externally". For example, it is framed as a "crisis" only when it reaches a certain scale or intensity declared nationally or picked up by media and defined by these sources (Roitman, 2013; Calhoun, 2004). This is in stark contrast to people living in villages or peri-urban areas reflecting on drought conditions outside of key events, or on more localised or lower-intensity events such as uneven rains that are made significant by climate change. More broadly, crises are commonly normalised in poorer communities. Whose voices are heard in crises contexts and who receives help often reflect political decisions made by those in power.

These caveats in mind, we use the term "intersecting crises" (or "polycrisis") to describe how multiple crises—like conflict, climate-related disasters and economic instability—increasingly overlap and reinforce each other. Our definition recognises that these intersections are often rooted in deeper structural and political issues as well as fundamental systemic shifts in global systems, norms and institutions that themselves characterise and reinforce crises. Our use is pragmatic, recognising the rising frequency of these crises in the context of climate change and how they compound to affect people's lives and systems.

It is worth noting that the focus on climate-related disasters, violent conflict and economic crises—embedded often in challenging geopolitical and governance contexts—is intentional, and distinct from other emerging scholarship on polycrisis noted above. While there are certainly other crises operating in these contexts and reflected in the wider polycrisis discourse (e.g. public health crises, technological crises), drawing attention to these three crises helps bound the analysis and focus on a set of crises consistently prevalent in a number of low- and lower middle-income countries. There are also various shocks, including ill health, and stressors that interact with or may be a consequence of these crises. This book is nevertheless focused on macro-level crises—i.e. those that are large-scale events impacting populations and sectors more broadly and requiring national or international responses. We consider the relationship of these macro-level crises with micro-level poverty dynamics to complement other studies that investigate how more localised household shocks can combine to negatively affect poverty dynamics. At the same time, recognising that macro-level crises can drive the salience of micro-level shocks to worsen macro-level crises, we acknowledge this interplay and its effects especially in Chapter 5.

As noted above, some argue that these macro-level intersections are not new (Henig and Knight, 2023). However, though multiple crises have been common historically, there is now a structural basis for change, as Chapters 3–6 acknowledge. In other words, there are more fundamental systemic shifts in global systems, norms and institutions, and coupled with the increasing frequency and intensity of climate-related disasters these add urgency to the issue. Indeed, this book argues that the interrelated intersections of crises today are contributing to increasingly precarious pathways out of poverty. Yet theoretical contributions on these issues to date have limitations, as considered in Chapter 2, which in turn motivate a stronger processual focus on multi-scalar, dynamic systems of change through which polycrisis may constrain pathways out of poverty and instead drive downward mobility or persistent poverty. These processes are then empirically analysed and policy implications derived in the subsequent chapters.

1.2 Mixed methods evidence

This book draws on mixed methods evidence carried out by CPAN—where the author is based—in 15 low- and middle-income country contexts (Afghanistan, Bangladesh, Cambodia, Ethiopia, India, Kenya, Malawi, Nepal, Niger, Nigeria, the Philippines, Rwanda, Tanzania, Zambia and Zimbabwe) across regions of sub-Saharan Africa and South and Southeast Asia. There is thus a richness of multi-country as well as multi-author collaboration behind much of the work on poverty dynamics (see Annex Table B2). The 15 countries capture around 40% of the world's population in poverty according to latest (typically 2018–22) figures and offer the ability to draw out common threads around poverty eradication in challenging contexts. The mixed methods data sources that are analysed in Chapters 3–6 are presented in Table 1.1 and comprise household survey data and panel datasets, life history interviews, focus group discussions and key informant interviews.

In Cambodia, Nepal, the Philippines, Rwanda and Zimbabwe, we only rely on qualitative survey data due to the absence of shock modules (e.g. in Cambodia and Zimbabwe), consumption aggregates (Nepal) or data access limitations (Rwanda, the Philippines). The qualitative data conducted by CPAN in these countries are summarised below:

- Cambodia: 60 LHIs, 36 FGDs, 24 KIIs in 2018; 35 LHIs, 8 FGDs, 4 KIIs in 2021.
- Nepal: 40 LHIs, 8 FGDs, 18 KIIs in 2017; 20 sentinel household interviews,[1] 5 KIIs in 2020.
- Philippines: 40 LHIs, 8 FGDs, 19 KIIs in 2018; 20 sentinel household interviews in 2021.
- Rwanda: 229 LHIs, 42 FGDs, 35 KIIs in 2017/19; 20 sentinel household interviews in 2022.
- Zimbabwe: 60 LHIs, 8 FGDs, 10 KIIs in 2021.

Finally, the mixed methods data is complemented by a rapid mapping of programmatic responses to polycrisis in the same 15 countries, identifying programmes that respond to more than one of the three crises simultaneously. This mapping is the basis of the analysis presented in Chapter 7.

Table 1.1 Countries and data sources analysed in this book

Country	*Data (years/households)*		*Qualitative (sample/date)*		
	Dataset and years	*Number (HH)*	*LHI*	*FGD*	*KII*
Afghanistan	Income, expenditure and labour force survey: 2019/20	8,139	42 (2021)	N/A	28
Bangladesh	Bangladesh Integrated Household Survey: 2011/12, 2015, 2019	5,019	40 (2020)	14	23
	PPRC-BIGD COVID-19 livelihoods survey 2020/21 (5 rounds)	3,380	60 (2024)	9	N/A
Ethiopia	LSMS—Ethiopia Socioeconomic Survey: 2018/19, 2021/22	4,875	98 (2017)	10	13
			20 (2021)	N/A	6
India	India Human Development Survey: 2004/05, 2011/12	40,018	31 (2020)	6	11
			39 (2021)	3	20
Kenya	Kenya Integrated Household Budget Survey 2015/16	21,773	60 (2017)	4	15
			20 (2020)	N/A	N/A
Malawi	LSMS Malawi Integrated HH Panel Survey: 2010/11, 2013	3,079	40 (2018)	8	23
			20 (2021)	N/A	7
Niger	LSMS National Survey on Household Living Conditions and Agriculture (ECVM/A): 2011, 2014/15	3,436	40 (2018)	8	13
			49 (2020)	16	4
Nigeria	LSMS General Household Survey: 2010/11, 2012/13, 2015/16, 2018/19	1,326	N/A (2021)	N/A	35
	National Longitudinal Panel Survey 2020–21 (12 rounds)	1,472	120 (2023)	24	26
	NLPS phase 2, 2021–22 (5 rounds)	2,181			
Tanzania	LSMS National Panel Survey: 2008/09, 2010/11, 2012/13, 2014/15, 2018/19	771	80 (2017)	32	44
	High frequency phone surveys 2020–24 (11 rounds)	1,003	54 (2022)	24	18
Zambia	Living Conditions Measurement Survey: 2022	8,307	146 (2020)	27	16
			20 (2021)	N/A	5

Note: in Afghanistan, Kenya and Zambia, we rely on cross-section quantitative survey data in the absence of panel data. All surveys are nationally representative, except Bangladesh which is representative only of rural areas. See Annex B (Table B2) for list of organisations and team leads for the qualitative data collection. HH = households, LHI = life history interview, FGD = focus group discussion, KII = key informant interview.

1.2.1 Methodological approach

The approach relies primarily on recent mixed methods data especially since 2010, combining quantitative panel data analysis with in-depth insights from the lived experiences of people in and near poverty within contexts of intersecting crises. The CPRC promoted and developed the systematic use of this Q-squared approach involving panel data and the encouragement of its integration with qualitative life history methods to understand chronic poverty (Shaffer, 2013). CPAN further built on this tried-and-tested approach across its 17 partner countries, and it was then adapted by the author in some countries to better explore the salience and effects of intersecting crises. In all cases, research ethics have been considered when designing the research and collecting the qualitative data. We also secured in-country ethical approvals where relevant and submitted ethics forms within organisations where CPAN was hosted during the time of research. The methods are further discussed in a range of existing CPAN poverty dynamics country studies and summarised below.

Quantitative analysis

CPAN's mixed methods analysis typically begins with secondary quantitative data, comprising publicly available and nationally representative household panel survey datasets. Panel surveys repeatedly visit the same households over a number of years and thus enable the tracking long-term of changes in poverty and wellbeing (i.e. they allow households' poverty trajectories to be constructed). The surveys also include modules on negative events that households experience in the 12 months preceding the survey, from which we extract variables across the survey period reflecting environmental, economic and social crises, for example:

- Environmental: drought, flood, storm, crop diseases/pests, livestock disease, cyclone, irregular rainfall, landslides, river erosion, earthquakes.
- Economic: loss of regular job or business, inability to access inputs, unusually low price for agricultural outputs, unusually high costs of agricultural inputs, unusually high prices for food, large decrease in price of agricultural products.
- Social: violence, conflict, local unrest, ethnic clashes, insecurity, theft (e.g. of crops, livestock, business assets or other belongings).

In this book, the self-reported data on these crises are harmonised across countries. In Bangladesh, Nigeria and Tanzania, these household surveys were further merged with actual data on violent conflict events and fatalities, alongside climate-related data on precipitation and flooding spanning the entire panel period.[2]

Across countries, the final dataset is then analysed descriptively and through regression-based methods utilising a harmonised set of correlates of poverty trajectories. Descriptively, this book newly disaggregates poverty trajectories across countries by the intersection of different types of crises within our polycrisis framing. We also rely primarily on a multinomial logistic regression model to assess correlates of poverty trajectories amidst intersecting crises. This model is selected given the categorical unordered outcome and its common use in assessing correlates of poverty trajectories (e.g. Diwakar and Shepherd, 2022). Our main model of interest is conditional on exposure to climate-related disasters (focused on floods and droughts where possible[3] to disaggregate). In our main model:

$$\ln\left(\frac{Pr(Poverty_i = j)}{Pr(Poverty_i = J)}\right) = \beta_{0j} + \beta_{1j}\ Crises_i + \beta_{2j}\ \mathrm{Div_i}\ +$$

$$\beta_{3j}\ (Crises_i \times \mathrm{Div}_i) + \beta_{4j}\ H_i + \beta_{5j}\ Area_i$$

estimated conditional on household exposure to climate-related disasters, where

- captures whether household is chronically poor, experiences poverty transience, or the base category *j* of resilience. (Given the absence of panel data in Afghanistan, Kenya and Zambia, it instead refers to household poverty status);
- is a vector capturing the presence of conflict or economic crises (marked by price and/or revenue shocks);
- includes diversified livelihoods or assets of the household head (whether they own an non-farm enterprise, livestock, cultivable land, and the head's level of education), given its centrality to building household resilience (see Box 2.1);
- is a vector of other household controls (religion, gender, age and age-squared, household size, work in agriculture, asset value, electricity, and receipt of remittances) selected due to its salience in the wider literature on poverty correlates.
- is a vector covering whether the household lives in an urban or rural area, and the region in which the household resides.

Our models cluster standard errors at the enumeration area. Deeper dives on crises and poverty trajectories in Bangladesh, Nigeria and Tanzania also complement this with various sensitivity measures and models, and further descriptive analysis from the COVID-19 period (see Diwakar and Brzezinska, 2023; Diwakar and Brzezinska, 2024; Diwakar, 2025). We also account for heterogeneity by disaggregating the analysis or drawing on disaggregated analysis in existing country studies, based on area of residence, gender and in some cases youth status where balancing criteria in the survey data permits.

Alongside our main conditional model, we also run alternative specifications. These include a specification with the same set of non-interacted regressors on the full unconditional sample (Annex Tables D1–D2). It also includes a specification with three-way interactions (four-way in the case of Nigeria and Afghanistan given the presence of triple crises) between intersecting crises and potential diversification-focused moderators on the full sample (Annex Tables D3–D7).

Across quantitative models and methods, it is worth stressing that our analysis is not causal but descriptive and/or indicative of correlations between key variables. Even so, they remain important in providing insights into the presence of poverty dynamics and wellbeing amidst polycrisis and the bundles of factors linked to poverty dynamics.

Qualitative data collection and analysis

The poverty trajectories identified from the panel data allowed for a selection of subnational areas for qualitative investigation that was carried out by CPAN researchers[4] between 2016 and 2024. Subnational areas were identified with a view to having a balanced coverage of regions with a high level of poverty escapes, those with high chronic poverty, and others with high impoverishment. Following this, the in-country qualitative research team helped narrow down the site selection to specific wards, villages or peri-urban or urban neighbourhoods that reflected the broader regions in which they were based. For example, if the region was selected as representing a relatively high share of sustained escapes from poverty, there was an attempt to choose a village or urban neighbourhood that similarly experienced high poverty escapes over a timeframe comparable to the panel survey.

The qualitative data comprises life history interviews, gender-disaggregated focus groups, discussions with long-term community residents and key informant interviews. Our life history sample per country is balanced by gender, area of residence (commonly rural, peri-urban and urban sites) and across our poverty trajectories of interest. On the latter, we selected respondents such that around 30–40% had experienced sustained poverty escapes, 40% had experienced impoverishment or transitory poverty escapes, and 20–30% had experienced chronic poverty. The life history respondents were also selected to represent a variety of livelihoods relevant in our study sites and the wider regions in which they were embedded. In Nigeria and Bangladesh, where qualitative interviews explicitly focused on intersecting crises were conducted, we also identified sites with recent violent conflict and/or climate-related disasters as a basis for data collection.

The focus of the qualitative data was to better understand the pathways and processes that kept: 1) some households entrenched in chronic poverty while 2) others escaped or remained out of poverty in the contexts of uncertainty and rapid change that increasingly characterise our world today, and 3) others, not surprisingly, fell into poverty. Alongside this, sentinel households were reinterviewed in a subset of countries during COVID-19 to understand changing wellbeing over time. This data is not meant to be representative in a statistical sense. Except for Nigeria and Bangladesh, the purpose of data collection was also not focused on understanding intersecting macro-level crises, though meso- and micro-level shocks and stressors have nevertheless long been key drivers of chronic poverty and impoverishment. Nevertheless, starting with lived experiences and poverty trajectories and inductively examining the salience of polycrisis across countries provides a powerful means of understanding how structural vulnerabilities shape pathways into and out of poverty amidst polycrisis.

This set of interviews was analysed using coding software to identify common attributions characteristic of different pathways into and out of poverty, and process tracing methods to examine the sequence and interaction of events that affected household poverty trajectories. This multi-scalar approach—spanning individual, household, community and district and national levels—is summarised in da Corta et al. (2021). Pre-pandemic qualitative data was first coded by a CPAN coding specialist (Eichsteller, see Acknowledgements) in country-level studies of poverty dynamics. The author reanalysed that coded qualitative dataset for this book to identify key attributes specific to polycrisis. This was undertaken alongside process tracing methods and a new analysis of qualitative data during and since the COVID-19 pandemic to present a longitudinal understanding of change from 2010 to present.

Iteration and integration

The qualitative data collection and analysis was used to iteratively probe the quantitative panel data around discrepancies, newly uncovered issues, and areas for further investigation. This combination of retrospective longitudinal data allows for a sound understanding of correlates of nationally representative poverty dynamics alongside a deeper focus on the causal sequences and pathways that affect people's ability to escape or remain out of poverty. With the qualitative findings validating the quantitative analysis and also providing new lines of inquiry, there is a stronger robustness to the conclusions that are drawn.

This approach is methodologically underpinned by a commitment to matrix thinking, to enable the type of intersectional, multi-level longitudinal analysis covered in this book. Matrix thinking may be defined as "the dynamic juxtaposition of complex symbolic structures, gradients, analogies, narratives, and entire paradigms" in ways that allow researchers to "focus upon their differences, similarities, and connections" (Corbally and Rappaport, 2015; Wynn and Coolidge, 2011). It is applied in this book as a meta-methodological lens—that is, not just combining methods, but enabling reflexive movement across paradigms (e.g. economic vs participatory framings of poverty), scales and temporalities. In doing so, it enables the analysis of overlapping frameworks of poverty (e.g. defined through monetary absolute metrics alongside participatory wealth rankings) and the layering of this across time to allow an assessment of change through panel data and life histories, an analysis of multiple scales from individual narratives up to policy discourse, and the integration of different types of quantitative and qualitative data across these scales.

1.2.2 Strengths and limitations

There are some caveats to bear in mind in this analysis. The timeframes of analysis are different across countries, in terms of first and last panel waves but also the number of waves per country, which affect the rates of poverty dynamics estimated using panel data. The quantitative analysis explores polycrisis through the presence of self-reported climate-related disasters, conflict or insecurity, and price or revenue shocks in the year preceding the survey, which ignores crises in other years, may involve reporting bias or be endogenous if self-reporting is influenced by poverty trajectories. However, we also consider the actual exogenous presence of floods, droughts and violence-related fatalities in Tanzania, Bangladesh and Nigeria across the panel period, where a deeper analysis, including sensitivity tests, was produced in country-level mixed methods studies. Our goal with these analyses is not for causal inference or cross-country comparative analysis of salience of polycrisis, but for examining relationships between polycrisis and poverty dynamics.

In all cases, polycrisis is defined through the presence of more than one crisis which may intersect at any point over the survey period, which again is affected by the number of waves and different timeframes that may sometimes reflect sequential rather than intersecting crises. We nevertheless also consider crises intersections over the same year in the cross-section datasets. Moreover, our conceptual recognition of crises as structural rather than episodic—discussed in Chapter 2—motivates this focus on crises across the panel period. This recognises crises as ongoing over long periods (e.g. climate change unfolding across the entire panel period) and the roots of crises in long-term systemic inequalities, governance failures and often entrenched exclusions rather than their being short-term or one-off events.

Regarding the poverty measure, the quantitative and qualitative data rely on different definitions of poverty which may lead to different trajectories being constructed even of similar types of households. Data quality considerations also mean that in some countries (Tanzania, Nigeria) a relative poverty status and trajectory is constructed (e.g. based on whether households are in the bottom two consumption quintiles) rather than comparing consumption to a national or international poverty line.[5] National poverty lines also vary somewhat across countries, though not hugely as they are based on nutritional measures within certain boundaries.

Finally, the participatory wealth ranking exercise to establish poverty levels and dynamics in the qualitative data collection also reduces comparability across and even within countries—albeit less so if a universal category benchmark is used. Indeed, there is significant similarity in the categorisations which emerge from participatory definitions in high-poverty low- and lower middle-income countries (see Annex B).

Though strict comparability may not be possible from this multi-country mixed methods dataset, it nevertheless does allow for contextually relevant, people-centred understandings of pathways into and out of poverty amidst crises, and some intuitive comparison where the indicators are similar. There are also other important strengths of this approach worth highlighting in its application to analysing polycrisis. First, focusing on dynamism (of poverty and of polycrisis) is central to better understanding the pathways and processes that keep some households entrenched in chronic poverty while others may escape or remain out of poverty in the contexts of uncertainty and rapid change that increasingly characterise our world today.

Second, an emphasis on multi-scalar drivers of poverty dynamics, bridging macro and micro discourses on the maintainers and interrupters of poverty, is important in better conceptualising and responding to the interplay of poverty and crises. Poverty dynamics—for example the degree of impoverishment or downward mobility compared to the experience of sustained upward mobility and the formation of a middle class—also affect the fortunes of the socio-political contract and resulting potential or actual political violence. As an example of this, in northern Nigeria long-term entrenched poverty and exclusion from government support, downward mobility and impoverishment, growing inequality, and resource competition underlie the origins and spread of conflict in the region. As such, the relationship is often bidirectional between poverty dynamics and crises.

Finally, by providing a conceptual, empirical and also practical basis to develop more holistic policies aimed at sustained poverty eradication, this book and the methods on which it draws attempt to act as a bridge between readers in research and policy.

1.3 Conclusion and contributions

The book makes key contributions to the literature. First, the literature on poverty dynamics does not systematically consider overlapping effects of or responses to conflict, climate-related disasters and economic crises. A key limitation of single-crisis studies is that they often treat all subsequent problems as cascading from that one crisis. For example, some attribute currency devaluation solely to a climate disaster, when it typically results from a mix of interacting factors—such as rising global fuel prices, poor economic management and pre-existing fiscal instability. These intersect in different ways across contexts. In Zambia, for instance, international and domestic economic pressures had already led to devaluation even before the COVID-19 pandemic and the severe 2024 drought.

Ignoring these intersections is an important limitation especially given the widespread impoverishment, economic precarity and destitution processes that crises and their intersections generate. "Maladaptive economic policies", a term developed and discussed in Chapter 3, may moreover emerge to respond to polycrisis but end up causing more harm and impoverishment. In the absence of attention to research on polycrisis and poverty, scholars and practitioners alike do not adequately understand (or seek to understand) the ways in which crises intersect to affect impoverishment or downward mobility more broadly. They are also unable to learn from outliers, for example where individuals may have managed to escape poverty in these challenging contexts. Relatedly, poverty eradication policies remain focused on pushing people out of poverty and much less so on preventing people from falling into poverty.

This book offers a corrective to more narrowly-focused, single-topic research works. It helps move beyond simplified causal narratives to show how climate, economic and conflict crises can overlap, reinforce one another and jointly shape outcomes like inflation, poverty or institutional breakdown. Its analysis of these pathways provides the basis for an underlying argument to move international discourse to consider poverty as an emergency.

In line with this, Chapter 2 draws attention to new ways of conceptually understanding the interplay between crises and poverty eradication, especially from 2010 to present. Chapters 3–6 then adopt a dynamic mixed methods investigation of different types of crises (economic, social and environmental) and how they variably intersect across space and time to affect people's pathways into and out of poverty. This is an application of the conceptual framework presented in Chapter 2.

Chapters 7 and 8 extend the conceptual lens discussed earlier to consider policy and programmatic responses to poverty reduction amidst polycrisis. These chapters offer a topical analysis of existing interventions in focus countries, from which it is possible to identify effective practices to support poverty eradication in challenging contexts. With the Sustainable Development Goals (SDGs) nearing their deadline but falling official development assistance (ODA) budgets weakening international support to poor countries grappling with polycrisis, there is a renewed urgency needed to support the reduction and eradication of global poverty.

Second, while there has been growing attention to impacts of polycrisis in international development (e.g. World Bank, 2024), this operates at different scales. Namely, there remains a separation between the literature focused on mainly micro-level drivers of poverty dynamics and institutionally focused macro-level research on polycrisis. The latter, as considered in Chapter 2, is often captured in multidimensional indices of state fragility (e.g. World Bank, 2023; OECD, 2022; Fund for Peace, 2022) or other research on crises that is primarily practitioner-focused (e.g. operational humanitarian reports such as post-disaster needs assessments) or with limited conceptual development. Instead, there remains limited explicit engagement with *how* different macro-level crises intersect to affect people's wellbeing over time (and differentially by gender, age, religion and ethnicity intersecting with poverty).

In this book, we consider how macro-level crises may interact with micro- and meso-level shocks and stressors to reinforce negative poverty trajectories to round out this multi-scalar focus, as discussed in Chapter 5. We also consider how macro-level crises interact with household-level livelihood correlates of poverty trajectories in Chapters 3–6. Together, this helps expose the conflation of root causes of poverty with its proximate drivers, which otherwise obscures the role of global interdependencies, entrenched inequalities and historical processes in shaping vulnerabilities experienced during polycrisis today. These juxtapositions are important because they can also help to understand the ways in which crises evolve, become crises and intersect, and the preventive and recovery-focused solutions to polycrisis. This pursues the theme of bidirectionality and treating poverty as an emergency as discussed above, an important contribution of this analysis. Indeed, this book does not just argue though that crises cause poverty, but that structural poverty and vulnerability already exist and are amplified when multiple crises intersect.

Consideration of multiple scales and demographics is also important for the study of crises. In terms of demographics, the book regularly disaggregates results by intersecting inequalities (e.g. due to gender, poverty status and area of residence). In many ways, these intersecting inequalities at the micro-level mirror the context of polycrisis at the macro-level.

In terms of scale, while crises are structural, all three types of crises examined (environmental, social, economic) can be highly localised and much more intense in specific areas and for specific groups, even when national-level data or media narratives do not reflect this. For instance, qualitative data from a district in Zambia pointed to successive droughts so severe that they were described locally as a "famine" despite it not being classified as a national drought year during the period of data collection. The same holds with regards to different types of subnational conflict in Nigeria, or for rural versus urban dimensions of economic crises. The case studies in this book make an argument for more consideration to be accorded to these localised dimensions of crises.

Third, data on wellbeing amidst polycrisis is patchy at best. Regarding quantitative data, even where household surveys are conducted in conflict-affected contexts, they rarely cover the most insecure areas experiencing heightened violence within countries due to access and security concerns. There are advances in merging these datasets with the actual prevalence of violence and climate-related disasters, but fine-tuned area-based disaggregated data even on the more tractable economic crises remain scarce in household surveys or other repositories.

In terms of qualitative data, too, lived experiences of people in and near poverty amidst polycrisis—especially those experiencing intersecting inequalities—are also inadequately captured. Yet qualitative and participatory insights can considerably strengthen our understanding of the processes, pathways and sequences through which complex crises intersect to affect poverty dynamics, as demonstrated by the COVID-19 bulletins published in near-real-time by CPAN during the pandemic (CPAN, 2020).

A holistic conceptual framework that investigates global polycrisis and in its application links these with meso- and micro-level shocks and stressors can help contribute to more effective policies aimed at sustained poverty reduction in the years ahead. Indeed, as this book argues, the impact of crises on poverty is now so severe that "normal" slow-paced development responses are no longer adequate. Empirical analysis along these lines can also improve our applied understanding of these challenges, their bidirectionality (as discussed in Chapter 2) and potential entry points for policymaking and programming. This book bridges macro and micro discourses on poverty drivers. It does this with a view towards providing a more holistic, multi-scalar understanding of the causes of, and in turn solutions to, sustained poverty reduction that accounts for the complexity and uncertainty underpinning lived experiences in today's complex context of polycrisis.

Notes

1 Strategically chosen households balanced across gender, livelihoods and poverty trajectories to act as a sample for re-interviews.
2 This merging based on geocoded data (based on a 20-kilometre radius of the household for conflict and floods, and 55-kilometre radius for precipitation given the varying granularity of these datasets) was done as part of country-level studies on intersecting crises and poverty dynamics in these three countries, and presented in Diwakar and Brzezinska, (2023); Diwakar and Brzezinska, (2024); Diwakar, (2025). This merged dataset was harmonised and re-analysed for this book. In India, actual data on violent conflict fatalities due to Naxalite violence was also merged at the district level, as the household survey shocks module did not capture violence.
3 This was possible everywhere except Afghanistan, Kenya and India, where self-reported data did not enable disaggregation by floods and droughts.
4 In Bangladesh, India, Nepal, the Philippines and Kenya, the author was directly involved in the qualitative data collection and qualitative coding with research partners. In other cases, the author was part of a wider mixed methods team, with the qualitative coding instead conducted by Marta Eichsteller (see Acknowledgements). In this book, the full spread of qualitative data is re-analysed using the already coded datasets.
5 This is because of limited comparability of the consumption aggregate between survey waves. The relative definition means that some households may be poor based on being in the bottom two welfare quintiles but still live above the absolute poverty line, or vice versa. See Diwakar and Adedeji (2021) for discussion. Finally, in rural Bangladesh, the then $1.90 international poverty line (since updated) was used due to its inclusion in the panel survey. In other countries relying on absolute poverty lines, the national poverty line was used.

References

Adam, H. and Rena, R. (2025) *Polycrisis and economic development in the Global South*. Routledge.

Albert, M.J. (2024) *Navigating the polycrisis: Mapping the futures of capitalism and the Earth*. MIT Press.

Boin, A., Lodge, M. and Luesink, M. (2020) 'Learning from the COVID-19 crisis: An initial analysis of national responses'. *Policy Design and Practice*, 3(3): 189–204. doi:10.1080/25741292.2020.1823670.

Calhoun, C. (2004) 'A world of emergencies: Fear, intervention, and the limits of cosmopolitan order'. *Canadian Review of Sociology and Anthropology*, 41(4): 373–395.

Corbally, C. and Rappaport, M.B. (2015) 'Matrix thinking: An adaptation at the foundation of human science, religion, and art'. *Academia*. https://www.academia.edu/18598284/MATRIX_THINKING_AN_ADAPTATION_AT_THE_FOUNDATION_OF_HUMAN_SCIENCE_RELIGION_AND_ART.

CPAN (2020) COVID-19 Poverty Monitor. https://www.chronicpovertynetwork.org/covid-19.

da Corta, L., Diarra, A., Diwakar, V., Eichsteller, M., Harouna, A. and Poggi, C. (2021) 'Youth inclusion in labour markets in Niger: Gender dynamics and livelihoods'. Working Paper. https://www.chronicpovertynetwork.org/resources/2021/6/29/youth-inclusion-in-labour-markets-in-niger-gender-dynamics-and-livelihoods.

Davies, M. and Hobson, C. (2023) 'An embarrassment of changes: International relations and the COVID-19 pandemic'. *Australian Journal of International Affairs*, 77 (2): 150–168. doi:10.1080/10357718.2022.2095614.

Diwakar, V. (2025) 'Poverty dynamics amidst intersecting crises in Tanzania'. *Data and Evidence to End Extreme Poverty (DEEP) Working Paper*. https://povertyevidence.org/resources/poverty-dynamics-amidst-intersecting-crises-in-tanzania/.

Diwakar, V. and Adedeji, A. (2021) 'Poverty dynamics and social protection in Nigeria'. *Chronic Poverty Advisory Network Working Paper*. https://www.chronicpovertynetwork.org/resources/2021/6/28/poverty-dynamics-and-social-protection-in-nigeria.

Diwakar, V. and Brzezinska, I. (2023) 'Poverty dynamics amidst multiple crises in Nigeria'. *DEEP Working Paper 17*. doi:10.55158/DEEPWP17.

Diwakar, V. and Brzezinska, I. (2024) 'Poverty dynamics amidst intersecting crises in rural Bangladesh'. *DEEP Working Paper 22*. https://povertyevidence.org/wp-content/uploads/2024/06/Poverty-dynamics-amidst-multiple-crises-in-Bangladesh.pdf.

Diwakar, V. and Shepherd, A. (2022) 'Sustaining escapes from poverty'. *World Development*, 151: 105611. doi:10.1016/j.worlddev.2021.105611.

Diwakar, V., Walker, J.-A., Turnwait, M., Eichsteller, M. and Adeniran, A.P. (2025) 'Poverty dynamics and social assistance amidst intersecting crises in Nigeria'. *BASIC Research Working Paper 35*. Institute of Development Studies. doi:10.19088/BASIC.2025.004.

Fraser, N. and Vogel, L. (2017) 'Crisis of care? On the social-reproductive contradictions of contemporary capitalism'. In T. Bhattacharya (Ed.), *Social reproduction theory: Remapping class, recentering oppression*. Pluto Press. doi:10.2307/j.ctt1vz494j.6.

Fund for Peace (2022) Fragile States Index. https://fragilestatesindex.org/.

Harvey, D. (2012) 'The urban roots of financial crises: Reclaiming the city for anti-capitalist struggle'. *Socialist Register*, 48. https://socialistregister.com/index.php/srv/article/view/15644.

Henig, D. and Knight, D.M. (2023) 'Polycrisis: Prompts for an emerging worldview'. *Anthropology Today*, 39: 3–6. doi:10.1111/1467-8322.12793.

Justino, P, Brück, R. and Verwimp, P. (2013) *A micro-level perspective on the dynamics of conflict, violence and development*. Oxford University Press.

Klein, N. (2008) *Shock doctrine: The rise of disaster capitalism*. Penguin.

Moloney, K., Billingsley, G., Jeong, B.G., Sanabria-Pulido, P., Thornton, T.E. and Zeemering, E. (2025) *The Routledge handbook on crisis, polycrisis and public administration*. Routledge.

Morin, E. and Kern, A.B. (1999) *Homeland Earth: A manifesto for the new millenium*. Hampton Press.

Nixon, R. (2011) *Slow violence and the environmentalism of the poor*. Harvard University Press.

OECD (2017) 'Gender equality and women's empowerment in fragile and conflict-affected situations: A review of donor support'. *OECD Development Policy Papers No. 8.*

OECD (2022) 'States of fragility 2022'. OECD Publishing. https://www.oecd.org/en/publications/2022/09/states-of-fragility-2022_9ee73e08.html.

Pauchant, T. and Mitroff, I. (1992) *Transforming the crisis-prone organization: Preventing individual, organizational, and environmental tragedies.* Jossey-Bass.

Roitman, J. (2013) *Anti-crisis.* Duke University Press.

Sen, A. (1980) 'Famines'. *World Development*, 8(9): 613–621. doi:10.1016/0305-750X(80)90053–90054.

Shaffer, P. (2013) 'Ten years of 'Q-squared': implications for understanding and explaining poverty. *World Development*, 45: 269–285. doi: 10.1016/j.worlddev.2012.12.008

Shepherd, A., Scott, L., Mariotti, C., Kessy, F., Gaiha, R., da Corta, L. (2014) 'The chronic poverty report 2014–2015: The road to zero extreme poverty'. CPAN. https://www.chronicpovertynetwork.org/resources/2014/6/13/the-chronic-poverty-report-2014-15-the-road-to-zero-poverty.

Tooze, A. (2022) 'Welcome to the world of the polycrisis'. *Financial Times*, 28 October. https://www.ft.com/content/498398e7-11b1-494b-9cd3-6d669dc3de33.

Vigh, H. (2008) 'Crisis and chronicity: Anthropological perspectives on continuous crisis and decline'. *Ethnos*, 73(1): 5–21. doi:10.1080/00141840801927509.

Williamson, F. and Courtney, C. (2018) 'Disasters fast and slow: The temporality of hazards in environmental history'. *International Review of Environmental History*, 4 (2): 5–11. https://search.informit.org/doi/10.3316/informit.276681008839464.

World Bank (2023) 'Classification of fragile and conflict-affected situations'. *Brief.* https://www.worldbank.org/en/topic/fragilityconflictviolence/brief/classification-of-fragile-and-conflict-affected-situations.

World Bank (2024) *Pathways out of the polycrisis. Poverty, prosperity, and planet report 2024.* World Bank.

da Corta, L., Diarra, A., Diwakar, V., Eichsteller, M., Harouna, A. and Poggi, C. (2021) 'Youth inclusion in labour markets in Niger: Gender dynamics and livelihoods'. *Working Paper.* https://www.chronicpovertynetwork.org/resources/2021/6/29/youth-inclusion-in-labour-markets-in-niger-gender-dynamics-and-livelihoods.

Davies, M. and Hobson, C. (2023) 'An embarrassment of changes: International relations and the COVID-19 pandemic'. *Australian Journal of International Affairs*, 77 (2): 150–168. doi:10.1080/10357718.2022.2095614.

Diwakar, V. (2025) 'Poverty dynamics amidst intersecting crises in Tanzania'. *Data and Evidence to End Extreme Poverty (DEEP) Working Paper.* https://povertyevidence.org/resources/poverty-dynamics-amidst-intersecting-crises-in-tanzania/.

Diwakar, V. and Adedeji, A. (2021) 'Poverty dynamics and social protection in Nigeria'. *Chronic Poverty Advisory Network Working Paper.* https://www.chronicpovertynetwork.org/resources/2021/6/28/poverty-dynamics-and-social-protection-in-nigeria.

Diwakar, V. and Brzezinska, I. (2023) 'Poverty dynamics amidst multiple crises in Nigeria'. *DEEP Working Paper 17.* doi:10.55158/DEEPWP17.

Diwakar, V. and Brzezinska, I. (2024) 'Poverty dynamics amidst intersecting crises in rural Bangladesh'. *DEEP Working Paper 22.* https://povertyevidence.org/wp-content/uploads/2024/06/Poverty-dynamics-amidst-multiple-crises-in-Bangladesh.pdf.

Diwakar, V. and Shepherd, A. (2022) 'Sustaining escapes from poverty'. *World Development*, 151: 105611. doi:10.1016/j.worlddev.2021.105611.

Diwakar, V., Walker, J.-A., Turnwait, M., Eichsteller, M. and Adeniran, A.P. (2025) 'Poverty dynamics and social assistance amidst intersecting crises in Nigeria'.

BASIC Research Working Paper 35. Institute of Development Studies. doi:10.19088/BASIC.2025.004.

Fraser, N. and Vogel, L. (2017) 'Crisis of care? On the social-reproductive contradictions of contemporary capitalism'. In T. Bhattacharya (Ed.), *Social reproduction theory: Remapping class, recentering oppression*. Pluto Press. doi:10.2307/j.ctt1vz494j.6.

Fund for Peace (2022) Fragile States Index. https://fragilestatesindex.org/.

Harvey, D. (2012) 'The urban roots of financial crises: Reclaiming the city for anti-capitalist struggle'. *Socialist Register*, 48. https://socialistregister.com/index.php/srv/article/view/15644.

Henig, D. and Knight, D.M. (2023) 'Polycrisis: Prompts for an emerging worldview'. *Anthropology Today*, 39: 3–6. doi:10.1111/1467-8322.12793.

Justino, P, Brück, R. and Verwimp, P. (2013) *A micro-level perspective on the dynamics of conflict, violence and development*. Oxford University Press.

Klein, N. (2008) *Shock doctrine: The rise of disaster capitalism*. Penguin.

Moloney, K., Billingsley, G., Jeong, B.G., Sanabria-Pulido, P., Thornton, T.E. and Zeemering, E. (2025) *The Routledge handbook on crisis, polycrisis and public administration*. Routledge.

Morin, E. and Kern, A.B. (1999) *Homeland Earth: A manifesto for the new millenium*. Hampton Press.

Nixon, R. (2011) *Slow violence and the environmentalism of the poor*. Harvard University Press.

OECD (2017) 'Gender equality and women's empowerment in fragile and conflict-affected situations: A review of donor support'. *OECD Development Policy Papers No. 8*.

OECD (2022) 'States of fragility 2022'. OECD Publishing. https://www.oecd.org/en/publications/2022/09/states-of-fragility-2022_9ee73e08.html.

Pauchant, T. and Mitroff, I. (1992) *Transforming the crisis-prone organization: Preventing individual, organizational, and environmental tragedies*. Jossey-Bass.

Roitman, J. (2013) *Anti-crisis*. Duke University Press.

Sen, A. (1980) 'Famines'. *World Development*, 8(9): 613–621. doi:10.1016/0305-750X(80)90053–90054.

Shepherd, A., Scott, L., Mariotti, C., Kessy, F., Gaiha, R., da Corta, L. (2014) 'The chronic poverty report 2014–2015: The road to zero extreme poverty'. CPAN. https://www.chronicpovertynetwork.org/resources/2014/6/13/the-chronic-poverty-report-2014-15-the-road-to-zero-poverty.

Tooze, A. (2022) 'Welcome to the world of the polycrisis'. *Financial Times*, 28 October. https://www.ft.com/content/498398e7-11b1-494b-9cd3-6d669dc3de33.

Vigh, H. (2008) 'Crisis and chronicity: Anthropological perspectives on continuous crisis and decline'. *Ethnos*, 73(1): 5–21. doi:10.1080/00141840801927509.

Williamson, F. and Courtney, C. (2018) 'Disasters fast and slow: The temporality of hazards in environmental history'. *International Review of Environmental History*, 4(2): 5–11. https://search.informit.org/doi/10.3316/informit.276681008839464.

World Bank (2023) 'Classification of fragile and conflict-affected situations'. *Brief*. https://www.worldbank.org/en/topic/fragilityconflictviolence/brief/classification-of-fragile-and-conflict-affected-situations.

World Bank (2024) *Pathways out of the polycrisis. Poverty, prosperity, and planet report 2024*. World Bank.

Wynn, T. and Coolidge, F.L. (2011) 'The implications of the working memory model for the evolution of modern cognition'. *International Journal of Evolutionary Biology*: 1–12. doi:10.4061/2011/741357.

2 Conceptualising polycrisis and poverty dynamics

This chapter highlights current research and practice-oriented approaches to understanding polycrisis that acknowledge different intensities of crises implicitly or explicitly, such as through indices of state fragility and concepts of sustainable development. It outlines key limitations of these approaches in relation to understanding poverty and socio-economic mobility, a process which forms the basis for the introduction of a conceptual framework linking crises to poverty and wellbeing. This framework draws on insights from fragility and sustainable development concepts and uses an intersectional lens to focus on the multi-scalar processes and dynamic systems of change through which crises may rapidly combine, amplify vulnerabilities, and/or create uncertainties for poverty eradication. The chapter then relies on cross-country quantitative indicators to provide an international overview of the state of poverty dynamics and the prevalence of different types of crises today.

The chapter proceeds as follows: Section 2.1 critically assesses existing conceptual entry points to understanding poverty/wellbeing and crises, introducing a new conceptual framework guiding the analysis in the empirical chapters that follow. Section 2.2 then presents key statistics on poverty and crises, especially over the last 15 years. Section 2.3 offers concluding remarks.

2.1 A crisis of sustainability

2.1.1 Disciplinary approaches to conceptualising crises

Climate-related disasters, violent conflict and economic crises are amongst the most prevalent types of global crises facing our world today. Different paradigms and disciplines have different ways of conceptualising crisis, some of which were touched on in Chapter 1. For example, critical theory points to crises as structural (Harvey, 2010), anthropological approaches recognise its processual dimensions and local coping responses (Roitman, 2013; Calhoun, 2004), feminist and decolonial scholars point to its temporality and intersectional impacts (Nixon, 2011; Crenshaw, 1991), while development studies draw attention to vulnerability and resilience shaped by access, entitlement and governance (Sen, 1981; Béné et al., 2014; Cannon and Müller-Mahn, 2010; Scoones, 1998).

DOI: 10.4324/9781003503125-3

Different disciplines rooted in the three crises domains also have different foci. Economic crises are the subject of much macroeconomic literature, as preventing such crises is perhaps the single most important objective of macroeconomic policy. Economic crises in turn are attributed to various reasons, including inadequate demand (Keynes, 1936; Krugman, 1999), central bank failures linked to supply-side disturbances (Friedman and Schwartz, 1963; Lucas, 1977), unfiltered expansion of credit that distorts markets (Rothbard, 1963; Hayek, 1931), exploitation and inequality in capital accumulation (Marx, 1867) and increased risk-taking that drives instability (Minsky, 1986). There is some recognition furthermore of people in poverty being disproportionately affected (Ruel et al., 2010; Heltberg et al., 2012).

The literature on climate crises recognises their anthropogenic dimensions (i.e. driven by human activities), the increasing of greenhouse gas emissions beyond planetary boundaries (IPCC, 2021; Hansen et al., 2012; Rockström et al., 2009) and tipping points and feedback loops (Cox et al., 2000). There is also a recognition of a complex and dynamic system underlying these processes, and accordingly a range of assessment models have been developed to forecast impacts, most notably in the Intergovernmental Panel on Climate Change (IPCC) reports. The IPCC has also re-framed its conception of vulnerability as a function of exposure, sensitivity, and adaptive capacity, to situating it in a broader risk framework acknowledging its interactions with hazard and exposure (IPCC, 2021). Issues related to vulnerability and resilience are also often highlighted in climate discourses (Adger, 2006; Folke, 2006), drawing attention to the unequal impacts of climate change and crises (Roberts and Parks, 2007).

The conflict literature meanwhile recognises structural and proximate causes of violence (Kalyvas, 2006) alongside their microeconomic impacts on households (Justino et al., 2013). A seminal framing on conflict drivers distinguishes greed-driven conflicts, which emerge from control over resources and may be linked to the resource curse, from grievance-based conflicts, which can stem from exclusion, injustice and/or relative deprivation (Collier and Hoeffler, 2004). Some works link these issues furthermore to horizontal inequalities—i.e. those between identity groups (Stewart, 2008; Østby, 2008). Central to these framings is often a recognition of state fragility and/or the preceding concepts on which it builds (e.g. weak or failed states). This draws attention to weak capacity, legitimacy or authority to govern, uphold security, and deliver the goods and services that advance the interests of citizens (Rotberg, 2004). There are also various historic and geopolitical dimensions underlying the different types of crises analysed in this book.

2.1.2 Conceptualising multiple crises

Some work attempts to conceptualise multiple crises, for example in relation to economic crises and climate-related disasters and drawing attention to ex-ante and ex-post actions to minimise shock exposure and impacts (Skoufias, 2003; Antoniades et al., 2022), the conflict–climate nexus examining how climate change affects conflict and vice versa (Homer-Dixon, 1994; Kahl, 2006) or through conceptions of state fragility that recognise conflict, climate-related disasters and sometimes also economic crises (Box 2.1).

Fragility has received much attention in development discourse, with its scholars acknowledging its bidirectional relationship with poverty. Indeed, poverty rates are higher in fragile states on average. Moreover, countries that are consistently experiencing state fragility over time also have higher rates of poverty than those that used to be fragile in the early 2000s but then escaped this categorisation. In the latter, poverty rates have declined from 44% in 2000 to 19% in 2019. However, in countries experiencing chronic fragility, poverty rates hovered around nearly half of the population in the decade pre-pandemic (Corral et al., 2020).

Box 2.1 Crisis as multidimensional fragility

Concepts of fragility have been developed alongside an attempt to operationalise their definitions through indices of state fragility. Amongst the most prominent of these are produced by the World Bank, the OECD and the Fund for Peace (Figure 2.1). These lists have many differences emerging from conceptual heterogeneity as to what constitutes fragility and the indicators used for its proxy. For example, just 25 countries appear across the three lists, while 31 other countries appear on just one of the lists. It is clear from Figure 2.1 that the OECD's "States of Fragility" report contains the most expansive definition, comprising many countries, especially in Africa and Asia, that only appear on its list.

A focus on multi-crisis frameworks offers some useful perspectives, insofar as it acknowledges different dimensions of risk and uncertainty and draws attention to institutional weaknesses that may generate crisis-like conditions. However, such framings have also been criticised on the grounds of ambiguity. This is particularly pronounced in critiques of fragility, as showcased through the lack of consensus in the lists of countries presented in the three indices above, and which limits their operationalisation across countries (Shields and Paulson, 2019). Some argue furthermore that these concepts are Eurocentric in placing strong emphasis on formal institutions which neglect the important role of informal and traditional systems of governance that may drive state legitimacy in parts of the Global South (Booth, 2012; Chandler, 2006). There is thus potential scope for refinement to a degree, through a more inclusive, non-Eurocentric and widely-agreed definition between the different institutions.

At the same time, all these dominant framings obscure key issues. For example, the operational indices often mean that fragility (or crisis) is commonly viewed with pre-defined categorical thresholds, obscuring its fluidity, context-specificity and temporal dimensions. Relatedly, root causes and long-term or

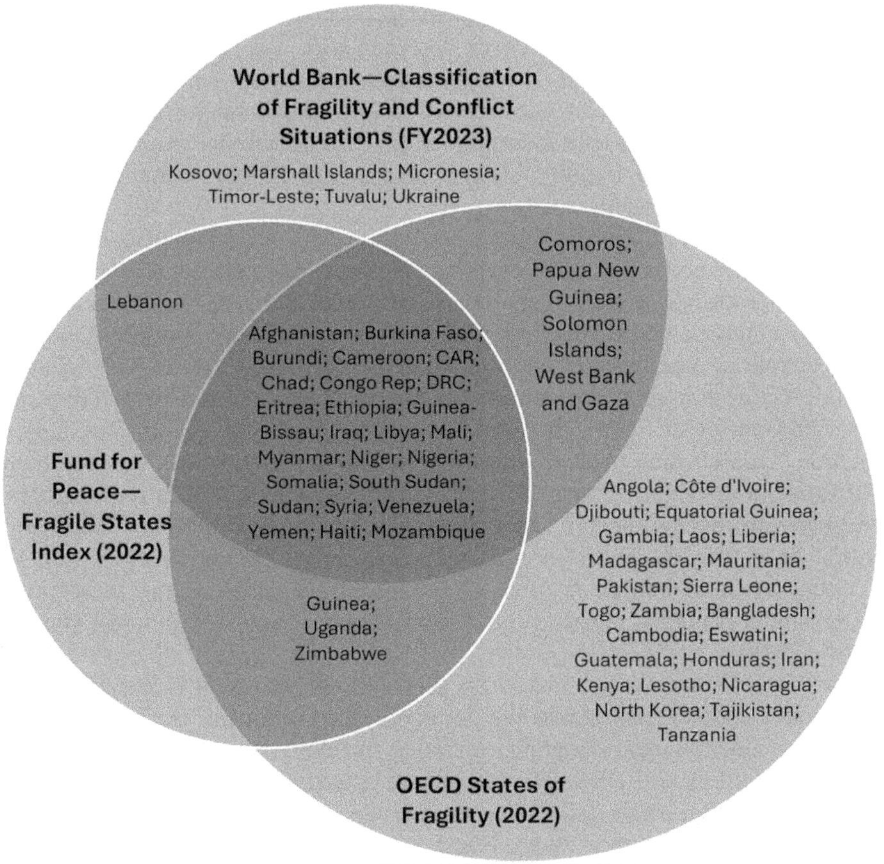

Figure 2.1 Fragile states based on number of international lists on which they appear
Note: Fund for Peace Fragile States Index relies only on the countries classified under "alert" levels.
Source: identification based on fragility indices by World Bank (2023a), OECD (2022) and Fund for Peace (2022).

historic inequalities generating crises may be overlooked or conflated with fragility itself, as the human dimension of the OECD's fragility framing suggests. Nevertheless, this framing does at least implicitly begin to consider poverty as having crisis-like dimensions, an argument that this book develops and advances.

2.1.3 Moving towards intersections of "unsustainability"

The three crises this book focuses on relate to climate-related disasters, violent conflict, and high inflation and economic instability linked to a cost-of-living crisis, embedded within varied governance structures and political challenges. There is thus an emphasis on environmental, socio-political (i.e. recognising conflict as a socio-political process) and economic dimensions to the three crises noted, respectively. Moreover, together with our desire to understand the impact of crises on poverty dynamics and vice versa—hence with a strong temporal element linked to questions of intergenerational justice—this work drives us towards an applied sustainability lens, remaining informed by the broader literature on fragility in its consideration of institutional weakness and multi-dimensional risk.

Sustainable development, often a proxy for sustainability, refers to "meeting the needs of people today without comprising the ability of future generations to meet their own needs" (WCED, 1987). This school of thought emerged especially from the analysis of natural resource degradation linked to unchecked economic and population growth. The idea of social, economic and environmental sustainability is not new (Barbier, 1987; Brown et al., 1987; Boyer et al., 2016; Purvis et al., 2019). It may include "goals" that stick to the aforementioned sustainable development definition and occur within the three dimensions mentioned; for example, through promoting social inclusivity, ecological sustainability and economic transformation within planetary boundaries (Diwakar et al., 2025). A focus of these models is often of intersecting systems across these three dimensions, bringing together multi-disciplinary schools of thought (Purvis et al., 2019).

Notions of sustainability matter for this analysis because it is the absence of sustainability that characterises the polycrisis analysed in this book. For example, environmental unsustainability underlies the climate crisis, as does the challenge of adapting to it. This can lead to social unrest as resource scarcity and displacement exacerbate grievances, thus driving social unsustainability (Kahl, 2006; Collier and Hoeffler, 2004). It can also lead to economic unsustainability by depressing economic activities and increasing market volatility (IMF, 2020). Critiques of sustainable development similarly point to its failure to reconcile environmental concerns with economic development.

Economic unsustainability in turn partly reflects the market distortions and inequalities in capital accumulation that can drive instability. It may emerge from a prioritisation of immediate economic growth over long-term investments in human development, climate adaptation or infrastructure development that again can drive unrest and social unsustainability. Similarly, inequalities in capital accumulation may run concurrent with a prioritisation of material wealth that leads to environmental degradation. Finally, social unsustainability may be marked by a breakdown in the social contract. This can weaken collective action around natural resource management and precipitate environmental unsustainability. A weak social contract can also undermine trust, including in economic institutions, which can then propel economic unsustainability.

This book implicitly argues that it is important to focus on the intersections of unsustainability across economic, social and environmental dimensions. This "negative" sustainability or "unsustainability" is under-evidenced in the literature or is viewed only through a singular dimension (Nebbia, 2012; Theodoro and Leonardos, 2021). However, the intersections can amplify vulnerability, erode coping mechanisms and create negative feedback loops that reinforce systemic failures that create and maintain negative poverty trajectories. This focus, combined with a relative absence of multi-scalar analysis of polycrisis, its heterogeneous pathways and impacts and strained coping mechanisms, motivates the development of a conceptual framework linking polycrisis to poverty dynamics. This is outlined next.

2.2 Introducing an integrated framework

Figure 2.2 introduces a conceptual framework to understand polycrisis and poverty dynamics (see Chapter 1 for definitions). We begin by outlining the intersecting crises, then discuss their direct impacts, before finally examining coping mechanisms. This framework is informed by insights from the literature on poverty dynamics (e.g. Shepherd et al., 2014; Hulme and Shepherd, 2003; Narayan et al., 2009; Carter and Barrett, 2006; Diwakar and Shepherd, 2022) and polycrisis (e.g. Morin and Kern, 1999; Tooze, 2022; Fraser and Vogel, 2017) alongside case studies presented in this book. It also draws from and builds on the wider literature on sustainable livelihoods, vulnerability and coping (e.g. Scoones, 1998; Devereux, 2001; Chambers, 1983; Heltberg et al., 2012; Davies, 1993; Adams et al., 1998).

The figure starts with a recognition of environmental crises as an overarching concern, given the increasing frequency and intensity of climate-related disasters. On top of this, it recognises that economic crises and social crises may each intersect with environmental crises to further amplify their effects, including through additional pathways beyond those from environmental crises alone, as detailed in Section 2.2.1. Within the social crisis dimension, the book focuses on violent conflict, categorised as a social process as outlined in Chapter 1.

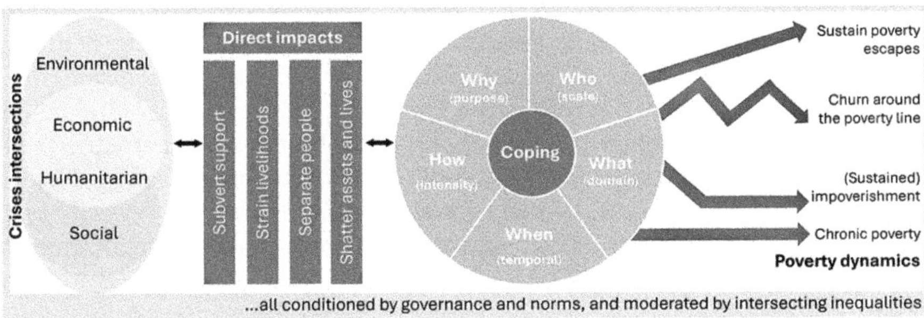

Figure 2.2 Polycrisis and poverty, an integrated conceptual framework
Note: there is bidirectionality and feedback loops across the components—e.g. poverty can affect coping responses and also drive new crises or amplify existing crises.
Source: author's own.

The direct effects of these intersecting crises include government support being diverted or even intentionally subverted away from pro-poor programming and policies, livelihoods being strained, people becoming separated including through forced displacement thus undermining social cohesion, and assets and lives being irrevocably shattered. These are effects directly on people, their assets and means of production, and the structures in place that support these, thus operating through multiple scales. They can also generate or themselves intersect with micro-level shocks and stressors, such as where ill health may be driven by government support for healthcare being subverted or diverted.

In response to the direct impacts of polycrisis, individuals and households adopt a range of coping mechanisms. Some do this out of strategic choice or agency. Others, who have no real alternatives, are forced to draw down on the bare minimum needed to survive, which can inadvertently aggravate direct impacts of crises. Polycrisis can thus push even the chronically poor into deeper destitution through survival coping. Gender, youth, ethnicity and class critically shape access to and consequences of these coping mechanisms, as these groups may have differential access to resources and experience marginalisation that reinforces these inequalities and in turn crises' impacts. Figure 2.2 accordingly points to bidirectionality between crises, impacts and coping. At the same time, coping responses and resulting poverty trajectories can also undermine longer-term resilience, in turn making individuals and households more vulnerable to future crises. As such, the directionality is much more complex than illustratively outlined in Figure 2.2.

The polycrisis, its direct impacts, the resultant coping responses and the interactions of these are shaped by (and shape) underlying governance and norms—which also have differential implications for certain groups based on gender, youth, ethnicity and class. Based on these factors, households are variably able to sustain escapes, though more commonly amidst crises intersections they end up churning around the poverty line, becoming impoverished, remaining in chronic poverty and/or falling more deeply into destitute forms of chronic poverty. As noted in Chapter 1, these negative poverty dynamics affect the fortunes of the socio-political contract and the nature of sustainable growth from below, which combine to produce or amplify polycrisis. For example, grievances related to sustained impoverishment or chronic poverty can drive conflict, as observed in Nigeria (see Chapter 5), or push people to adopt environmentally degrading livelihoods in the absence of alternatives, as observed in Cambodia (see Chapter 3). This bidirectional poverty–polycrisis trap in turn constrains preventive and recovery-focused solutions.

The sub-sections below elaborate on the direct impacts and coping responses to polycrisis.

2.2.1 Direct impacts of polycrisis

Figure 2.3 elaborates on this high-level framing by outlining direct pathways of impact through which crises and their intersections may differentially affect

	Subvert (support)	Strain (livelihoods)	Separate (people)	Shatter (assets, lives)
Environmental crises	• Resources shifted from development to emergency relief responses • Public service investments diverted to relief	• Loss of crops, livestock e.g. from floods or drought • Loss of fish stocks e.g. from storm surges • Loss of grazing land	• Climate-induced displacement or distress migration, leading to thinning of networks	• Land, livestock, agricultural implements, roads destroyed • Health (incl WASH) and education facilities overwhelmed, destroyed, used as shelters • High disease burdens, death
Economic crises (on top of climate crisis)	• Reduced government spending on healthcare and education • Reductions in aid spend due to austerity measures	• Rising costs e.g. inputs, food, transport • Currency devaluation • Weak industry/ service sector, power outage, supply disruption • Job/ business loss, market slump	• Rural-to-urban forced migration • Evictions • Pressures on low-income urban informal settlements	• Depreciation of asset quality and value (including due to disrepair from climate crises, inflation) • Increase of some asset values (e.g. real estate, commodities) • Increased user costs of assets e.g. education
Social crises (i.e. conflict, *on* top of climate crisis)	• Spending subverted to military sectors • Co-opted public services • Reduced FDI • Obstructed access to insecure areas	• Market collapse due to insecurity, destroyed infrastructure • Co-opted/ disrupted supply chains • Added care responsibilities	• Forced/ mass internal displacement or refugees • Separation of families, weak social cohesion	• High mortality, demographic change (e.g. widows/orphans) • Deliberate destruction of homes, farms, livestock, NFEs • Looting by armed groups • Scorched-earth strategies • SGBV, psychosocial illbeing
Humanitarian crises (climate/econ /social)	• Development to emergency aid shift • Failed/ weak state provision • Donor fatigue	• Widespread unemployment, loss of livelihoods • Economic collapse, market failures	• Chronic/ multiple displacements • Permanent separation • Statelessness	• Amplified mortality • Intensified loss of productive, physical, financial assets, infrastructure destruction

Figure 2.3 Examples of direct impacts of polycrisis on poverty, a 4S framework
Note: each row includes the additional effect of other crises on top of environmental crises, which is often more intense than a purely additive effect. As such, the row on economic crises should be viewed alongside the row on environmental crises to understand the compounding consequences of crises intersections.
Source: author's own based on insights from the wider literature and analysis presented in this book.

poverty. In each intersection, the focus is on additional pathways that go beyond the baseline of environmental crises; in other words, the row relating to economic crises draws attention to direct impacts generated by the addition of economic crises in contexts of climate related disasters. As such, it should be viewed alongside the first row on environmental crises. For example, conflict-induced displacement can considerably undermine the social networks households rely on to cope with crises, while a large-scale flood can further strain the ability of entire communities to provide this support.

The key point is that there are likely to be more intense or long-lasting effects when crises intersect, and also different effects depending on which crises intersect. These effects may be additive, compounded, or display unexpected results, pointing to the complexity of directionality. For example, a flood can devastate harvests, while economic crises can drive job loss through different additive pathways. However, more commonly, there may be compounded or cascading effects, where for example government resources amidst conflict may be subverted by warring parties which could lead to the effects of flooding being more severe. Unequal access to relief in turn can sometimes unexpectedly drive new or amplified exclusion with long-term effects. The compounded effects can moreover differ between types of crises, where for example rapid-onset flooding can have more immediately depressing effects compared to slow-onset drought.

As the introductions to Chapters 3–5 highlight, crises can also generate crises, where for example drought can aggravate competition over water or grazing land which may be a basis for violence, as observed in farmer–herder conflicts. These pathways can be group specific. For example, droughts in Asia and Africa have contributed to sustaining conflict for agriculturally dependent and political excluded groups in poor countries (von Uexkull et al., 2016). Feedback loops may also be present, where such conflicts might drive environmental degradation triggering an intensification of climate-related disasters. All three intersecting crises can become situations to which a humanitarian response is given. Finally, the sequence also matters; for example, the COVID-19 pandemic was followed by (and in part drove) inflation, which often prevented recovery from the COVID-19 pandemic.

The direct multi-scalar impacts of these intersecting crises are further disaggregated by the "4S" framework—introduced to distinguish between crises impacts that severely strain individual livelihoods, separate people from their resources and networks, shatter assets (tangible and intangible—such as education, health, and environmental assets) and lives, and subvert institutional support, as reflected in shrinking aid budgets, rising needs and weakened capacity. These "4S" impacts vary depending on the pre-existing vulnerability of individuals up to systems, as discussed in the next sub-section. The strands of the 4S framework align largely with similar categories recently put forward in the literature, around conflict effects that distinguish between destruction, deterioration, disruption, diversion, devaluation and dissaving due to conflict, or some groupings of these (Vesco et al., 2025; Lind et al., 2025).

There are nevertheless some notable differences. Our 4S framework uniquely considers how intersecting crises have direct impacts on poverty. We draw attention to the subversion of institutional support, to highlight the intentionality of these often politically motivated processes in times of polycrisis that can actively sabotage support to populations in need, as discussed in Section 2.2.4. Moreover, our focus on separation rather than displacement places an emphasis on the human and social dimension accompanying the physical movement of people during crises.

These 4S elements thus operate at multiple scales, with gendered impacts on individuals, households, community networks and government capacity. As partly reflected in the impact of "shattered assets", some of this refers to intangible assets and outcomes—like mental health and social cohesion—that can in turn deepen poverty and contribute to its persistence across generations. Chapters 3–5 provide further detail on conceptual and applied insights around how specific crises uniquely intersect with one another and amplify each other, especially for marginalised or vulnerable groups.

It is worth noting that Figure 2.3 does not depict secondary effects of crises on wellbeing, such as through loss of livelihoods or crops from environmental and economic crises driving food insecurity. Moreover, it does not elaborate on the heterogeneous impacts noted above or the shocks and stressors that intersect with these crises, both of which effects are cross-cutting and considered in the mixed methods analysis in Chapters 3–6. Even so, it offers a schema for understanding direct impacts of polycrisis on poverty and wellbeing and vice versa, i.e. the impacts of poverty dynamics on polycrisis.

2.2.2 Coping with crises

Alongside the direct impacts on poverty outlined above, polycrisis can also erode people's coping mechanisms over time, which has the potential to drive negative feedback loops, further amplifying crises' effects. Indeed, a key aspect of intersecting and sequential crises is the contribution to the erosion—or collapse—of informal support systems over time, which may be irretrievable. A single crisis might be recoverable, but when shocks keep coming, especially covariate ones, people's support networks deteriorate. This is especially clear in cases of displacement, where people lose access to their longstanding kin and community networks altogether.

There have been many ways of conceptualising coping mechanisms in the literature, each with different emphases (e.g. Heltberg et al., 2012; Davies, 1993; Adams et al., 1998). For example, coping is sometimes distinguished by the intensity of the response, at one extreme being erosive where households have few alternatives and so are forced to respond to crises in ways that undermine current and longer-term wellbeing, as Chapter 6 highlights. The temporal dimensions of coping—when people are building and using their coping mechanisms—also affects poverty dynamics. Those who build capacities ex-ante may be better placed to mitigate polycrisis effects, whereas those who react to crisis after crisis may see their coping abilities sequentially erode.

All of this is typically conditioned by households' degree of diversification, assets and area of residence, demographic factors and access to networks and institutional support—which in turn is also affected by crises. Indeed, a wealthier household selling assets to maintain wellbeing may not be at risk of downward mobility, while a poorer household doing the same amidst increasing regularity of crises is likely reinforcing a poverty trap. This means that not only can different coping responses vary across different socio-economic groups including differentially based on gender and intersecting inequalities, but the implementation of these responses may be itself shaped by the frequency, intensity and waxing and waning of crises. These distinctions inherently draw on different framings based on agency and capacity (e.g. forced, survival or distress responses) and those based on outcomes such as adverse or erosive coping, which describe responses that deepen vulnerability. Both are important to consider in the analysis of coping responses.

A fuller understanding of coping emerges from moving beyond isolated categories to consider an integrated framework acknowledging both capacity and outcomes. This is illustrated through the introduction of a new "crisis coping wheel" (Figure 2.4, left) bringing together key dimensions of coping according to:

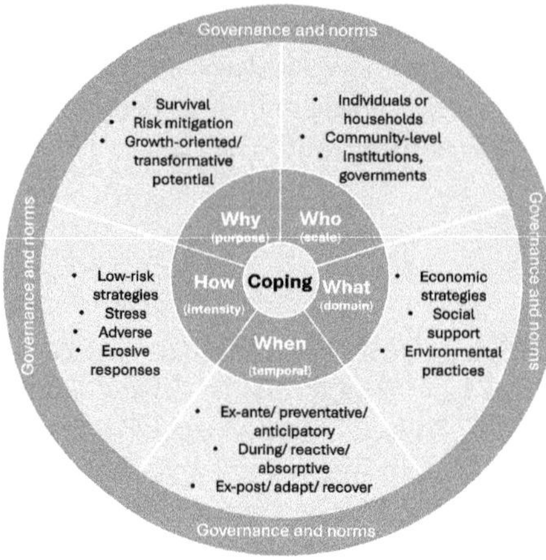

Dim.	Individual/household	Institutional
Economic	• Obtain credit, migrate, diversify income • AE: Child labour • AE: Reduce food • AE: Asset sales	• Macroeconomic management • Public works • Unemployment insurance • Extension services
Social	• Support from friends and family, savings groups • AE: Withdraw children from school • AE: Early marriage	• Social protection • Expansion of public services • Conflict resolution, peacebuilding • Anti-discrimination
Environment	• Change agricultural practices • AE: Exploit natural resources • AE: Relocate to hazard-prone areas	• Disaster risk reduction • Green infrastructure • Risk insurance • Payment for ecosystem services

Figure 2.4 Crisis coping wheel (left) and example of coping dimensions (right)
Note: "AE" in the figure on the right refers to adverse or erosive responses. Moreover, all these responses are furthermore conditioned by individual and systemic vulnerabilities, discussed in the main text.
Source: author's own based on insights from the wider literature and analysis presented in this book.

- **who is coping**: e.g. individuals (women, men, young adults, people experiencing intersecting inequalities, etc.), households, communities (including ethnic and class categories) or governments.
- **what domain of coping they rely on**: social (e.g. aid, friends and family, including psychosocial pathways such as through faith, and involving institutions), economic (e.g. relying on savings, credit or work, government and private transfers) or environmental (e.g. adopting climate-smart agricultural practices or instead relying more on exploitation of natural resources).
- **when they are coping**: preventative responses that reduce risk before crises, responses during crises and ex-post coping seeking to manage its immediate impacts and recover (note that these broadly reflect anticipatory, adaptive and absorptive resilience capacities in the broader literature).
- **how intensely they are coping**: are they able to adopt more agency-driven low-risk strategies (e.g. drawing on savings, accessing formal safety nets) or at the other extreme are they compelled to engage in intense erosive responses to survive but that involuntarily undermine longer-term well-being (e.g. skipping meals, withdrawing children from school, selling productive assets, engaging in transactional sex).
- **why they are coping**: is the purpose to survive or to adapt and grow, the latter often more of a choice and the former typically characterised by the absence of choice.

Shaping these responses, furthermore, are underlying governance arrangements and social norms and processes that condition the ability of individuals and households to take up specific responses, linked to household socio-economic status and the presence of intersecting inequalities. The crisis coping wheel thus bridges analytic gaps to present a more holistic, flexible way of understanding coping mechanisms, including in response to polycrisis.

Figure 2.4 (right) presents an example of how some of these coping dimensions can be brought together. The columns provide examples of institutions enabling household coping with crises (the "who" in Figure 2.4, left), while the rows refer to the pathways (the "what"). Moreover, it also presents examples of low risk (e.g. diversifying income), stress (taking a loan to cope) and adverse or erosive responses ("AE" categories in Figure 2.4, right) that reflect the intensity of coping mechanisms (the "how"). It is worth stressing that the crisis coping wheel is conditioned by governance and norms and moderated by intersecting inequalities including those based on socio-economic differences.

A key distinction in terms of coping with polycrisis compared to one-off shocks, stressors or crises, is that coping with polycrisis may be additive or compounded, and there may also be trade-offs. On the latter, for example, households coping with drought may not have the resources to additionally cope with high inflation or conflict-induced insecurity. The sequentially eroded capabilities may be particularly pronounced for households experiencing destitution or extreme poverty, reinforcing the bidirectionality of coping responses and negative poverty dynamics.

In this context, adverse or erosive responses may become more common during polycrisis over time as individuals and households are increasingly forced to react to crises in a survival mode that impoverishes or prolongs poverty, rather than develop preventative coping mechanisms. Indeed, those facing polycrisis—especially the severely impoverished, chronically poor or those pushed into destitution—often lack access to such coping options across the social, economic and environmental domains. Social, economic, political and environmental exclusion—particularly after climate disasters—can thus severely constrain the ability to cope. These often are furthermore shaped by gendered and ethnic background factors. In many cases, *inability to cope* is a defining feature, with only marginal forms of response available. For example, lacking assets or social support and being faced with adverse gender norms may leave women in poverty with no choice but to draw down on their health—by reducing food intake for themselves and their children just to survive.

Having examined the direct effects of and coping responses to polycrisis, Section 2.3.3 outlines the poverty dynamics that may emerge as a result of this interplay.

2.2.3 Poverty dynamics

The relationship portrayed in Figure 2.2 between crises and the outcome poverty dynamics is complex, bidirectional and often mutually reinforcing. For example, considering singular crises, poverty can be a trigger for conflict, but conflict can also impoverish or keep people poor. Similarly, people in poverty may be driven to live in areas where land is cheaper, or on informal land or government land, on account of commonly occurring natural hazards. This might include areas such as riverbanks, coastal areas, floodplains or urban valleys. People in poverty may also have no alternative but to live in homes built with poor quality materials. This can mean that damage from flooding or other natural hazards can be severe and escalate into disasters for these communities. Concurrently, floods can damage assets and livelihoods that can impoverish households. Finally, poverty can increase vulnerability to economic crises, where for example the types of informal employment people in and near poverty engage in, or their limited access to financial services, can reduce their ability to cope with crises, while inflation can erode their purchasing power and deepen poverty.

When these crises combine, the effects can be amplified as the crises can reinforce each other. Moreover, they can also reinforce direct impacts, erosive and reactive coping, and negative poverty trajectories, which in turn further amplifies vulnerability to polycrisis. For example, violent conflict in a drought-affected area can drive displacement and constrain access to services, which may force households to withdraw children from school to complement household labour amidst prevalent insecurity, as observed in Borno, Nigeria (Chapter 6). This can have implications for the intergenerational persistence of poverty. Climate shocks can also more easily push people into poverty in conflict-affected contexts where institutions may already be weak.

Similarly, hyperinflation during or caused by drought (e.g. as harvests fail and lead to food price spikes) can be mutually reinforcing, forcing households to engage in a distress sale of assets including land and livestock in order to cope, thus undermining key protective factors and driving impoverishment. Moreover, distress sales of assets often happen when market prices are at their lowest—like in flooded cattle markets where many households are selling at the same time—so these sales potentially yield very little, deepening the loss.

In this way, there can be feedback loops within crises themselves as well as with the impacts and coping responses they generate, to in turn shape gendered poverty dynamics. These negative poverty trajectories finally can heighten individual and household vulnerability to subsequent crises, reflecting a polycrisis–poverty trap. This trap creates a downward spiral towards destitution in the absence of supportive mechanisms, including institutions. It also provides a strong rationale to start treating poverty as an emergency with a view to generate stronger proportional responses to deprivation.

At the same time, to emphasize, there is considerable heterogeneity as populations are not equally affected by crises; rather, systemic marginalisation and pre-existing social inequalities shape exposure and the ability of individuals and households to cope with crises (Mangubhai et al., 2021; Few et al., 2020). Related to this is the added challenge of intersecting inequalities, where the effects of polycrisis may be particularly pronounced for groups facing inequalities based on wealth or socio-economic status *alongside* gender, area of residence, ethnicity, disability status or other dimensions of inequality. For example, women and girls living in poor households may face limited access to healthcare and education, have care responsibilities that are accentuated due to crisis-driven suspension or disruption of essential services, or experience increased risk of sexual and gender-based violence. Similarly, ethnic minorities in poverty may already experience political marginalisation or live in remote areas that are often neglected in policymaking. They may accordingly experience dual sources of discrimination and marginalisation during times of polycrisis when priorities may shift to support easy-to-reach populations or those closer to the poverty line, thus deepening the exclusion and persistent poverty of those left or pushed behind.

2.2.4 Governance, norms and inequalities

Governance and causal pathways

Global governance structures, financing and norms may all facilitate or limit potential responses to crises and household poverty trajectories. For example, weak state capacity can constrain the effectiveness of disaster management or conflict resolution, as seen in Ethiopia's response to the war in Tigray intersecting with COVID-19 and rising inflation (Tafere et al., 2023). Applied to the conceptual framework (Figure 2.2), the conflict subverted resources away from the pandemic response and other forms of support to address rising inflation. Clientelist practices and politicised institutions can also affect who receives support, often with marginalised groups within countries excluded in this process, as evidenced in Nigeria (Chapter 5). Policies can also ignore vulnerabilities of marginalised groups and so create barriers to accessing relief to cope with crises, as observed in our qualitative data in terms of smallholders often being excluded from flood relief in Bangladesh (Chapter 6). There are thus various causal pathways through which governance weaknesses or failures can exacerbate the direct effects of polycrisis or operate to weaken coping responses.

These governance structures are also shaped by geopolitics. Some countries may be protected much better than others by some global actors because of history and bilateral relationships. Yet, as we are witnessing at the moment, those protections can suddenly disappear. At subnational level, much depends on central–local relationships (e.g. constitutional, financial, level of decentralisation or devolution)—in other words, responses are dependent on the level of authority or agency that local authorities have (e.g. through devolution) as well as the central government's responsibility to provide financial support to enable local response. Local authorities are often the implementers of relief, raise the alarm when a crisis is hitting, and are in touch with people experiencing crises and so can provide feedback.

Political regimes and crises

Political regimes and political crises can accordingly contribute as well as respond to polycrisis. More inclusive regimes that attempt to respond to structural injustice through redistributive measures and institutional reform may see their ability to enact change constrained, for example due to pressures of global economic crises or vested elite interests that gain a foothold during crises. Taken further, the presence of polycrisis can be leveraged to strengthen authoritarian control, through consolidating chief executive and elite power, disregarding accountability and empowering military personnel (Regilme and Parthenay, 2024; Lührmann et al., 2020).

Arrests in the Philippines and Zimbabwe during the pandemic provide examples of strengthened control. The Philippines also passed the Anti-Terrorism Act of 2020 to silence opposition (Hilhorst and Mena, 2021). Such responses indicate a worrying move towards using times of emergencies to pass through legislation that could counteract civil liberties and democratic processes. Moreover, the transition in power in Afghanistan discussed in Chapter 5 reflects a return to increased repression and amplified human rights crises experienced by women and other marginalised groups, which heightens structural challenges that weaken the ability of individuals, households and systems to build resilience to crises.

The discussion so far implicitly speaks to a broader literature on whether democracies or authoritarian forms of governance are better at addressing (multiple) crises. Earlier literature on this argued that democracies should be better at preventing famines due to the downward accountability mechanisms built into their structures, a free press and strong civil society (de Waal, 2000). Moreover, in some cases authoritarian governments have been replaced by democratic regimes as a reaction—as observed in Sudan in 1985 or in the example of Indian independence being hastened by the 1943 famine.

At the same time, studies on the COVID-19 response indicate mixed results. On the one hand, countries with authoritarian regimes were able to implement measures to curb transmission rates more quickly. However, this was also inherently harmful given it was typically not accompanied by measures to mitigate the negative socio-economic effects of the pandemic on people living in and near poverty (Shepherd et al., 2023). In addition, though democracies often struggle with timely action, they tend to have more inclusive participation and accountability mechanisms built in. The stage of a crisis and state capacity can also influence crisis responses across different regime types (Mao, 2021).

Inequalities and adverse social norms during crises

The instrumentalisation of crises or pendulum swings towards authoritarian control can also be supported by reshaped norms during these times of macro-level threats. Indeed, crises have been linked to an uptick in conservative attitudes, moving in some instances towards endorsement of less democratic government types (Severen et al., 2024; Laustsen and Petersen, 2017). This is true moreover of different types of crises, including economic crises, violent conflict or terrorism, and climate-related disasters (Ballard-Rosa et al., 2022; Asbrock and Fritsche, 2013; Russo et al., 2020).

Norms are not only important in relation to crisis governance, but also importantly shape micro- and meso-level responses to polycrisis. An example of this is seen through the frequent resistance of urban local authorities to absorb migrants or people due to crises. Social norms that reduce women's mobility can additionally condition coping capacities. In Bangladesh, mortality rates during cyclones are higher for women, shaped by delayed evacuation among women who face restricted mobility or have care responsibilities that limit their capacity to prepare for cyclones or mitigate their consequences (Chowdhury et al., 2022).

The discussion above reflects the role that socio-demographic characteristics more broadly play in the framework, in terms of leading to differential impacts, intensifying pre-existing vulnerabilities and moderating coping capacities in ways that can amplify crises' impacts and constrain recovery. For example, women and girls face increased responsibilities during crises and heightened risk of gender-based violence. Older adults and persons with disabilities may face mobility constraints and be especially susceptible to illness and mortality as evidenced during the COVID-19 pandemic. Young children may lack access to education, as the pandemic's school closures illustrated, but also to critical sources of nutrition when crises strike. Minority groups, for example based on ethnicit,y may also experience severe marginalisation. These dimensions moreover may intersect, including with socio-economic status. They are critical to how people experience and respond to crises. The impacts of polycrisis—and people's capacity to cope and recover—are profoundly shaped by these intersecting inequalities.

In this way, governance structures and norms and longstanding intersecting inequalities can directly influence not only the salience of crises but also the coping mechanisms households are able to draw on in response to crises. Moreover, weak governance and adverse social norms can influence who is most vulnerable to the impacts of polycrisis, as the examples from South Asia and the wider international COVID-19 responses discussed above highlighted.

2.3 Country-level analysis of crises and poverty in focus countries

2.3.1 Environmental, economic and social crises

Many of the countries at the intersection of the lists presented in Figure 2.1 are countries experiencing chronic "unsustainability" due to crises, or for whom it is underlying the crises they experience. Tables 2.1 to 2.3 outline the crises and governance contexts experienced in the book's focus countries. As Table 2.1 highlights, these crises occur against a backdrop of structural constraints, such as unpredictable rainfall, poor market access, high food prices driving food insecurity, weak governance and poor healthcare variably across countries. These crises also intersect with trends like the speed of population growth and its impact on resources and urbanisation.

Of the focus countries, Afghanistan, Ethiopia, Niger and Nigeria are very regularly captured by indices of state fragility outlined in Section 2.1. On the other hand, Rwanda, Malawi, Nepal, India and the Philippines are typically not reflected in these international indices of state fragility. However, even in these cases, sources of subnational or temporal fragility remain, as highlighted in Table 2.1, for example due to post-conflict legacies and/or climate-related disasters.

The crises described in Table 2.1 alongside thresholds of crises intensity (see Annex A for indicator definitions and thresholds) and coping capacities marked by the indicators in Tables 2.2 and 2.3 motivate the placement of countries along a typology of crises intersections aligned with the left-hand side of our conceptual diagram (Figure 2.2). It is worth noting from Table 2.2 that there is some heterogeneity in the degree to which countries are prone to climate-related disasters. However, our starting point as noted above is a recognition of the increasing intensity and frequency of climate-related disasters given climate change, onto which economic crises and violent conflict may germinate. The types of self-reported crises referenced in Chapters 3–6 lend credence to this starting point, where many households report climate-related disasters relative to other types of crises. Moreover, as Figure 2.5 highlights, all focus countries except Rwanda have fatalities due to climate-related disasters that are higher than the global average, while Rwanda nevertheless still experiences high climate vulnerability. Together, these insights motivate the salience of climate crises in the focus countries.

On top of climate-related disasters, both Afghanistan and Nigeria experience very high growth volatility or very high inflation alongside violent conflict—and thus deal with a strong triple crisis. Another set of countries—Ethiopia, India, Kenya, Niger and the Philippines—all experience a very high threshold of conflict-related crises alongside the climate crises. Bangladesh may also be a contender for this category, but its high human hazard score is primarily on account of the Rohingya refugee population within Cox's Bazaar—a relatively localised focus that is not covered in our mixed methods data and is distinct from the types of more violent conflict within countries characterising the other contexts.

Table 2.1 Crises contexts in focus countries

Country	*Climate-related disasters*	*Violent conflict and insecurity*	*Economic crises*	*Governance challenges and context*	*Sources*
Asia					
Afghanistan	Frequent floods, driving vector-borne diseases Severe and repeated droughts (e.g. 2018, 2021, 2022), water scarcity, heat waves	Pre-transition high rates of insurgent activities and fatalities 2021 political transition driving climate of fear, including gendered death threats Suppression of political dissent	High inflation, aid dependency Disruption to core services during political transition Exchange rate depreciation, international sanctions, liquidity crisis	Fragmentation of power for decades, weak institutions Volatility in public service provision affected further by external environment Donor funding reliance De facto authorities not formally recognised by many countries—isolation Political parties banned	World Bank, 2022b; BTI, 2022; Burattini et al., 2022; HRW, 2022; OCHA, 2022
Bangladesh	Frequent floods (e.g. 2017, 2019, 2020), cyclones (Amphan 2020), drought, storm surge, landslides, fire, riverbank erosion Experiences amongst the highest maximum temperatures in Asia	Some political unrest (2013–14, 2020–25), including student-led protests and fall of Sheikh Hasina's government Protracted refugee context— displaced Rohingya population, mostly in Cox's Bazar	Inflation concerns COVID-19 economic contraction, global inflation affected fuel and food prices Export decline during pandemic and job loss in informal sector	Clientelist practice, governance disruptions during political transition Interim government mandated to draft inclusive constitution, with push-back	World Bank, 2021; World Bank, 2024; Pollman, 2018; Basu et al., 2018; IWGIA, 2025

Country	*Climate-related disasters*	*Violent conflict and insecurity*	*Economic crises*	*Governance challenges and context*	*Sources*
Cambodia	Highly vulnerable to floods (e.g. 2020, 2021), storms, typhoons, periodic droughts (e.g. in the Tonle Sap Basin), heatwaves and epidemics	Relatively low to moderate levels of political tensions Opposition suppressed, arbitrary arrests and critics harassed	Real growth contraction by 3.1% in 2020 driving recession for first time in three decades Dependence on garment and tourism—affected by COVID-19 pandemic	Authoritarian political environment, dynastic control, suppression of civil society Expanded social protection, but hampered by erosion of public trust alongside weak subnational institutions	World Bank, 2022a; CDRI, 2012; Nguyen et al., 2020; ADB et al., 2021
India	Floods (e.g. 2018 in Kerala, 2020 in Assam), recurrent droughts (e.g. in western India and southern states), heatwaves (e.g. 2015, 2016, 2022), cyclones (e.g. Amphan 2020)	Regional conflicts (e.g. Naxal violence in central and eastern India), ethnic violence in Manipur, tensions and conflict with Pakistan over Kashmir (including missile strikes, 2025 cross-border attacks) Farmer protests against farm laws	GDP contraction during COVID-19, alongside rising unemployment Inflation in 2022–23 linked to rising oil prices, currency depreciation, credit crunch, high debt burden of farmers, rural credit crisis	Clientelist political practices Lack of transparency and accountability, weak stakeholder engagement Poverty reduction programme implementation (e.g. PDS) weakened by corruption and wastage	BBC, 2024; Reuters, 2024; Eynde, 2018; Rath et al., 2023; Clary, 2025
Nepal	Landslides, earthquakes (e.g. 2015), "altitude effect" driving temperature increase, droughts (e.g. Terai region), glacial lake outburst floods	Maoist violence (1996–2006) Periodic protests and strikes (e.g. Terai region)	Strong reliance on remittances which make it vulnerable to shocks GDP contraction during COVID-19 Recovery lag post-2015 earthquake	Decentralisation brings limited finances for provincial/local government Government turnover drives political instability Political trust low Calls for political change (e.g. through protests)	Sah, 2024; Pokhrel, 2022; Sneddon 2019

Country	*Climate-related disasters*	*Violent conflict and insecurity*	*Economic crises*	*Governance challenges and context*	*Sources*
The Philippines	Floods, drought (e.g. 2019–20), tropical cyclones including super typhoons (e.g. Goni 2020, Vamco 2020), earthquakes, dry spells Highest disaster risk in the world	Low-level insurgencies (e.g. in Mindanao) Marawi siege (ISIS-affiliated militants) in 2017 Military operations against insurgent groups ongoing	One of world's longest and strictest lockdowns during COVID-19 Recurrent volatility and variations in food price inflation (e.g. in 2023) mean food prices 23% higher than 2017–18 average	Dynastic politics, frequent leadership changes Misused or underutilised funds amidst political gridlocks Rising public debt Reliance on political networks to identify aid beneficiaries leads to co-option	World Food Programme, 2023a, 2023b; Bündnis Entwicklung Hilft and IFHV, 2024; Babst, 2025
Africa					
Ethiopia	Recurrent droughts (2020–21, worst drought in decades in 2015–16), regular floods (e.g. 2020, 2021 in southern and eastern parts), desertification	Tigray war 2020–22 Conflicts in Oromia and Somali regions Amhara conflict 2023–present Al-Shabaab incursion 2022 Third largest refugee population in Africa (mainly from South Sudan, Somalia, Eritrea, Sudan)	Aid reliance Government reforms (e.g. stock market and currency reform/devaluation) with adverse effects—rising inflation but no mitigation strategy for vulnerable populations Tigray conflict disrupted infrastructure	Crackdowns in 2020 and 2024 (e.g. of government critics) harmed political pluralism Journalist arrests, anti-terrorism laws used to suppress dissent Limited federal control over conflict-affected areas Unequal resource distribution	World Food Programme, 2023a; World Bank, 2020; Freedom House, 2025

Country	*Climate-related disasters*	*Violent conflict and insecurity*	*Economic crises*	*Governance challenges and context*	*Sources*
Kenya	Droughts (2017, 2022) and consecutive below-average rainy seasons, flash floods (e.g. 2024, intensified by El Niño patterns), pandemics and epidemics	Al-Shabaab violence and cross-border attacks (especially northeast) Pastoral militias Inter-ethnic conflict Political violence linked to land rights, election-related violence Protracted refugee situation (mainly from Somalia, South Sudan)	Staple food price rises (e.g. maize and beans 60–90% more expensive than five-year average in February 2023) COVID-19 economic slowdown High debt burden driving austerity measures	Repression of youth activism Considerable political and economic reforms, but implementation challenges Patronage, weak citizen participation Vote buying, bribes common to procure contracts, bail out arrested individuals—bribes higher in poorer counties	International Organization for Migration, 2024; United Nations Office for the Coordination of Humanitarian Affairs, 2023; ACLED: 2024; UNHCR, 2023
Malawi	Droughts (e.g. 2016–18), floods (2015, 2019), cyclones (e.g. Tropical Cyclone Freddy impacts in 2023 and Tropical Storm Ana contributing to the threat of cholera)	Low levels of political tensions Civil unrest related to economic challenges Occasional border tensions with Mozambique	Long-standing macroeconomic imbalances, debt and balance-of-payments crisis, low growth High inflation (e.g. 32.3% year-on-year for April 2024) and elevated food prices, devaluation of Malawi Kwacha since late 2023	Dependency on donor aid including for social protection programming Infrastructure deficits but some progress in roads and agricultural development Narrow political settlement Rents dispersed to tribesmen entrenched in public sector Contracts for government programmes used as vote-buying	Médecins Sans Frontières, 2023; World Bank, 2023b; United Nations, 2024

Country	*Climate-related disasters*	*Violent conflict and insecurity*	*Economic crises*	*Governance challenges and context*	*Sources*
Niger	Droughts (2018, 2019), heavy precipitation (e.g. torrential rains in 2020, 2024), floods, landslides, wildfires, desertification, epidemics, insect infestation	Terrorist activities, illicit trafficking, protracted conflict Jihadist insurgency July 2023 military coup ousting President Bazoum Large share of refugees from Nigeria, Mali, Burkina Faso Security situation worsened post-coup	Drastic sanctions in response to coup Inflation, including due to trade disruptions due to border closure with Benin (year-on-year rise from 1.7% in June 2023 to 15.5% in June 2024) High debt burden Sanctions following coup	Coups and transitions lead to instability of development efforts, including recent military coup dissolving democratic processes Weak inclusive governance Public finance reforms in health and education, but constrained by aid suspension	UNDP, 2021; UNHCR, 2024; World Bank, n.d.; Babatounde and Kanta, 2024
Nigeria	Droughts and desertification (especially in the north), extreme heatwave, floods (especially Niger and Benue River basins, e.g. 2012, 2017 Benue, 2020, 2022, 2023 Borno)	Boko Haram insurgency in northeast Farmer–herder violence in Middle Belt, aggravated by 2017 anti-grazing laws Renewed militancy in Niger Delta, ethnic militias, armed banditry Plateau state massacres 2023	Oil dependency and sharp drop in oil prices Record high inflation (40.9% for food and 34.2% for all items in June 2024) Devaluation of currency Fuel subsidy removal Cashless policy Economic mismanagement	Corruption scandal at highest levels of social protection decision-making "Stomach infrastructure politics"—mobilise voters with food items and other necessities Poor governance and weak investment in social development and infrastructure	World Bank, 2017; International Crisis Group, 2018; World Food Programme, 2024; Okoi and Iwara, 2021

Country	*Climate-related disasters*	*Violent conflict and insecurity*	*Economic crises*	*Governance challenges and context*	*Sources*
Rwanda	Floods (2018, 2020, 2023— impact of El Niño-induced heavy rains and flooding), landslides, drought (2016–17), unpredictable rainfall, rising temperature	Protracted refugee presence Some regional instability due to supporting M23 rebel groups in DRC	Price spikes (e.g. of fertilisers, with doubling of prices during 2022) Export bans, supply chain disruptions increasing food prices (59.2% annual year-on-year inflation for food items reported in 2022)	Centralised decision-making, challenges related to political freedoms Prioritisation of poverty reduction in Vision 2020 and social policies (e.g. health insurance free for poorest) Compulsion for small payments to access social services exerts pressure	World Bank, 2019b; Namit and Poulsen, 2023; Rosenbach and Spielman, 2022
Tanzania	Rising temperatures, longer dry spells and drought (especially southern and central regions, e.g. 2015–16), more intense heavy rainfall and sea level rise, flash floods	Refugees mainly from Burundi and DRC Decline in peaceful protests when Magufuli took office but rise in politically motivated riots and civilian targeting by unidentified armed groups Insurgency in south, albeit small-scale	Ignored COVID-19 for majority of the pandemic Yet COVID-19 impacts especially on manufacturing, tourism Inflationary pressures, especially on food and fuel	Challenges on policy implementation Weak public service delivery, driven also by low government spending (e.g. on health and education) Opposition leader arrested in 2025, political climate volatility	World Bank, 2023c; da Corta et al., 2022; Banks, 2016

Country	*Climate-related disasters*	*Violent conflict and insecurity*	*Economic crises*	*Governance challenges and context*	*Sources*
Zambia	Droughts (e.g. El Niño droughts in 2016, 2019, 2020, 2024), heavy rains and floods (2017, 2020), low water levels also affect hydropower reservoirs	Political competition and “gassing” incidents Some protests during election periods Border incidents along DRC border	Debt crisis and default, continued high debt burden Currency depreciation High inflation spiking during e.g. drought periods of 2015–16, 2019, COVID-19 Sharp drop in copper prices in 2015 Economic stagnation	Weak fiscal governance and revenue mobilisation Current government more committed to poverty reduction Presence of civil society network for poverty reduction Weak administrative capacity in rural areas	World Bank, 2019a; Shepherd et al., 2021; ACAPS, 2025
Zimbabwe	El Niño induced droughts (2019, 2020), floods (e.g. 2020), cyclones (e.g. Cyclone Ana in 2022, Cyclone Idai in 2019), water scarcity, “January disease”, fall armyworm outbreaks, cholera	Political instability and repression of opposition and civil society Protests over economic challenges (e.g. due to massive fuel price hikes)	History of and ongoing hyperinflation, currency instability, severe economic crisis Loss of investor confidence, low FDI	Weak public policies Diversion of resources away from poverty reduction Neopatrimonialism Declining public satisfaction Some slow progress (e.g. infrastructure development)	WFP and FAO, 2025; Green Climate Fund, 2019; SIVIO Institute, 2024

Note: the table presents crises related to the key dimensions being explored in this book, though there are of course other crises not mentioned (e.g. public health crises, the spillovers from the war in Ukraine and COVID-19, the latter of which is variably mentioned but was present across countries, and the emergence of IDPs resulting from these crises but itself with crisis dimensions).

Table 2.2 Crises across focus countries according to cross-country indices and indicators

	Climate crises		*Economic crises*		*Social crises*		*Climate-crises intersection*		
Country	*Natural hazard*	*Climate vulnerability*	*Growth volatility*	*Headline consumer price inflation*	*Global Peace Index*	*Human hazard*	*Economic*	*Conflict*	*Triple*
Afghanistan	High	High	V. high	High	V. low	V. high			X
Nigeria	Medium	Low	High	V. high	V. low	V. high			X
Ethiopia	Medium	Medium	High	V. high	Low	V. high		X	
India	V. high	Low	High	High	Medium	V. high		X	
Kenya	Medium	Low	Medium	High	Low	V. high		X	
Niger	Medium	V. high	High	Medium	Low	V. high		X	
Philippines	V. high	Low	High	Medium	Medium	V. high		X	
Bangladesh	V. high	High	Medium	High	Medium	V. high	X		
Cambodia	Medium	Low	High	Medium	Medium	V. low	X		
Malawi	Medium	High	Medium	V. high	Medium	V. low	X		
Nepal	Medium	Low	High	High	Medium	V. low	X		
Rwanda	Low	High	High	High	Medium	Low	X		
Tanzania	Medium	Medium	Medium	Medium	Medium	Low	X		
Zambia	Low	Low	High	V. high	Medium	V. low	X		
Zimbabwe	Medium	Medium	V. high	V. high	Low	Low	X		
Source	INFORM	ND-GAIN	WDI	WDI	IEP	INFORM			
Year of reference	2025	2022	2023	2023	2024	2025			

Note: see Annex A for indicator definitions.

Table 2.3 Country-level institutional coping capacities

Crises	*Country*	*Disaster risk reduction*	*Economic management*	*Government effectiveness*	*Voice and accountability*
Triple	Afghanistan	V. low	V. low	V. low	V. low
	Nigeria	N/A	Medium	Low	Low
Climate–conflict	Ethiopia	Low	V. low	Low	V. low
	India	Medium	N/A	V. high	V. high
	Kenya	Medium	High	Medium	Medium
	Niger	V. low	Medium	Low	Low
	Philippines	High	N/A	V. high	Medium
Climate–economic	Bangladesh	High	Medium	Low	Low
	Cambodia	Low	High	Medium	V. low
	Malawi	High	V. low	Low	V. high
	Nepal	V. low	Medium	Low	Medium
	Rwanda	N/A	High	V. high	Low
	Tanzania	Low	High	Medium	Low
	Zambia	V. low	V. low	Low	Medium
	Zimbabwe	Medium	V. low	V. low	V. low
	Source	INFORM	WB CPIA	WGI	WGI
	Year of reference	2014–24	2023	2023	2023

Note: India and the Philippines are not included in the CPIA as they qualify for non-concessional International Bank for Reconstruction and Development (IBRD) lending (i.e. they are not eligible for International Development Association (IDA) funding, which is a criterion for World Bank Country Policy and Institutional Assessment (WB CPIA) coverage). See Annex A for indicator definitions. WGI = Worldwide Governance Indicators.

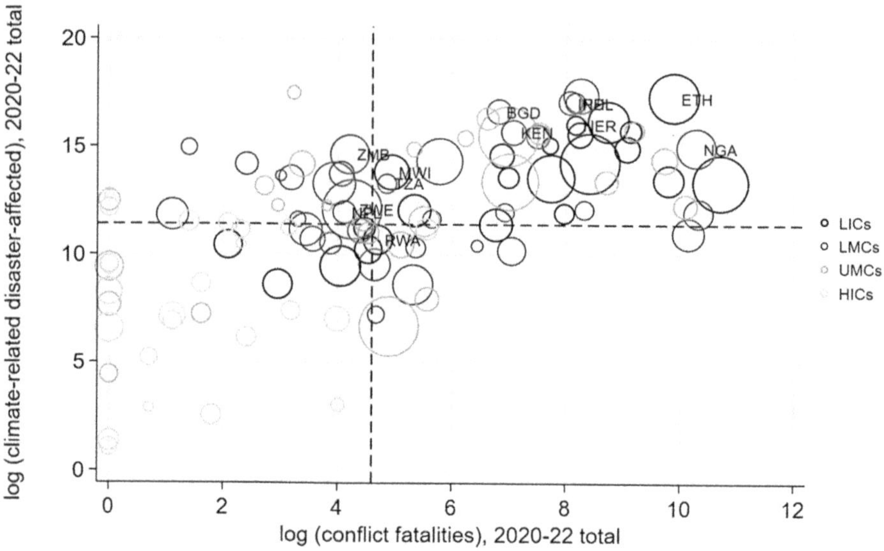

Figure 2.5 Populations affected by climate-related disasters and conflict by country (2020–22), weighted by average headline consumer price inflation rates (2020–22)

Note: LICs = Low-income countries; LMCs = Lower middle-income countries; UMCs = Upper middle-income countries; HICs = High-income countries.
Source: authors' analysis of Armed Conflict Location & Event Data (ACLED) (2020–22), Emergency Events Database (EM-DAT) (2020–22) and World Development Indicators (WDI) (2020–22) data.

Finally, other countries with low conflict-related crises—Cambodia, Malawi, Nepal, Rwanda, Tanzania, Zambia and Zimbabwe—typically have high economic crises indicators alongside variable climate crises. An exception is Tanzania, though our mixed methods data on self-reported shocks and crises (e.g. Table 3.1 in Chapter 3) motivates its inclusion in this category alongside its poor capacity to deal with climate-related disasters.

There are various caveats to Table 2.2. The dates of the sources and the definitions applied can result in different categories. For example, Zambia's low climate hazard and vulnerability score does not appear to capture well the massive drought and dry years experienced recently. Additionally, very large countries might be peaceful across extensive areas of the country but may be defined as high conflict due to localised intense conflict. Nevertheless, Table 2.2 offers some indication of the country-level presence of or proxies for crisis conditions.

2.3.2 Capacity to respond to crises

As the example from Tanzania above suggests, alongside existing crises profiles, it is also important to consider country-level preparedness to manage crises. This is because countries experiencing severe crises but with strong governance capacity backed by institutional management strategies may be better placed to cope with crises. Table 2.3 presents a stoplight scorecard for the focus countries in terms of their ability to cope with climate-related disasters, economic crises and violent conflict, proxied by institutional-level indicators defined in Annex Table A1.

An immediate observation is the heterogeneity of voice and accountability scores across countries when disaggregated by the type of polycrisis. This suggests that citizen demands for accountability may have less of a consistent effect in strengthening institutional responses to crises. Indeed, research on inclusive, sustainable economic transformation similarly found this to be less of a factor in driving sustainability across the broader three categories of social, economic and environmental sustainability in low- and lower middle-income countries (Diwakar et al., 2025).

In terms of countries experiencing triple crises, Afghanistan scores poorly in terms of its ability to manage crises. Its adoption and implementation of national disaster risk reduction (DRR) strategies are weak, it experiences poor economic management, weak government effectiveness and low voice and accountability. Nigeria—albeit without information on its DRR capacity—also receives weak scores in terms of its government effectiveness and voice and accountability, but an average score in terms of its economic management. However, the intensity of these weak coping capacities is not as severe as in Afghanistan. The two countries are also varied in terms of underlying governance challenges (Table 2.3). Afghanistan has been affected by decades of power fragmentation and the erosion of state legitimacy and its institutional capacities, leading to weak service delivery and externally driven poverty reduction interventions. In contrast, Nigeria is a more stable state with established federal structures and state-delivered services for poverty reduction, albeit undermined by corruption and patronage politics.

In terms of countries affected by the climate–conflict nexus, there is a bimodal distribution. On one end are Niger and Ethiopia, which have relatively weak DRR capacity and low government effectiveness, while Ethiopia also experiences poor economic management. Both countries also experience low voice and accountability scores. India, Kenya, and the Philippines at the other end of the spectrum fare relatively well across dimensions where data is available. Thus, even though these three countries score poorly on social crises (Table 2.2), their relatively stronger coping capacities may make them better placed to manage conflict.

Finally, for countries experiencing climate-related disasters with economic crises, there is more heterogeneity in coping capacities. Zimbabwe performs particularly weakly on its economic management and government effectiveness, though adequately in terms of its disaster risk reduction capacity. Yet when compared to Table 2.2, the combination of high risk of economic crises with poor economic and government coping capacities make for a particularly challenging institutional context.

Taken together, Malawi, Zambia and Zimbabwe perform poorly in terms of economic management, while Zambia and Nepal have weak DRR capacities. This set of four countries also have weak government effectiveness. On the other hand, Cambodia, Rwanda and Tanzania appear to be doing relatively strongly on economic management and government effectiveness, though poorly in terms of DRR. Finally, Bangladesh faces the opposite challenge—strong on its DRR but weak on economic management and government effectiveness. These variations are particularly interesting when viewed alongside their crises profiles (Table 2.2)—where for example Bangladesh scores poorly on climate crises yet has strong DRR capacity, and Rwanda scores poorly on economic crises yet has strong economic management capacity and broader government effectiveness. This suggests that these countries may be able to better institutionally manage the effects of crises when they strike.

2.3.3 Convergence of polycrisis and poverty?

At a cross-country level, there is a clear correlation between the number of people affected by climate-related disasters and the number of fatalities due to violent conflict. Moreover, the rate of inflation is generally high towards and into the top right quadrant of Figure 2.5 (as measured by the larger size of the circles on average), especially amongst low-income countries. This quadrant is also where the numbers of people affected by conflicts and disasters are highest. It's worth noting more broadly that the data covers the time since COVID-19, when a global public health crisis was also prevalent, and where inflation rates also soared due to the economic crisis it produced. Together, these results point to the presence of intersecting climate-related disasters, violent conflict and economic crises.

Moreover, absolute numbers of people in poverty are often higher in countries with more deaths due to climate-related disasters or conflict (Figure 2.6). These results are in part a function of large population sizes. Though biased against populous countries, this nevertheless points to the added challenges that populous low- and lower middle-income countries in particular face due to crises and poverty. Moreover, this positive relationship is still observed especially in low-income countries when measuring conflict- and disaster-affected people as a share of the total population. This points to a convergence of poverty with polycrisis, providing some indication of a polycrisis–poverty trap.

Poverty rates of focus countries are next presented in Figure 2.7 for focus countries. There is wide heterogeneity in poverty profiles, with extreme poverty rates consistently lower in South and Southeast Asia compared to the focus countries in Africa. This reflects the regions' strong poverty reduction at the turn of the century. However, there are exceptions, where for example national poverty rates based on thresholds equivalent to approximately a third of the international poverty line point to 47.1% of people living in

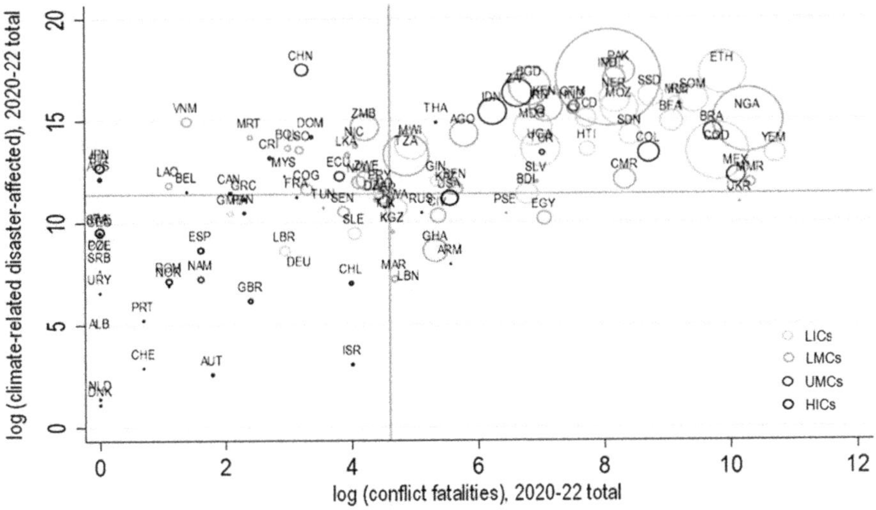

Figure 2.6 Populations affected by climate-related disasters and conflict by country, 2020–22, weighted by number of population in poverty pre-pandemic

Source: authors' analysis of ACLED (2020–22), EM-DAT (2020–22) and Poverty and Inequality Platform (PIP) (latest year after 2010) data, first presented in Diwakar et al. (2023).

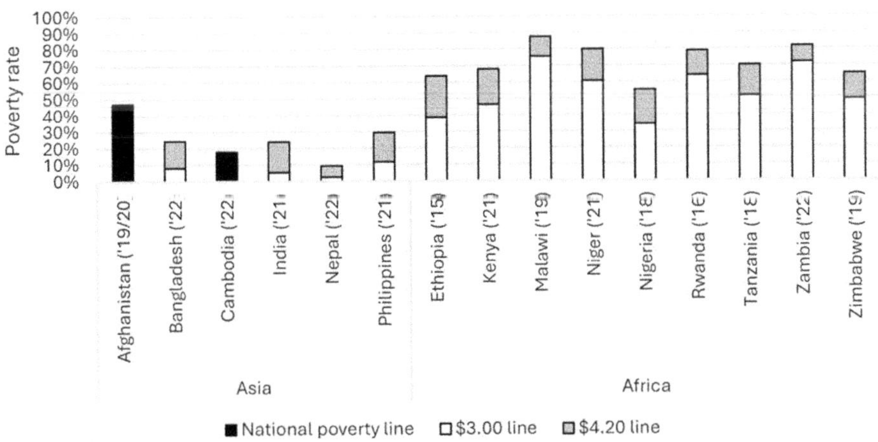

Figure 2.7 Extreme and moderate poverty headcount ratios at international poverty lines (IPLs)

Note: IPL data not available for Afghanistan and Cambodia, so poverty rates based on national poverty lines are presented (equivalent to approximately US$1.00/day in Afghanistan and US$2.70/day in Cambodia).

Source: author's visualisation of data from World Bank Poverty and Inequality Platform, 2025.

poverty in 2019–20 in Afghanistan. Interestingly, there is a relatively comparable share of people living above the extreme poverty line but still in moderate poverty across countries, with rates lower in Nepal, Zambia and Malawi—though in the latter two this is on account of high extreme poverty.

Figure 2.8 illustrates the high degree of mobility underpinning the static estimates of poverty presented above. It points to considerable heterogeneity in the types of movements into and out of poverty across countries. Box 2.2 summarises the latter based on CPAN evidence. Chronic poverty is particularly low in rural Bangladesh while sustained escapes are highest in India, again both South Asian countries with considerable poverty reduction in the early 2000s period captured by the data. Chronic poverty is highest in Niger and Malawi, though rates of downward mobility and churning around the poverty line are also high in Nigeria, Tanzania and to a lesser degree Ethiopia, likely on account of varied sources of risk. The drivers with a focus on the overlap of crises across these trajectories are investigated in the subsequent chapters.

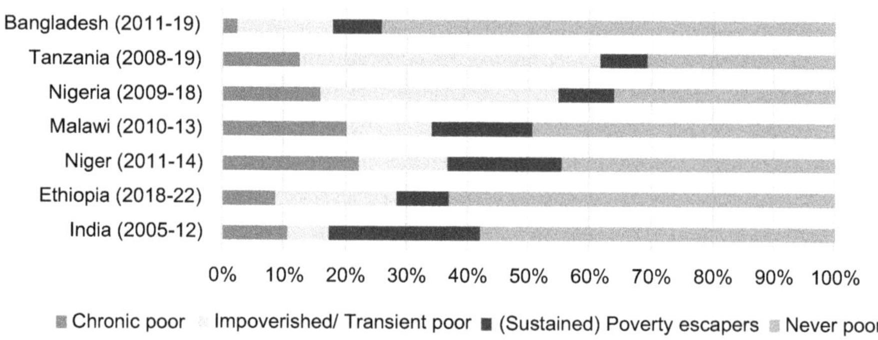

Figure 2.8 Poverty dynamics at reference poverty lines[1]
Source: author's analysis of panel data presented in Table 1.1.

Box 2.2 Factors enabling sustained poverty escapes

A mixed methods analysis from nine countries in parts of East Africa, South Asia and Southeast Asia in the 2010s (see Diwakar and Shepherd, 2022) points to the importance of livelihood trajectories emphasising economic diversification—in agriculture and off-farm sectors, and commonly also involving internal migration—in sustained pathways out of poverty. Underpinning these strategies were forms of asset development, especially of farm or business assets, electricity and livestock, or of education as an intangible asset. Livestock for example could act as a store of value but also was commonly used as insurance or sold during times of crises. Education, especially the completion of at least lower secondary education of the household head, has been of instrumental importance in these pathways, more so when combined with these positive livelihood strategies.

The role of social networks within and outside of the family complements these strategies. Within the family, spousal collaboration was identified as supporting sustained poverty escapes, whether through mutual support, transfers of capital and investment of savings, economic partnerships and shared decision-making.

Finally, the enabling environment also helped determine the degree to which sustained rather than transitory escapes from poverty could be supported:

> Interactive features of this environment that are conducive to sustained escapes include context-specific pro-poor policy and infrastructure, for example around livestock insurance, climate-smart agriculture alongside predictable disaster risk management, universal health coverage, and supporting a negotiated approach to norm change.
>
> (Diwakar and Shepherd, 2022)

2.4 Conclusion

This chapter introduced an integrated conceptual framework for improving our understanding of polycrisis and poverty dynamics. This framework was informed by concepts of state fragility alongside the antithesis of "sustainability", which is argued here as reflecting crises along the three dimensions examined in this book: environmental, economic and social. However, unlike existing frameworks of fragility or sustainability which focus largely on the macro-level, our focus is on bridging this with the micro-level poverty dynamics that are generated amidst and due to polycrisis. We thus incorporate a focus on direct impacts alongside coping mechanisms that are often a cause and consequence of heightened vulnerability and that can reinforce negative poverty trajectories.

The chapter also presented country-level insights on the salience of the three crises, poverty and its dynamics within the subset of countries that are the focus of subsequent chapters. The convergence of polycrisis and poverty observed here points to a reinforcing relationship. Crises are widely prevalent and coping strategies often weak in low- and lower middle-income countries. Partly as a result, this is likely to reinforce conditions of vulnerability that can worsen the emergence and amplification of crises.

These reflections which relate centrally to the conceptual framework are revisited in the empirical chapters that follow. Chapters 3–5 draw attention to the outer ends of the processual framework—the direct impacts of polycrisis on negative poverty trajectories. Chapter 6 focuses especially on coping responses and pathways out of poverty amidst polycrisis.

Note

1 Bangladesh's data is a rural survey that relies on the $1.90 line; Tanzania and Nigeria's data is based on a relative measure where the bottom 40% of households

per wave are defined as living in poverty; and Malawi, Niger, Ethiopia and India's data is based on national poverty lines, albeit with a reliance on just two waves meaning it can only calculate poverty escapes and not whether these were sustained.

References

ACAPS (2025) 'Zambia: Update on the impact of drought'. https://www.acaps.org/fileadmin/Data_Product/Main_media/20250116_ACAPS_Zambia_-_Update_on_the_impact_of_drought_.pdf.

ACLED (2024) 'Situation Update April 2024. Kenya: Kenyan security forces combating al-Shabaab, pastoralist militias, and mob violence'. https://acleddata.com/2024/04/19/kenya-situation-update-april-2024-kenyan-security-forces-combating-al-shabaab-pastoralist-militias-and-mob-violence/.

Adams, A.M., Cekan, J. and Sauerborn, R. (1998) 'Towards a conceptual framework of household coping: reflections from rural West Africa'. *Africa: Journal of the International African Institute*, 68(2): 263–283.

ADB, UNICEF and World Food Programme (2021) 'Socio-economic impact assessment of Covid-19 in Cambodia'. World Food Programme. https://docs.wfp.org/api/documents/WFP-0000137166/download/?_ga=2.253509696.878333279.1646741780-1361699286.1641794423.

Adger, W.N. (2006). 'Vulnerability'. *Global Environmental Change*, 16(3): 268–281.

Antoniades, A., Antonarakis, A.S. and Kempf, I. (Eds.) (2022) *Financial crises, poverty and environmental sustainability: Challenges in the context of the SDGs and COVID-19 recovery.* Springer Nature.

Asbrock, F. and Fritsche, I. (2013) 'Authoritarian reactions to terrorist threat: Who is being threatened, the me or the we?' *International Journal of Psychology*, 48(1): 35–49.

Babatounde, M. and Kanta, M.S. (2024) 'Turning governance challenges into opportunities: how reforms are transforming lives in Niger'. World Bank. https://blogs.worldbank.org/en/africacan/turning-governance-challenges-into-opportunities-how-reforms-are-transforming-lives-in-niger.

Babst, A. (2025) 'In the Philippines, the president and vice president are threatening each other'. *NZZ*, 25 February. https://www.nzz.ch/english/philippine-political-feud-brings-death-threats-and-gridlock-ld.1872662.

Ballard-Rosa, C., Jensen, A. and Scheve, K. (2022) 'Economic decline, social identity, and authoritarian values in the United States'. *International Studies Quarterly*, 5(1): 1–14. doi:10.1093/isq/sqab027.

Banks, N. (2016) 'Youth poverty, employment and livelihoods: Social and economic implications of living with insecurity in Arusha, Tanzania'. *Environment & Urbanization*, 28(2): 437–454. doi:10.1177/0956247816651201.

Barbier, E.B. (1987) 'The concept of sustainable economic development'. *Environmental Conservation*, 14(2): 101–110. https://www.jstor.org/stable/44519759.

Basu, I., Devine, J. and Wood, G. (Eds.) (2018) *Politics and governance in Bangladesh: Uncertain landscapes.* Routledge.

BBC (2024) 'Why India farmers are protesting again'. *BBC*, 13 February. https://www.bbc.co.uk/news/world-asia-india-68282270.

Béné, C., Newsham, A., Davies, M., Ulrichs, M. and Godfrey-Wood, R. (2014). 'Resilience, poverty and development'. *Journal of International Development*, 26(5): 598–623.

Booth, D. (2012) *Development as a collective action problem: Addressing the real challenges of African governance.* Overseas Development Institute.

Boyer, R.H.W., Peterson, N.D., Arora, P. and Caldwell, K. (2016) 'Five approaches to social sustainability and an integrated way forward'. *Sustainability*, 8(9): 878. doi:10.3390/su8090878.

Brown, B.J., Hanson, M.E., Liverman, D.M. and Merideth, R. (1987) 'Global sustainability: Toward definition'. *Environmental Management*, 11: 713–719. doi:10.1007/BF01867238.

BTI (2022) 'Country report: Afghanistan'. https://bti-project.org/fileadmin/api/content/en/downloads/reports/country_report_2022_AFG.pdf.

Bündnis Entwicklung Hilft and IFHV (2024) 'WordRiskReport 2024'. Bündnis Entwicklung Hilft. https://reliefweb.int/report/world/worldriskreport-2024-focus-multiple-crises.

Burattini, B., Guerreiro Osorio, R., Wagner, L., Markhof, Y. and Arruda, P. (2022) 'Afghanistan: Needs assessment'. *Research Report, No. 66*. International Policy Centre for Inclusive Growth. https://ipcid.org/sites/default/files/pub/en/RR66_Afghanistan_Needs_assessment.pdf.

Calhoun, C. (2004) 'A world of emergencies: Fear, intervention, and the limits of cosmopolitan order'. *Canadian Review of Sociology and Anthropology*, 41(4): 373–395.

Cannon, T. and Müller-Mahn, D. (2010) 'Vulnerability, resilience and development discourses in context of climate change'. *Journal of International Development*, 22 (2): 220–233.

Carter, M.R. and Barrett, C.B. (2006) 'The economics of poverty traps and persistent poverty: An asset-based approach'. *The Journal of Development Studies*, 42(2): 178–199. doi:10.1080/00220380500405261.

CDRI (2012) 'Understanding poverty dynamics: Evidence from nine villages in Cambodia'. *CDRI Working Paper Series No. 69*. http://www.cdri.org.kh/webdata/download/wp/wp69e.pdf.

Chambers, R. (1983) *Rural development: Putting the last first*. Longman.

Chandler, D. (2006) *Empire in denial: The politics of state-building*. Pluto Press.

Chowdhury, T.J., Arbon, P., Gebbie, K., Muller, R., Kako, M. and Steenkamp, M. (2022) 'Lived experience of women's well-being in the cyclone shelters of Coastal Bangladesh'. *Prehosp. Disaster Med.*, 37(4): 437–443. https://pmc.ncbi.nlm.nih.gov/articles/PMC9280069/pdf/S1049023X2200070Xa.pdf.

Clary, C. (2025) 'Four days in May: The India-Pakistan crisis of 2025'. Stimson. https://www.stimson.org/2025/four-days-in-may-the-india-pakistan-crisis-of-2025/.

Collier, P. and Hoeffler, A. (2004) 'Greed and grievance in civil war'. *Oxford Economic Papers*, 56(4): 563–595.

Corral, P., Irwin, A., Krishnan, N., Mahler, D. and Vishwanath, T. (2020) 'Fragility and conflict: On the front lines of the fight against poverty'. World Bank Group. http://documents.worldbank.org/curated/en/375651583211667808.

Cox, P.M., Betts, R., Jones, C., Spall, S. and Totterdell, I. (2000) 'Acceleration of global warming due to carbon-cycle feedbacks'. *Nature*, 408(6809): 184–187.

Crenshaw, K. (1991) 'Mapping the margins: intersectionality, identity politics, and violence against women of color'. *Stanford Law Review*, 43(6): 1241–1299.

da Corta, L., Kayunze, K.A., Kahamba, J.S., Simba, C.G., Shepherd, A., Mangi, H. O. (2022) 'Covid-19 monitoring in rural Tanzania: The pandemic exacerbated pre-existing factors negatively affecting wellbeing'. *CPAN*. https://www.chronicpovertynetwork.org/resources/2022/11/7/covid-19-monitoring-in-rural-tanzania-the-pandemic-exacerbated-pre-existing-factors-negatively-affecting-wellbeing.

Davies, S. (1993) 'Are coping strategies a copout?' *IDS Bulletin*, 24(4): 60–72.

Devereux, S. (2001) 'Livelihood insecurity and social protection: A re-emerging issue in rural development'. *Development Policy Review*, 19(4): 507–519.

de Waal, A. (2000) 'Democratic political process and the fight against famine'. *IDS Working Paper 107*. IDS.

Diwakar, V. and Shepherd, A. (2022) 'Sustaining escapes from poverty'. *World Development*, 151: 105611. doi:10.1016/j.worlddev.2021.105611.

Diwakar, V., Bizoza, A., Lenhardt, A., Shepherd, A., Moonga, A., Shahan, A. (2023) 'Equitably responding to and recovering amid polycrisis'. In A. Shepherd *et al.* (Eds.), *Chronic Poverty Report 5 – Pandemic poverty.* Institute of Development Studies (IDS). doi:10.19088/CPAN.2023.021.

Diwakar, V., Kamninga, T., Kelsall, T., Pickard, S., Raga, S., Shepherd, A. (2025) 'Inclusive and sustainable economic transformation: Ways forward in low- and middle-income countries'. *ODI*. https://odi.org/en/publications/inclusive-and-sustainable-economic-transformation-ways-forward-in-low-and-middle-income-countries.

Eynde, O.V. (2018) 'Targets of violence: Evidence from India's Naxalite conflict'. *The Economic Journal*, 128(609): 887–916. doi:10.1111/ecoj.12438.

Few, R., Chhotray, V., Tebboth, M., Forster, J., White, C., Armijos, T. (2020) 'COVID-19 crisis: Lessons for recovery. What can we learn from existing research on the long-term aspects of disaster risk and recovery?' *The British Academy*. https://www.thebritishacademy.ac.uk/publications/covid-19-crisis-lessons-recovery/.

Folke, C. (2006). 'Resilience: The emergence of a perspective for social–ecological systems analyses'. *Global Environmental Change*, 16(3): 253–267.

Fraser, N. and Vogel, L. (2017) 'Crisis of care? On the social-reproductive contradictions of contemporary capitalism'. In T. Bhattacharya (Ed.), *Social reproduction theory: Remapping class, recentering oppression*. Pluto Press. doi:10.2307/j.ctt1vz494j.6.

Freedom House (2025) 'Ethiopia' . *Freedom in the World 2025*. https://freedomhouse.org/country/ethiopia/freedom-world/2025.

Friedman, M. and Schwartz, A.J. (1963). *A monetary history of the United States, 1867–1960*. Princeton University Press.

Fund for Peace (2022) Fragile States Index. https://fragilestatesindex.org/.

Green Climate Fund (2019) 'Funding proposal. SAP007: Integrated climate risk management for food security and livelihoods in Zimbabwe focusing on Masvingo and Rushinga districts. Zimbabwe. World Food Programme. B.23/10'. https://www.greenclimate.fund/sites/default/files/document/funding-proposal-sap007-wfp-zimbabwe.pdf.

Hansen, J., Sato, M. and Ruedy, R. (2012) 'Perception of climate change'. *Proceedings of the National Academy of Sciences*, 109(37): E2415–E2423.

Harvey, D. (2010) *Enigma of capital and the crises of capitalism*. Profile Books.

Hayek, F.A. (1931) *Prices and production*. George Routledge & Sons.

Heltberg, R., Hossain, N., Reva, A. and Turk, C. (2012) 'Coping and resilience during the food, fuel and financial crises'. *The Journal of Development Studies*, 49(5): 705–718.

Hilhorst, D. and Mena, R. (2021) 'When Covid-19 meets conflict: Politics of the pandemic response in fragile and conflict-affected states'. *Disasters*, 45(Suppl. 1): S174-S194. doi:10.1111/disa.12514.

Homer-Dixon, T.F. (1994) 'Environmental scarcities and violent conflict: Evidence from cases'. *International Security*, 19(1): 5–40.

HRW (2022) 'Afghanistan: Economic roots of the humanitarian crisis'. https://www.hrw.org/news/2022/03/01/afghanistan-economic-roots-humanitarian-crisis.

Hulme, D. and Shepherd, A. (2003). 'Conceptualising chronic poverty'. *World Development*, 31(3): 403–423.

IEP (2024) *Global Peace Index* [*Dataset*]. Institute for Economics & Peace.

IMF (2020) 'Climate change and financial risk'. https://www.imf.org/external/pubs/ft/ar/2020/eng/spotlight/climate-change/.

INFORM (2025) *INFORM Risk Index* [*Dataset*]. European Commission, Joint Research Centre (JRC).

International Crisis Group (2018) 'Stopping Nigeria's spiralling farmer-herder violence' (*Report No. 262*). https://www.crisisgroup.org/africa/west-africa/nigeria/262-stopping-nigerias-spiralling-farmer-herder-violence.

International Organization for Migration (2024) *Kenya crisis response plan 2024*. https://crisisresponse.iom.int/response/kenya-crisis-response-plan-2024.

IPCC (2021) *Climate change 2021: The physical science basis*. Cambridge University Press.

IWGIA (2025) 'The Indigenous World 2025: Bangladesh'. https://iwgia.org/en/bangladesh/5652-iw-2025-bangladesh.html.

Kahl, C.H. (2006) *States, scarcity, and civil strife in the developing world*. Princeton University Press.

Kalyvas, S.N. (2006) *The logic of violence in civil war*. Cambridge University Press.

Keynes, J.M. (1936) *The general theory of employment, interest and money*. Macmillan.

Krugman, P. (1999) 'The return of depression economics'. *Council on Foreign Relations*, 78(1): 56–74.

Laustsen, L. and Petersen, M. B. (2017) 'Perceived conflict and leader dominance: Individual and contextual factors behind preferences for dominant leaders'. *Political Psychology*, 38(6): 1083–1101. doi:10.1111/pops.12403.

Lenton, T.M., Held, H., Kriegler, E., Hall, J., Lucht, W., Rahmstorf, S. (2008) 'Tipping elements in the Earth's climate system'. *Proceedings of the National Academy of Sciences*, 105(6): 1786–1793.

Lind, J., Holland-Szyp, C., Sabates-Wheeler, R., Teshome, Y. and Otto Naess, L.O. (2025) 'Can social protection programmes promote livelihoods and climate resilience in conflict-affected settings? Evidence from Ethiopia's Productive Safety Net Programme'. *BASIC research working paper 37*. IDS. doi:10.19088/BASIC.2025.006.

Lucas, R.E. (1977) 'Understanding business cycles'. In K. Brunner & A.H. Meltzer (Eds.), *Stabilization of the domestic and international economy* (Vol. 5, pp. 7–29). North-Holland.

Lührmann, A., Edgell, A.B. and Maerz, S.F. (2020) 'Pandemic backsliding: Does Covid-19 put democracy at risk?'. *V-Dem Institute Policy Brief No. #23*. V-DEM Institute.

Mangubhai, S., Nand, Y., Reddy, C. and Jagadish, A. (2021) 'Politics of vulnerability: Impacts of Covid-19 and Cyclone Harold on Indo-Fijians engaged in small- scale fisheries'. *Environmental Science & Policy*, 120: 195–203. doi:10.1016/j.envsci.2021.03.003.

Mao, Y. (2021) 'Political institutions, state capacity, and crisis management: A comparison of China and South Korea'. *International Political Science Review*, 42(3): 316–332. doi:10.1177/0192512121994026.

Marx, K. (1867) *Capital: A critique of political economy*.

Médecins Sans Frontières (2023) 'Malawi: MSF responds to medical needs following Cyclone Freddy'. https://www.doctorswithoutborders.org/latest/malawi-msf-responds-medical-needs-following-cyclone-freddy.

Minsky, H.P. (1986) *Stabilizing an unstable economy*. Yale University Press.

Morin, E. and Kern, A.B. (1999) *Homeland Earth: A manifesto for the new millenium*, Hampton Press.

Namit, K. and Poulsen, T. (2023) 'How could rising food prices impact education outcomes in Rwanda – and what can be done?' *Education for Global Development*, 16 February. World Bank. https://blogs.worldbank.org/en/education/how-could-rising-food-prices-impact-education-outcomes-rwanda-and-what-can-be-done.

Narayan, D., Pritchett, L. and Kapoor, S. (2009) *Moving out of poverty, Vol. 2: Success from the bottom up*. Palgrave Macmillan/World Bank.

ND-GAIN (2022) Notre Dame Global Adaptation Initiative Country Index [Dataset]. University of Notre Dame.

Nebbia, G. (2012) 'The unsustainability of sustainability'. *Capitalism Nature Socialism*, 23(2): 95–107.

Nguyen, T.T., Nguyen, T.T., and Grote, U. (2020) 'Multiple shocks and households' choice of coping strategies in rural Cambodia'. *Ecological Economics*, 167. doi:10.1016/j.ecolecon.2019.106442.

Nixon, R. (2011) *Slow violence and the environmentalism of the poor*. Harvard University Press.

OCHA (2022) 'Humanitarian response plan Afghanistan'. https://reliefweb.int/report/afghanistan/afghanistan-humanitarian-response-plan-2018-2021-2020-year-end-monitoring-report#:~:text=In%202020%2C%20%24564.5%20million%20(50,the%20country%20throughout%20the%20year.

OECD (2022) *States of Fragility 2022*. https://www.oecd.org/en/publications/2022/09/states-of-fragility-2022_9ee73e08.html.

Okoi, O. and Iwara, M-A. (2021) 'The failure of governance in Nigeria: An epistocratic challenge'. *Georgetown Journal of International Affairs*, 12 April. https://gjia.georgetown.edu/2021/04/12/the-failure-of-governance-in-nigeria-an-epistocratic-challenge/.

Østby, G. (2008) 'Polarization, horizontal inequalities and violent civil conflict'. *Journal of Peace Research*, 45(2): 143–162.

Pokhrel, J. (2022) 'Impact of COVID-19 on economy of Nepal'. *Shaheed Smriti Peer Reviewed Journal*, 11(8): 20–27.

Pollman, D. (2018) 'The anatomy of violence in Bangladesh'. ACLED, 9 November. https://acleddata.com/2018/11/09/the-anatomy-of-violence-in-bangladesh/.

Purvis, B., Mao, Y. and Robinson, D. (2019) 'Three pillars of sustainability: In search of conceptual origins'. *Sustain. Sci.*, 14: 681–695. doi:10.1007/s11625-018-0627-5.

Rath, D.B., Muduli, S. and Shekhar, H. (2023) 'Low Stagflation Risk in India'. *RBI Bulletin*, 77(12): 93–104. https://ssrn.com/abstract=4670597.

Regilme, S.S. and Parthenay, K. (2024) 'COVID-19 pandemic and competitive authoritarian regimes: Human rights and democracy in the Philippines and Nicaragua'. *Political Geography*, 115: 103212. doi:10.1016/j.polgeo.2024.103212.

Reuters (2024) 'As landslides hit Kerala, a look at India's extreme weather events'. Reuters, 30 July. https://www.reuters.com/world/india/india-extreme-weather-events-landslides-kerala-state-2024-07-30/.

Roberts, J.T. and Parks, B.C. (2007) *A climate of injustice: Global inequality, North–South politics, and climate policy*. MIT Press.

Rockström, J., Steffen, W., Noone, K., Persson, A., Chapin, F., Lambin, E. (2009) 'A safe operating space for humanity'. *Nature*, 461(7263): 472–475.

Roitman, J. (2013) *Anti-crisis*. Duke University Press.

Rosenbach, G. and Spielman, D. (2022) 'The global food and energy price crisis and implications for Rwanda'. International Food Policy Research Institute (IFPRI). https://rwanda.ifpri.info/2022/06/03/the-global-food-and-energy-price-crisis-and-implications-for-rwanda/.

Rotberg, R.I. (Ed.) (2004) *When states fail: Causes and consequences.* Princeton University Press.

Rothbard, M.N. (1963) *America's Great Depression.* D. Van Nostrand Company.

Ruel, M., Garrett, J., Hawkes, C. and Cohen, M. (2010) 'The food, fuel, and financial crises affect the urban and rural poor disproportionately: A review of the evidence'. *The Journal of Nutrition*, 140(1): 170S-176S.

Russo, S., Mirisola, A., Dallago, F. and Roccato, M. (2020) 'Facing natural disasters through the endorsement of authoritarian attitudes'. *Journal of Environmental Psychology*, 68: article 101412.

Sah, R.K. (2024) 'Preserving Nepal's mountains: Climate change, migration, and youth's role in the future'. International Organization for Migration, 5 June. https://environmentalmigration.iom.int/blogs/preserving-nepals-mountains-climate-change-migration-and-youths-role-future.

Scoones, I. (1998) 'Sustainable rural livelihoods: A framework for analysis'. *IDS working papers 72*. https://www.ids.ac.uk/publications/sustainable-rural-livelihoods-a-framework-for-analysis/.

Sen, A. (1981). *Poverty and famines: An essay on entitlement and deprivation.* Oxford University Press.

Severen, R.V., Roets, A., Van Muylem, D., Haesevoets, T., Van Hiel, A. and Wauters, B. (2024) 'Democratic and authoritarian government preferences in times of crisis: An experimental investigation'. *Social Psychology*, 55(1). https://econtent.hogrefe.com/doi/10.1027/1864-9335/a000538.

Shepherd, A., Bond, V., Bwalya, C., Bwalya, R., Chapoto, A., da Corta, L. (2021) 'Layered crises preventing poverty reduction: An analysis of Zambian poverty dynamics and policy implications'. In A. Antoniades *et al.* (Eds.), *Financial crises, poverty and environmental sustainability.* Springer.

Shepherd, A., Diwakar, V. Bizoza, A., Lenhardt, A., Moonga, A., Shahan, A. (2023) 'Chronic Poverty Report 5 – Pandemic poverty'. *CPAN, Institute of Development Studies.* https://DOI:10.19088/CC.2023.006.

Shepherd, A., Scott, L., Mariotti, C., Kessy, F., Gaiha, R., da Corta, L. and Hanifnia, K. (2014) 'The chronic poverty report 2014–2015: The road to zero extreme poverty'. *CPAN.* https://www.chronicpovertynetwork.org/resources/2014/6/13/the-chronic-poverty-report-2014-15-the-road-to-zero-poverty.

Shields, R. and Paulson, J. (2019) 'Analysing donor conceptualisations of state fragility'. *Education and Conflict Review*, 2: 20–27.

SIVIO Institute (2024) 'Navigating slow progress: The Government of Zimbabwe's performance in 2024'. *SIVIO Connect.* https://connect.sivioinstitute.org/2025/02/26/navigating-slow-progress-the-government-of-zimbabwes-performance-in-2024/.

Skoufias, E. (2003) 'Economic crises and natural disasters: Coping strategies and policy implications'. *World Development*, 31(7): 1087–1102.

Sneddon, A. (2019) 'Earthquakes and Landslides in Nepal'. *Practical Action.* https://practicalaction.org/wp-content/uploads/2019/07/SHEAR-Snapshot-Nepal-Earthquake.pdf.

Stewart, F. (2008) *Horizontal inequalities and conflict: Understanding group violence in multiethnic societies.* Palgrave Macmillan.

Tafere, Y., Shahan, A., Rahem, R. and Diwakar, V. (2023) 'The role of local resources in mitigating the impact of Covid-19'. *CPAN policy brief.* CPAN. https://hdl.handle.net/20.500.12413/18035.

Theodoro, S.H. and Leonardos, O.H. (2021) 'The unsustainable sustainability'. *Anais da Academia Brasileira de Ciências*, 93(1): e20181226.

Tooze, A. (2022) 'Welcome to the world of the polycrisis'. *Financial Times*, 28 October. https://www.ft.com/content/498398e7-11b1-494b-9cd3-6d669dc3de33.

UNDP (2021) 'Project document: Strengthening capacities for disaster risk reduction and adaptation for resilience in the Sahel region: Fostering risk-informed solutions for sustainable development'. https://www.undp.org/media/1057496/download?inline.

UNHCR (2023) *Government of Kenya SHIRIKA Plan*. https://data.unhcr.org/es/documents/download/104460.

UNHCR (2024) 'Operational Update: Niger – July 2024'. https://data.unhcr.org/en/documents/download/110817.

United Nations (2024) 'ROSEA 20240724 Malawi El Niño drought flash appeal update'. https://malawi.un.org/sites/default/files/2024-07/ROSEA_20240724_MALAWI_EL%20Nino_Drought_Flash_Appeal_Update.pdf.

United Nations Office for the Coordination of Humanitarian Affairs (2023) *Kenya Drought Response Plan 2023*. https://humanitarianaction.info/plan/1137/article/kenya-drought-response-plan-2023.

Vesco, P., Baliki, G., Bruck, T., Doring, S., Eriksson, A., Fjelde, H. (2025) 'The impacts of armed conflict on human development: A review of the literature'. *World Development*, 187: 106806.

von Uexkull, N.V., Croicu, M., Fjelde, H. and Buhaug, H. (2016) 'Civil conflict sensitivity to growing-season drought'. *PNAS*, 113(44): 12391–12396. https://www.pnas.org/doi/10.1073/pnas.1607542113.

WCED (1987) 'Report of the World Commission on Environment and Development: Our common future'. *World Commission on Environment and Development*. https://www.are.admin.ch/are/en/home/media/publications/sustainable-development/brundtland-report.html.

WDI (2023) *World Development Indicators* [*Dataset*]. World Bank.

WFP and FAO (2025) 'Hunger hotspots. FAO–WFP early warnings on acute food insecurity: June to October 2025 outlook'. doi:10.4060/cd5684en.

World Bank (2017) 'Multi-Sectoral Crisis Recovery Project for North Eastern Nigeria: Project Appraisal Document (Report No. PAD1992)'. https://documents1.worldbank.org/curated/en/720891490278540329/pdf/final-Project-Appraisal-Document-PAD-P157891-2017-03-06-15-07-03092017.pdf.

World Bank (2019a) 'Zambia – Transforming landscapes for resilience and development project: Project appraisal document'. https://documents1.worldbank.org/curated/en/341331558231295072/pdf/Zambia-Transforming-Landscapes-for-Resilience-and-Development-Project.pdf.

World Bank (2019b) 'Rwanda: Socio-Economic Inclusion of Refugees and Host Communities Project: Project Appraisal Document on a Proposed Credit in the Amount of SDR 25.1 million (US$35 million equivalent) and a Proposed Grant in the Amount of SDR 17.9 million (US$25 million equivalent) to the Republic of Rwanda. Report No: PAD3172'. https://documents1.worldbank.org/curated/en/222811556935409836/pdf/Rwanda-Socio-Economic-Inclusion-of-Refugees-and-Host-Communities-in-Rwanda-Project.pdf.

World Bank (2020) 'Ethiopia – Urban Productive Safety Net and Jobs Project: Project Appraisal Document'. https://documents1.worldbank.org/curated/en/438581601776877012/pdf/Ethiopia-Urban-Productive-Safety-Net-and-Jobs-Project.pdf.

World Bank (2021) 'Climate risk country profile: Bangladesh'. https://climateknowledgeportal.worldbank.org/sites/default/files/country-profiles/15502-WB_Bangladesh%20Country%20Profile-WEB.pdf.

World Bank (2022a) 'Cambodia Southeast Asia Disaster Risk Management Project 2. Report No: PAD4726'. https://documents1.worldbank.org/curated/en/879561653594041489/pdf/Cambodia-Second-Southeast-Asia-Disaster-Risk-Management-Project.pdf.

World Bank (2022b) 'Afghanistan Community Resilience and Livelihoods Project: Project Appraisal Document'. https://documents1.worldbank.org/curated/en/099941005092220009/pdf/IDU0ba95440800fb504e13083fc077d4132723aa.pdf.

World Bank (2023a) 'FY23 List of Fragile and Conflict-affected Situations'. *Classification of Fragility and Conflict Situations.* World Bank. https://www.worldbank.org/en/topic/fragilityconflictviolence/brief/classification-of-fragile-and-conflict-affected-situations.

World Bank (2023b) 'New Malawi Economic Update calls for urgent action to address macroeconomic imbalances and increase energy access'. https://www.worldbank.org/en/news/press-release/2023/07/19/new-afe-malawi-economic-update-calls-for-urgent-action-to-address-macroeconomic-imbalances-and-increase-energy-access.

World Bank (2023c) 'Tanzania – The second productive social safety nets project – additional financing (P179701)'. https://documents1.worldbank.org/curated/en/099042623152532740/pdf/P17970105b60ed0708c460d8541a3ce69e.pdf.

World Bank (2024) 'Host and Rohingya Enhancement of Lives Project: Project Appraisal Document. Report No: PAD00204'. https://documents1.worldbank.org/curated/en/099050924092013437/pdf/BOSIB1b5f078a00961a7d11c833d7c55328.pdf.

World Bank (n.d.) 'Niger overview: Development news, research, data'. https://www.worldbank.org/en/country/niger/overview.

World Food Programme (2023a) 'Microinsurance and social protection: Ethiopia country case studies'. https://docs.wfp.org/api/documents/WFP-0000145513/download/.

World Food Programme (2023b) 'Country brief: The global food and economic crisis' impact on food system resilience in the Philippines'. https://reliefweb.int/report/philippines/country-brief-global-food-and-economic-crisis-impact-food-system-resilience-philippines-november-2023.

World Food Programme (2024) 'Economic hardship, the climate crisis and violence in the northeast projected to push 33.1 million Nigerians into food insecurity in 2025'. *Press release*, 8 November. https://www.wfp.org/news/economic-hardship-climate-crisis-and-violence-northeast-projected-push-331-million-nigerians.

Part II

Mixed methods evidence on poverty dynamics in times of polycrisis

3 Poverty dynamics and economic crisis in a changing climate

Climate-related disasters and economic crises are interlinked. Climate-related disasters on their own can lead to loss of crops and livestock, overwhelmed health facilities due to increased disease burdens and fatalities, health or education facilities being used as shelters thus disrupting human development, and the shifting of government resources to relief responses (Deutsch et al., 2018; Mall et al., 2017; Guihenneuc et al., 2023). However, climate-related disasters can also drive economic crises, for example by disrupting supply chains, damaging roads and other infrastructure thus reducing mobility including the ability to bring crops to market or seek work, and driving short-term spikes in food prices and other essential goods in a manner that disproportionately hurts people in and near poverty (da Corta et al., 2018; Ghadge et al., 2019; de Abreu et al., 2022; Odongo et al., 2022).

On the other hand, economic vulnerability can also precede and shape exposure to climate impacts. For example, economic crises can induce labour-market shifts, such as where formal job losses are high and workers are forced to take on more precarious work that can weaken their recovery prospects and reinforce vulnerability to climate-related disasters and other crises (Darvas, 2023). Furthermore, wage stagnation or currency devaluation can reduce households' resilience when climate shocks hit and market distortions during times of economic crises, such as through price volatility or exploitative lenders, can amplify this vulnerability.

At the same time, there is also broader economic inflation not directly caused by climate, such as international supply chain disruptions (e.g. due to the Ukraine war or COVID-19), which create external price shocks and deepen poverty. In other words, it is important to distinguish economic crises caused by climate impacts (e.g. droughts, floods) and economic crises driven by external/global factors (e.g. inflation, conflict, supply shocks).

In addition, both types of crises interact to shape future vulnerability and deepen poverty. Economic crises overlaid with climate-related disasters can drive distress migration amidst depressed labour markets. This can devalue currencies, driving inflationary pressures as households are no longer able to readily draw on savings or assets amidst a crisis of liquidity and asset destruction (Rastogi, 2023; Cooper, 1993). These intersections can push

DOI: 10.4324/9781003503125-5

governments to adopt austerity measures or policy responses that (inadvertently or intentionally) drive uneven recovery amidst the absence of effective safety nets. Macro-crises can also converge with micro-level shocks and stressors to reinforce deprivation and force households to adopt environmentally and economically unsustainable measures that drive or amplify crises in a mutually reinforcing relationship. Where such crises are severe, countries may be driven to take international loans that reinforce debt dependency and constrain investments in resilient infrastructure and systems, thus limiting their ability to reduce poverty over the long term (Chelwa et al., 2024; Chuku et al., 2023).

This chapter investigates how the intersection of climate-related disasters and economic crises drive negative poverty trajectories, drawing on insights from Bangladesh, Cambodia, Nepal, Malawi, Tanzania, Zambia and Zimbabwe. Section 3.1 considers how these intersections can drive households to churn around the poverty line based on the analysis of nationally representative quantitative panel data. The two subsequent sections undertake a mixed methods analysis, critically synthesising insights from CPAN studies (e.g. da Corta et al., 2018; Diwakar, 2018; Bird, Diwakar, Manjengwa et al., 2023; Bird, Diwakar, Roth et al., 2023; Shepherd et al., 2025; Shepherd et al., 2021) alongside a new cross-country re-analysis of the mixed methods data. In particular, Section 3.2 relies on mixed methods data to investigate the changing role of agriculture, which faces growing environmental and price pressures and yet helps households in extreme or chronic poverty with marginal landholdings survive during times of heightened crises. Section 3.3 next considers how government responses to the polycrisis, often through economic policymaking in times of austerity, could inadvertently or intentionally reinforce downward income mobility. Section 3.4 concludes.

3.1 Churning and chronic poverty amidst climate-related disasters and economic crises

3.1.1 Economic crises, low-stressor insecurities and a changing climate

Climate-related disasters are prevalent across the countries in Figure 3.1, with the highest rate in rural Bangladesh, largely on account of data measurement differences.[1] However, despite their prevalence, there are interesting differences between poverty trajectories within the countries being discussed. In Zambia, Malawi and Bangladesh, households that were never in poverty during the survey period are least likely to report climate crises or their intersection with economic or conflict-related crises, though most likely in Tanzania (discussed below). Amongst the upwardly mobile in Tanzania and Malawi, moreover, there is a larger share of households reporting only climate-related disasters relative to the downwardly mobile. This suggests that households are still able to develop pathways out of poverty amidst climate-related disasters, relative to crises intersections. Results may also reflect the ability of richer households to

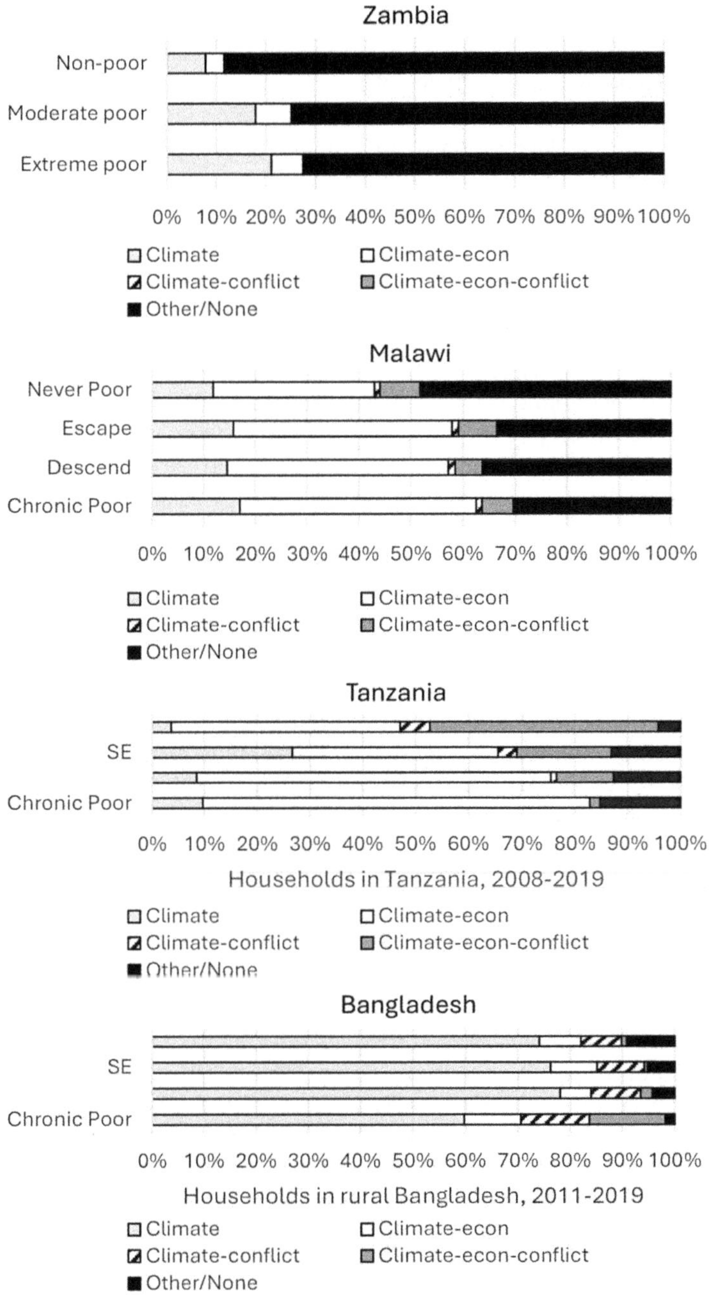

Figure 3.1 Climate-related disasters and polycrisis in Zambia, Malawi, Tanzania and rural Bangladesh, disaggregated by poverty status/trajectory

Note: climate and conflict data in Tanzania and Bangladesh are based on actual geo-coded data, while elsewhere they are based on self-reported shock modules (see Chapter 1).

Source: author's analysis of panel survey data presented in Table 1.1.

reside in or migrate to areas less affected by polycrisis, or with more stable jobs that enable them to better weather price shocks, each of which can guard against experiencing crises or their intersections.

Instead, the intersection of climate and economic crises appears to be prolonging poverty. The presence of climate-related and economic crises is clearly pronounced amongst households that are living in chronic or extreme poverty and/or those that are falling into poverty or experiencing its transience. This is evident in Bangladesh, Malawi, Tanzania and Zambia. For example, climate and economic shocks are more commonly reported amongst households in moderate or extreme poverty in Zambia, amongst the chronic poor in Malawi and Bangladesh, and amongst the transient poor and chronic poor in Tanzania (Figure 3.1). Taken together, these results give an early indication that the salience of economic crises and climate-related disasters may be a factor driving chronic poverty or its transience, a point we return to below.

Insecurity, alongside climate-related disasters and economic crises, is variably evident in these countries, although the type of insecurity is low-intensity or more localised and distinct from the conflict-affected contexts discussed in Chapter 4. In Malawi, insecurity in the survey data is mostly reported for experiences of theft. In Tanzania, where we rely on the presence of actual fatalities rather than self-reported data, fatalities are often due to violence against civilians, many of whom are politicians, journalists or local leaders (analysis of ACLED data). It is perhaps for this reason that the intersection of this type of insecurity with climate-related disasters and economic shocks is more frequently reported by wealthier households, especially in Tanzania where over two in five households (43%) experienced these triple crises across the panel period.

3.1.2 Climate-related disasters and economic crises in Tanzania

In Tanzania, amongst the subset of households who were in poverty in 2008, sustained escapers into 2019 were least prevalent amongst households who had experienced both climate-related disasters and economic shocks. Instead, more of these households that started in poverty and then experienced climate-related disasters and economic crises were identified to have escaped but then fallen back into relative poverty (Figure 3.2). Similar results hold when focusing on drought as a subset of climate-related disasters (Diwakar, 2025).

Such descriptive analysis is reinforced in the regression results, where households experiencing both drought and economic crises over the 2008 to 2019 survey period experienced a higher probability of churning around the poverty line relative to just experiencing drought. This may be due to the seasonal nature of some economic shocks—like rising food prices during lean periods—where a drought intensifies the impact, but households might partially recover the following year if conditions improve. Households experiencing drought with economic crises were also less likely to be able to sustain escapes from poverty conditional on beginning the period in relative poverty,

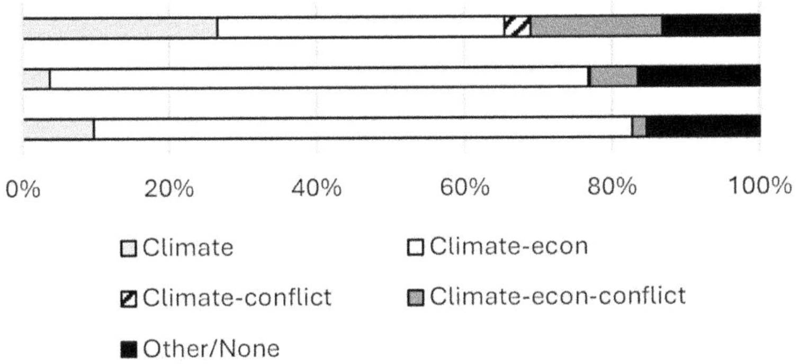

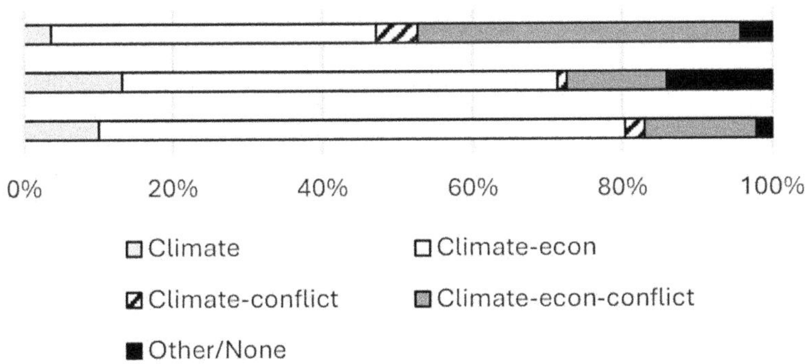

Figure 3.2 Climate-related disasters and polycrisis in Tanzania, disaggregated by households beginning the survey period in poverty (top) and beginning the survey period non-poor (bottom)

Note: drought, floods and insecurity draw on actual data from CRU-TS, Global Flood Observatory and ACLED, respectively.

Source: analysis of TNPS (2008–19), ACLED (2008–19), Global Flood Observatory (2008–18) and CRU-TS (2008–20), first presented in Diwakar (2025).

relative to experiencing just drought. Drought with economic shocks was also associated with a higher probability of chronic poverty as well as impoverishment in Tanzania (Figure 3.3).

Into and beyond the COVID-19 pandemic, moreover, price shocks increased in frequency. In Tanzania, an increase in the price of food items affected 57% of households by 2024 and was particularly common amongst urban households (Figure 3.4). Climate shocks were also common, affecting nearly one in three households over the same period. Both climate and economic shocks were also the most common self-reported shocks prior to the pandemic in Tanzania (Diwakar, 2025). It is then unsurprising that more households, especially those experiencing climate-related and economic crises (compared to just one crises), felt that they had become financially worse off during the year preceding the survey (Figure 3.5).

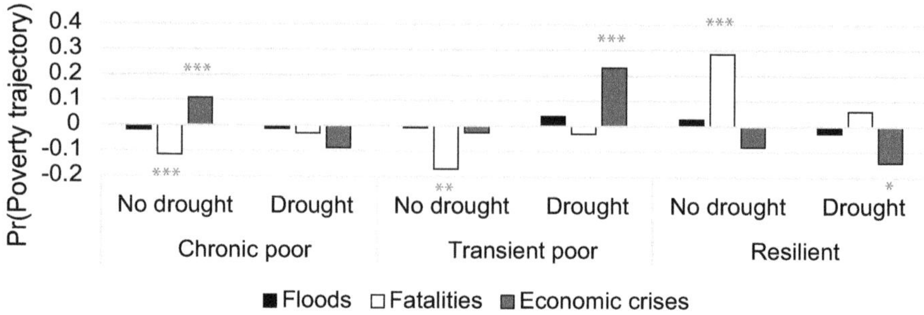

Figure 3.3 Relationship between crises (2008–19) and poverty trajectories, by drought in Tanzania

Note: average marginal effects are presented. Figure refers to three models, examining the intersection of drought with 1) floods, 2) fatalities and 3) economic shocks. Asterisks refer to results that are statistically significant at conventional levels (*** p<0.01, ** p<0.05, * p<0.1). All controls are the same as in the main equation.

Source: analysis of TNPS (2008–19), ACLED (2008–19), Global Flood Observatory (2008–18) and CRU TS (2008–19), first presented in Diwakar (2025).

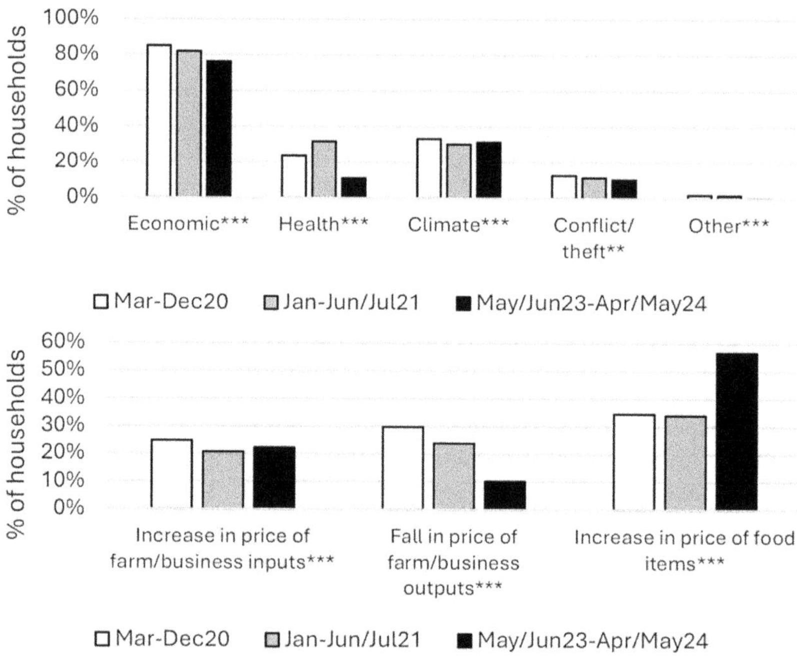

Figure 3.4 Self-reported shocks by survey period in Tanzania, 2020–24

Note: difference in means based on adjusted Wald test where *** p<0.01, ** p<0.05, * p<0.1.

Source: analysis of HFPS balanced panel, first presented in Diwakar (2025).

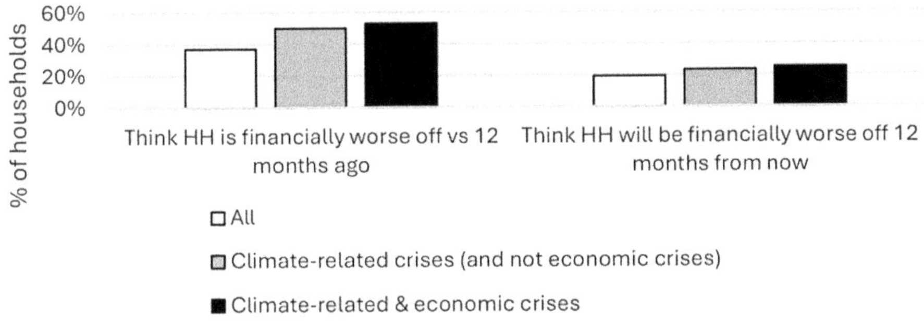

Figure 3.5 Economic sentiments disaggregated by climate and economic crises in Tanzania

Source: analysis of HFPS balanced panel, first presented in Diwakar (2025).

3.1.3 Polycrisis and poverty persistence in Bangladesh

In contrast to Tanzania, the triple crises was most prevalent amongst households living in chronic poverty relative to other trajectories in rural Bangladesh, and least prevalent amongst households sustaining poverty escapes. It affected 15% of chronically poor households in the country and less than 1% of sustained escapers. More than half (57.5%) of the population in Bangladesh are exposed to high flood risk (Rentschler et al., 2022), which was also the main type of climate-related disaster identified in the survey data. Insecurity was most reported in the form of violence against civilians and riots (analysis of ACLED data). Interestingly, though, it is also the context where climate shocks alone (i.e. without intersections of insecurity and economic crises) had the lowest salience amongst the chronic poor. Regression results further reinforce these findings, where floods with violence, or floods with economic shocks, are associated with a higher probability of chronic poverty, relative to experiencing only floods (Diwakar and Brzezinska, 2024).

Taken together, these descriptive results could reflect Bangladesh's successful history of disaster risk management for flooding (Rumpa et al., 2023). However, as these results suggest, the intersection of floods or drought with economic crises or insecurity remains a potent combination in potentially driving poverty persistence. Finally, the results disaggregated by starting poverty status (Figure 3.6) suggest that while the climate–economic intersection may be manageable and enable households to escape poverty to a degree, it is the intersection of insecurity which creates particularly challenging downward pressures in rural Bangladesh.

Finally, during the pandemic, 73% of rural respondents and 87% of urban respondents who were categorised as being vulnerable but non-poor became impoverished in April 2020, with a drop in monthly income of around 66% (PPRC-BIGD, 2020; UNDP, 2021). This drop in income was largest for temporary workers, ethnic minorities and persons with disabilities, reinforcing the heterogenous impacts of crises often being worst felt by groups already experiencing marginalisation.

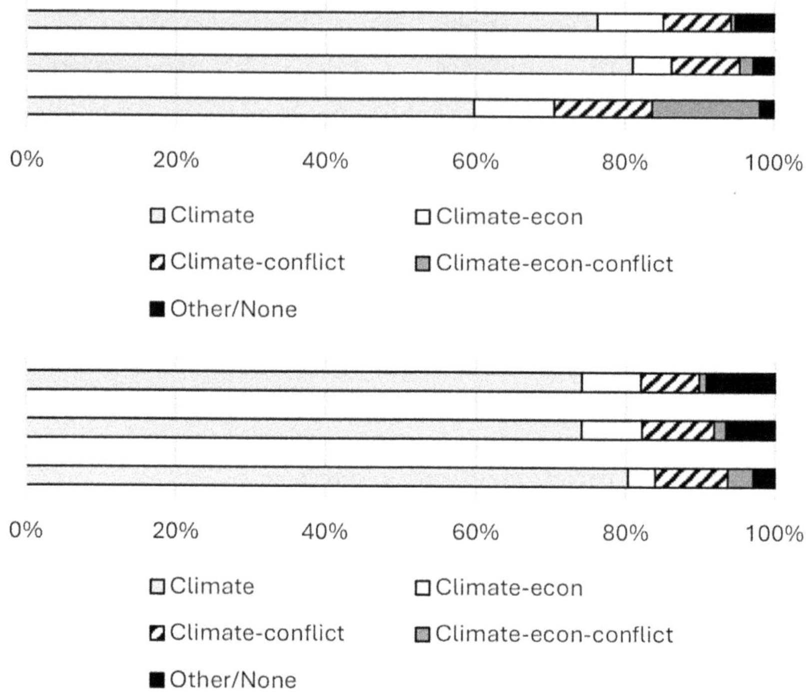

Figure 3.6 Climate-related disasters and polycrisis in rural Bangladesh, disaggregated by households beginning the survey period in poverty (top) and non-poor (bottom)

Note: drought, floods and insecurity draw on actual data from CRU-TS, Global Flood Observatory and ACLED, respectively.

Source: analysis of BIHS (2011–19), ACLED (2011–19), Global Flood Observatory (2010–18) and CRU-TS (2010–20), first presented in Diwakar (2025).

3.1.4 Heterogenous impact pathways

The intersection of climate-related disasters and economic crises can have heterogeneous impacts within countries, as well as ethnicity, age, youth, gender and other socio-demographic characteristics. Differential impacts of these polycrisis by gender, for example, stem in great part from gendered divisions of labour, care responsibilities and access to resources. Women are often overrepresented in informal work, subsistence agriculture and unpaid care work that may be particularly vulnerable to polycrisis. Care responsibilities may increase if schools close amidst climate-related disasters or where these crises drive ill health. In addition, women often are less likely to own land, access credit or engage in decision-making that could otherwise support their needs (Agarwal, 2018; Fothergill, 1996).

The area of residence too can drive fundamental differences in impact pathways. Urban households living in poverty may reside in low-income settlements that are flood-prone, where disasters can easily displace them and put intense pressures on the already weak infrastructure. When economic crises amplify, their cost of food—typically purchased—can skyrocket. Residency in informal settlements moreover can bring with it a threat of forced eviction amidst land disputes or corruption. Indeed, in the qualitative data in Bangladesh conducted in 2024, land-grabbing in Dhaka by government authorities and private companies was observed.

On the other hand, rural households in extreme poverty may rely on subsistence agriculture that could cushion price shocks. However, this cushion may be overwhelmed by the downward pressures associated with climate-related disasters such as drought or floods that can destroy crops and livestock and drive distress migration and repeated cycles of borrowing to purchase inputs. This cycle of debt is elaborated on in Chapter 6.

At the same time, in some urban but especially in rural areas where agriculture is a mainstay, this livelihood is often combined with other strategies, such as through microenterprise development or migration. Such complementarities between agricultural and other livelihood strategies are a form of adaptation that can strengthen household resilience, as is discussed in Chapter 6. For example, provision of remittances from migrating household members can offer a key buffer for households in time of distress. Small-scale non-farm enterprises can also help smooth consumption when harvests fail, though as Section 3.3 notes below, non-farm enterprises (NFEs) also face considerable risk, including price volatility in contexts of economic crises.

The next section elaborates on what might drive the negative poverty dynamics noted above.

3.2 Changing role of agriculture in poverty dynamics amidst climate-related disasters and economic crises

3.2.1 Heightened vulnerability and strained agricultural livelihoods amidst dual crises pre-pandemic

Agriculture is often a mainstay of people living in poverty in rural areas. In the context of intersecting climate-related disasters and economic crises, agriculture faces amplified challenges, as noted in the introduction to this chapter. This stems in part from the complex link between agricultural production, market access and poverty. For example, roads or transport may be damaged or destroyed during flooding, which can weaken market access, thus limiting the ability of smallholder farmers to sell produce or access inputs.

Indeed, agricultural livelihoods were coming under increased strain amidst climate-related disasters and economic crises, according to the qualitative data in many countries. For example, climate-related disasters like drought in Zimbabwe considerably strained livelihoods, driving harvest failure and widespread food insecurity, as stores of value eroded and livestock diseases and crop pests abounded. In addition, price inflation for food and agricultural inputs, transport and school fees further drove destitution processes, when layered onto climate shocks in 2019 (Bird, Diwakar, Manjengwa et al., 2023).

Such challenges in many cases are pronounced especially amongst poorer households given underlying conditions of vulnerability, including reliance on subsistence agriculture. In Zimbabwe, around three quarters of households in the poorest quintile listed agriculture as their primary source of income in the survey data from 2017. Yet though this was a common source of income, it was also associated with a higher probability of poverty in 2017 and lower per capita welfare across the distribution based on regression analysis, when compared to heads deriving income from casual, salaried or wage labour (Diwakar and Pindiriri, 2022). This relationship may reflect agriculture being a mainstay for the rural poor, rather than causality.

Even so, large-scale irrigation for crops that could help mitigate exposure to risk was out of reach for households in and near poverty; instead, reliance on hand-irrigation was widespread (Bird, Diwakar, Manjengwa et al., 2023). Moreover, crop pests can undermine agriculture even in the context of irrigation, where for example it caused disproportionate loss of maize income in Zimbabwe (CABI, 2021). In addition, the poorest households often do not have land. Many may rely on fishing and landless labour. Some of these groups can also be located within households, such as landless youth agricultural labourers, reflecting intra-household precarity.

The confluence of macro-level polycrisis with micro shocks has also been widely prevalent. In Zimbabwe, for example, where hyperinflation has been historically prevalent, health and additional dimensions of economic crises can drive destitution processes and weaken coping mechanisms. In CPAN interviews from 2021, this often was attributed in the qualitative data to the loss of remittances during economic crises that were otherwise used to support health needs, inflation eroding household purchasing power, and households being less able to rely on casual labour markets or social supports during lockdown. Moreover, these crises occurred on the back of economic and climate shocks in 2019 that led to food price increases and already contributed to a rise in extreme poverty, which was then aggravated during the pandemic (Bird, Diwakar, Manjengwa et al., 2023).

In Malawi, macro-level crises and micro-level shocks converged to amplify polycrisis impacts. One interviewee (INT40-MW, female, transitory escape, rural Malawi) managed to escape poverty amidst ladders of investment in farming and using its proceeds to diversify her livelihoods (Figure 3.7). However, successive droughts in 2016 and 2017 left her with poor harvests and drove low output prices. The drought affected her agricultural yields, while market failure marked by low prices and exploitative vendors amplified her economic collapse, where even crops that remained despite drought were faced with poor returns:

> That is the period I don't forget. Of course we did not produce enough maize due to the drought but I had a lot of pigeon peas and groundnuts but imagine the vendors buying our pigeon peas at K20/Kg? This was the beginning of our downfall.
>
> (CPAN LHI with INT40-MW, first presented in da Corta et al., 2018)

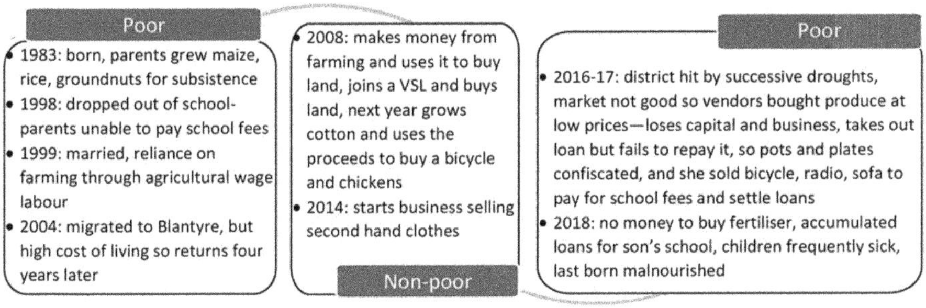

Figure 3.7 A transitory poverty escape amidst economic crises and successive droughts
Source: summary of CPAN LHI with INT40-MW (female, transitory escape, rural Malawi) in 2018.

This forced her to progressively sell off assets and fall into moderate and then extreme poverty. As she reflected: "All the assets are gone, and my house is just like a football pitch". Frequent illnesses for her children combined with these macro-level crises to hasten asset sales and ultimately led to the collapse of her business. In other words, for INT40-MW, macro-level climate impacts and global crop price losses triggered a cascading series of micro-level shocks, adverse coping responses and further crisis-type events.

These results collectively reflect a context where the direct impacts of crises (Figure 2.2 in Chapter 2) are evident: 1) agricultural livelihoods are under extreme pressure, 2) livestock as a store of value is being eroded amidst diseases, 3) government support is inadequate, notable in its limited references in interviews, and 4) inflationary pressures further strain livelihoods and means of survival. Indeed, qualitative data points to the simultaneous hit of "declining farm foundations" (deteriorating farm size, soil fertility and yields), rising costs of living (including transport, food and inputs) with the growing commodification of natural resources alongside inflationary pressures, and monetisation of basic needs (da Corta et al., 2021; Filmer and Fox, 2014; Banks, 2016).

An added challenge reflected in the examples above is that the polycrisis not only affects the context in which people live, but that it operates alongside or amplifies personal micro-level crises—of which ill health is a near universal denominator—amongst those affected. These together point to cascading crises, for example, where macro crises driving ill health require medical costs, loss of income from breadwinners and caregivers, debt, and asset sales. Micro-level crises determine how people cope within the larger structural conditions and crises that drive poverty dynamics. They can also aggregate to create macro-level crises, for example where ill health and rapid transmission of COVID-19 became a pandemic of national proportions. This is discussed next.

3.2.2 The COVID-19 pandemic and its legacies amidst climate-related disasters

Another example of climate–economic crises intersections was during the COVID-19 pandemic, which was a public health as well as economic crises. On the one hand, agriculture was an important source of subsistence for many households, when many urban or international migrants returned to rural areas amidst lockdowns and border closures. However, agriculture also experienced severe disruptions linked to the economic dimensions of the COVID-19 pandemic, with for example transport restrictions interrupting agricultural supply chains and input prices rising and output prices being highly volatile,. There was large-scale destabilisation of formal and informal sectors, particularly pronounced in specific service sectors such as domestic work and for informal workers, many whom were women and young adults living in poverty. When overlaid with climate-related disasters, this further reinforced harvest loss and created acute pressures that hastened downward mobility.

In Zambia, reasons that extreme poor households reported being worse off in 2022 compared to a year preceding the survey included exposure to drought, lack of agricultural inputs, and low agricultural production (Figure 3.8). In the qualitative data, lack of inputs was commonly linked to prices of these inputs being too high. During the pandemic, moreover, Zambia's lockdown reduced business income following lower demand, increased the cost of basic needs due to both the devaluation of the Kwacha and high maize prices on the back of the 2019 drought, and increase cost of farm inputs (CPAN, 2021b). These results point to drought-induced higher input prices—reflecting the role of climate-related crises in driving economic shocks that together strain livelihoods—but also drought following economic crises marked by the COVID-19 pandemic.

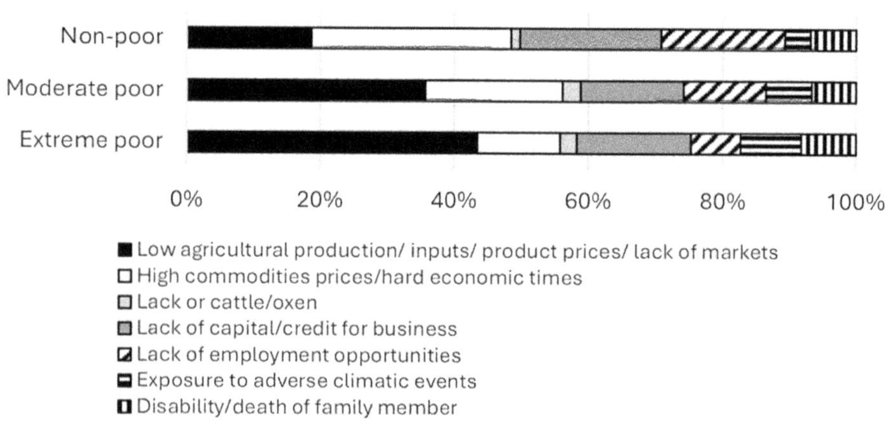

Figure 3.8 Subjective reasons households are "worse off" in Zambia, 2022 vs 2021
Source: analysis of LCMS (2022).

Similarly, in Cambodia, a dramatic increase in the cost of inputs during the pandemic, such as the price of oil or fertilisers, coupled with floods, drought, pest attacks and volatility in farmgate prices, left farmers with low profits and drove indebtedness—a coping response further detailed in Chapter 6. To cope with this, many smallholders changed their planting patterns, pausing rice for a season until more rains came (Bird, Diwakar, Roth et al., 2023). However, this adaptation stems from resource scarcity rather than a position of resilience.

> Growing rice is not profitable because the price of oil doubled from 50,000 to 100,000 riels and fertiliser prices increased from between 60,000 and 80,000 riels to between 170,000 and 200,000 riels, while the price of rice has remained around 800–1,000 a kg (2020–2022). Therefore, we have had to pause growing rice for one season and wait until May and October when there will be more rain, which reduces the need for fertiliser.
>
> (INT8-KH, male, transitory escape, rural Cambodia, 2018 LHI, first presented in Bird, Diwakar, Roth et al., 2023)

In many countries, the legacy effects of the pandemic remained even after restrictions imposed by governments had eased. For example, in Malawi, on the one hand, many respondents referred to an increase in the harvest yields from major staple crops in 2021, coinciding with government relaxation of lockdowns and other restrictions (CPAN, 2021a). At the same time, though, low market prices were consistently mentioned by interviewees:

> I feel that we are still feeling the pinch of the COVID-19 pandemic. You see we are complaining of low prices of produce on the market because the market is full of vendors. For maize, the demand for the crop is low—leading to lower prices as the vendors from Zambia (who buy at good prices) are still not coming here because the borders are still closed. In addition, because many people struggled during the peak of the pandemic, we have few buyers on the market and people are not spending.
>
> (INT9-MW, female, sustained escape, rural Malawi, 2021 LHI, first presented in CPAN, 2021a)

On top of this, some agricultural households were faced with crop infestations that reinforced downward mobility and obstructed recovery pathways even after the height of the COVID-19 pandemics: "Honestly, my wellbeing has gone down. This year I did not harvest a lot because my garden was infested with armyworms. I only harvested four bags [of maize] compared to the ten bags which I harvested last year" (INT5-MW, female, transitory escape, rural Malawi, 2021 LHI, first presented in CPAN, 2021a).

Reflecting pandemic legacies, moreover, certain groups saw existing vulnerabilities exacerbated, for example due to increased care responsibilities that women took up, learning gaps for marginalised children, and informal workers left without economic protections. There is a temporality to this, driving long-term structural shifts in labour markets and livelihood diversification. For example, youth labour force participation significantly dropped in some contexts, and erosive coping mechanisms drove the intergenerational persistence of poverty and vulnerability. Recovery trajectories in low-income countries were also far behind richer countries, aggravated by rising debt, constrained fiscal space and continued climate-related disasters and other crises.

3.2.3 Uninsured agricultural asset risks

In the context of unanticipated climate-related disasters, COVID-19 legacy effects of inflation and economic crises, and with uninsured agricultural risk, many households find themselves becoming inescapably indebted (see Section 6.1.1 for debt-related coping responses). As a result, they have been falling deeper into poverty from moderate to extreme levels, and sometimes towards destitution. These processes are linked to declining land holdings and livestock diversification as a common strategy becoming increasingly under threat amidst polycrisis, which we treat in turn.

Firstly, land is an asset in decline due to land grabbing and small landholdings coupled with pressures on these due to crises. Land grabbing by private companies in Cambodia was noted especially in the 2010s. It is likely on account of this intensified risk environment and weak coping mechanisms that agriculture is no longer a main source of household income for many households in rural areas of Cambodia (Bird, Diwakar and Roth, 2023). Indeed, in the panel data, amongst households sometimes in poverty between 2008 and 2017, average land holding sizes in rural Cambodia ranged from 1.1–1.5 hectares across poverty trajectories (Bird et al., 2019).

Livestock ownership has been a common livelihood diversification strategy and wealth status across low- and lower-middle income countries, though may be coming under threat amidst climate-related and other intersecting crises. It has historically had numerous benefits well-documented in the literature, such as acting as a store of value, ladder of investment, and helping cushion household consumption during times of distress (Upton, 2004; Otte et al., 2012). Amidst polycrisis, the role of livestock can also be critical. For example, amongst the subset of households experiencing climate-related disasters, livestock is associated with a lower probability of chronic poverty in Malawi, and higher probability of transient poverty in rural Bangladesh where economic crises are also reported (Figure 3.9). Amongst the full sample, livestock is furthermore associated with a lower probability of negative poverty trajectories (chronic or transient poverty rather than resilience) in Zambia, significant for households living in areas affected by climate-related disasters and reporting economic crises (Annex Table D3).

However, livestock is highly vulnerable to economic shocks and disease, which may be a function of climate change. In areas affected by either droughts or floods in Tanzania, rural Bangladesh and Zambia, though,

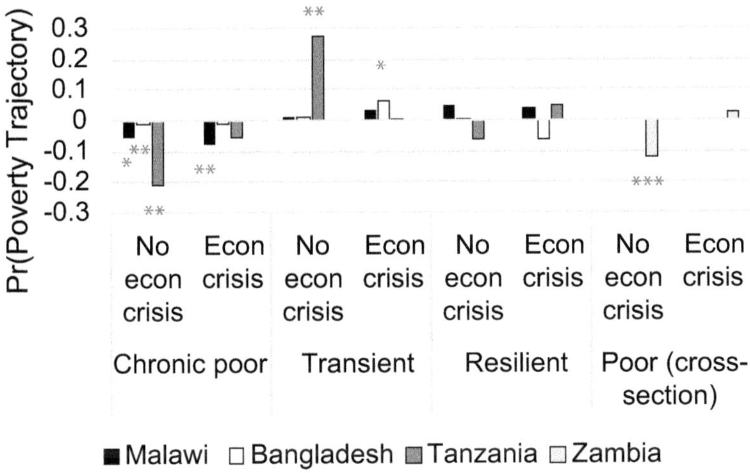

Figure 3.9 Relationship between livestock ownership and poverty (trajectories), by economic crises, in areas affected by climate-related disasters

Note: average marginal effects are presented. The figure refers to four models (one per country), examining the intersection of livestock ownership with economic crises, for the subset of households experiencing floods or drought. Asterisks refer to results that are statistically significant at conventional levels (*** $p<0.01$, ** $p<0.05$, * $p<0.1$). All controls are the same as in the main equation presented in Section 1.2.1 of Chapter 1.

Source: analysis of datasets referenced in Table 1.1.

livestock is only a statistically significant protective factor for households that do not report economic crises. In rural Bangladesh, moreover, livestock ownership is instead associated with a higher probability of negative poverty trajectories (chronic or transient poverty rather than resilience) in the full sample, significant for households living in areas affected by climate-related disasters and reporting economic crises (Annex Table D3).

The lack of significance for the poorest households reporting economic crises amongst the subset of households affected by climate-related disasters could reflect market distortions during economic crises that lower the price of livestock or increase the price of its feed, thus eroding its profit margins. Indeed, during drought or amidst inflation, households may be driven to sell many cattle or small ruminants, which can drive sharp declines in the price of livestock. Crop failures can also increase the cost of livestock feed. These effects could occur on top of livestock disease or death that may be increased due to pests or other natural hazards like flooding. Indeed, livestock is not a significant correlate of resilience amidst climate–economic crises in any of the countries investigated (Figure 3.9). Taken together, these results point to the mixed role of livestock, with potential to guard against dual climate–economic crises for the poorest households in some contexts, but with limited effects in supporting household resilience more broadly.

Besides the market distortions mentioned above, there are various other risks to livestock rearing, especially in the absence of insurance. Theft of livestock has been common across countries, especially amidst deepening widespread poverty. This was so both during and in post-conflict contexts. On the latter, INT11-NP's family in Nepal was attacked twice, but the family did not go to the police due to perceptions of a lack of justice accorded to people in and near poverty:

> Once, they stole the bicycle. Then, they also stole our buffalo. Next, they tried to attack my grandfather. He had some money with him … So, they tied him to the bed and robbed his money … There wouldn't be much police investigation, since we are poor.
>
> (INT11-NP, male, transitory escape, urban Nepal, 2018 LHI, first presented in Diwakar, 2018)

Livestock diseases and deaths can also wipe out household savings. In Zimbabwe, for example, qualitative respondents reported severe loss from January disease and Blackleg disease in 2019–20:

> Between 2002 and 2018 a cattle disease decimated herds. Most farmers lost all their cattle. These farms were mostly female-headed, and they have further moved down from the poor category to the destitute extreme poor category because they no longer had draft power. Also, a chicken disease killed chickens during the same time as the cattle disease.
>
> (KII in 2021, rural Zimbabwe, first presented in Bird, Diwakar, Manjengwa et al., 2023)

Livestock disease can also be a function of a changing climate (ACAPS, 2025; Bwalya et al., 2024). Such diseases not only restrict the income-generating potential of livestock as a ladder helping households out of poverty but also curtails the ability of the asset to act as a store of value through its savings (a coping mechanism) for poor households in times of crises.

3.2.4 Heterogeneity at the bottom of the welfare distribution

There are various gendered effects of these polycrisis including on agricultural livelihoods. For example, asset theft including of livestock was particularly prevalent amongst women-headed households and older heads of households in poverty across a number of countries. Moreover, where climate change has partly driven erratic water supply that can negatively impact health as observed in Zimbabwe, these effects can also be highly gendered where care responsibilities typically fall on women (Bird, Diwakar, Manjengwa et al., 2023). This in turn can restrict women's time for paid work and their mobility. Somewhat relatedly, during droughts in Muzarabani, Zimbabwe, girls were often taken out of school for productive work including on the farm, or early marriage (UNDP, 2017), while some women and girls were pushed into transactional sex (Williams, 2022). Such coping responses are elaborated on in Chapter 6.

At the same time, there is a bimodal relationship between agriculture and extreme and/or chronic poverty. On the one hand, as noted above, agricultural livelihoods are facing increasing precarity amidst climate-related disasters and economic crises. However, running concurrent to this is some evidence of its cushioning effects observed for the poorest households during times of heightened crises. For example, following the COVID-19 pandemic and successive drought in Zambia leading into 2022, the household head's engagement in agriculture was no longer a significant correlate of poverty (Shepherd et al., 2025). In Tanzania, amidst reporting economic shocks, household heads engaged in agriculture and residing in drought-affected areas was also not a significant correlate of chronic poverty (Diwakar, 2025). Relatedly, in Malawi, cultivable land ownership is not a statistically significant correlate of poverty trajectories for households that experience economic shocks and live in areas reporting floods or droughts (Figure 3.10).

The lack of significance in the relationship between agriculture and chronic poverty amidst polycrisis may reflect its role as a viable strategy for poor households with farmland, given its self-provisioning element even during polycrisis. During COVID-19, the small patches of land owned by rural and peri-urban households in poverty was identified to help cushion the impacts of the pandemic on people in poverty, alongside the shorter duration of lockdowns

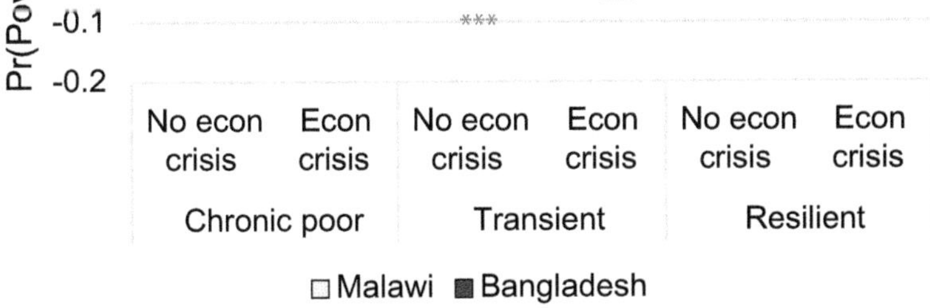

Figure 3.10 Relationship between cultivable land ownership and poverty trajectories, by economic crises, in areas affected by climate-related disasters

Note: average marginal effects are presented. The figure refers to two models (one per country), examining the intersection of cultivable land ownership with economic crises, for the subset of households experiencing floods or drought. Asterisks refer to results that are statistically significant at conventional levels (*** $p<0.01$, ** $p<0.05$, * $p<0.1$). All controls are the same as in the main equation presented in Section 1.2.1 of Chapter 1.

Source: analysis of datasets referenced in Table 1.1.

imposed in Tanzania (da Corta et al., 2022). In Bangladesh, too, cultivable land ownership appears to be a protective factor amidst floods or drought intersecting with price or revenue shocks. In particular, regression results points to its association with a lower probability of transient poverty and higher probability of resilience for disaster-affected households experiencing economic crises (Figure 3.10). It is also associated with a lower probability of negative poverty trajectories (chronic or transient poverty rather than resilience) in the full sample in rural Bangladesh, significant for households living in areas affected by climate-related disasters and reporting economic crises (Annex Table D3). Thus, land can still act as an important asset supporting resilience amidst climate–economic crises, while agricultural livelihoods may be important at least for its survival function for the poorest households.

3.3 "Maladaptive" economic policies across rural–urban divides reinforce downward mobility

Economic policies aimed at addressing intersecting climate and economic crises can be harmful—sometimes worsening rather than reducing impoverishment in both rural and urban areas. This book terms these as "maladaptive economic policies". Maladaptive economic policies exacerbate issues they aim to solve, including poverty, motivating in turn the need to start considering poverty as an emergency. They do this primarily by undermining or obstructing resilience pathways, thus widening existing inequalities, amplifying vulnerability and exclusion or creating new risks. These maladaptive policies also relate to the wider discussion around political regimes and governance arrangements in Chapter 2. It is discussed in more detail in Chapter 5 focused on humanitarian contexts, though is also evident amidst climate and economic crises in the absence of violent conflict as discussed below.

Examples of maladaptive economic policies include: government austerity measures that cut spending on health, education, and social protection and in doing so remove key safety nets and human development access; subsidy cuts without adequate mitigation or compensation measures for people in and near poverty; regressive taxation; social protection interventions that are narrowly targeted amidst high need and/or exclude informal workers; and agricultural policies that neglect smallholder farmers. These policies may be universally applied or narrowly targeted, but in each case, they have profound effects on people in and near poverty who already experience limited buffers. Political exclusion may also underlie these economic policy responses to drive their maladaptive effects. More detail on some of these maladaptive economic policies and the underlying structural conditions that generate them are presented below.

3.3.1 Restrictions and regulations

Perhaps the most blatant cross-country example of "maladaptive" economic policies came during and in response to the COVID-19 pandemic. Attempts to curb the transmission of COVID-19 through border closures and lockdowns were not accompanied by measures to better support returnee migrants or those targeting the many informal workers who were left without access to social protections (Shepherd et al., 2023). Such maladaptive policies obstructed common resilience pathways out of poverty through migration or enterprise development amidst border closures and some highly repressive lockdowns. When climate-related disasters were overlaid, moreover, as observed during Cyclone Amphan in India and Bangladesh in 2020, or drought in Zambia in 2020, resources for disaster relief were stretched and sometimes absent, a point we return to in Chapter 7.

Other examples of country-specific maladaptive policies are evident in times of polycrisis. In Rwanda, even pre-pandemic there have been various agricultural restrictions on where and what households could plant and many smallholders were priced out of cooperatives and thus did not benefit from access to rising share prices or marketing (see Table 3.1). This sequence was identified as a driver of harvest failure. When coupled with repeated drought, floods and landslips, this further hastened downward income mobility (da Corta, Simons and Shepherd, 2018). Outside of agriculture, too, government restrictions on vending in Kigali and cost barriers to trade, alongside user costs of "free" primary education were often cited by interviewees, reflecting multidimensional challenges associated with government compulsion. Perhaps because of the former, rural migration to urban settings was not a strong correlate of poverty escapes in the regression results in Rwanda (da Corta, Simons and Shepherd, 2018).

As another example, in the last phase of villagization in Rwanda, the government attempted to incentivise people to relocate to become closer to services and infrastructure. This was carried out with partial enforcement, requiring new households to build homes within village boundaries (Ansoms et al., 2017). Impoverishment was a common result of households not eligible for housing subsidies (Box 3.1). These processes collectively reflect the increasing centralisation of decision making that comes with demands on

Table 3.1 Economic policy issues reported by interviewees as driving downward mobility in Rwanda

District	*Rural villagisation costs or urban relocation and renting property*	*Restrictions on what and where to plant and land reforms*	*Inability or cost barriers to trade or cost barriers to trade in Kigali*
Gakenke	5	5	0
Nyarugenge	6	0	9
Bugesera	5	0	0
Nyamasheke	10	2	1
Total (out of 80 LHs)	26	7	10

Source: Bird (2019).

local communities to invest in government programmes (Ansoms and Rostagno, 2012; Gaynor, 2014). It raises an important question about the legitimacy of this "fast-track reform process" (Gaynor, 2014).

Box 3.1 Temporary escape and impoverishment in rural Rwanda

INT5-RW and his wife initially benefitted first from cash from the construction work made available by villagisation, building agglomerations of residences after the 1994 genocide and war. The savings from this work enabled an escape sequence out of extreme poverty. However, recently, the need to buy a new room in the model village where dwellings were very small at high building standards (cement floors and plastered walls) was part of the cause of their land sales. He is concerned that he may not be able to bounce back through the same route.

In 2016, he sold another plot because they had eight kids by then who were getting bigger and so they couldn't fit into the very small dwellings in the agglomeration. He thus decided to extend his existing house further, with electricity installation because his kids needed light to do their homework at night. The problem is with no money left for lighting fixtures, his electricity cable is only used to charge his mobile phone.

In 2017, after these land sales, he is now in level 2 (extreme poor—see Annex Table B1), dependent on selling labour in construction. He hopes that he might bounce back after saving from construction labour and renting in land. But he is 47 and his wife 39: much older now, and they have costs associated with secondary school. Given the lack of rains and rising consumption needs of the family, his wife is not optimistic about their future wellbeing.

Source: INT5-RW, male, impoverished, rural Rwanda, 2019 LHI, first presented in Bird, (2019)

3.3.2 Underfunded social protection and political exclusion

There are also various examples of underfunded social protection and underlying political exclusion that drives maladaptive policy responses. In Zimbabwe, a history of hyperinflation, institutional failure, infrastructure weakness and collapse, the worsening impacts of climate change, all affect and are affected by underfunded government programmes (Bird, Diwakar, Manjengwa et al., 2023; Larochelle et al., 2014). Political exclusion and the limited provision of public services have had particularly detrimental effects on the poorest populations. Moreover, loss of remittances—mainly from South Africa—during the lockdown measures amidst COVID-19 impoverished many interviewed households. Informal cross-border traders, typically women, were unable to access new stock amidst lockdown border closures

(Bird, Diwakar, Manjengwa et al., 2023). Cash transfers provided by the government was moreover perceived to be of too low a value to act as a mitigation measure.

Box 3.2 Urban informality amidst polycrisis

Economic crises especially but also climate-related disasters can also increase urban (as well as rural) informality, driven by formal job loss or business collapse. Indeed, shares of informal sector work regularly increases during economic instability (World Bank, 2019). On the one hand, informality can be a survival response or a common pathway to improving wellbeing at the bottom of the distribution. Informal work may be more accessible than formal employment, especially for individuals with low education levels or without formal legal status. A challenge however is that informal workers usually are outside of formal social protection or other systems to guarantee their rights, and often informal firms are credit constrained (La Porta and Shleifer, 2014; Busso et al., 2012). Informal workers are partly as a result susceptible to exploitation that can drive low wages, as well as exclusion from relief or recovery programming.

In urban areas, many people in poverty work in the informal sector and lack social protection. They may reside in overcrowded low-income neighbourhoods and informal settlements that furthermore lack basic services such as water, sanitation and hygiene (WASH). These contexts can also be highly vulnerable to flooding and disease outbreak due to inadequate infrastructure, which can drive poverty persistence. Households in and near poverty often prioritise low-cost mitigation strategies, which may be temporary fixes that emerge from conditions of precarity. This includes, for example, efforts to raise pit latrines, use sandbags, and dig secondary drains, with varying effectiveness (Nchito, 2024). However, inflation during economic crises erodes the already weak purchasing power of households to adopt effective measures.

Reflecting some of these processes, in Rwanda, price rises and climate change constrained households' ability to recover from the pandemic due to the successive sequencing of crises:

> Imagine the one who was doing a business bar, he/she has spent all most one year and a half without opening, and those who used to work there at the bar as a part-time job were not able to work and then after that price increased without any saving to his/her. Finally, after the coronavirus, it was a time of making recover ourselves, but now we are facing the problem of climate change and even the war in Ukraine.
>
> (KII with health officer in 2023, Rwanda, first presented in Shepherd et al., 2023)

In addition, evidence points to slower recovery due to weak job growth in informal growth post-crisis. (Grover and Pereira-Lopez, 2023). The gendered nature of certain types of informal work, such as for care responsibilities or domestic work, can mean that women face compounded vulnerabilities—earning less on account of engagement in informal work, without protection, and taking on added care responsibilities during times of crises.

Some of the institutional responses, such as cash transfers, are certainly an attempt to promote economic recovery; however, in the context of government austerity, recovery becomes uneven due to underfunding, limited coverage, not adjusting for inflation, and failing to respond to large-scale impoverishment caused by polycrisis. A key example of this is in Zambia. Debt servicing over the years leading to debt default in 2020 was overlaid with significant droughts in 2016, 2019 and 2023–25, as well as the COVID-19 pandemic which sequentially decimated farm and informal sector incomes (Shepherd et al., 2021). High food prices and soaring inflation coupled with price controls for farm produce amidst successive droughts further constrained upward mobility for extreme poor households. The government's load shedding of electricity in partial response to drought further affected small and medium businesses even before the pandemic hit (Shepherd et al., 2021).

It is perhaps for this reason that NFEs are significantly associated with a lower probability of poverty in Zambia only for households not reporting economic crises, conditional on reporting flooding or drought (Figure 3.11).

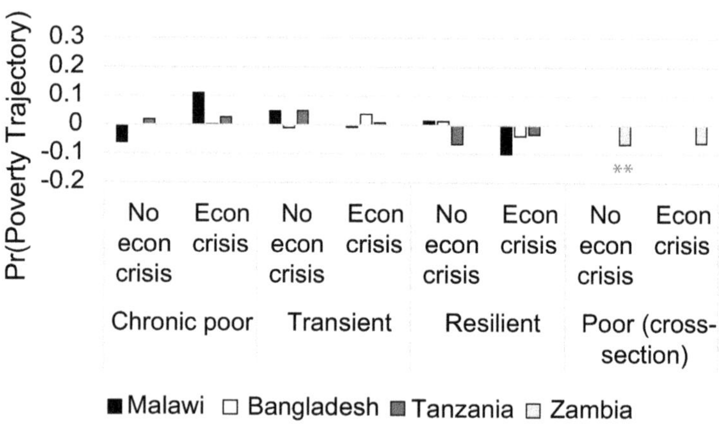

Figure 3.11 Relationship between NFE ownership and poverty trajectories, by economic crises, in areas affected by climate-related disasters

Note: average marginal effects are presented. The figure refers to four models, examining the intersection of NFE ownership with economic crises, for the subset of households experiencing floods or droughts. Asterisks refer to results that are statistically significant at conventional levels (*** $p<0.01$, ** $p<0.05$, * $p<0.1$). All controls are the same as in the main equation presented in Section 1.2.1 in Chapter 1.

Source: analysis of datasets referenced in Table 1.1.

Even so, when we zoom out to the full sample in Zambia, NFEs are associated with a lower probability of negative poverty trajectories (chronic or transient poverty rather than resilience), which remains significant for households living in areas affected by climate-related disasters and reporting economic crises (Annex Table D3). These two results suggest that in areas where climate vulnerability may already be high, additional economic crises may offset the protective role of NFE ownership. Indeed, NFE ownership also lacks significance across the subset of households reporting floods or drought in Malawi, rural Bangladesh and Tanzania, regardless of whether they report economic crises. The latter suggests more broadly that there may be various risks as well as rewards permeating these contexts during climate-related disasters that prevent NFEs from contributing to poverty escapes.

3.3.3 Fines, asset loss and debt pronounced for those experiencing intersecting inequalities

Outside of Southern and Eastern Africa, there are also examples of maladaptive economic policy responses that drove downward mobility in the context of polycrisis. For instance, in Cambodia, amidst climate-related disasters and environmental degradation, agricultural land has become less common over time as the dominant source of income for many households in and near poverty. This has driven poor and rural households to other types of livelihoods including risky alternatives, like illegal logging. However, these activities are also subject to huge fines if caught, when assets can furthermore be confiscated (Bunthoeurn, 2021). Indeed, rural interviewees in poverty speak of hand tractors being seized and loggers required to pay a fine, necessitating borrowing at high interest rates from moneylenders (Bird et al., 2019).

The lost income, asset confiscation, and climate-related disasters constraining the ability of households to repay debt in the context of limited viability of land for income has driven widely prevalent debt spirals placing a strain on the national economy. Indeed, Cambodia has the world's highest microfinance debt-per-capita in the world (CEIC, 2022; Goldstein and Sea, 2024), reflecting an aggregation of micro-level shocks into macro-level economic crises. On top of this, illegal logging can drive biodiversity loss and worsen climate-related disasters for example due to lack of canopy cover. In this way, the negative poverty dynamics caused by crises and their maladaptive policy responses can further amplify polycrisis and generate emergency-like conditions.

There are again heterogenous impacts in this, where poorer households may be compelled to borrow for consumption (rather than production) and then be unable to repay loans when faced with crises, women may have limited decision-making power over use of loans due to adverse gender norms, and displaced people may lack the networks through which to borrow from friends or family rather than exploitative moneylenders. This also inherently reflects a spectrum of types of debt, where informal debt from friends and family may be low-interest or interest-free in many cases, support from Village Savings and Loans Associations (VSLAs) and other group-based mechanisms can offer flexible support, microfinance may be less flexible or shock-responsive, while exploitative moneylending can be a particularly harmful source for loans in the absence of alternatives. In all of this, socio-economic differences and gradations of poverty can also affect people's coping capacity, as well as the outcomes that may deepen vulnerability or undermine resilience. This is discussed further in Chapter 6.

In all of the above, market distortions (e.g. price volatility, monopolistic behaviour, exploitative lenders, supply disruptions) is a crucial pathway through which economic crises on top of climate-related disasters affect poverty. However, as the examples above indicate, it is not purely temporary shocks but rather structural including institutional weaknesses and policy failures that generate market failures. As noted above, market access can be severely curtailed amidst climate-related disasters that weaken already inadequate market and transport infrastructure. Market concentration can become more pronounced amidst crises, where regulation may be weak or non-existent. In this context, "maladaptive" policy shifts reflect an avoidable harm amplifying crises. Moreover, these failures affect the poorest (e.g. extreme or chronically poor) households in particular who have the least buffer against crises, typically without access to credit or insurance and without land tenure security.

3.4 Conclusion

This chapter drew attention to how agricultural livelihoods are facing amplified challenges in the context of successive climate-related disasters combined with and driving price volatility and inflation. Agricultural livelihoods were particularly risky in the absence of insurance mechanisms and amidst inadequate social safety nets and contexts of macro-level debt further limiting social service provisioning. The intersection thus of climate–economic crises was observed to contributes to churning and the chronicity of poverty.

At the same time, the chapter acknowledged that macro-level crises often intersect with micro-level shocks such as ill health, which when aggregated could also strain national systems and generate crises. This was observed during the COVID-19 pandemic. Alongside this, low-stressor often meso-level experiences of insecurity, variably prevalent across countries in contexts of economic hardship, can also drive poverty persistence as households in and near poverty—typically informal work—lack protections to guard against crises. All of this operates in contexts with relatively weak insurance provisioning and limited equity in disaster risk management (DRM) that reinforces a poverty–polycrisis trap—points we return to in the policy analysis presented in Chapters 7 and 8.

The role of agricultural assets was still important in enabling extreme and chronically poor households to survive. This may be particularly pronounced in rural and remote areas that may experience isolation during crises that could limit their access to recovery programming. This may also be a cushion for migrating households that may be driven to return to rural areas and their landholdings (for those who have it) amidst labour market shifts linked to climate-related disasters and/or economic crises. We return to this provisioning role of land in Chapter 6 as it is also an important asset for other intersections of crises.

Without government support in contexts of climate–economic crises, recovery can be uneven. However, even with government support, there can be unintended or adverse consequences. Indeed, the chapter highlighted how government regulations, emerging in part to contain sources of vulnerability and promote growth and recovery amidst climate-related disasters and economic crises, can instead reinforce downward mobility. It introduced the concept of "maladaptive economic policies" to reflect this phenomenon, showcasing strong bidirectionality whereby the negative poverty dynamics outcomes they generate could in turn amplify polycrisis. Maladaptive policy formulation though can be mitigated through sounder consideration of equity in policy development amidst polycrisis, which we further reflect on in Chapter 8.

The next chapter considers a different intersection of crises, focused on climate-related disasters with violent conflict, and considers its relationship with negative poverty dynamics.

Note

1 In Bangladesh, the survey focuses on rural areas that are accordingly more susceptible to the negative effects of floods or drought given the importance of agricultural livelihoods in these contexts. As such, cross-country comparability should be viewed with caution, and so we focus more on within-country comparisons of crises across poverty trajectories.

References

ACAPS (2025) 'Zambia: Update on the impact of drought'. https://www.acaps.org/fileadmin/Data_Product/Main_media/20250116_ACAPS_Zambia_-_Update_on_the_impact_of_drought_.pdf.

Agarwal, B. (2018) 'Gender equality, food security and the sustainable development goals'. *Current Opinion in Environmental Sustainability*, 34: 26–32.

Ansoms, A., Marijnen, E., Cioffo, G. and Murison, J. (2017) 'Statistics versus livelihoods: Questioning Rwanda's pathway out of poverty'. *Review of African Political Economy*, 44(151): 47–65. doi:10.1080/03056244.2016.1214119.

Ansoms, A. and Rostagno, D. (2012) 'Rwanda's Vision 2020 halfway through: What the eye does not see'. *Review of African Political Economy*, 39(133): 427–450. doi:10.1080/03056244.2012.710836.

Atkinson-Sheppard, S. (2019) *The gangs of Bangladesh. Palgrave advances in criminology and criminal justice in Asia*. Palgrave Macmillan. doi:10.1007/978-3-030-18426-1_4.

Banks, N. (2016) 'Youth poverty, employment and livelihoods: Social and economic implications of living with insecurity in Arusha, Tanzania'. *Environment & Urbanization*, 28(2): 437–454. doi:10.1177/0956247816651201.

Bird, K. (2019) 'Understanding poverty trends and poverty dynamics in Rwanda: Qualitative report'. *CPAN.* https://www.chronicpovertynetwork.org/resources/2020/6/3/understanding-poverty-trends-and-poverty-dynamics-in-rwanda.

Bird, K., Diwakar, V. and Roth, V. (2019) 'Resilience and sustainable poverty escapes in rural Cambodia'. *CPAN/USAID.* https://www.chronicpovertynetwork.org/resources/2019/1/16/resilience-and-sustained-poverty-escapes-in-rural-cambodia.

Bird, K., Diwakar, V., Manjengwa, J., Pindiriri, C., Chamunogwa, A., Ndlovu, N. (2023) 'Understanding poverty dynamics in Zimbabwe in the context of COVID-19'. *CPAN.*

Bird, K., Diwakar, V., Roth, V., San, S., Sean, C., Shepherd, A. (2023) 'Cambodia poverty dynamics and Covid-19'. *Institute of Development Studies.* https://hdl.handle.net/20.500.12413/18059.

Bunthoeurn, O. (2021) 'Forestry crimes up last year, official vows law enforcement'. *The Phnom Penh Post*, 14 January. https://www.phnompenhpost.com/national/forestry-crimes-last-year-official-vows-law-enforcement.

Busso, M., Fazio, M. and Algazi, S. (2012) '(In) formal and (un) productive: the productivity costs of excessive informality in Mexico'. *IDB Working Paper No. IDB-WP-341.* https://papers.ssrn.com/sol3/papers.cfm?abstract_id=2207240.

Bwalya, B., Chiluba, B.C. and Mwanza, K. (2024) 'Livestock ownership among smallholder farming households in Eastern Zambia: A gendered pathway for enhancing climate resilience?' *Front. Sustain. Food Syst.*, 8: 1487798. doi:10.3389/fsufs.2024.1487798.

CABI (2021) 'Households in Zimbabwe affected by fall armyworm are 12% more likely to experience hunger'. *Phys. Org.*, 15 March. https://phys.org/news/2021-03-households-zimbabwe-affected-fall-armyworm.html.

CEIC (2022) 'Cambodia household debt: % of GDP'. https://www.ceicdata.com/en/indicator/cambodia/household-debt–of-nominal-gdp#:~:text=Key%20information%20about%20Cambodia%20Household,an%20increased%20of%203.6%20%25%20YoY.

Chelwa, G., Kaulule, N.S. and Renzio, P.D. (2024) 'External forces and Zambia's permanent debt crisis'. *Development.* doi:10.1057/s41301-025-00431-z.

Chuku, C., Samal, P., Saito, J., Hakura, D.S., Chamon, M.D., Cerisola, M.D. (2023) 'Are we heading for another debt crisis in low-income countries? Debt vulnerabilities: Today vs the pre-HIPC era'. *IMF Working Paper No. 2023/079.* IMF. https://www.imf.org/en/Publications/WP/Issues/2023/04/04/Are-We-Heading-for-Another-Debt-Crisis-in-Low-Income-Countries-Debt-Vulnerabilities-Today-531792.

Cieslik, K., Barford, A. and Vira, B. (2021) 'Young people not in employment, education or training (NEET) in Sub-Saharan Africa: Sustainable development target 8.6 missed and reset'. *Journal of Youth Studies*, 25(8): 1126–1147. doi:10.1080/13676261.2021.1939287.

Cooper, R. (1993) 'Currency devaluation in developing countries'. In J.M. Letiche (Ed.), *Economic Theory, Econometrics, and Mathematical Economics, International Economic Policies and their Theoretical Foundations* (2nd Edition). Academic Press (pp. 740–772). https://www.sciencedirect.com/science/chapter/edited-volume/abs/pii/B9780124442818500362.

CPAN (2021a) 'Malawi Covid-19 Poverty Monitor: December 2021'. https://www.chronicpovertynetwork.org/covid19-poverty-monitor/malawi-december.

CPAN (2021b) 'Zambia Covid-19 Poverty Monitor: September 2021'. https://www.chronicpovertynetwork.org/covid19-poverty-monitor/zambia-september.

da Corta, L., Diarra, A., Diwakar, V., Eichsteller, M., Harouna, A. and Poggi, C. (2021) 'Youth inclusion in labour markets in Niger: Gender dynamics and livelihoods'. *Working paper.* https://www.chronicpovertynetwork.org/resources/2021/6/29/youth-inclusion-in-labour-markets-in-niger-gender-dynamics-and-livelihoods.

da Corta, L., Kayunze, K.A., Kahamba, J.S., Simba, C.G., Shepherd, A., Mangi, H.O. (2022) 'Covid-19 monitoring in rural Tanzania: The pandemic exacerbated pre-existing factors negatively affecting wellbeing'. *CPAN.* https://www.chronicpovertynetwork.org/resources/2022/11/7/covid-19-monitoring-in-rural-tanzania-the-pandemic-exacerbated-pre-existing-factors-negatively-affecting-wellbeing.

da Corta, L., Scott, L., Eichsteller, M. and Gondwe, A. (2018) 'Resilience and sustainable poverty escapes in Malawi'. *USAID.* https://www.chronicpovertynetwork.org/resources/2019/2/18/resilience-and-sustainable-poverty-escapes-in-malawi-national-report.

da Corta, L., Simons, A. and Shepherd, A. (2018) 'Understanding impoverishment and supporting sustained pathways out of chronic poverty in Rwanda: National report'. *CPAN/IPAR.*

Darvas, Z. (2023) 'Two crises, two continents: How the labour-market impacts have differed'. *Bruegel.* https://www.bruegel.org/analysis/two-crises-two-continents-how-labour-market-impacts-have-differed#:~:text=Two%20once%2Din%2Da%2D,output%2C%20especially%20during%20the%20pandemic.

de Abreu, V.H.S., Santos, A.S. and Monteiro, T.G.M. (2022) 'Climate change impacts on the road transport infrastructure: A systematic review on adaptation measures'. *Sustainability,* 14(14): 8864. doi:10.3390/su14148864.

Deutsch, C.Tewksbury, J.Tigchelaar, M., Battisti, D., Merrill, S.C., Huey, R. (2018) 'Increase in crop losses to insect pests in a warming climate'. *Science,* 361: 916–919. doi:10.1126/science.aat3466.

Diwakar, V. (2018) 'Resilience and sustainable poverty escapes in Nepal – national report'. *CPAN.* https://www.chronicpovertynetwork.org/resources/2018/6/11/resilience-and-sustainable-poverty-escapes-in-nepal-national-report.

Diwakar, V. (2025) 'Poverty dynamics amidst intersecting crises in Tanzania'. *CPAN.* https://povertyevidence.org/resources/poverty-dynamics-amidst-intersecting-crises-in-tanzania/.

Diwakar, V. and Brzezinska, I. (2024) 'Poverty dynamics amidst intersecting crises in rural Bangladesh'. *DEEP Working Paper 22.* DEEP. https://povertyevidence.org/wp-content/uploads/2024/06/Poverty-dynamics-amidst-multiple-crises-in-Bangladesh.pdf.

Diwakar, V. and Pindiriri, C. (2022) 'Poverty in Zimbabwe, 2011–2017: Analysis of dynamics, correlates, and welfare across the distribution'. *Background paper.* CPAN/ODI.

Filmer, D. and Fox, L. (2014) 'Youth employment in Sub-Saharan Africa'. Africa Development Series. World Bank. doi:10.1596/978-1-4648-0107-5.

Fothergill, A. (1996) 'Gender, risk and disaster'. *International Journal of Mass Emergencies and Disasters,* 14(1): 33–55.

Gaynor, N. (2014) '"A nation in a hurry": The costs of local governance reforms in Rwanda'. *Review of African Political Economy,* 41(sup1): S49–S63. doi:10.1080/03056244.2014.976190.

Ghadge, A., Wurtmann, H. and Seuring, S. (2019) 'Managing climate change risks in global supply chains: A review and research agenda'. *International Journal of Production Research,* 58(1): 44–64. doi:10.1080/00207543.2019.1629670.

Goldstein, L. and Sea, E. (2024) 'Green bonds, red flags: Cambodia's microfinance crisis deepens amid sustainability push'. *Dialogue Earth,* 10 October. https://dia

logue.earth/en/climate/green-bonds-red-flags-cambodias-microfinance-crisis-deepens-amid-sustainability-push/.

Grover, A. and Pereira-Lopez, M. (2023) 'Does informality depress investments and job recovery? Firm-level evidence from the COVID-19 crisis in South Asia'. *Policy Research Working Paper 10580*. World Bank. https://openknowledge.worldbank.org/server/api/core/bitstreams/9bb3091a-a583-4167-97d1-3185e67ec687/content.

Guihenneuc, J., Ayraud-Thevenot, S., Roschnik, S., Dupuis, A. and Migeot, V. (2023) 'Climate change and health care facilities: A risk analysis framework through a mapping review'. *Environmental Research*, 216(3): 114709. doi:10.1016/j.envres.2022.114709.

La Porta, R. and Shleifer, A. (2014) 'Informality and development'. *Journal of Economic Perspectives*, 28(3): 109–126. doi:10.1257/JEP.28.3.109.

Larochelle, C., Alwang, J. and Taruvinga, N. (2014) 'Inter-temporal changes in well-being during conditions of hyperinflation: Evidence from Zimbabwe'. *Journal of African Economies*, 23(2): 225–256. doi:10.1093/jae/ejt028.

LCMS (2022). *Living Conditions Measurement Survey* [*Dataset*], Zambia. ZamStats.

Mall, R.K., Gupta, A. and Sonkar, G. (2017) 'Effect of climate change on agricultural crops'. *Current Developments in Biotechnology and Bioengineering*: 23–46. doi:10.1016/B978-0-444-63661-4.00002-5.

Nchito, W. (2024) 'Flood risk adaptation among poorer households in Lusaka, Zambia'. *Urban Climate Change Research Network*. https://academiccommons.columbia.edu/doi/10.7916/d2nj-9q44/download.

Odongo, M.T., Misati, R.N., Kamau, A.W. and Kisingu, K.N. (2022) 'Climate change and inflation in Eastern and Southern Africa'. *Sustainability*, 14(22): 14764. doi:10.3390/su142214764.

Otte, J., Costales, A., Dijkman, J., Pica-Ciamarra, U., Robinson, T., Ahuja, V. (2012) 'Livestock sector development for poverty reduction: An economic and policy perspective – Livestock's many virtues'. Food and Agriculture Organization. https://www.fao.org/4/i2744e/i2744e00.pdf.

PPRC-BIGD (2020) 'Phase I: Livelihoods, coping, and support during Covid-19 crisis'. PPRC and BRAC Institute of Governance and Development Rapid Response Research. https://bigd.bracu.ac.bd/wp-content/uploads/2020/06/PPRC-BIGD-Final-April-SurveyReport.pdf.

Rastogi, P. (2023) 'Currency devaluation and its global impact: An in-depth descriptive analysis'. *Gyanshauryam International Scientific Refereed Research Journal*. https://gisrrj.com/paper/GISRRJ23667.pdf.

Rentschler, J., Salhab, M. and Jafino, B.A. (2022) 'Flood exposure and poverty in 188 countries'. *Nature Communications*, 13(1): 3527. doi:10.1038/s41467-022-30727-4.

Rumpa, N.T., Real, H.R.K. and Razi, M.A. (2023) 'Disaster risk reduction in Bangladesh: A comparison of three major floods for assessing progress towards resilience'. *International Journal of Disaster Risk Reduction*, 97: 104047. doi:10.1016/j.ijdrr.2023.104047.

Shepherd, A., Bond, V., Bwalya, C., Bwalya, R., Chapoto, A., da Corta, L. (2021) 'Layered crises preventing poverty reduction: an analysis of Zambian poverty dynamics and policy implications'. In A. Antoniades *et al.* (Ed.), *Financial crises, poverty and environmental sustainability*. Springer.

Shepherd, A., Bwalya, R., Chapoto, A., da Corta, L., Eichsteller, M., Diwakar, V. (2025) (forthcoming) 'Zambian poverty dynamics and climate resilience: A growing policy agenda through a period of crises'. CPAN.

Shepherd, A., Diwakar, V., Bizoza, A., Lenhardt, A., Moonga, A., Shahan, A. (2023) 'Chronic Poverty Report 5 – Pandemic poverty'. CPAN/Institute of Development Studies. doi:10.19088/CC.2023.006.

UNDP (2017) 'Climate change and human development: Towards building a climate resilient nation. Zimbabwe Human Development Report 2017'. https://hdr.undp.org/system/files/documents/undpzw2017zhdrfull.pdf.

UNDP (2021) 'Addressing Covid-19's uneven impacts on vulnerable populations in Bangladesh: The case for shock-responsive social protection'. *UNDP Global Policy Network Brief.* https://www.undp.org/library/dfs-addressing-covid-19s-uneven-impacts-vulnerable-populations-bangladesh-case-shock-responsive.

Upton, M. (2004) 'The role of livestock in economic development and poverty reduction'. *PPLPI Working Paper No. 10*. Food and Agriculture Organization. https://www.gov.uk/research-for-development-outputs/the-role-of-livestock-in-economic-development-and-poverty-reduction.

Williams, C. (2022) 'How climate change forces women and girls in Zimbabwe into sex work'. *Independent Online*, 15 February. www.iol.co.za/news/africa/how-climate-change-forces-women-and-girls-in-zimbabwe-into-sex-work-82c761a5-55d4-4765-9f81-eb63224489be.

World Bank (2019) 'Promoting business registration with Entreprenant status in Benin'. https://www.worldbank.org/en/programs/competitiveness-policy-impact-evaluation-lab/brief/benin-impact-evaluation-of-the-entreprenant-status.

4 Poverty dynamics amidst the climate–conflict nexus

There is a mutually reinforcing relationship between violent conflict, climate-related disasters and negative poverty dynamics, which can contribute to the amplified and protracted nature of polycrisis. Violent conflict can degrade the environment, destroy infrastructure, limit mobility and often subvert governance and services in ways that limit macro and micro capacities to manage natural resources (Solomon et al., 2018; Aysan et al., 2023). This can increase individual and household vulnerability and turn natural hazards into disasters. At the same time, climate-related disasters can increase resource scarcity, limit livelihood options and displace populations. This can drive or sustain violent conflict over resources such as water or land (Burrows and Kinney, 2016; von Uexkull et al., 2016).

There can be certain "threshold effects" whereby the impact of one crisis becomes significantly worse once another crisis intersects. For example, a drought in a stable context could drive malnutrition, though this can be mitigated through access to health services. Amidst conflict, however, this access can be curtailed and/or services destroyed, which may result in acute levels or a larger scale of malnutrition. The effects can moreover be worse for specific groups, such as those who are displaced and lack social networks or access to aid, people in extreme poverty who may have limited support structures to cope, or women and girls who may face increased care responsibilities during crises. These compounding risks as well as their heterogeneous impacts point to the importance of understanding climate–conflict crises intersections.

What makes the climate–conflict nexus unique from the climate–economic crises intersections of the preceding chapter? The climate–conflict nexus more commonly can result in forced displacement, drive a vicious cycle of resource competition and poverty, and obstruct access to aid due to prevalent insecurity. Its conflict roots can moreover affect government authority, legitimacy and capacity as governance institutions erode and power vacuums emerge into which armed groups may consolidate control (Ide et al., 2016; Raleigh and Linke, 2018). Violence can moreover undermine social cohesion important to coping with conflict and other crises, though some literature also points to the opposite where conflict strengthens cooperation and social

DOI: 10.4324/9781003503125-6

cohesion of citizens (Fiedler, 2023; Blattman, 2009). It can have heterogenous impacts, reinforcing vulnerabilities for politically marginalised groups who may be intentionally excluded or residing in areas of insecurity where the effective distribution of aid is constrained. The psychological trauma from these effects can be severe (Stevens et al., 2013; Abbasi, 2022), constraining recovery pathways.

In these direct impacts is a deliberate focus, as noted in Chapter 2—such as through wanton destruction of economic infrastructure, homes, farms, livestock and other assets, looting by armed groups, displacement and the forced separation of people undermining their social networks and cohesion, and the disruption of government spending as this is diverted or even subverted to respond to violence alongside reduced external investments. This deliberate focus lends a stronger motivation to view poverty as an emergency in these contexts. Together, these direct impacts can make recovery more challenging and lead to the emergence of poverty traps, as conflict on top of climate-related disasters (and because of it) directly impacts both the means of production and means of survival necessary to maintaining human wellbeing.

This chapter centres around the nexus of violent conflict and climate-related disasters, drawing on data from India, the Philippines, Kenya, Ethiopia and Niger. Afghanistan and Nigeria also experience these crises alongside economic instability and are dealt with separately in Chapter 5. In this chapter, sections 4.1 and 4.2 consider the amplification of downward mobility amidst the climate–conflict nexus and how competition over resources can be heightened due to environmental stressors and instability, driving poverty and reinforcing a vicious cycle between the climate–conflict nexus and deprivation. In Section 4.3, it then highlights how even low-intensity conflict-induced disruptions can create conditions characteristic of economic crises, further reinforcing hardships amidst environmental stressors. Section 4.4 examines human development consequences at the climate–conflict nexus before Section 4.5 concludes.

4.1 The amplification of downward mobility amidst the climate–conflict nexus

4.1.1 Conflict dynamics shape intersectional poverty impacts

In areas of new or persistent conflict, households can become impoverished or find it difficult to escape chronic poverty. Indeed, CPAN research points to rates of these negative poverty trajectories being higher in areas affected by violent conflict in India and Nigeria (Diwakar et al., 2017), reinforcing the bidirectional relationship between conflict and poverty. The risk of impoverishment was moreover found to be higher in the Autonomous Region in Muslim Mindanao—a conflict-affected part of the Philippines—compared to elsewhere in the country (Diwakar, 2018). Contexts of violent conflict can also extend to perceptions of prevalent insecurity. Households who newly felt "unsafe" in Pakistan and Uganda in 2015 compared to 2012 experienced a reduction in their asset holdings (Diwakar et al., 2017). The examples on impoverishment especially indicate that conflict is not just a problem for people living in poverty. Instead, people who are wealthier may also have a lot to lose from conflict (Verwimp et al., 2019).

There is moreover a heterogeneity of poverty outcomes that emerge depending on the waxing and waning of conflict—in other words both its dynamics and intensities. Countries experiencing chronic conflict have much higher monetary and multidimensional poverty rates compared to those who escaped conflict (Corral et al., 2020). Even within countries, areas of low-intensity conflict or insecurity may not experience the same level of impoverishment as those in high-intensity conflict zones. The latter may drive widespread displacement and asset loss, markets may be depressed or face destruction, and the scale of systems collapse may be acute. Amidst low-intensity or localised insecurity, in contrast, there may still be livelihoods coming under strain and driving income loss, but on a lesser scale.

Another moderator of conflict impacts depends on ideology. The type of ideology might be linked to specific types of conflict. Ideologies can motivate ethnic clashes or violence, as the literature on horizontal inequalities illustrates (Stewart, 2002; Cederman et al., 2014). These ideologies may be religious (including caste-based or those with certain interpretations that justify violence), ethnic, nationalist or other types of political ideologies (e.g. liberal authoritarian and class-based Marxist, Maoist/Naxalite, neoliberal ideologies). State maladaptive policies embedded in neoliberal ideology that drives chronic underfunding of social protection and disaster risk management can also spur on conflict-based reactions from below. This can be through dividing groups along ethnic lines and situating certain groups as superior or experiencing grievances. Motivating this, higher rates of structural and chronic poverty are typically observed for marginalised ethnic groups such as indigenous Janajatis or lower caste Hindus in Nepal (Wagle, 2016), linked for example to inequalities in education or regional development (Gradin, 2016). Such ethnic tensions are frequently exploited for political gain and can drive conflict, as observed for example in Kenya (Peace Direct, 2017; Oino and Kioli, 2014; Nyaura, 2018).

The ideologies of warring parties can also create unexpected outcomes either during conflict or through its legacies. For example, in Nepal and India, violent conflict linked to Maoist ideologies was associated with a higher probability of girls' enrolment in Nepal and learning outcomes of girls in poor households in India (Valente, 2014; Diwakar, 2023b). In the qualitative data in India, for example, INT20-IN (female, impoverished, rural India, 2020 LHI) recalled how Naxals kidnapped her school's headmaster for many days, interrogating him about the school and threatening him to make him improve facilities for tribal students. Upon his return, teachers began to return notes to tribal students on time, and improved teaching processes (Diwakar, 2023b). However, even where these unexpected results were observed, they were overshadowed by the broader negative outcomes and downward mobility characteristic of conflict contexts and driven by its widespread and deliberately destructive nature.

4.1.2 Climate–conflict nexus: heterogeneity amongst poverty trajectories

Conflict can create its own downward pressures that drive negative poverty trajectories—with grievances linked to the often-associated breakdown of the social contract fuelling violence and generating conflict traps. However, conflict can also interact with other types of crises that it generates or otherwise intersects with. Figure 4.1 presents the intersection of conflict, climate-related disasters and economic crises in Kenya, Ethiopia, Niger and India.

Some interesting observations emerge. The intersection of climate-related disasters with conflict appears to be pronounced amongst the poorest households in Kenya (i.e. amongst households in extreme poverty) and in India (amongst households in chronic poverty). In India, there is a gradient favouring wealthier households when disaggregating poverty trajectories by starting positions. In other words, chronically poor households tend to experience more conflict–climate crises than other households, including compared to households escaping poverty. Households falling into extreme poverty in India instead tend to experience marginally more conflict–climate crises compared to households remaining never poor.

As another example, in Kenya, conflict dynamics have been largely climate-driven but compounded by other stressors. On top of the farmer–herder conflicts, households in Kenya faced a series of climate-related slow- and rapid-onset disasters that are inherently linked to these conflicts. For example, drought in 2016 affected wellbeing and livestock rearing, forcing herders to move to other areas in search of grazing lands, driving conflict (Scott et al., 2018). This was followed in 2017 by hailstones leading to lower food production, and fall armyworms further damaging maize fields. Erratic rainfall also worsened production and contributed to a threefold increase in food prices, generating economic crisis conditions with the government driven to subsidising the price of maize and flour. On top of this, student strikes over the same period damaged school infrastructure, with parents often bearing the brunt of replacing destroyed facilities (analysis of FGDs conducted in Kenya in 2018). Political uncertainties linked to this prevailing insecurity also scared investors leading to even higher food prices than through the channel of erratic rainfall alone. Much of these polycrisis effects were pronounced for poorer households, as the clear gradient in Figure 4.1 indicates.

The climate–conflict nexus alongside the presence of economic crises is especially prevalent amongst households falling into poverty in Ethiopia in Figure 4.1. This result perhaps reflects the presence of economic crisis-like conditions generated by conflict (see Section 4.3). The conflict refers to the war in the Tigray region erupting in 2020 alongside unrest in Oromia and other regions especially in northern Ethiopia. The conflict–climate nexus was also relatively more prevalent in Ethiopia for households sometimes or always in poverty across the panel period, compared to households never in poverty (Figure 4.1). This again reinforces the bidirectional relationship between conflict and poverty often expounded in the literature (Justino, 2011; Diwakar, 2023a).

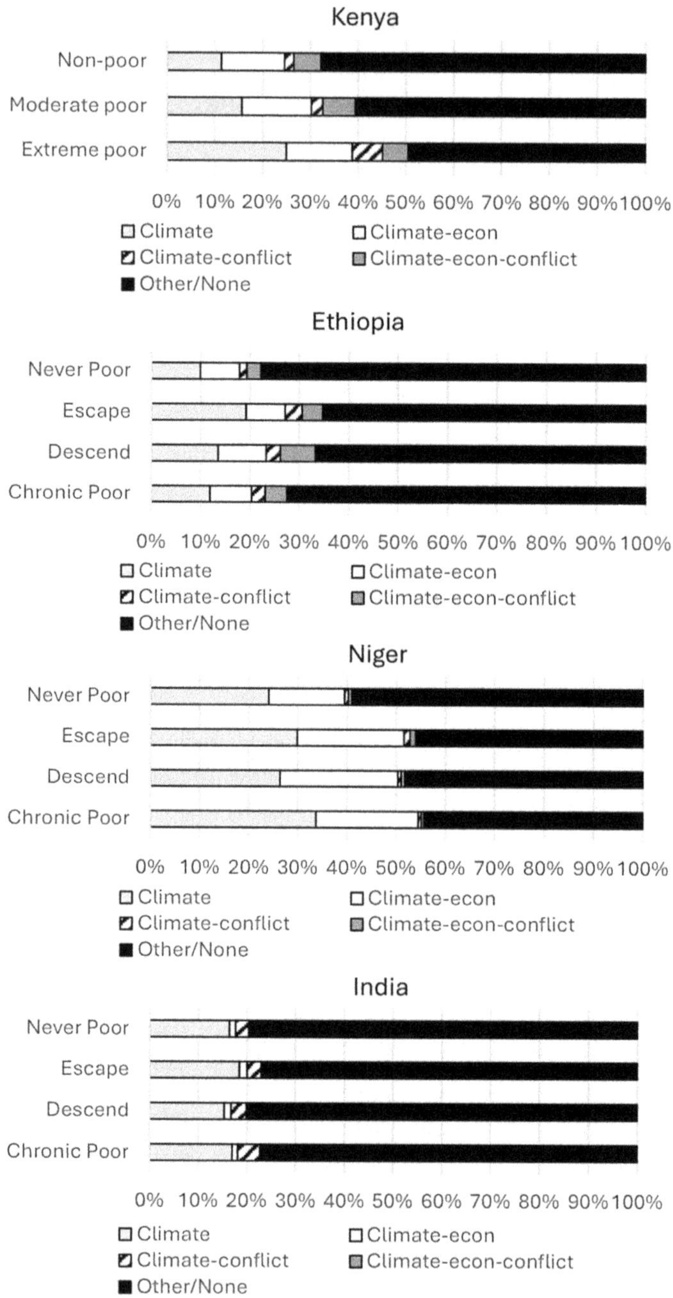

Figure 4.1 Climate-related disasters and polycrisis in Kenya, Ethiopia, Niger and India, disaggregated by poverty status/trajectory

Note: conflict data in India based on actual geocoded data, while elsewhere is based on self-reported shock modules (see Chapter 1).

Source: author's analysis of panel survey data presented in Table 1.1.

In Niger, the climate–conflict nexus was not apparent based on the panel survey data (Figure 4.1). Instead, climate-related disasters and economic crises were slightly more common amongst households falling into poverty relative to other trajectories. This salience likely reflects the severity instead of the drought Niger experienced in 2010, driving large-scale food insecurity in the country and possibly also driving poverty descents. Revenue shocks are also often linked to climate-related disasters that drive price changes (da Corta et al., 2021). Revenue shocks were more pronounced in the panel data amongst households headed by youth that had fallen into poverty, pointing to a double whammy where these households typically also have fewer assets due to their life course stage. Alongside this, insecurity especially in the form of theft were more frequently reported by impoverished youth-headed households relative to other households that had fallen into poverty (da Corta et al., 2021). Instead, the relative absence of violent conflict can reflect the localised nature of fighting alongside the relatively safer period of data coverage, discussed below.

4.1.3 A critical eye on conflict data

We also consider how these intersections, disaggregated by poverty trajectory, stack up against the intersections presented in Figure 3.1 in Chapter 3. Interestingly, more households report that they did not experience climate-related disasters, conflict or economic crises amidst the climate–conflict nexus compared to the climate-economic crises nexus examined in Chapter 3. This result very likely reflects data issues, namely: 1) limited data availability on particularly insecure areas within countries, where for example Tigray was excluded in the 2022 survey wave on account of the security situation; 2) self-reported data often underestimating the presence of conflict due to its focus on identifying often severe negative direct effects on households; and 3) the period of data coverage. On the second point, in India, shocks data was only collected for the 2012 wave of the India Human Development Survey (IHDS) panel and presented in high level categories that excluded conflict. It included "job loss" but no responses related to price shocks that may have proxied broader economic stressors. This points to the need for localised surveys rather than national ones and highlights how the localised intensity of a polycrisis is just as (if not more) important as broader but less intense national-level impacts.

The period of data coverage in part can explain the relative absence of conflict reported in Niger. The data from Niger reflects the early 2010s period (2011–14) where conflict-related fatalities and violence were much lower than present, as noted above. Indeed, Tillaberi in Niger—bordering Mali and Burkina Faso—has been more affected by insecurity since 2017 due to jihadist groups, while Diffa—bordering Nigeria and Chad—has experienced spillovers from the Boko Haram insurgency especially since 2015 (analysis of ACLED data). The panel data coverage in Niger thus precedes rising insecurity in the country.

The types of insecurity mentioned in these datasets nevertheless refer to higher-intensity conflict than that observed in Chapter 3. For example, in Kenya common responses under the conflict category include theft and robbery but also conflict and ethnic/clan clashes. In Niger, conflict/violence/insecurity was referenced, albeit by just a few households given the panel period. In Ethiopia, local unrest/violence were commonly experienced by households. In India, the absence of self-reported conflict data motivated inclusion of data on Naxal-violence related fatalities. These results accordingly point to more severe forms of violent conflict, compared to the lower-intensity theft and insecurity covered in Chapter 3.

4.2 Competition over resources at the climate–conflict nexus

4.2.1 Resource scarcity and competition

The analysis of Kenya in the preceding section refers to farmer–herder conflicts, which represent a key phenomenon at the intersection of the climate–conflict nexus. This is certainly not new, with roots in historical land tenure systems during colonial role that displaced more traditional land management in favour of land privatisation and territorial encroachment (Pkalya et al., 2003). Over time, this privatisation eroded traditional systems built on symbiotic social interactions, driving in its place environmental degradation and resource scarcity, worsened by urbanisation (Davidheiser and Luna, 2008). This degradation is also driven by livelihoods under severe strain from conflict amongst people in and near poverty, in turn amplifying environmental crises and further driving resource-related conflicts. In other words, negative poverty dynamics stemming from this nexus affects the patterns of growth and environmental degradation that in turn amplify crises.

While the conflicts are not new, the intensification of the climate crisis has worsened resource scarcity of grazing land and water, further fuelling these conflicts amongst pastoralists and also between pastoralists and farmers (di Santo et al., 2022; Evans, 2010). For example, in Kenya, Niger, Tanzania and other countries in regions of sub-Saharan Africa (see a discussion of these conflicts in Nigeria in Chapter 5), persistent drought has led to herders moving livestock to areas with higher rainfall which is often where farmers are traditionally located (Kimaro et al., 2018). In Kenya for example, competition is the north is centred around access to water and grazing lands amongst pastoralist groups. Instead, in southern Niger, contemporary land disputes between armer and pastoralists are often linked to population growth and desertification, though again with historical, political and ethnic roots. While Tanzania was identified in our typology as being situated primarily at the intersection of climate-related disasters and economic crises (see Chapter 2), there are localised experiences of farmer–herder conflicts that are not well captured by existing data and so we discuss its dimensions here, albeit drawing on partial insights from interviews with farmers.

At the same time, farmer–herder conflicts are only one albeit highly common type of competition over resource scarcity. Indeed, resource scarcity and competition is a driver of both conflict and poverty and amplified in contexts of environmental crises. Contested resource types or sectors that drive competition often centre around pastoralism, agriculture, water resources, and forests.

With regards to farmer–herder conflicts, structural challenges marked by the absence of adequate land tenure security, property rights and conflict resolution in countries experiencing these types of conflict have created a context where livestock are able to demolish fields with herders unlikely to risk punishment (da Corta et al., 2018; Hussein, 1998; Mwamfupe, 2015). This brutal power dynamic was observed in several FGDs in Tanzania, which some respondents likened to creating conditions similar to slavery:

> If cattle die on your farm, the Maasai will camp in your farm, and ensure they capture and kill you even if you are not the cause of the death. As a result, farmers fear pastoralists and their livestock to the extent that there was a time when the cattle were very weak due to lack of water and wandering in the farmers' fields and farmers had to fetch water for the cattle to ensure that they did not die in their farms. Fetching water for the cattle was a strategy for the cattle to gain energy and move out of their farms for fear of the Maasai's brutality. This is slavery.
>
> (FGD, rural Tanzania, 2017, first presented in da Corta et al., 2018)

Farmers in turn were driven to stop growing certain crops, accentuating the strain that their livelihoods were already facing. For example, factories in study sites in Tanzania that processed sugarcane had to accordingly reduce their period of operation, driving job loss and impoverishment (da Corta et al., 2018).

> For instance, Mtibwa Sugar Company used to operate for nine months per year in the past with a closure for only three months for cleaning and maintenance. This was possible because the company could get raw materials from sugarcane out-growers. With the invasion of the pastoralists, out-growers have stopped producing sugarcane, which means the factory is not getting enough raw materials. In 2016, the factory operated for only three months (from July to September 2016) and until now (March 2017) it is closed, which is not normal … One reason is failure to get raw materials because out-growers have stopped producing sugarcane. The community has been affected by loss of employment opportunities which we used to enjoy in working in the factory and in cutting sugarcane.
>
> (KII, rural Tanzania, 2017, first presented in da Corta et al., 2018)

4.2.2 Weak governance driving extreme poverty during crises

Weak governance and corruption have reinforced a cycle of extreme poverty at the conflict–climate nexus. In Tanzania, farmers noted that pastoralists were able to collectively organise and sell a cow to pay a bribe to the police or government officials (da Corta et al., 2018). In Kenya, a positive correlation was identified between county-level poverty rates and average bribe values at the county level in the mid-2010s, with highest bribes being paid to procure contracts and employment, as well as to bail out arrested individuals, and to secure social security benefits (Figure 4.2). More broadly, government institutions in conflict-affected areas may be weak or co-opted, and so when climate-related disasters occur, communities may be left with limited support. The governance vacuum can in turn prompt rebel forces to gain a foothold, further reinforcing poverty traps.

Weak governance may be observed through corruption, low state capacity to provide services, and political instability. This can facilitate the exploitation of resources or subvert aid distribution in conflict zones or in areas affected by climate-related disasters. For example, Kenya is just one of many countries with a history of politicians transferring aid to offshore accounts for personal use (Himbara, 2020). This can limit the support needed for operationalising critical services during crises. In other words, governance conditions can determine the mechanisms through which poverty may be prevented or reinforced during crises.

There were moreover intersections of crises that with differential government responses drove the resulting poverty traps. For example, pastoral destruction of assets and crops (enabled through corruption and weak

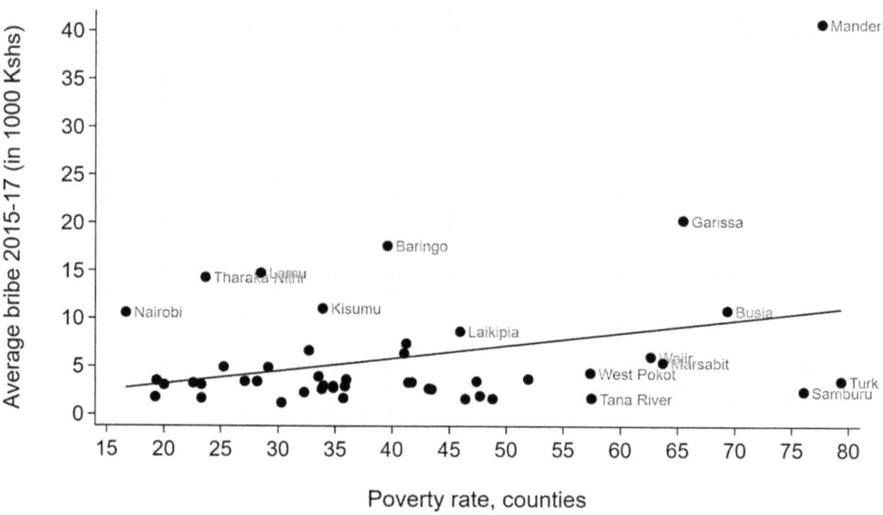

Figure 4.2 Average bribe and poverty rate by county

Note: county names presented for those with the top quintile rates of poverty and value of bribes.

Source: analysis based on KIHBS (2015/16) and EACC (2018) in Diwakar and Shepherd (2018).

governance) were often combined with government confiscation of farms, which in turn were followed by loan institutions seizing homes or land as collateral for unpaid debt taken out for farming in the first instance (da Corta et al., 2018). The prevalence of drought or high inflation of food prices or of agricultural inputs were added climate-related disasters linked to economic crises that also motivated loan procurement that reinforced these poverty traps in the qualitative data.

These examples thus point to structural dimensions of polycrisis that have considerable direct impacts for example in straining livelihoods and annihilating assets. Their underlying historical processes have shaped vulnerabilities households experience during polycrisis today. These vulnerabilities further combine to amplify polycrisis, as noted at the start of the section, which in turn obstructs recovery pathways out of poverty. They may also generate other crises outside of the conflict–climate nexus, as discussed next.

4.3 Crises-like economic conditions generated by conflict

4.3.1 Depressed labour markets due to conflict and aggravated by climate-related disasters

As noted in Figure 2.2 (Chapter 2), conflict on its own and on top of climate-related disasters can place livelihoods under considerably strain. This can occur through supply and demand-side mechanisms, where conflict can lead to a collapse of markets, weaken economic infrastructure and disrupt supply chains (Jagtap et al., 2022; Ali et al., 2016). This can variably increase price volatility and contribute to a context of broader insecurity, pointing to the bidirectional relationship between conflict and economic crises.

As with the cases discussed in Chapter 3, the COVID-19 pandemic was a key example of an economic crisis that—when interacting with violent conflict—hastened downward mobility. For example, in Ethiopia, despite restrictions on market trading and transportation easing following COVID-19, people in and near poverty reported that the price of food and transport remained high. This was followed by the war in Tigray which had spillovers in neighbouring Amhara where conflict was prevalent especially along the borders. A respondent noted:

> Because of the ongoing war, we hear that people are getting displaced … There is not much movement and transaction, people are overwhelmed by fear … The living cost has increased steadily … There is no attempt from the government to control and stabilize the market, and the way prices are increasing is beyond imagination.
>
> (Sentinel household INT8-ET in 2021, Ethiopia, first presented in CPAN, 2021)

As a result of these effects, the respondent perceived the war was significantly overshadowing the effect of the COVID-19 pandemic.

For those further away from the epicentre of violence, conflict was not typically directly present in their narratives. For example, INT12-ET in Oromia, Ethiopia (sentinel household interview in 2021), had to stop sending their children to school during the onset of COVID-19, but was unable to send them back in the following year due to their declining economic condition. They attributed declining finances and resulting food insecurity to COVID-19 and the shortage of rains. This is an important point regarding potential misattribution by respondents who are aware of the proximate causes of their economic condition but unaware of the meso- and macro-level drivers, such as conflict. This lack of awareness may also affect survey responses; rural individuals might state that conflict has had no impact on their lives at all, in contrast to more visible issues like climate change or the impacts of COVID-19 on the local economy.

Indeed, broader literature also situates these outcomes in the context of disrupted trade, with Oromia's central location in the country being negative affected by conflict through regular clashes, roadblocks and supply chains being affected (Gebremedhin, 2024). Agriculture in the region was also affected by conflict-induced displacement and insecurity alongside drought, wreaking havoc on markets and land access for farmers (Tiruneh, 2021). These economic distortions constitute important indirect effects of conflict even far from hotspots of violence within countries.

The interaction between conflict and climate crises can also lead to market distortions or failures. For example, during flooding in a conflict-affected context, trade may be restricted due to blockades stemming from insecurity or transport being affected. There could also be externally imposed sanctions due to conflict. Food price volatility can be especially high, for example due to limited supply amidst drought but also uncertainties linked to conflict that may obstruct import substitution. In all of this, certain market types may be more prone to failure. For example, agricultural markets can be affected by climate-related disasters affecting yields, and conflict affecting access to farmland. Both crises can drive food price volatility as noted above. Limited formal regulation or protection of informal markets can also make them susceptible to volatility and extortion. Cross-border and trade markets are other types of markets that can experience challenges when violence spills over across borders driving border closures, or mobility is restricted amidst disasters affecting transport routes.

As an example of these pathways of impact, in Zinder, Niger, interviewees pre-pandemic referred to poor rainfall and irregular growing seasons, layered on with livestock epidemics, crop infestation, conflict spillovers and economic crises. On the latter, the demolition of the Dolé market was noted by many interviewees. The Dolé market was the key market in the region for food and goods, where petty traders operated. However, in December 2016, the government sought to renovate the market and formalise it, requiring traders to pay registration and rental fees. This ended up excluding many small-scale traders—predominantly women in poverty— unable to afford these fees (McCullough and Diwakar, 2018). On top of this, cross-border trade, for example in palm weaves to Nigeria, also suffered on account of the Naira devaluation, which furthermore led to loss of remittances for many in the country. These conditions can limit recovery pathways even once markets are rehabilitated. Finally, the Boko Haram insurgency also had spillover effects by driving conflict-induced reverse migration. Box 4.1 illustrates how these polycrisis contributed to INT10-NE's impoverishment.

Box 4.1 Impoverishment in rural Niger

INT10-NE and her husband used to farm sorghum, millet, beans and peanuts—the latter two sold in the village or at the market. Her children continue to farm today and send them money, as she and her husband are in post-productive ages. She noted during the interview in 2018 that "there are lower harvests now compared with the last 20 years. There is not a lot of rainfalls, there are many crop enemies like insects. This year, it attacked our crops at the advanced period ... Each field became white. In 2016, we experienced food shortage due to rain misallocation".

INT10-NE instead raises poultry, though this has been affected by livestock epidemics. "Only God knows how many hens I lost. The disease was very contagious. I lost all of my poultry. Some years ago, we recovered by selling harvest. When the poultry was sick, we used some tablet but unsuccessfully".

Insecurity and economic crises in neighbouring Nigeria also affected their wellbeing in Niger. In 2013, the interviewee's brother-in-law returned to Niger because of the Boko Haram crisis in Nigeria. In 2015, one of her sons also returned from Nigeria on account of the Naira devaluation. "He was working in a road construction company. His work consisted of unloading ground from the truck. The salary became lower when he exchanged it to CFA [the currency in Niger]. So he preferred to come back to home. [Traders came less frequently] ... and then they stopped [altogether]. This is a result of Naira devaluation".

On top of this, today they were doing market gardening through irrigation. They were selling market gardening products in Dolé market in Zinder. They had been doing this activity for 15 years. When Dolé market collapsed, they lost their client base. They were still trying to gain it back unsuccessfully at the time of interview.

Source: INT10-NE, female, impoverished, rural Niger, 2017 LHI.

In contexts where conflict intersects with climate shocks, ownership of productive assets does not always lead to resilience—markets are disrupted or depressed, demand falls, and households may turn to exploitative intermediaries. In India, life history interviews conducted by the author from early 2020 just prior to the pandemic point to fluctuation in the price of crops stemming from violent conflict dynamics during their lives—Naxalite violence that peaked in the early 2000s. These dynamics led many households in turn to rely on exploitative middlemen. Businesses also commonly lost profits or went under due to insecurity, whether because of depressed demand and/or changes in supply patterns to mitigate widespread insecurity.

It is perhaps for this reason that we see mixed results between productive assets and livelihoods with the poverty trajectories they drive. Indeed, for households reporting conflict amidst climate-related disasters, cultivable land ownership and livestock ownership are also both associated with a higher probability of chronic poverty and lower probability of resilience in India (Figure 4.3). The same is true for the full sample in India (Figure 4.3). In other countries, however, the relationship lacks statistical significance amidst polycrisis. Livestock is associated though with a higher probability of transient poverty in India, but a lower probability of poverty in Kenya at the climate–conflict nexus (Figure 4.3). These relationships also persist amongst the full sample (Annex Table D4).

NFE ownership is associated with a lower probability of poverty in Kenya, again at the climate–conflict nexus (Figure 4.3). This result persists in the full sample (Annex Table D4). However, the relationship between NFE ownership and poverty escapes is not significant for households in other countries reporting conflict. This reflects a reality where amongst informal firms in conflict-affected contexts, businesses can be very risky, and the risk of default can be particularly high (Benjamin, 2023). As a result, recovery pathways out of poverty through off-farm diversification amidst polycrisis can be constrained.

Instead, for areas not affected by conflict albeit experiencing climate-related disasters, the relationship between land or NFE ownership and poverty trajectories is more intuitive (Figure 4.3). For example, land ownership is associated with a lower probability of transitory poverty (India), higher probability of resilience (India, Niger), and lower probability of poverty (cross-section data in Kenya) for households experiencing only climate-related disasters. There are still mixed results in India regarding livestock accumulation. Finally, where significant, NFE ownership is associated with a lower probability either of chronic poverty (Ethiopia), transient poverty (India, Ethiopia) or poverty status overall (Kenya, based on cross-section data). Together, these results point to strategies that households are able to draw on during climate-related disasters that may be eroded amidst depressed labour markets characteristic of conflict-affected contexts.

4.3.2 Insecurity and crime along the conflict spectrum vary by intersecting inequalities

Insecurity and crime are both associated with conflict, related to a breakdown in state institutions or absence of legitimate governance structures. In turn, conflict reinforces poverty through its long-term impacts on livelihoods and labour

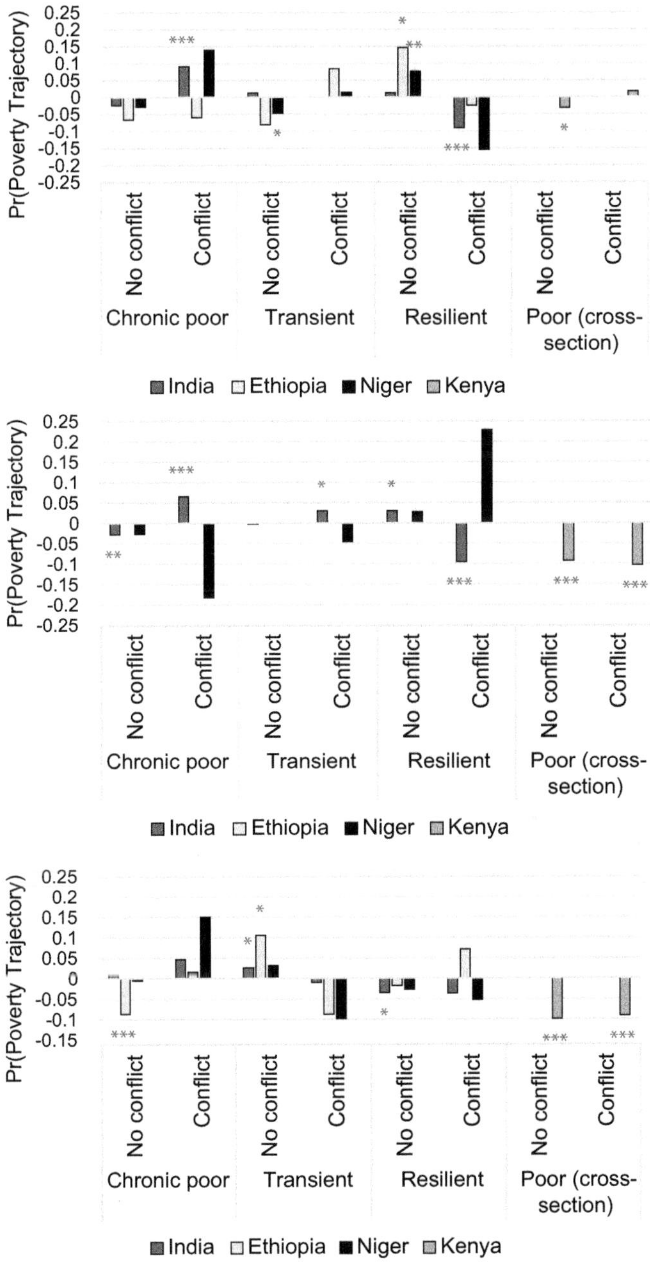

Figure 4.3 Relationship between cultivable land (top), livestock (middle) and NFE ownership (bottom) and poverty trajectories, by conflict, in areas affected by climate-related disasters

Note: average marginal effects are presented. There are four models per figure, examining the intersection of different variables (cultivable land, livestock and NFE ownership) with economic crises, for the subset of households experiencing floods or drought. Asterisks refer to results that are statistically significant at conventional levels (*** $p<0.01$, ** $p<0.05$, * $p<0.1$). All controls are the same as in the main equation presented in Chapter 1.
Source: analysis of survey datasets referenced in Table 1.1.

market opportunities (e.g. by increasing theft, land-grabbing or extortion). These effects can persist even after the conflict formally ends. In other words, there may be legacies of this violence that persist into post-conflict contexts.

Indeed, while theft can contribute to the depressed labour markets noted above it can also be due to it. Land-grabbing and burglaries were prevalent in the qualitative data in the Autonomous Region in Muslim Mindanao (ARMM, more recently transitioned into the Bangsamoro Autonomous Region in Muslim Mindanao) in the Philippines. This was often linked in narratives to limited job opportunities reflecting depressed labour markets driven by conflict-related insecurity. For example, INT8-PH's (male, initial poverty escape, rural Philippines, 2018 LHI, first presented in Diwakar, 2018) family experienced repeated burglaries. Bandits also threatened his family at gunpoint to extort money during harvest. This drove his parents to downsize their livelihood by limiting time spent on fields, corn planted and harvested, and by selling livestock as "it was hard to maintain them … and we became more afraid due to the crime". Even so, the family avoided destitution due to other diversified livelihoods they maintained.

Instances of theft amidst conflict can also be higher for specific demographic groups. In Kenya, poor households headed by youths between the ages of 15–24 years old were more likely to report shocks related to conflict and theft during the 2010–15/16 period, especially in urban areas. For many in the country, theft is now accordingly perceived as "a normal burden of citizenship" (Ombaka, 2015, p. 13). Other groups more likely to report theft or conflict were Muslims and religious minorities such as such as Hindus and Traditionalists in the country, where 12% of such households reported theft or conflict, compared to 8% for other religious groups (Diwakar and Shepherd, 2018).

4.3.3 Infrastructure deficit and structural economic constraints amidst the climate–conflict nexus

As a result of violence and other forms of crime and insecurity, conflict-affected contexts can experience an infrastructure deficit that can limit the scope for economic recovery and reinforce the structural basis of economic crises. This deficit can come from the destruction of existing infrastructure, reduced government spending on social and economic services, and/or a decline in external investments. On the latter, in Kenya, post-election violence and associated political uncertainties meant that investors were scared to invest even in the capital, leading to high food prices (FGDs in Scott et al., 2018). In study sites in the Philippines, insurgent groups terrorised private contractors who refused to pay the revolutionary tax. In the conflict-affected Mindanao region, this tax was imposed on businesses and other individuals operating in their areas and was obtained to fund insurgent activities. This often meant that private contractors were less willing to come into the area and build key infrastructure such as roads (Diwakar, 2018).

The infrastructure deficit also reinforces cycles of poverty and contributes to the intergenerational persistence of poverty. In the Philippines, typhoons and other natural hazards was linked to lower private investments that could otherwise help drive growth. This vacuum enabled armed groups to step in and insecurity to heighten (Sganzerla, 2016). It is unsurprising in turn that studies have found a strong relationship between climate change or armed conflict and chronic poverty in the country (Bayudan-Dacuycuy and Baje, 2017). In India, this infrastructure deficit moreover restricted teacher recruitment from coastal areas. Amidst insecurity and poor road infrastructure, many teachers were unwilling to migrate or travel to schools in conflict-affected areas (Diwakar, 2023b). These results reinforce the presence of a poverty–polycrisis trap, where not only is there a bidirectional relationship, but certain crises like climate-related disasters can precipitate other crises like violent conflict.

In a qualitative study site in southern Odisha, India, the infrastructure deficit that stemmed from the fear of investors and contractors to enter areas affected by Naxal violence "took the district four to five years back in development, if you compare it with the other districts" (KII with agricultural NGO in 2020, India). Despite receiving government funds for school facilities, a schoolteacher reflected: "no contractor is coming in fear of Naxal violence, and in the absence of road and communication infrastructure, even chips, iron and so on cannot be transported into the areas" (KII with schoolteacher in 2020, India). Another teacher noted that contractors who did come were warned or killed. The perception was that infrastructure development would enable police to move more easily to the jungle terrains where Naxals were hiding (Diwakar, 2023b). What this meant, however, was that the resulting poverty–polycrisis trap significantly constrained recovery prospects due to obstructing infrastructure development, disrupting school functioning and deepening intergenerational poverty.

The next section outlines other education outcomes constrained at the climate conflict nexus.

4.4 Human development outcomes at the climate–conflict nexus[1]

4.4.1 Education of school-going children amidst disasters and conflict: intersectional insights

While education can act as a portable asset, it is also often under stress during polycrisis. Indeed, negative human development outcomes can be amplified at the conflict–climate nexus. As noted earlier in Figure 2.2, there can be deliberate attacks on schools amidst violent conflict, while climate-related disasters can also destroy school infrastructure or cause it to be used as shelters. These supply-side impacts can result in overcrowding in remaining schools, putting pressures on the education system. Certain groups, such as girls and children with disabilities, may self-exclude due to the challenges linked to insecurity or limited access. Early marriages may result as families for example marry girls in neighbouring areas less affected by violence and insecurity. On the demand side, some children may also drop out of school to help complement household welfare amidst the depressed labour markets noted above (Diwakar, 2023c).

In India, armed conflict and disasters together are associated with a decrease in years of schooling for girls and boys (Figure 4.4). Residence for girls and boys in districts that newly became conflict affected in 2012 and experienced a disaster was associated with a statistically significant decrease in the years of schooling. Boys in districts experiencing chronic conflict and living in a village affected by a disaster in the leadup to the second survey wave tended to have the lowest years of schooling. For both boys and girls, differences were least severe where they were residing in areas that did not experience armed conflict in either survey year, though results lack statistical significance.

Intuitively, it could be that these shocks are separate but together act to amplify effects on conflict. However, it is more likely that disasters itself might contribute to an increase in conflict. Indeed, a meta-analysis of the emerging literature on climate change and conflict found that changes from moderate temperatures and precipitation increased the risk of conflict (Hsiang et al., 2013). In India, in contexts of drought there may be reduced returns from agricultural activities, for example, which could fuel grievances and increase support for Naxalism.

There are differential impacts based on the type of disaster. When disaggregating to common shocks, drought is associated only with a decline in years of schooling that is statistically significant for girls, though flooding is typically accompanied by reductions in schooling for girls and boys. It could be that drought creates conditions that require girls to engage in certain time use activities that may require additional effort during disasters. Especially amidst slow-onset disasters, households in patriarchal contexts may have more time to re-allocate intra-household labour to respond in ways that maintain a differential in favour of boys. Descriptively, in 2012 and for the same subset of children, women in these households living in areas that had experienced drought spent 34 minutes per day on average fetching and collecting water (including waiting in line), compared to 25 minutes for women in areas without drought. For men, they typically spent 15 minutes per day with water tasks in drought-prone areas. Overall, these numbers were even higher for women (and men) in poor households. In the wider literature in India, too, there is evidence to suggest that girls may be taken out of school in response to conditions of drought to assist with family and care responsibilities (Singh et al., 2013; Mishra, 2007; Sam et al., 2016).

Such results highlight the direct impacts of climate-related disasters and violent conflict in terms of weakening intangible assets like education and reinforcing time poverty. Results also point to the intergenerational dimensions of these impacts generated by short-term adverse coping responses where children may be taken out of school and thus be less able to develop longer-term recovery capacities. There are heterogeneous impacts in all of

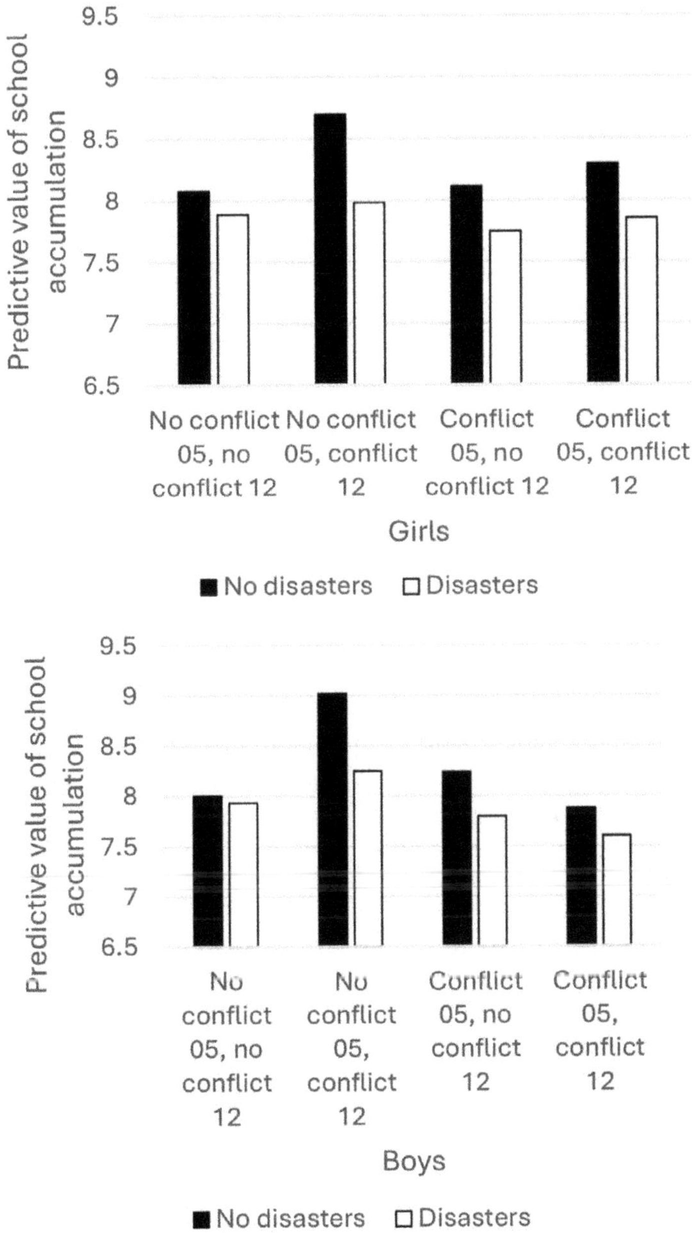

Figure 4.4 Relationship between conflict dynamics, climate-related disasters and school accumulation

Source: analysis of IHDS 2004/05–2011/12 data.

this, especially disadvantaging girls in poor and remote households. In many ways, then, these intersecting inequalities (e.g. due to gender, extreme or moderate poverty status, and area of residence) at the micro-level mirror the context of polycrisis at the macro-level. There are multiple crises affecting the context in which people live, and multiple sources of vulnerability amongst those most affected.

4.4.2 Health, trauma and intangible outcomes

These multiple sources of vulnerability can also extend to less tangible dimensions. INT10-IN's experience (Box 4.2) points to conflict and economic crises that negatively affected his mental health and education. This reflects the very real psychological stressors that can exist amidst conflict and linked to conditions of violence as well as economic crises or precarity more broadly. Indeed, the literature points to trauma from violence contributing to dropouts, lower test scores, and self-exclusion from education (Bruck et al., 2019; Poutvaara and Ropponen, 2018; UNESCO, 2006; Monteiro and Rocha, 2017). There are clear gender differentials, where girls may experience worse outcomes in terms of mental health but also gender-based violence, further reinforced by gender-blind health system responses amidst conflict (Percival et al., 2018).

Box 4.2 Trauma amidst climate and economic crises in India

When Naxalite violence increased in the area in which INT10-IN lived, it peaked in an attack on a famous contractor, followed by the blasting of two Border Security Force commanders inquiring into the attack. The killing of government forces amplified villagers' fears. INT10-IN recalls that many girls left school as a result, particularly those from other villages, while others would attend irregularly for the months that followed. Villagers locked themselves at home after 5pm, bus services were discontinued for days, and the weekly market was also disturbed for a few weeks.

As a result, his mother's vegetable business lost profits and was shut down due to lower demand coupled with market insecurities and price volatility reflective of economic crises-like conditions. With these conflict-induced financial and domestic difficulties prompting destitution, INT10-IN was unable to concentrate and failed his class 10 exam, dropping out of school. It was the combination of economic and psychological shocks resulting from conflict insecurities that prompted him to drop out of school and help his family by working.

Source: INT10-IN, male, initial poverty escape, rural India, 2020 LHI, first presented in Diwakar, 2023b.

There are so many conflict- and polycrisis-driven impacts on intangible outcomes—like education, mental health and social cohesion—that in turn can deepen poverty and contribute to its persistence across generations.

Indeed, alongside this is a wider context of hopelessness, fear and anxiety that permeates many life histories amidst contexts of polycrisis and is visible in the quantitative analysis, as the next chapter elaborates. Moreover, where conflict can drive internal displacement or migration, the resulting weakening of social cohesion can amplify these effects, as the next chapter also highlights.

Thus, macro-level crises can drive micro-level mental ill health and hopelessness. Given the aggregate salience of mental ill health amidst conflict and polycrisis, coping systems may be overwhelmed and underprepared to deal with the scale of challenge. It is important though not to conflate proximate drivers of extreme poverty—in this case ill health—with root causes linked to structural conditions and entrenched inequalities generating violent conflict. Instead, these juxtapositions can improve our understanding of how crises evolve or become crises, and their solutions (see Chapter 7).

4.5 Conclusion

This chapter investigated some of the ways in which conflict dynamics generated negative poverty trajectories, and how this was moreover affected by the intersection of climate-related disasters. On the former, conflict characteristics, including its duration, intensity and changes in this intensity over time, extent of civilian casualties, and ideologies behind the violence can interact to shape its dynamics and legacies into periods well beyond the end of violence. At the same time, climate-related disasters can intersect with conflict, shaping and being shaped by its dynamics. This is exemplified by farmer–herder conflicts in regions of sub-Saharan Africa. Amidst these conflicts, weak local government institutions sometimes prompted corruption, leading to high bribes and loan procurement to help pay bribes. The co-option of weak local governance by conflict parties was also observed in these contexts, further eroding social cohesion.

Resource competition can also emerge from and contribute to crises-like economic conditions. Indeed, the chapter drew attention to depressed labour markets and other forms of insecurity and crime that disrupted these markets further. Informal work in these contexts can be a survival strategy but also face considerable risk with limited protections. Prevalent insecurity in turn limited external and local investment at the climate–conflict nexus, which in turn amplified polycrisis. This limited investment also extends to critical human development infrastructure, of which education facilities were presented as an example. The study pointed to how education was undermined as conflict- and climate-related disasters converged to drive heterogenous reallocations in the labour of girls and boys resulting in gender-differentials in school withdrawals amidst crises, but also trauma further driving negative education outcomes. Trauma was also a common consequence driving negative education outcomes as exemplified in this chapter; however, more broadly there is a host of other negative impacts of mental health issues in reducing the ability of individuals to engage in economic activities or manage households.

Together, the findings in this chapter point especially to deliberate strain and even destruction of livelihoods and infrastructure at the climate–conflict nexus, motivating a focus on treating poverty itself as an emergency in these contexts. The chapter highlighted a bidirectional and forward-reinforcing relationship with poverty, marked by its effects on intangible harms perpetuating poverty's intergenerational persistence. Together, these relationships drive a poverty–polycrisis trap. Even where investors may show appetite, conflict can prevent access to insecure areas which can obstruct reconstruction and the recovery pathways these could otherwise support. Climate-related disasters can amplify these challenges by making it even more difficult to reach marginalised populations, leading to entrenched poverty traps.

The next chapter investigates the presence of humanitarian crises where violent conflict, economic crises and climate-related disasters can converge, and its relationship in turn with negative poverty dynamics.

Note

1 Some of the text in this section is taken from the author's PhD thesis, with further elaboration and analysis.

References

Abbasi, K. (2022) 'Understanding the complexity of conflict trauma: A systematic review'. *South Asian Journal of Social Sciences and Humanities*, 3(5). doi:10.48165/sajssh.2022.3510.

Ali, R., Barra, A.F., Berg, C.N., Damania, R., Nash, J.D. and Russ, J. (2016) 'Infrastructure in conflict-prone and fragile environments: Evidence from the Democratic Republic of Congo'. *World Bank Policy Research Working Paper No. 7273*. https://ssrn.com/abstract=2607773.

Aysan, A.F., Bakkar, Y., Ul-Durar, S. and Kayani, U.N. (2023) 'Natural resources governance and conflicts: Retrospective analysis'. *Resources Policy*, 85(Part A): 103942. doi:10.1016/j.resourpol.2023.103942.

Bayudan-Dacuycuy, C. and Baje, L. (2017) 'Chronic and transient poverty and weather variability in the Philippines: Evidence using components approach'. *Discussion Paper Series No. 2017–24*. Philippine Institute for Development Studies.

Benjamin, N. (2023) 'Dealing with informality in conflict and fragile settings: Technical report'. *Donor Committee for Enterprise Development*. https://www.researchgate.net/profile/Nancy-Benjamin/publication/371952385.

Blattman, C. (2009) 'From violence to voting: War and political participation in Uganda'. *American Political Science Review*, 103(2): 231–247. doi:10.1017/S0003055409090212.

Bruck, T., Di Maio, M. and Miaari, S. (2019) 'Learning the hard way: The effect of violent conflict on student academic achievement'. *Journal of the European Economic Association*, 17(5): 1502–1537. doi:10.1093/jeea/jvy051.

Burrows, K. and Kinney, P.L. (2016) 'Exploring the climate change, migration and conflict nexus'. *International Journal of Environmental Research and Public Health*, 13(4): 443. doi:10.3390/ijerph13040443.

Cederman, L-E., Gleditsch, K.S. and Buhaug, H. (2014) *Inequality, grievances, and civil war*. Cambridge University Press. https://www.cambridge.org/core/books/inequality-grievances-and-civil-war/39F26D12EFEE2D7D621A59DF74DED496.

Corral, P., Irwin, A., Krishnan, N., Mahler, D. and Vishwanath, T. (2020) 'Fragility and Conflict: On the front lines of the fight against poverty'. *World Bank Group*. http://documents.worldbank.org/curated/en/375651583211667808.

CPAN (2021) 'Ethiopia Covid-19 Poverty Monitor: August 2021'. https://www.chronicpovertynetwork.org/covid19-poverty-monitor/ethiopia-august.

da Corta, L., Kessy, F., Ruhinduka, R., Shepherd, A. and Scott, L. (2018) 'Understanding and supporting sustained pathways out of extreme poverty and deprivation: Tanzania national report'. *CPAN*. https://www.chronicpovertynetwork.org/resources/2018/9/14/understanding-and-supporting-sustained-pathways-out-of-extreme-poverty-and-deprivation-tanzania-national-report.

da Corta, L., Diarra, A., Diwakar, V., Harouna, A. and Poggi, C. (2021) 'Youth inclusion in labour markets in Niger: Gender dynamics and livelihoods'. *CPAN*. https://www.chronicpovertynetwork.org/resources/2021/6/29/youth-inclusion-in-labour-markets-in-niger-gender-dynamics-and-livelihoods.

Davidheiser, M. and Luna, A.M. (2008) 'From complementarity to conflict: A historical analysis of Farmer-Fulbe relations in West Africa'. *African Journal on Conflict Resolution*, 8(1): 77–104. doi:10.4314/ajcr.v8i1.39421.

di Santo, N., Russo, I. and Sisto, R. (2022) 'Climate change and natural resource scarcity: A literature review on dry farming'. *Land*, 11(12): 2102. doi:10.3390/land11122102.

Diwakar, V. (2018) 'Resilience and sustainable poverty escapes in the Philippines'. *USAID*.

Diwakar, V (2023a) 'Ending extreme poverty amidst fragility, conflict, and violence'. *DEEP Working Paper 2. DEEP.* https://povertyevidence.org/wp-content/uploads/2023/07/Ending-extreme-poverty-amidst-fragility-conflict-violence-Thematic-paper.pdf.

Diwakar, V. (2023b) 'Learning outcomes and mediating pathways in conflict-affected areas in India'. *International Journal of Educational Research*, 119: 102159. doi:10.1016/j.ijer.2023.102159.

Diwakar, V. (2023c) 'Interrogating dynamic, intersecting inequalities in education amidst armed conflict'. *Research in Comparative and International Education*, 18(4): 528–546. doi:10.1177/17454999231212714.

Diwakar, V. and Shepherd, A. (2018) 'Understanding poverty in Kenya: A multidimensional analysis'. *CPAN*. https://www.chronicpovertynetwork.org/resources/2019/3/14/understanding-poverty-in-kenya-a-multidimensional-analysis-1.

Diwakar, V., Shepherd, A. and Sturge, G. (2017) 'Conflict, pro-poorest growth, and wellbeing: A subnational analysis'. *CPAN Challenge Paper*. CPAN.

Evans, A. (2010) 'Resource scarcity, climate change and the risk of violent conflict'. *World Development Report background papers*. World Bank. http://documents.worldbank.org/curated/en/351651468337157443.

Fiedler, C. (2023) 'What do we know about how armed conflict affects social cohesion? A review of the empirical literature'. *International Studies Review*, 25(3). doi:10.1093/isr/viad030.

Gebremedhin, A.E. (2024) 'Impact of the civil war in Ethiopia on the export economy in Oromia, Amhara, and Tigray'. *Borkena*, 29 May. https://borkena.com/2024/05/29/impact-of-the-civil-war-in-ethiopia-on-the-export-economy-in-oromia-amhara-and-tigray/.

Gradin, C. (2016) 'Poverty and ethnicity in Asian countries'. In J. Silber and G. Wan (Eds.), *The Asian 'Poverty Miracle'*. Edward Elgar Publishing (pp. 253–320). doi:10.4337/9781785369155.00017.

Himbara, D. (2020) 'Kenya: Study reveals scale of foreign aid diversion offshore'. *The Africa Report*, 18 March. https://www.theafricareport.com/24282/kenya-study-reveals-scale-of-foreign-aid-diversion-offshore/#:~:text=Put%20another%20way%2C%20ruling%20politicians,Settlements%20.

Hsiang, S.M., Burke, M. and Miguel, E. (2013) 'Quantifying the influence of climate on human conflict'. *Science*, 341(6151). doi:10.1126/science.1235367.

Hussein, K. (1998) 'Conflicts between farmers and herders in the semi-arid Sahel and East Africa: A review'. Oversees Development Group and School of Development Studies, University of East Anglia. http://pubs.iied.org/pdfs/7386IIED.pdf.

Ide, T., Michael Link, P., Scheffran, J. and Schilling, J. (2016) 'The climate-conflict nexus: Pathways, regional links, and case studies'. In H.G. Brauch *et al.* (Eds.), *Handbook on sustainability transition and sustainable peace*. Springer (pp. 285–304). doi:10.1007/978-3-319-43884-9_12.

Jagtap, S., Trollman, H., Trollman, F., Garcia-Garcia, G., Parra-López, C., Duong, L. (2022) 'The Russia-Ukraine conflict: Its implications for the global food supply chains'. *Foods*, 11(14): 2098. doi:10.3390/foods11142098.

Justino, P. (2011) 'The impact of armed civil conflict on household welfare and policy'. *Working Paper 384*. Institute of Development Studies. https://www.ids.ac.uk/download.php?file=files/dmfile/Wp384.pdf.

Kimaro, E.G., Mor, S.M. and Toribio, J-A.L.M.L. (2018) 'Climate change perception and impacts on cattle production in pastoral communities of northern Tanzania'. *Pastoralism*, 8: 19. doi:10.1186/s13570-018-0125-5.

McCullough, A. and Diwakar, V. (2018) 'Resilience and sustainable poverty escapes in Niger'. *Overseas Development Institute/USAID*. https://www.chronicpovertynetwork.org/resources/2019/1/17/resilience-and-sustainable-poverty-escapes-in-niger-national-report.

Mishra, S. (2007) 'Household livelihood and coping mechanism during drought among Oraon Tribe of Sundargarh district of Orissa, India'. *Journal of Social Science*, 15(2): 181–186. doi:10.1080/09718923.2007.11892580.

Monteiro, J. and Rocha, R. (2017) 'Drug battles and school achievement: Evidence from Rio de Janeiro's favelas'. *Review of Economics and Statistics*, 99: 213–228.

Mwamfupe, D. (2015) 'Persistence of farmer-herder conflicts in Tanzania'. *International Journal of Scientific and Research Publications*, 5(2). https://www.ijsrp.org/research-paper-0215/ijsrp-p3862.pdf.

Nyaura, J.E. (2018) 'Devolved ethnicity in the Kenya: Social, economic and political perspective'. *European Review of Applied Sociology*, 11(16): 17–26. https://ideas.repec.org/a/vrs/erapso/v11y2018i16p17-26n2.html.

Oino, P.G. and Kioli, F.N. (2014) 'Ethnicity and social inequality: A source of under-development in Kenya'. *International Journal of Science and Research*. https://www.ijsr.net/archive/v3i4/MDIwMTMzOTc=.pdf.

Ombaka, D.M. (2015) 'Explaining Kenya's insecurity: The weak state, corruption, banditry and terrorism'. *International Journal of Liberal Arts and Social Science*, 3 (3): 11–26. https://ir-library.ku.ac.ke/items/d4ff6f6e-e194-4741-8508-3ed7179927f7.

Peace Direct (2017) 'Kenya'. *Peace Insight*. https://www.peaceinsight.org/conflicts/kenya/.

Percival, V., Dusabe-Richard, E., Wurie, J., Namakula, J., Ssali, S. and Theobald, S. (2018) 'Are health systems interventions gender blind? Examining health system reconstruction in conflict affected states'. *Globalization and Health*, 14: 90. doi:10.1186/s12992-018-0401-6.

Pkalya, R., Adan, M. and Masinde, I. (2003) 'Conflict in northern Kenya: A focus on the internally displaced conflict victims in Northern Kenya'. https://practicalaction.org/docs/region_east_africa/conflict_in_northern_kenya.pdf.

Poutvaara, P. and Ropponen, O. (2018) 'Shocking news and cognitive performance'. *European Journal of Political Economy*, 51: 93–106. doi:10.1016/j.ejpoleco.2017.03.006.

Raleigh C. and Linke, A. (2018) 'Subnational governance and conflict: An introduction to a special issue on governance and conflict'. *Political Geography*, 63: 88–93 doi:10.1016/j.polgeo.2017.09.014.

Sam, A., Kumar, R., Kachele, H. and Miller, K. (2016) 'Quantifying household vulnerability triggered by drought: evidence from rural India'. *Climate and Development*, 9(7): 618–633. doi:10.1080/17565529.2016.1193461.

Scott, L., Miller, R., Eichsteller, M., Diwakar, V., Njagi, T. and Nyukuriet, E. (2018) 'Resilience and sustainable poverty escapes in rural Kenya – Country report'. *CPAN*. https://www.chronicpovertynetwork.org/resources/2018/6/13/resilience-and-sustainable-poverty-escapes-in-rural-kenya-country-report.

Sganzerla, T. (2016 [updated 2022]) 'Meet the small-town mayor risking her life to fight for peace in rural Philippines'. *Quartz*, 28 January. https://qz.com/605631/meet-the-small-town-mayor-risking-her-life-to-fight-for-peace-in-rural-philippines.

Singh, R., Feroze, S. and Ray, L. (2013). 'Effects of drought on livelihoods and gender roles: A case study of Meghalaya'. *Indian Journal of Gender Studies*, 20(3): 453–467. doi:10.1177/0971521513495293.

Solomon, N., Birhane, E., Gordon, C., Haile, M., Taheri, F. and Azadi, H. (2018) 'Environmental impacts and causes of conflict in the Horn of Africa: A review'. *Earth-Science Reviews*, 177: 284–290. doi:10.1016/j.earscirev.2017.11.016.

Stevens, G., Eagle, G., Kaminer, D. and Higson-Smith, C. (2013) 'Continuous traumatic stress: Conceptual conversations in contexts of global conflict, violence and trauma'. *Peace and Conflict: Journal of Peace Psychology*, 19(2): 75–84. doi:10.1037/a0032484.

Stewart, F. (2002) 'Horizontal inequalities: A neglected dimension of development'. *CRISE Working Paper*. Centre for Research on Inequality, Human Security and Ethnicity (CRISE). https://assets.publishing.service.gov.uk/media/57a08cba40f0b652dd0014fa/wp1.pdf.

Tiruneh, M. (2021) 'Conflict, displacement hinders agriculture'. *Ethiopian Business Review*, 99. https://ethiopianbusinessreview.net/conflict-displacement-hinders-agriculture/.

UNESCO (2006) 'Education in emergencies: The gender implications'. *Advocacy brief*. UNESCO Office Bangkok and Regional Bureau for Education in Asia and the Pacific. https://unesdoc.unesco.org/ark:/48223/pf0000148908.

Valente, C. (2014) 'Education and civil conflict in Nepal'. *World Bank Economic Review*, 28(2). World Bank. http://hdl.handle.net/10986/23544.

Verwimp, P., Justino, P. and Bruck, T. (2019) The microeconomics of violent conflict. *Journal of Development Economics*, 141: 1–6. doi:10.1016/j.jdeveco.2018.10.005.

von Uexkull, N.V., Croicu, M., Fjelde, H. and Buhaug, H. (2016) 'Civil conflict sensitivity to growing-season drought'. *PNAS*, 113(44): 12391–12396. https://www.pnas.org/doi/10.1073/pnas.1607542113.

Wagle, U.R. (2016) 'The caste/ethnic bases of poverty dynamics: A longitudinal analysis of chronic and structural poverty in Nepal'. *Journal of Development Studies*, 53 (9). doi:10.1080/00220388.2016.1224850.

5 Humanitarian contexts, extreme polycrisis and acute poverty frontiers

A humanitarian emergency is an "event or series of events that represents a critical threat to the health, safety, security or wellbeing of a community or other large group of people, usually over a wide area" (Humanitarian Coalition, n.d.). This type of emergency thus can refer to different types of contexts, such as conflict zones, post–climate disaster settings and/or areas with mass displacement. Crises in humanitarian contexts are different to the crises mentioned in earlier chapters due to: the scale, intensity, number and types of crises; the scale of human suffering stemming from mass inability to meet basic needs including of an often large share of populations, including those forcibly displaced; and the weaknesses of governance structures to respond thus often necessitating international humanitarian aid.

Deeply challenged humanitarian contexts are an increasingly important poverty frontier where large numbers of people in acute poverty reside, yet where data on poverty and its dynamics are especially limited. These are historically contexts of rapid change, but increasingly also sites of protracted, multiple crises that contest traditional delineations between humanitarian and development approaches (Policinski and Kuzmanovic, 2019; Sabates-Wheeler et al., 2022). In spite of this, responses in humanitarian contexts remain largely reactive and short-term, rather than addressing root causes of crises.

The direct impacts of the intersections of climate-related disasters, economic crises and violent conflict in humanitarian contexts can be particularly severe. As noted in Chapter 2, this can include economic collapse or widespread market failures, heightened waves of displacement, statelessness and high rates of mortality, reinforced by weak state provision and/or donor fatigue amidst chronic crises. A key distinction is that the prevalence and intensity of humanitarian crises usually go well beyond the effects of the climate–conflict contexts alone. This is because the convergence of these crises can generate overlapping vulnerabilities that reinforce structural constraints and successively erode coping mechanisms to trap populations in severe and sustained poverty—reinforcing the crisis-like dimensions of poverty. Systems over time are weakened yet the scale of needs and human suffering remain highest in these contexts. The inadequacy of support is often catastrophic and continues to respond largely to

DOI: 10.4324/9781003503125-7

immediate survival needs rather than complementing this with longer-term recovery and development efforts.

This fifth chapter builds on themes from the preceding chapter, in particular investigating multi-scalar drivers of chronic (i.e. longer-term) and acute (i.e. more severe) poverty amidst polycrisis with a focus on complex humanitarian settings. It deepens analysis from country studies by the author in collaboration with partners in Afghanistan and Nigeria (e.g. Nemat et al., 2022; Diwakar et al., 2025).[1] It highlights systemic vulnerabilities that predate crises and helps emphasise crises as embedded in longer-term structural inequality with mutually reinforcing dimensions, rather than episodic events.

Sections 5.1 and 5.2 rely on mixed methods analysis of polycrisis in Afghanistan and Nigeria, respectively. The chapter identifies the role of structural challenges—such as weak governance, exclusion of marginalised groups and a fragmented aid environment—that provide a backdrop against which climate-related disasters, violent conflict and economic crises can come together and be reinforced by micro-level shocks and stressors to drive negative poverty trajectories. These trajectories include downward mobility that is increasingly giving way to chronic poverty, and the acuteness of this chronic poverty and deprivation. The chapter then draws attention to the heterogenous impacts of the effects of polycrisis, with a focus on internally displaced persons (IDPs), young adults and women in poverty, with a view to considering how demographic variations can shape exposure and vulnerability amidst humanitarian crises. This is followed by a brief conclusion in Section 5.3.

5.1 Afghanistan: insights on the acuteness of poverty

5.1.1 Structural challenges provide an incubator for polycrisis

Pre-transition Afghanistan

Humanitarian contexts are typically characterised by deep structural challenges. These may be identified through reliance on quantitative indices (e.g. WGI, fragility indices—see Chapter 2), expert assessments and local perceptions. In Afghanistan, violence and insecurity over the decades has combined with structural vulnerabilities including climate change, economic fragility and significant donor dependence. Related to this, weak security, displacement, growth volatility, international sanctions and asset/aid freezes, droughts and flash floods, the COVID-19 pandemic and a fragmented aid environment have contributed over decades to heighten vulnerability and processes towards destitution.

Power has also long been fragmented in the country and reinforced by repeated international interventions and instability and conflict. For example, the Bonn Agreement signed in 2001 after the fall of the Taliban had reconstruction and institution-building as central tenets to state-building. However, it was in part ineffective on account of Western technocratic models attempting to replace informal institutions that had helped limit exclusion—for example through informal credit mechanisms or conflict mediation (Huot and Pain, 2017; SIGAR, 2021; Allouche et al., 2022). Additionally, it was further undermined by predatory action by those in power who used aid to exert influence in politics and over the economy, including through corruption and off-budget grants in the name of security. This meant that service delivery for health, education and other population needs was often sidelined (Allouche et al., 2022).

There is also a crisis of human rights that humanitarian contexts experience. Even prior to the shift in power to the Taliban in 2021, Afghanistan was regularly in the top ten countries globally in terms of discrimination against women in social institutions (OECD, 2023). As one KI interviewed before the transition in 2021 noted, insecurity "has highly impacted women. Girls even stopped going to schools in addition to leaving jobs outside; they are not able to walk out of home" (Diwakar et al., 2022). It is then unsurprising that women-headed households experienced a higher probability of extreme food poverty and hunger in the country according to the analysis of 2019/20 survey data (Diwakar, 2022).

The socio-political exclusion of certain groups is also a key symptom of the structural challenges that Afghanistan faces. For example, religious and ethnic minorities, the Kuchi population, and other minority identities continue to experience persistent marginalisation amidst polycrisis. For example, Shi'a Hazaras in the country have been discriminated against over decades, facing exclusion from social, political and economic roles in Afghanistan, while Hindus and Sikhs have also experienced rising persecution in recent years (Hasrat, 2019; Chiovenda, 2014; TOLO news, 2016). Nomadic groups such as Kuchis and Pashtuns, despite experiencing less political exclusion, often lack access to key infrastructure and services including education and health, which correlates with their monetary poverty. Conflict and drought have decimated livestock and affected Kuchi migration routes and worsened during the pandemic lockdowns. Moreover, limited land tenure policy and rights have also contributed to vulnerability of Kuchi herders (FAO, 2020).

Regime change deepening structural constraints

The Taliban's rapid and ideologically driven regime change in mid-2021 deepened these crises: collapsing public institutions, massive oppression of women and girls, cutting off aid, worsening food insecurity and creating widespread fear and social control. This was a rapid, nationwide military takeover that reshaped the entire society and state along ultra-conservative religious lines—essentially erasing women's rights and freedoms almost entirely. This is one of the most extreme systems of gender-based social control in recent history, setting Afghanistan apart as a uniquely severe and ideologically enforced humanitarian crisis.

Indeed, since the political transition, the lack of rule of law and human rights abuses forcibly prevent the ability of women and other marginalised groups to develop pathways out of poverty (Barr, 2024; Albrecht et al., 2022).

Women's rights have been reversed including through measures that limit their access to employment and education. INT8-AF (female, impoverished, rural Afghanistan, 2022 sentinel household interview) reflected:

> Women are more vulnerable than all. Women become more dependent on men. They are not allowed to work outside and have no more income. They have to wait for men to provide them food, cloth and other needs ... They don't have freedom. They have to sit at home and do household tasks; they will not be able to get income by doing household tasks ... these economic crises and poverty put more pressure on women.

The whole governance system—courts, civil service, security—was dismantled or rebuilt to fit this ideology. The Afghan economy prior to August 2021 was three-quarters dependent on foreign assistance, which furthermore meant that the suspension of aid that year as a result of the transition in power led to salaries being cut off for essential workers including in education and healthcare (UNDP, 2021; HRW, 2022; Byrd, 2022; SIGAR, 2021). Interference by the regime further amplified challenges in service delivery:

> The interference of [local government] in our management and administrative work. The issue is more problematic during the time of staff recruitment. The interference ... prevents us from recruiting highly qualified people [and] that affect[s] our service delivery ... [Another issue] that we face and prevents us from providing high-quality services is no high-quality drugs are available in the market.
>
> (KII in Afghanistan, 2022 LHI, first presented in Diwakar et al., 2022)

All of this has furthermore contributed to a context of heightened volatility and cash liquidity crisis (UNDP, 2021; SIGAR, 2021). The resulting deep economic collapse, aid freeze and total isolation have made the scale of institutional and social breakdown unlike most other crises. The public punishments and widespread fear and repression also created a context of extreme polycrisis.

5.1.2 Acute poverty amidst humanitarian crises

The sequential and intersecting nature of these crises drove acute (i.e. more severe) poverty and the creation of a humanitarian context even before the shift in power. Using national poverty lines, 38.2% of Afghans lived in poverty in 2011, a figure that dramatically rose to 54.4% by 2016, before going down to 47.1% by 2020 and then being estimated as up to half of the population by 2023 (World Bank, 2023). The depth of poverty has also increased between 2007/08 and 2020, when the distance of people in poverty from the poverty line nearly doubled from 7.2% to 13.5% over the period on account of the gap rising in urban areas, while the intensity of poverty also more than doubled (World Bank, 2022a). It is worth noting that these figures are based on a very low national poverty line equivalent to about US$1 per day, pointing to the acuteness of poverty. This depth coupled with volatility in poverty has limited households' ability to plan for the future. As such, when subsequent crises strike, downward mobility into poverty or towards destitution is all too common.

Indeed, Figure 5.1 illustrates the salience of climate-related disasters, as well as that of these disasters intersecting with other crises, prior to the transition. This is pronounced amongst the poorest households, who also report the highest shares of climate-related disasters intersecting with economic crises. However, when focused on triple intersections alone, this appears to be more prevalent amongst less poor households—namely moderately poor and non-poor households in 2019/20—which may reflect broader impoverishment across the country. The sub-sections below reflect on these different intersections in more detail.

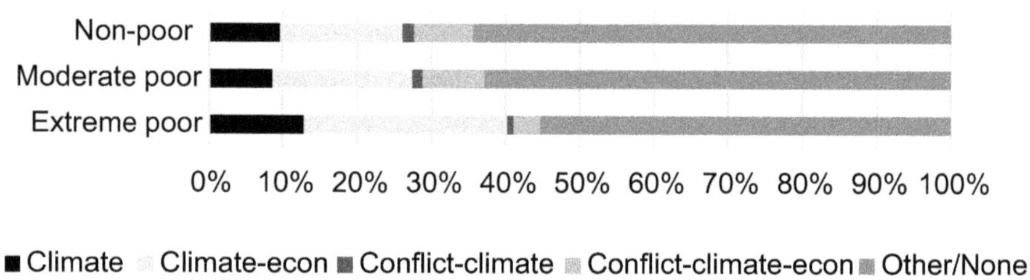

Figure 5.1 Climate-related disasters and polycrisis in Afghanistan (2019–20), disaggregated by poverty status
Source: author's analysis of IE&LFS 2019/20.

Conflict and disasters driving welfare loss and forced displacement

In Afghanistan, an analysis of household survey data from 2019/20 pointed to a higher probability of welfare loss in the summer of 2020 compared to earlier quarters. This represented a period when COVID-19 transmission rates were increasing alongside insecurity, while climate-related disasters remained prevalent. This probability of welfare loss was especially high in districts where a larger share of households reported insecurity (Diwakar, 2022). Speaking of this convergence prior to the transition, an interviewee reflected: "In the last one year, the case of theft, robbery and other criminal activities has reached its peak … Looking to the economic situation, the insecurity, drought, lack of work, we may have people who died because of hunger" (KII prior to the political transition in 2021, first presented in Nemat et al., 2022). This quote reinforces how even before the Taliban took over again, there was already a heavy atmosphere of fear from conflict, criminality and hunger.

As a result of intersecting crises, livelihood strategies have been largely ineffective. Indeed, regression analysis indicates that cultivable land, livestock and non-farm enterprise ownership are not significant correlates of poverty for the subset of households living in disaster-affected areas that reported experiencing economic crises and conflict (Figure 5.2). Results persist across the full sample (Annex Table D5). Amongst households living in disaster-affected areas, it is only those who do not experience conflict yet report economic crises who see significant moderators of these crises. In particular, livestock and non-farm enterprise ownership are associated with a lower probability of poverty for these households. This could reflect the role of livestock in cushioning the effects of economic crises so long as violence does not decimate herds or be related to the winners that can emerge in enterprise development amidst economic volatility so long as households remain shielded from direct violence. These results point to the hugely depressing role that conflict can have on livelihood strategies for those in and near poverty.

After the transition in power, there were fewer conflict fatalities but a renewed climate of fear: "The security situation is good, but people are living in terror. We are going out in a panic, or if any of my family members go out, I am worried until he/she comes back" (INT4-AF, female, impoverished, rural Afghanistan, 2022 LHI, first presented in Diwakar et al., 2022). As such, even though there may be fewer direct conflict deaths now, the sense of terror and immobility has deepened, with people facing personal punishments for breaking strict rules. This reflects a different kind of harm—less visible but just as serious.

At the same time, there were also noticeable intersections between climate-related disasters, economic crises marked by the COVID-19 pandemic, and

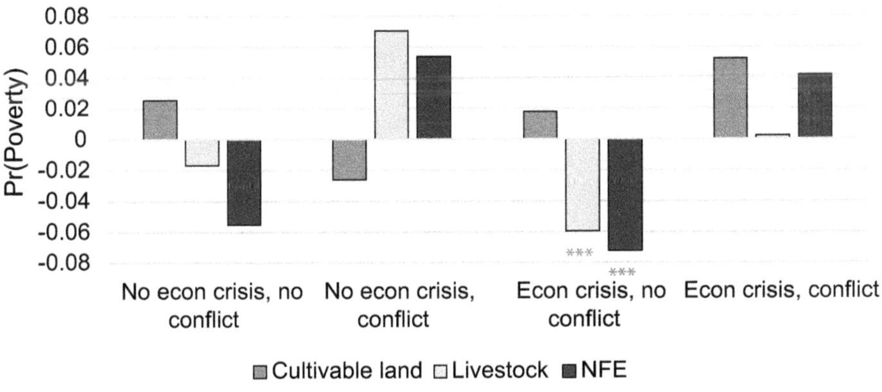

Figure 5.2 Relationship between livelihood strategies and poverty, by economic crises and conflict, in areas affected by climate-related disasters

Note: average marginal effects are presented. The figure refers to three models, examining the intersection of 1) cultivable land, 2) livestock and 3) NFE ownership with economic crises and conflict, for the subset of households experiencing floods or drought. Asterisks refer to results that are statistically significant at conventional levels (*** p<0.01, ** p<0.05, * p<0.1). All controls are the same as in the main equation presented in Section 1.2.1 of Chapter 1.

Source: analysis of IE&LFS dataset referenced in Table 1.1.

insecurity even prior to the transition. Shocks related to disasters, agriculture and/or food/farm prices were associated with a higher probability of welfare loss and poverty during the summer of 2020 (Diwakar, 2022). This could reflect the increasing vulnerability of the agricultural sector during the summer months when Kuchi herders were unable to migrate along their usual routes amidst the lockdown. Descriptively, too, the reduced availability of grazing areas and Kuchi migration routes was noted to be higher in the summer months relative to the preceding spring period within the survey, reinforcing these results. In addition, such shocks were compounded by insecurity and crime:

> In the early morning, when people want to bring milk to the market. They may sell their dairy product for AFN200 to AFN300, but there are thieves who stop people and take their mobile phone, which may cost AFN6,000; and they even took motorbikes from people. Such incidents happened a lot. [The] security situation has a lot of impact on farmers and everyone. As a result, it has affected our income and livelihood.
>
> (INT6-AF, male, sustained escape, rural Afghanistan, 2021 pre-transition LHI)

Climate-related disasters and conflict have driven large-scale displacements, where IDPs face increased precarity. This is often on account of limited social connections that in turn hampers access to economic opportunities and weakens the informal support structures that are so critical in maintaining wellbeing in the country. This was pronounced even prior to the transition.

> Our life was relatively better in our village … People knew us as a daily wage labourer. We were busying in people's land and gardens and had a sort of income to support our family … in Kandahar city, we lost our social connection. We cannot find daily wage labour and face a lot of hurdles and challenging times.
>
> (INT12-AF, male, impoverished, rural Afghanistan, 2021 pre-transition LHI)

> When we were in our village, we had a good connection with our relatives. In a time of need, I was getting help from them, and in financial issues, I was taking a loan from them. However, when displaced to Herat province, everything changed. I do know anyone in this place. Therefore, in a time of need, I cannot ask for help or a loan.
>
> (INT15-AF, male, impoverished, rural Afghanistan, 2021 pre-transition LHI)

Economic consequences of humanitarian crises

While the COVID-19 pandemic was not as strong by mid-2021, it left a legacy, especially in terms of high unemployment and inflation, that was amplified amidst other crises. As INT13-AF (male, impoverished, rural Afghanistan, 2021 pre-transition LHI) noted:

> Unemployment and being jobless is the main challenge and difficulty that affected our well-being. The economic condition of Afghanistan is getting worst.The drought increased the crises as well. We and the people in the village have nothing to eat. Extreme poverty exists in our district. Besides this, the prices have risen. We are not able to buy a kilo of chicken meat. Last year, three kg of oil was AFN320 but now three kg of oil is AFN600. You can find everything on the market, but the prices are high, and you cannot buy anything. There is no control, and all shopkeepers select a price, and no one controls them. We don't have access to health services and medicine.
>
> (Diwakar et al., 2022)

While some of these reflections point to direct COVID-19 legacies, the unemployment mentioned appears to stem more from broader economic conditions, including drought and possibly international shocks like rising oil prices, that converged with the pandemic to amplify impacts.

There was similarly a large and increasing share of households reporting that their economic situation at the time of survey (prior to the transition) was much worse than a year prior, pointing towards destitution processes (Figure 5.3). Self-reported reasons for income decline were commonly on

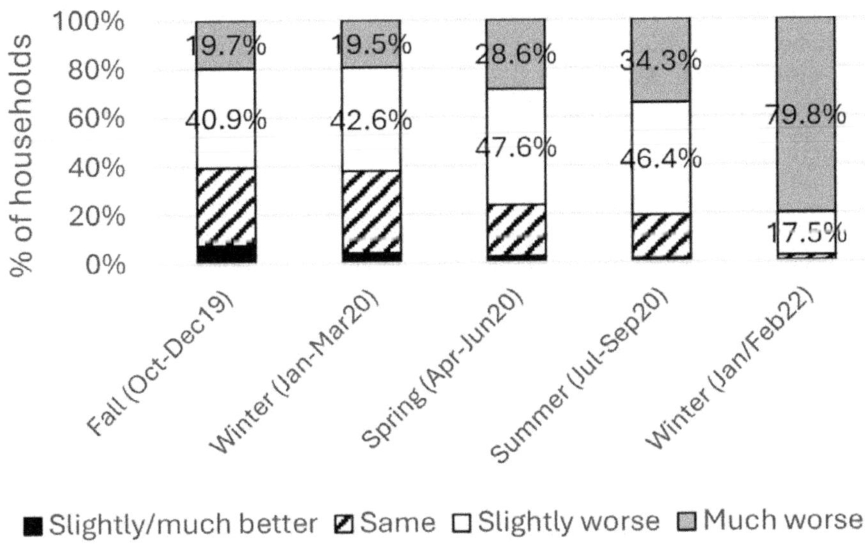

Figure 5.3 Self-reported economic situation at time of survey vs one-year prior

Note: the final column refers to self-reported "income" change of individuals, compared to the first four columns which ask specifically about the self-reported "economic situation" of households, so are not strictly comparable.

Source: analysis of survey data presented in Diwakar et al. (2022).

account of reduced employment opportunities (58%), followed by armed conflict (22%). Reduced employment was more commonly reported in urban areas, whereas conflict was more commonly reported in rural areas (WFP, 2022). These self-reported trends were furthermore corroborated by rising unemployment in urban areas and declining labour earnings more broadly, including for women. On the latter, 61% of women involved in income-generating activities lost their livelihoods in the six months before a late 2021 survey (World Bank, 2022a).

In humanitarian contexts and amidst protracted crises, infrastructure and assets are devastated, livelihoods placed under extreme strain, people are separated from their families and networks, as well as government support often subverted to respond to violence, as outlined in the conceptual framework guiding this analysis (see Chapter 2). This multi-layered crisis intersects moreover with longer-term vulnerabilities. In this context, people may have various needs that are not being met, as Figure 5.4 illustrates using data after the shift in power. This spans across material needs of food and shelter, but also institutional needs relating to education and economic infrastructure.

Intersecting shocks and stressors with crises

In addition to macro-level polycrisis, there are again a range of localised shocks and stressors in conflict situations that interact with these crises to maintain poverty or drive impoverishment, even in pre-transition Afghanistan. For example, INT12-AF (Figure 5.5) and his family members in rural Afghanistan had diverse income sources, including from agriculture and salaried employment. This meant that the regular ill health of his family did not initially drive impoverishment. However, given the successive nature of

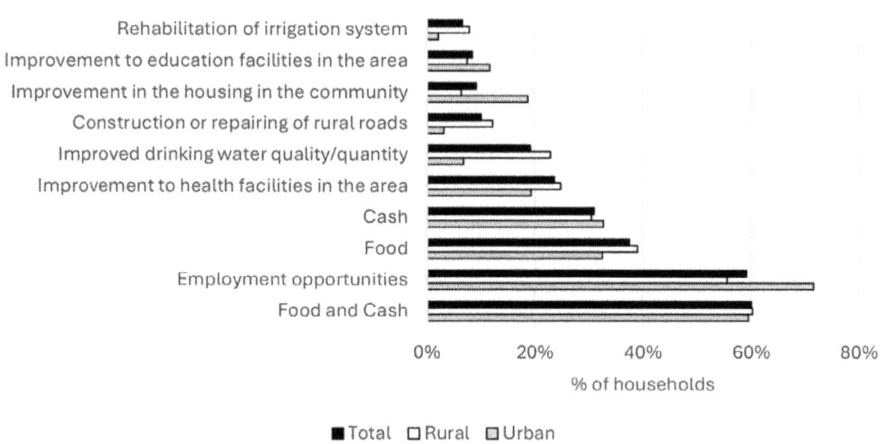

Figure 5.4 Top priority needs identified in Afghanistan
Source: Diwakar et al.'s (2022) visualisation of WFP's PLSA 2022 data.

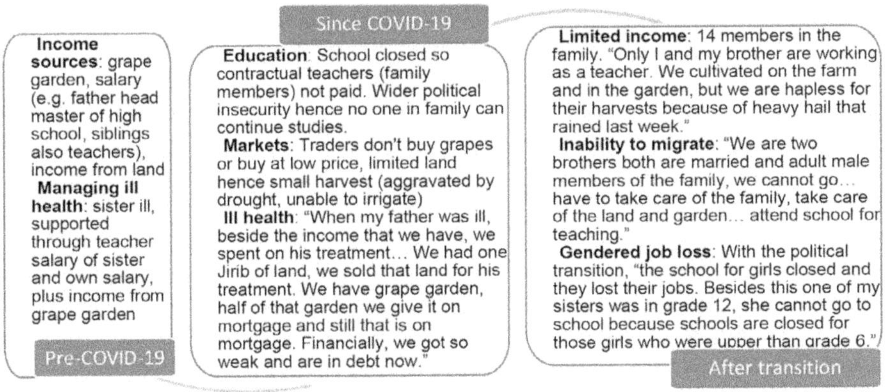

Figure 5.5 Intersecting vulnerabilities and shocks limit coping potential to ill health
Source: INT12-AF, male, impoverished, rural Afghanistan, 2021 pre-transition LHI, first presented in Diwakar et al. (2022).

shocks, his family mortgaged their land but were increasingly unable to pay back the mortgage on account of the macro-level crises marked by depressed labour markets during the COVID-19 pandemic. Once his father died, he and his brother were no longer able to migrate as they were now the main breadwinners. Layered on top of this, the political transition saw his sisters lose their salaried employment. These intersecting and successive economic and conflict-related crises meant that coping mechanisms were sequentially overwhelmed, especially in the face of ill health. Together, it drove the households deep into poverty over time.

5.1.3 Variations by demographic: spotlight on IDPs, young adults and gender

Young adults constitute a sizeable share of Afghanistan. People under the age of 35 years old constitute 80% of the Afghan population. Youth-headed households, that is those led by heads aged between 18 and 25 years, tend to have a lower asset base and experience higher food insecurity. The low asset base may reflect their stage of life, where they are forming households. Related to this, they also have fewer dependents, and perhaps as a result are less likely to be living in poverty. Nevertheless, they are highly susceptible to welfare loss, especially during times of heightened crises. For example, during the COVID-19 pandemic, youth heads of households were more likely to report that they were temporarily laid off compared to pre-pandemic, amongst the subset of heads that were not working or looking for a job. As INT9-AF reflected:

> Due to drought and lack of irrigation resources, I was losing my income. COVID has obliged people who were working in the factory and other manufacturing companies to quit their job as the companies are shut

> down. The income that we had from outside is now stopped. As a result, it has severely affected our livelihoods and economic situation.
>
> (INT9-AF, male, impoverished, rural Afghanistan, 2021 pre-transition LHI)

These circumstances reinforced the precarity of youth employment, in spite of the higher rates of secondary school completion amongst this subset. Young adults in the qualitative data in Afghanistan relatedly spoke of limited labour, resources, and thinning of social networks. Common means of coping were also blocked during the pandemic and into the political transition. For example, credit access was constrained amidst the thinning of social networks, and many households were displaced or migrated. This further eroded the important buffer that social capital otherwise provided.

Indeed, internal displacement was widespread before the shift in power. Forced displacement can be a common direct effect of polycrisis especially those involving violent conflict (see Figure 2.3), even pre-transition. Drought, environmental degradation, and the pre-transition ongoing conflict between Taliban and government forces forced many rural households to move to into urban informal settlements. IDPs experience heightened vulnerability, especially as a result of limited social connections and in the context of weak economic opportunities (Nemat et al., 2022). This pushed many young adults who had been forcibly displaced from their homelands to pursue risky work strategies:

> Since we have come here, our problems have increased. My husband doesn't have a proper and regular job; my sons are going to the streets to collect plastics. If they could collect some, they can get at least AFN10 per kg. Some people say not to send my sons on the streets; that it is not good for their health. But what can we do? If I don't send them what do we do to eat, we will die in poverty before dying by COVID.
>
> (INT11-AF, female, chronic poor, urban Afghanistan, 2021 pre-transition LHI)

The intersection of crises moreover differentially affected youth heads of households. For example, the intersection of households reporting climate-related disasters affecting them during the summer 2020 months of COVID-19 were seen to specifically disadvantage youth-headed households, according to regression analysis of IE&LFS 2019/20 data. Instead, for household heads that were beyond the youth age threshold, the absence of disasters was associated with a lower probability of welfare loss during the pandemic (Diwakar, 2022). At the same time, this is not to say that youth-headed households were consistently worse off. Indeed, during times of conflict-related insecurity, youth-headed households were observed to be marginally better off compared to other households during the pandemic (Diwakar, 2022). Older heads may have found it more difficult to escape insecurity or be targeted on account of higher asset and wealth holdings as descriptively observed above, thus making them particularly susceptible to welfare loss.

Finally, when disaggregating further by gender, young men during the COVID-19 pandemic were less likely to engage in economic activities compared to months preceding the pandemic (Figure 5.6). This aligns with the descriptive data above pointing to higher rates of layoffs amongst young adults. Moreover, while young women had much lower rates of economic activity compared to men, rates of economic activity instead increased for young women amidst insecurity, pointing to a slight narrowing of the gender differential in income generation. However, given that this is likely to be precarity-driven economic activity, this could be a sign of households moving deeper into poverty, forcing women to engage in income generation even on adverse terms. Indeed, women-headed households more broadly were more likely to be living in poverty or experiencing hunger in 2019–20. In addition, one of the responses that women were driven towards during earlier drought in the country between 2006 and 2008 was to intensify income-generation as a survival mechanism (Huot and Pain, 2017). These survival responses, discussed more in Chapter 6, highlights how changing gendered roles within households amidst contexts of polycrisis can reshape the vulnerability of women and their households.

There is also intersectionality of gender with other vulnerabilities. For example, the intersection of gender, ethnicity and religious identify has heightened the discrimination that Hazara women in Afghanistan face. Most

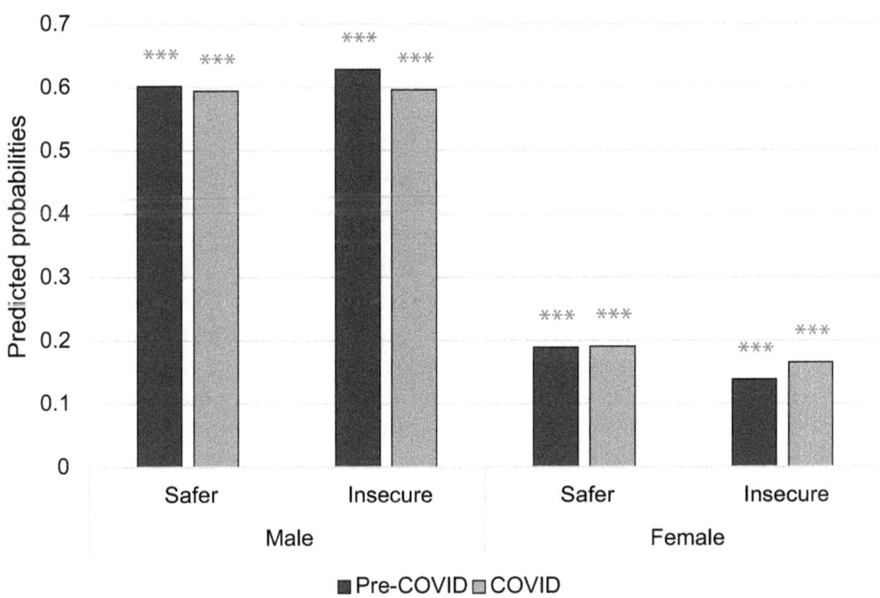

Figure 5.6 Predicted probability of economic activity, by gender, conflict and COVID-19 among youth

Note: Asterisks refer to results that are statistically significant at conventional levels (*** p<0.01, ** p<0.05, * p<0.1)

Source: visualisation of analysis of IE&LFS 2019/20 data, first presented in Diwakar (2022).

Hazaras are Shia Muslims, compared to the Taliban who are Sunni Muslims. Sectarian and ethnic differences used by the Taliban to accuse Hazaras of not being real Muslims (HRC, 2024). Taliban forces have regularly treated Hazara women and girls particularly harshly including through use of violence (Akbari and Moradi, 2024). These examples reinforce how intersecting inequalities also amplify vulnerability during crises.

The case of Afghanistan thus presents the clearest example of the book's argument, namely how polycrisis reinforce each other to drive, prolong and deepen poverty. The direct impacts are severe and interact with micro-level shocks and stressors to overwhelm coping systems and reinforce negative feedback loops that further amplify polycrisis. Certain marginalised groups including those facing intersecting inequalities are often the most affected in these contexts. Recovery pathways are moreover severely curtailed amidst large-scale suffering. Though international aid is present, the intractable crises constrain its effectiveness and may contribute to the challenges experienced given histories of fragmented power.

The next case study is of Nigeria, where again polycrisis generating a humanitarian context has emerged over the last decade, albeit with a stronger subnational dimension and relatively more established formal governance structures.

5.2 Nigeria: insights on chronic poverty and sustained impoverishment

5.2.1 Structural challenges provide an incubator for polycrisis

Nigeria faces entrenched challenges—including corruption, weak governance, oil dependence and major infrastructure gaps—which have long contributed to chronic poverty and remain highly relevant today (see also Brock et al., 2004). Governance is weak, as measured through perceptions of government effectiveness (WGI, 2025). Ethnic and regional tensions for political dominance intersect with pervasive systems of clientelism to drive limited effectiveness of pro-poor policymaking (Demarest, 2021). Corruption challenges are also rampant as a result, including at the highest levels of ministerial leadership (Aradi, 2024; Ojo, 2024). Weak coordination amongst aid actors results in limited gap-filling of national systems.

In terms of its economy, Nigeria is heavily dependent on oil revenues, which render it vulnerable to fluctuation in global oil prices. The government's removal of the long-standing fuel subsidy—while intended as a measure to alleviate the burden it placed on public finances—led to a drastic rise in the price of petrol and related transportation and energy costs (Addeh, 2024). As a result of its historic reliance on oil revenues, the country has experienced a "resource curse" resulting in limited diversification neglecting the growth of sectors like agriculture and manufacturing, as well as poor infrastructure, corruption, mismanagement, weak public services and high unemployment , which are all aggravated by a rapidly growing population without access to quality education adequately linked to labour market needs (Gbahabo and Oduro-Afriyie, 2017; Sala-i-Martin and Subramanian, 2013). In other words, its resource wealth has not translated into broad-based development.

Infrastructure deficits are a common structural challenge resulting from weak governance and a weak economy. For example, power outages were highly common in study communities across the six geopolitical zones of the country, negatively affecting people's livelihoods, with mitigating options constrained amidst the fuel subsidy removal. In 2022, the national grid collapsed at least four times, and this breakdown has continued into more recent years (BBC, 2023). In some cases, such outages have been crisis-induced: for example, Boko Haram destroyed the power grid in Maiduguri, Borno in January 2020, and prevented state attempts to revitalise it (Campbell, 2020). Power outages in various study sites have meant that the price to sustain businesses has increased. It also prevented households attempting to irrigate their farmland. To mitigate the effects of power outages, typically better-off households in study communities in the qualitative data relied on generators or other electricity sources to reduce dependency on the national grid. However, amidst the fuel subsidy removal, these strategies have come under strain, limiting people's agency in crafting pathways out of poverty.

Against this backdrop of structural challenges, crises are driving chronic poverty that is increasingly acute. Crises over the last two decades has included terrorist movements including Boko Haram, farmer-herder conflicts, banditry, and climate-related disasters including drought and floods. Nigeria is one of the ten most climate vulnerable countries globally (USAID, 2019). There are geographic and temporal variations to this, where for example drought is particularly common along Nigeria's eastern and central regions (Figure 5.8), the latter also a site of farmer–herder violence (Figure 5.7) amplified during the lean seasons (World Bank, 2022b; Adelaja and George, 2019). Instead, though different types of crime and insecurity are prevalent across Nigeria's zones, the epicentre of violence over the last two decades in particular has been in the northeast resulting from Boko Haram activities.

Structural challenges and resulting crises also often have strong ethnic dimensions. Poverty is lower amongst certain ethnic groups, such as the Igbo and Yoruba, reinforced by spatial divides amongst the richer southern regions in which they typically reside (Musa Abdu et al., 2018; Adegbami and Uche, 2015). On the other hand, certain groups experiencing ethnic marginalisation are found in some of the poorer northern regions. Boko Haram as an Islamist insurgency is tied to ethnic marginalisation, while the farmer–herder conflicts are often delineated across ethnic links with regular ethnic profiling (e.g. scapegoating Fulani pastoralists). These groups also typically have lower education levels alongside broader monetary and multidimensional deprivations prevalent in the northern states.

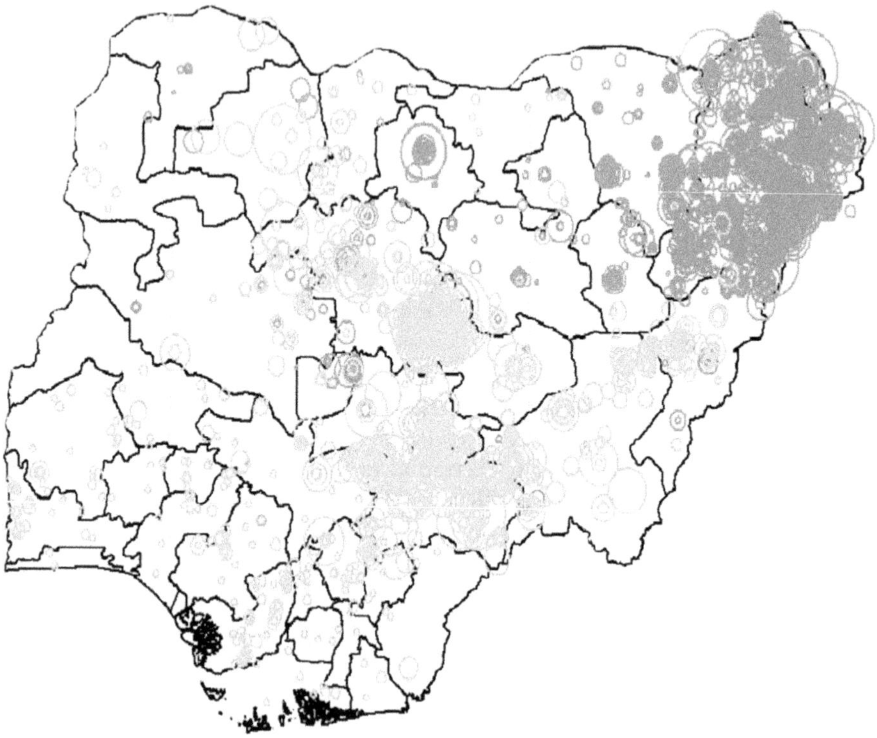

Figure 5.7 Boko Haram (darker) and herder–farmer conflict (lighter) fatalities, 2010–22
Note: Circles are weighted by the number of fatalities, within each conflict type.
Source: analysis of ACLED 2010–22 data, first presented in Diwakar and Brzezinska (2023).

5.2.2 Acute and chronic poverty amidst humanitarian crises

These crises have led to a host of negative poverty trajectories (Figure 5.9). A larger share of households in chronic poverty tend to experience climate-related disasters in Nigeria. The intersection of conflict or economic crises with climate-related disasters moreover is also much more pronounced amongst households that have fallen into poverty, are churning around the poverty line or are living in chronic poverty, relative to households never in poverty or those sustaining escapes from poverty. Amongst these negative trajectories, impoverished households tend to most commonly experience climate and economic crises intersections, followed by households escaping but falling back into poverty. Interestingly, households sustaining poverty escapes report no violent conflict, a point we return to in Chapter 6.

The next sub-sections outline ways in which these crises and their intersections drive negative poverty trajectories in Nigeria.

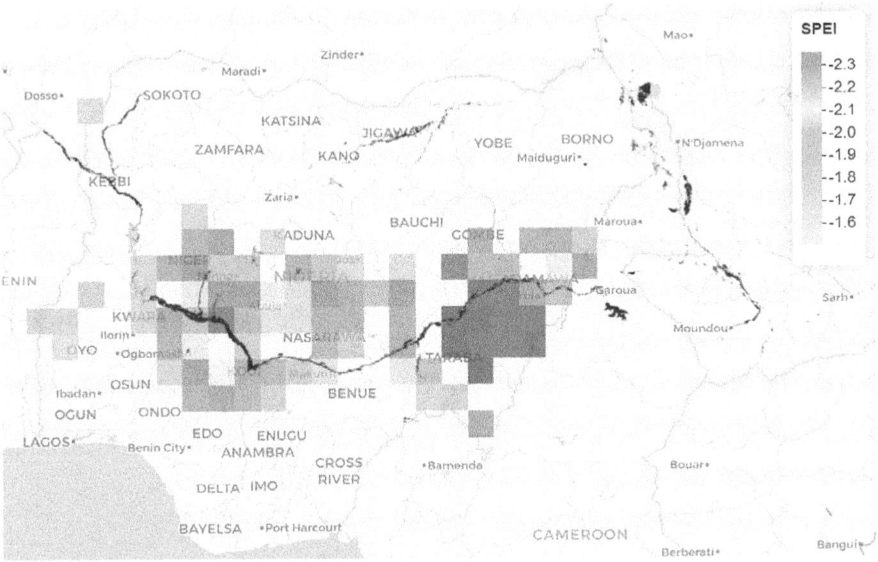

Figure 5.8 The worst experienced drought (SPEI < - 1.5) in the period 2010–20 and flooded areas in the period 2010–18

Source: analysis of Version 4 Climate Research Unit gridded Time Series (CRU-TS) 2010–20 and Global Flood Database 2010–18 data, first presented in Diwakar and Brzezinska (2023).

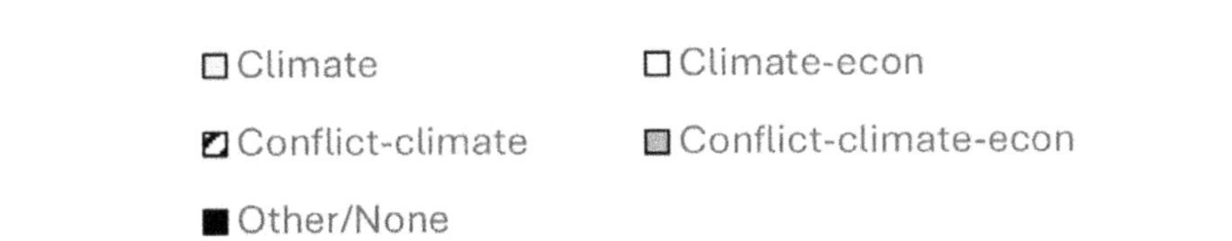

Figure 5.9 Climate-related disasters and polycrisis in Nigeria, 2010–19, disaggregated by poverty status

Note: I/TE = impoverished or transitory escapers; SE = sustained escapers.

Source: author's analysis of GHS panel merged with ACLED (2010–19), CRU-TS (2010–20) and Global Flood Database (2010–18) data.

Violent conflict drives chronic poverty and impoverishment

Violent conflict, especially pronounced in the northeast, has had devastating effects on people's livelihoods and wellbeing. Borno, which has been an epicentre for Boko Haram-related violence, experienced the brunt of conflict fatalities especially during the 2010s (analysis of ACLED data). Regression results point to a strong association between the long-term effects of Boko Haram-related fatalities between 2010 and 2014 (i.e. prior to the peak of violence) and chronic poverty, as well as violence being associated with a lower probability of resilience. northern states, with higher salience of conflict, are also those with higher rates of relative chronic poverty and transience (Figure 5.10). The relationship between violence and negative poverty trajectories was observed when relying on the presence of violence within a 20-kilometre radius of a household, as well as when identified as self-reported exposure to violence,[2] which was also dominant in the northeast.

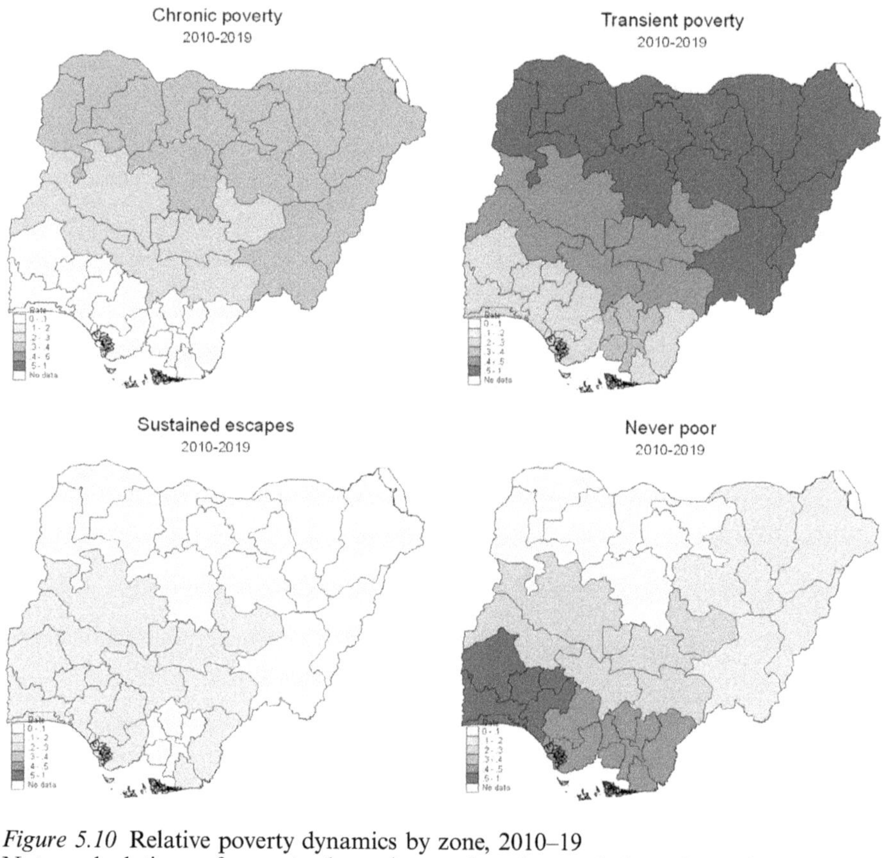

Figure 5.10 Relative poverty dynamics by zone, 2010–19
Note: calculations of poverty dynamics are based on a balanced panel across four waves of The Nigeria GHS Panel, covering years 2010/11, 2012/13, 2015/16 and 2018/19, first presented in Diwakar and Brzezinska (2023).

Similarly, focus groups and KIIs in Borno in 2023 spoke of security forces destroying markets, telecoms being cut off for six months, a power blackout for two years and the closure of the Maidiguri International Airport. Fish production—a key livelihood amongst people in poverty living along the Lake Chad basin—was also banned in 2014 for three years on grounds of security concerns, as militants were believed to go under the guise of fishermen to fund arms purchases and launch attacks having controlled areas along the lake (Garba and Dauda, 2017; FAO and Eni, 2021).

The insecurity households experienced on farmland is not unique to the qualitative data. Indeed, in the nationally-representative regression analysis, ownership of cultivable land is associated with a higher probability of chronic poverty (relative to not owning land) over the 2010–19 period, which could reflect the profiles of people in poverty often living in rural areas where agriculture is a mainstay, as noted in Chapter 3. Moreover, effect sizes are larger for self-reported victimised households (Diwakar and Brzezinska, 2023). This is again likely on account of half of self-reported victimisation acts taking place in the household or on the farm.

Climate-related disasters further intersect with violence to prolong poverty

On top of the challenges stemming from violence, climate-related disasters have exacerbated the vulnerability of already impoverished communities. Increased duration of drought especially along Nigeria's middle belt is leading to crop failures and diminished agricultural harvests, which directly affects people's incomes (Omokaro, 2025). Frequent floods also severely affect livelihoods, causing crop losses, infrastructure damage, and temporary displacement (OCHA, 2024). Many commercial farmers who invested their entire capital in their farms were previously categorised as WB5 (see Annex B) and WB4, but dropped to WB2 by 2023: "The flood of 2022 affected so many farmers. It caused so many farmers to lose their farming capital and has made some not farm this year. It has made some farmers start all over" (male FGD in rural northern Nigeria, 2023).

The flood also damaged non-farmlands, such as markets, shops, houses, and roads, causing businesses to halt for weeks and months. Box 5.1 highlights acute poverty at this convergence of conflict and climate-related disasters, even where conflict dynamics may have waned over time.

Box 5.1 Acute poverty at the climate–conflict nexus in Nigeria

In Borno, Nigeria, there are signs of poverty becoming increasingly acute for many households, marking downward mobility towards destitution. In a 2023 survey of two LGAs in the state, over one in ten households reported being affected by income disruptions that they attributed either to conflict or climate-related disasters in the year leading up to the survey. This is a relatively low share that may be attributed to subsiding conflict in the region, and households likely attributing income or asset loss to effects of conflict, rather than conflict fatalities themselves. Indeed, crime or landmines were most prevalent as a reason households attributed conflict contributing to income loss, whereas drought or irregular rainfall and limited employment opportunities were more prevalent amidst climate-related disasters.

Nevertheless, the scale of income loss has been severe. Of households who experienced either of these crises, 41% saw more than half of their income lost as a result. Moreover, besides income, asset destruction and disruption to agriculture was also a common consequence of these crises. Nearly half of surveyed households (43%) reported either income or agricultural disruptions or asset loss due to conflict, floods or drought. There are also demographic variations to this, where for example older heads of households aged 65 years or above more commonly experienced asset loss where they had reported conflict and polycrisis, relative to other heads of households.

Source: Diwakar et al. (2024)

In other cases, climate-related disasters and conflict are deeply intertwined, driving the acuteness of chronic poverty. For example, drought in the far north has led to the migration of herders to Benue State in search of water and grazing for their cows. However, this has devastated farmlands and crops owned by farmers in Benue. These farmer–herder conflicts resulted in the highest number of fatalities in West and Central Africa during the 2010s (Brottem, 2021).

In the regression analysis, amidst drought, a higher number of farmer–herder conflict fatalities is associated with a higher probability of poverty transience and lower probability of resilience. In the survey data, almost half (48%) of households between 2010 and 2018 that lived in areas of extreme or severe drought were living in close proximity to farmer–herder conflicts (Diwakar and Brzezinska, 2023). This is intuitive where drought may create pressures on agricultural and pastoralist livelihoods and related access to land. Indeed, other research also points to spikes in herder-farmer conflict fatalities during lean seasons (World Bank, 2022b).

Relatedly, ownership of cultivable land was associated with a higher probability of chronic poverty and a lower probability of resilience (relative to non-ownership) in areas with herder–farmer conflicts (Figure 5.11). The qualitative data have also highlighted pathways of impact, where climate-driven conflicts between the herders and farmers have resulted in acute chronic poverty through the displacement of host communities and loss of lives and livelihoods. For example, according to one interviewee spoken to in 2023, since 2017 she had not put much effort into farming as the Fulanis (nomadic herders) would not allow the community to go into their farms to harvest when crops were ripe. Now it was only on a piece of land surrounding the house that they could cultivate sweet potatoes, corn and groundnut for immediate consumption. Previously, she had farmed yam and rice in large scale (INT66-NG, female, chronic poor, rural northern Nigeria, 2023 LHI).

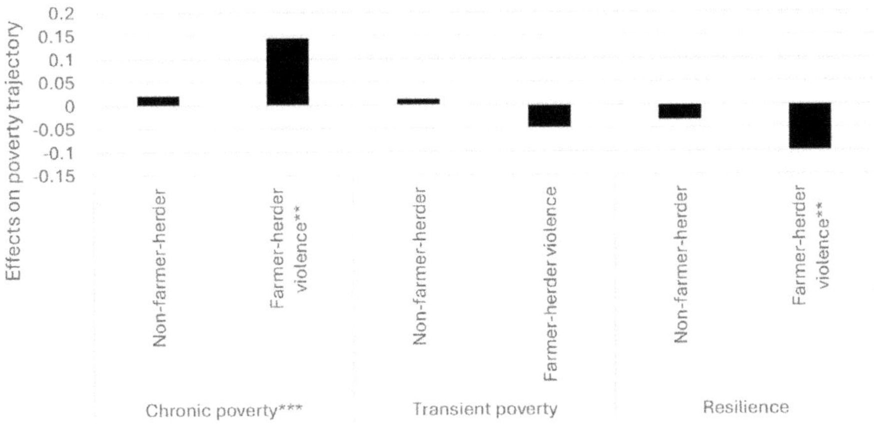

Figure 5.11 Average marginal effects of cultivable land ownership on poverty trajectory, by farmer–herder conflicts

Note: *** p<0.01, ** p<0.05, * p<0.1.

Source: analysis of Nigeria General Household Survey (GHS) 2010/11–2018/19 data merged with ACLED (2010–19) data, first presented in Diwakar and Brzezinska (2023).

Finally, when examining intersecting crises amongst the subset of households living in areas affected by climate-related disasters, the role of agricultural livelihoods in cushioning against risk and uncertainty is mixed. On the one hand, cultivable land is associated with a lower probability of poverty transience at the conflict-climate nexus so long as economic crises are not present (Figure 5.12). At the same time, diversification within agriculture seems to have limited potential to cushion households. Indeed, livestock is instead associated with a higher probability of chronic poverty (Figure 5.12). Amongst the full sample, moreover, results are not statistically significant (Annex Table D5).

The role of diversification into non-farm sources however may be more consistently positive provided the absence of violence. Non-farm enterprise ownership is associated with a lower probability of chronic poverty provided that violence is not present, even where economic crises is present (Figure 5.12). Amidst the conflict-climate nexus though in the absence of economic crises, non-farm enterprise ownership is associated with a lower probability of resilience. Again, among the full sample, results are not statistically significant (Annex Table D5). These results suggest that the presence of violence as one of multiple intersecting crises acts to constrain the potential of economic diversification as a means of supporting household resilience.

5.2.3 Maladaptive economic policies drive sustained impoverishment

The climate–conflict nexus noted above was associated with chronic and acute poverty. The intersection with economic crises has additionally driven non-poor

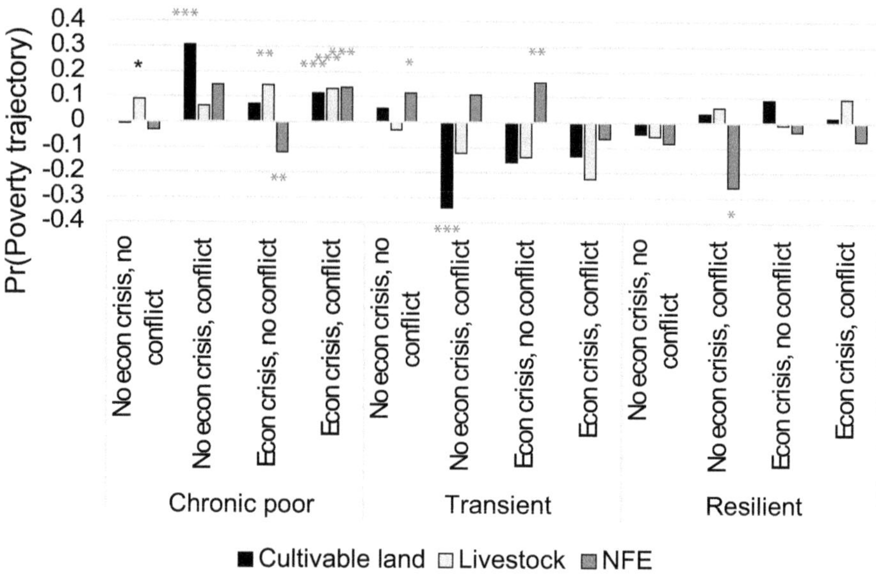

Figure 5.12 Relationship between livelihood strategies and poverty trajectories, by economic crises and conflict, in areas affected by climate-related disasters

Note: average marginal effects are presented. The figure refers to three models, examining the intersection of 1) cultivable land, 2) livestock, and 3) NFE ownership with economic crises and conflict, for the subset of households experiencing floods or drought. Asterisks refer to results that are statistically significant at conventional levels (*** $p<0.01$, ** $p<0.05$, * $p<0.1$). All controls are the same as in the main equation presented in Section 1.2.1 of Chapter 1.

Source: analysis of Nigeria General Household Survey (GHS) (2010/11–2018/19) data referenced in Table 1.1 merged with ACLED (2010–19) data and CRU-TS (2010–22) and Global Flood Observatory (2010–18) data.

households into sustained impoverishment. A sequence in recent years of the economic crises dimensions of the COVID-19 pandemic, followed by a cost-of-living crisis then amplified by the cashless policy, fuel subsidy removal and exchange rate reform has driven many households into unsustainable debt levels (Diwakar et al., 2025). This is driven by food price inflation alongside increased transport costs and limited access to cash (Ejechi, 2024). Households in these contexts are increasingly seeing their poverty becoming long-term, given that were already suffering from crime, banditry, violence, displacement limiting social cohesion and spurring asset loss, or climate-related disasters further wiping out agricultural production.

Economic crises noted above have arisen in part from economic policies that have been largely maladaptive, discussed in this section as well as Section 5.2.4 in relation to IDPs. Household impoverishment amidst continued post-pandemic inflationary effects of these maladaptive policies have been sustained over time, turning a temporary descent into chronic poverty. This sustained impoverishment amidst maladaptive economic policies is distinct from the churning that these policies may otherwise generate amidst climate-related disasters and economic crises alone. This is because the structural foundations of poverty in humanitarian contexts noted in Section 5.2.1 interact with these maladaptive policies to obstruct coping responses and reinforce vulnerability.

COVID-19 and border closures

For example, COVID-19 was itself a layered crisis of multiple dimensions—health and economic being most salient. For households in humanitarian contexts, this layered onto already often conflict or climate-related crises. The policy response to the pandemic affected the livelihoods especially of informal workers in and near poverty, disrupting trade and daily wage activities, leading to food insecurity and reduced income. Though agriculture in rural areas was relatively cushioned compared to urban livelihoods, the centrality of farming within the livelihood portfolio of both rural and urban households meant that a key source of stability was eroded:

> During the Covid pandemic it was a difficult period because we were afraid, we could not attend to our farms or purchase food stuffs because of the restriction of movement, fortunately we had access to water because the tap was in front of our house. Before the pandemic the community apportioned me a small piece of land where I grew beans and groundnut, but because the farms are located a few kilometres from the village due to the lockdown we could not access our farms. Some people even endured loses as the farms were taken over by weeds.
>
> (INT86-NG, female, chronic poor, rural northern Nigeria, 2023 LHI)

Border closures were implemented to curb transmission rates during the pandemic, putting extreme strain on livelihoods internationally, but such closures have been a common occurrence in Nigeria more generally. The government regularly closes borders in Nigeria due to different reasons often with unintended consequences on markets and the livelihoods dependent on these. For example, in 2019 the government closed borders as a means to curb smuggling of rice and illicit fuel exports to neighbouring countries—thus an attempt to address some of the structural challenges noted above. It then closed borders during the 2020 COVID-19 lockdowns as part of the policy toolkit to respond to the pandemic, and more recently as a result of the sanctions imposed more on neighbouring Niger (Kassa and Zeufack, 2020; Salmanu, 2024).

Yet these border markets are often thriving economic centres. These closures wreak havoc on trade, leading to scarcity and high demand for essential goods and commodities like rice and livestock (Kassa and Zeufack, 2020; Isah, 2020). This in turn creates higher prices for these goods, disproportionately affecting those with limited financial resources and potentially pushing them further into poverty, especially those who rely on cross-border trade with neighbouring countries.

Cashless policy, fuel subsidy removal and exchange rate reforms

The cashless policy which became effective in early 2023 in turn was regularly cited across interviews as a reason for households continuing to experience or sustain their impoverishment post-pandemic. The policy, which includes measures such as redesigning the Naira notes and restricting cash withdrawals to reduce the use of cash in transactions and promote digital payments, was introduced as measure to curb corruption and promote financial inclusion (Banwo and Ighodalo, 2023). However, it often meant that people had to pay high fees to access their money. Interviewees regularly spoke of the resulting cash shortage which made it difficult to buy food and other essentials. Some goods were sold at higher prices when purchased electronically. It also led to smuggling, barter trade, and charges being procured from POS agents.

In Akwa Ibom, for example, a discussion with long-term residents noted that people lost almost half of their money they needed to withdraw each time, due to the scarcity of the naira. Together, these results contributed to the depression of local markets, MSMEs shutting down, and widespread hunger. In all of this, households without bank accounts were hugely affected, characterising people in and near poverty especially in rural areas and working in the informal sector. The psychological toll of these economic difficulties also contributed to distress and suicide.

The cashless policy posed a new challenge to the entire country. There was no money in circulation, thus going about daily routines was difficult. One interviewee stated that the recent spike in fuel prices has caused his enterprises to be set back. He stated that when there was no power source, he used to buy fuel to use generators, but with the recent increase in the price of fuel, "we only wait and relay on grid power supplies to function". He added that previously for 3,000 Naira, he could buy enough fuel to last the entire day, while recently 6,000 Naira of fuel was no longer sufficient to operate our services (INT90-NG, male, impoverished, rural northern Nigeria, 2023 LHI).

Alongside this, the fuel subsidy removal and removing the currency peg to the US dollar both led to an increase in cost of living and the naira's value to plummet. The former, for example, is illustrated by the testimonial from a driver who, despite years of experience, struggled to make a meagre income due to soaring fuel prices following the subsidy removal: "I have been a driver for seven years, but this year, I bought fuel at N12,000, and after I had made everything, I made N14,800. So, everything is difficult right now; it affects the transportation business mostly" (respondent from male FGD, urban southern Nigeria, 2023). Poor implementation of the fuel subsidy removal has distorted the actual market value of fuel (Abdulrasaq et al., 2025).

The hike in prices of commodities and of transportation linked to this subsidy removal made basic necessities more expensive. For example, farmers found it difficult to afford the cost of transporting their produce to markets and buying necessary inputs like fertilisers and herbicides. Those travelling to nearby towns also saw their real income reduce as a result: "People cannot afford transport fare. Travelling to other towns and even within the metropolis has become challenging" (Respondent in long-term residents' female group interview, 2023). For low-income individuals, like the driver in the testimonial, these fluctuations erode their earnings and disposable income, making it increasingly challenging to afford essential goods and services.

Sustained impoverishment and chronic poverty amidst closely sequenced crises

This closely sequenced polycrisis has driven households to fall into poverty or remain entrenched in it as their ability to cope with new shocks has been steadily worn down. As a result, they turn increasingly to adverse or erosive coping, for example by selling assets, or their family and children going hungry. Indeed, households that pre-pandemic were in the bottom two welfare quintiles were more likely to engage in distress asset sales and experience hunger in response to negative shocks during the pandemic in 2020 relative to richer households (Diwakar and Adedeji, 2021). By 2022, these households were also likely to pay more petrol in 2022 during the economic crises, and report drought/delayed rains expected to negatively affect them into the summer of 2022, signalling lower expectations for managing future climate-related crises.

These intersections were also observed in richer southern parts of the country. Figure 5.13 illustrates one respondent's account of the sequence of crises affecting their livelihoods and wellbeing since 2013. They described a series of escalating and overlapping crises, including: salary loss, COVID-19 lockdowns (which triggered income loss and hunger), farm flooding leading to harvest failure, the cashless policy which considerably strained their ability to effectively carry out their livelihood and reduced effective demand for their services, and finally, the fuel price hike that hit their husband's small commercial business.

The intersections moreover have also driven poorer households to more commonly borrow money from friends or relatives during the pandemic, mainly to purchase food (analysis of NLPS 2020–22, first presented in Diwakar and Brzezinska, 2023). All of this—hunger, the distressed sale of

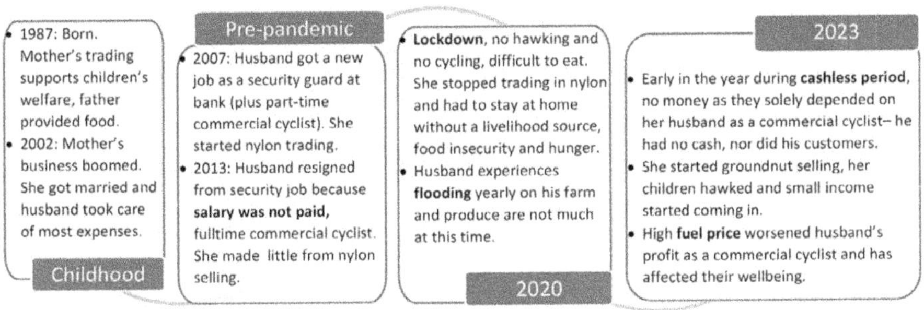

Figure 5.13 COVID-19, flooding and economic crises
Source: INT101-NG, female, chronic poor, urban southern Nigeria, 2023 LHI.

assets, worry about climate-related disasters, and price concerns linked to economic crises—collectively points to impacts of polycrisis on the longer-term persistence of poverty, for those already in poverty and those who newly fell into poverty during the pandemic and have been unable to escape it.

Intersecting shocks and stressors with polycrisis

Some of these direct impacts and eroded coping responses may be consequences of conflict itself. For example, a common consequence of conflict is displacement, where IDPs and forcibly displaced populations are a particularly vulnerable group likely to have high rates of poverty and multi-dimensional deprivations (Corral et al., 2020). In Nigeria, almost a quarter of households reporting direct victimisation[3] were displaced, with the prevalence higher amongst households that experienced only transitory escapes from poverty (Diwakar and Brzezinska, 2023).

INT86-NG (female, sustained impoverishment, rural northern Nigeria, 2023 LHI) experienced conflict, climate-related disasters, maladaptive economic policies and health shocks—thus macro level crises intersecting with micro-level shocks (Figure 5.14). While conflict initially impoverished, it was the intersection of crises and shocks that sustained her impoverishment over time, turning it into chronic poverty. In INT86-NG's case, her new female headship due to the death of her husband as the otherwise primary breadwinner led to a substantial loss in income and assets, including her land and home. More broadly, in the qualitative data, women within households were frequently affected by illness or its impacts, linked in part to heightened care responsibilities.

In addition to the example from INT86-NG, there are various life histories that illustrate the kinds of personal shocks and stressors (like illness or injury)

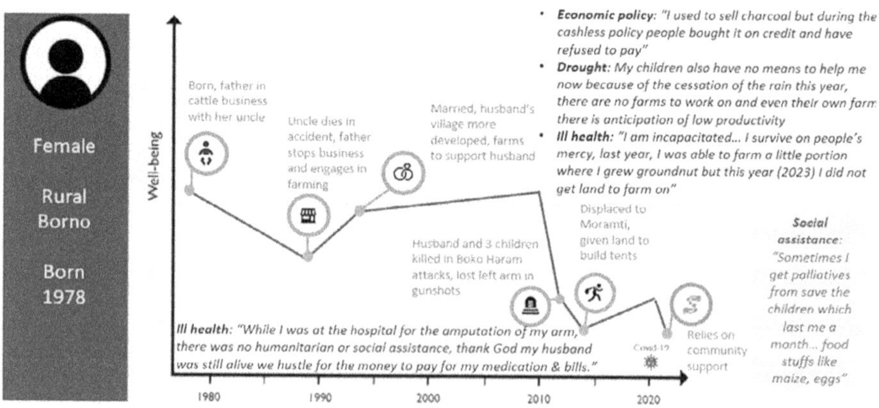

Figure 5.14 Shocks and stressors emerging from and operating alongside polycrisis
Source: INT86-NG LHI, first presented in Diwakar et al. (2025).

that emerge from or operate alongside broader polycrisis. Box 5.2 illustrates another example of this. Experiences of ill health show how personal shocks—like injury or illness—lead to loss of income from the injured breadwinner, loss of income from the caregiver, medical costs which take money away from investing responsibilities, livelihoods, and deeper poverty traps—leaving people more vulnerable to macro crises like climate shocks.

Box 5.2 Job loss, floods, death, illness convergence in Nigeria

Mr. B's life is characterised by a series of polycrisis that have affected his wellbeing and livelihood. At a young age, he lost his mother. In search of better opportunities, he migrated from his village to Cameroon, and then to Delta State, Nigeria. Initially, he found some stability working as a domestic staff and rubber tapper, but his progress was hindered by **unpaid wages**. Despite the increase in his income, he only managed to eat once or twice a day, and he did not acquire assets (except radio and mat) because he was saving money for his father's burial. He visited the village in 2009 to bury his father three years after his demise. He also sold his father's only piece of land to cater for the burial; he even borrowed and finished the burial in indebtedness.

In **2012 floods** affected the rubber plantations and forced him to abandon his job and return to his village, resulting in a drop in his wellbeing. As he attempted to recover from the flood, **illness struck**, further complicating his efforts to regain stability. He returned to Delta in 2019 to continue rubber tapping, but there was another **flood in 2022**. He lost his job and returned to the village with his wife and three kids. Because he had no skills to practice in the village, he took to menial jobs clearing and weeding farms for people until he started getting ill and had to manage his health condition to still work. Things became difficult and it was hard to feed and to send children to school.

The **loss of two brothers** in quick succession added to his burdens, as he took on the responsibility of caring for their children, further straining his already limited resources. Things are currently hard, some days they don't have anything to eat, sometimes they drink garri or buy foodstuffs on credit. He now does menial jobs whenever people call him to work in their farms but that is not consistent. The period of **COVID-19** brought difficulties to him. He was in Delta at the time. Currently, Mr. B struggles to provide for his family, often facing days without food and relying on menial jobs that are insufficient to meet their needs. He lives in a rented one-room apartment with his wife and six children, he has no assets to fall back on, leaving him at the lowest level of wellbeing.

Mr. B's story illustrates the compounding nature of crises, where each setback—extreme weather events, health issues or death of family members and the consequent familial responsibilities—intersects to create a cycle of poverty and deprivation that he finds difficult to escape.

Source: INT19-NG, male, chronic poor, rural southern Nigeria, 2023 LHI, first presented in Diwakar et al. (2025)

5.2.4 Variations by demographic: spotlight on IDPs and women

Similar to Afghanistan, IDPs in Nigeria often experienced heightened disadvantages driven by polycrisis. The qualitative data pointed to various instances of multiple displacements due to climate-related disasters, violence and infrastructure projects accompanied by forced evictions. Conflict- and climate-induced displacement has been particularly common in different parts of the country, and these crises combine regularly to drive displacement (IDMC, 2025). For example, INT19-NG (male, chronic poor, rural southern Nigeria, 2023 LHI) noted that "immediately after settling the debt in 2012 there was flooding which affected the whole community" and which forced him to stop work and return to the village, leaving everything he had, with the hope that he would return after the flood. However, the intensity of violence such as from the Boko Haram insurgency or farmer–herder conflicts in northern states often drove more prolonged displacement, with some ending up in IDP camps with limited access to services such as healthcare, education and housing, or livelihood opportunities (Diwakar et al., 2025; Okon, 2018). This highlights critical gaps in humanitarian response.

Another dimension to this relates to maladaptive recovery policies that have amplified vulnerability amongst IDPs. A key example is the Borno State government's controversial decision to shut down formal and informal IDP camps in the state. On the one hand, the initiative aimed to restore livelihoods including access to farmlands and improve living conditions of IDPs and stemmed from a desire to move away from humanitarian aid (Musa, 2025; People's Gazette, 2024). However, the closure of camps was not accompanied by adequate alternatives and so led to worsening hunger, begging, and limited access to housing (HRW, 2022).

Moreover, for those who had returned to homes or resettled whether due to the closure of camps but also more broadly, they continue to experience distress:

> Fulani herdsmen have not been allowing us to settle … it's not been long that we came back … When those Fulani herdsmen came and killed people, the livestock guards [a security force created by the former governor] came and carried all the cows and promised us that they are going to come back with palliatives but they went and never came back … [The Fulani] even burn our houses … Even the foods that are remaining that were not burnt there are other criminals that will invade the house and pack everything. Pack the goat, pack the cows and leave the empty house.
>
> (Female FGD in urban northern Nigeria, 2023)

The example illustrates continued insecurity that pervades narratives of returnees, that prevents recovery from crises. The conflict that continues may aggravate mental health impacts and trauma for people who already suffered through displacement but continue to experience direct violence upon their return.

Again, intersecting inequalities permeate these examples. For example, limited early warning systems, rocky terrains and physical barriers in the Plateau region made it challenging for persons with disabilities to flee homes when attacked due to violent conflict in Nigeria. A lack of alternatives for persons with disabilities experiencing extreme poverty amplify these challenges. IDPs with disabilities also experienced obstacles in accessing healthcare, work, food, clean water and toilet facilities once they had found a safer place to live. This was attributed to distance from services, discrimination and self-exclusion due to fear of violence (IDMC, 2020). Intersecting inequalities due to disability status and gender would in this case amplify exclusion and vulnerability. Women with disabilities in Nigeria also regularly experience challenges in meeting basic needs during economic crises and being subjected to gender-based violence (UN Women, 2022).

The intersection of crises also especially disadvantages women. For example, though women are increasingly entering paid work outside of the household, this is in part driven by increased unemployment of men and high cost of living (Eze, 2023). This has placed the burden of meeting essential household needs increasingly on women, who are finding it especially difficult to navigate these changing contexts marked by rising fuel prices and costs of goods.

> Fuel subsidies cause prices and cost of living to go high because you buy items at a high cost. When the traders add the cost of transportation to the cost of purchasing the item, the price will increase, and we don't have enough money to buy things, so life becomes hard for the women.
>
> (Long term residents' group interview, rural southern Nigeria, 2023)

Part of the challenge is that women often have fewer economic networks so are not privy to information that could enable their adaptability, such as was evident when the cashless policy came into effect. In this context, many women are looking to village savings groups to support their basic needs, though amidst crises contexts these can be risky as it can be prone to failure. "Women face a double whammy—they are often more affected by crises because of social norms that disadvantages them disproportionately, and these norms amplify the impact of these crises and deprivations" (Diwakar et al., 2025).

5.3 Conclusion

This chapter overviewed the structural challenges and systemic vulnerabilities that predate crises and into which polycrisis evolve. This framing helps emphasise crises as embedded in longer-term processual challenges of structural inequality and with mutually reinforcing dimensions, rather than episodic events.

In Afghanistan, this includes longstanding institutional fragility and fragmentation of power reinforced by repeated aid interventions, persistent insecurity and violence, a crisis of human rights, and the political exclusion of certain groups—these are structural vulnerabilities that predate the shift in power in August 2021. This has converged to drive welfare loss and acute poverty amidst violent conflict, climate-related disasters and economic collapse. The more acute, ideologically enforced repression and institutional collapse that followed the Taliban's return to power not only deepened polycrisis but fundamentally shifted this in character after the takeover, especially in relation to women's rights, service delivery, and governance structures.

In Nigeria, corruption, governance challenges, heavy dependence on oil and infrastructure deficits are some of the structural constraints against which crises develop. Institutions are not as unstable as in Afghanistan, though governance challenges nevertheless permeate. The confluence of triple crises has instead driven chronic poverty. Maladaptive economic policies, in particular, have contributed to new and sustained impoverishment over the last five years marked by COVID-19 and a range of successive economic policies. These policies have been implemented by the government to stabilise economic growth and increase its revenue which has experienced hits as a result of the intersections of crises. However, such policies have not been accompanied by adequate consideration of equity or mitigation measures to alleviate its effects on vulnerable populations.

In both contexts, the chapter considers how these dynamics have heterogeneous impacts that are particularly pronounced for certain groups such as IDPs, young adults and women. It also examines importantly the ways in which these crises can contribute to intersecting shocks and stressors and micro- and meso-levels to amplify the effects of macro-level crises and overwhelm coping systems, thus reinforcing negative feedback loops.

Across the two contexts, there is some normalisation of the climate-conflict nexus given its protracted histories, but economic crises layered on top of this nexus and with its maladaptive economic governance dimensions is reinforcing a structural dimension to these crises. This in turn erodes people's ability to cope with the crises let alone recover in the aftermath of its more intense periods and moves us towards consideration of poverty itself as an emergency in such contexts. The next chapter considers coping mechanisms and learns from outliers that have managed to escape poverty amidst polycrisis.

Notes

1 This chapter builds on and deepens work that the author carried out in collaboration with AREU in Afghanistan between 2020 and 2022 (Diwakar, 2022; Nemat et al., 2022) and with dRPC and CSEA in Nigeria between 2022 and 2025 (Diwakar et al., 2024; Diwakar et al., 2025).

2 For example, where a family member was killed, suffered physical aggression or sexual violence, was injured or disabled from a direct attack, forced to work for free, internally displaced, or captured/kidnapped/abducted or robbed between 2010 and 2015.

3 Self-reported in the Nigeria General Household Survey as a situation between 2010 and 2015 where a family member was killed, suffered physical aggression, or was injured or disabled from a direct attack, suffered sexual violence, was forced to work for free, was internally displaced, or was captured/kidnapped/abducted/robbed.

References

Abdulrasaq, K., Walker, J.-A., Ukpai, S. and Diwakar, V. (2025) 'Political perspectives of social assistance amidst economic shocks in Nigeria'. *BASIC Research Briefing 7.* Institute of Development Studies. doi:10.19088/IDS.2025.043.

Addeh, E. (2024) 'Energy prices continue rise, fuel transportation costs nationwide'. *This Day.* https://www.thisdaylive.com/2024/06/25/energy-prices-continue-rise-fuel-transportation-costs-nationwide/.

Adegbami, A. and Uche, C. (2015) 'Ethnicity and ethnic politics: An impediment to political development in Nigeria'. *Public Administration Research*, 4(1). https://pdfs.semanticscholar.org/c8ba/840ea30af0e99cdd31a0e669ce0ef7a5c9aa.pdf.

Adelaja, A. and George, J. (2019) 'Effects of conflict on agriculture: Evidence from the Boko Haram insurgency'. *World Development*, 117: 184–195. doi:10.1016/j.worlddev.2019.01.010.

Akbari, F. and Moradi, K. (2024) 'Hazara women: How gender and ethnicity intersect in the Taliban's repression'. *Just Security*, 7 March. https://www.justsecurity.org/93123/hazara-women-how-gender-and-ethnicity-intersect-in-the-talibans-repression/.

Albrecht, C., Rude, B. and Stitteneder, T. (2022) 'Women in Afghanistan: Developments over the last 20 years and the return of the Taliban'. *Ifo Institute.* https://www.ifo.de/DocDL/CESifo-Forum-2022-1-albrecht-et-al-afghan-women-january.pdf.

Allouche, J., Sida, L., Nelis, T. and Shahab, S. (2022) 'Needs and vulnerability in Afghanistan'. *Institute of Development Studies.* https://www.ukhih.org/documents/7/needs_and_vulnerability_in_afghanistan.pdf.

Aradi, G. (2024) 'Betta Edu probe: Nigeria recovers $24m in poverty minister investigation – EFCC'. *BBC*, 9 April. https://www.bbc.co.uk/news/world-africa-68759033.

Banwo and Ighodalo (2023) 'Naira redesign and cashless policy: Wither the role of Bank Neutral Cash Hubs?'https://www.lexology.com/library/detail.aspx?g=6f01a72a-5c2d-4071-92c2-263adce4f91e.

Barr, H. (2024) 'The Taliban and the global backlash against women's rights'. *Human Rights Watch.* https://www.hrw.org/news/2024/02/06/taliban-and-global-backlash-against-womens-rights.

BBC (2023) 'Nigeria hit by widespread blackout in "total system collapse"'. *BBC*, 14 September. https://www.bbc.co.uk/news/world-africa-66810202.

Brock, K., McGee, R. and Gaventa, J. (2004) *Unpacking policy: Knowledge actors and spaces in poverty reduction in Uganda and Nigeria.* Fountain Publishers.

Brottem, L. (2021) 'The growing complexity of farmer-herder conflict in West and Central Africa'. *Africa Security Brief No. 39.* Africa Center for Strategic Studies. https://africacenter.org/publication/growing-complexity-farmer-herder-conflict-west-central-africa/.

Byrd, W. (2022) 'How to mitigate Afghanistan's economic and humanitarian crises'. United States Institute of Peace. https://www.usip.org/publications/2022/01/how-mitigate-afghanistans-economic-and-humanitarian-crises.

Campbell, J. (2020) 'Boko Haram cuts electricity to Maiduguri in Northern Nigeria'. Council on Foreign Relations. https://www.cfr.org/blog/boko-haram-cuts-electricity-maiduguri-northern-nigeria#:~:text=On%20January%2020%2C%20the%20electric,Maiduguri%20from%20the%20national%20grid.

Chiovenda, M. (2014) 'The illumination of marginality: How ethnic Hazaras in Bamyan, Afghanistan, perceive the lack of electricity as discrimination'. *Central Asian Survey*, 33(4): 449–462. doi:10.1080/02634937.2014.987967.

Corral, P., Irwin, A., Krishnan, N., Mahler, D. and Vishwanath, T. (2020) *Fragility and conflict: On the front lines of the fight against poverty.* World Bank. http://hdl.handle.net/10986/33324.

Demarest, L. (2021) 'Elite clientelism in Nigeria: The role of parties in weakening legislator-voter ties'. *Party Politics*, 28(5): 939–953. doi:10.1177/13540688211030219.

Diwakar, V. (2022) 'Welfare of young adults amidst Covid-19, conflict, and disasters: Evidence from Afghanistan'. *CPAN Working Paper.* CPAN. https://www.chronicpovertynetwork.org/resources/2022/5/3/welfare-of-young-adults-amid-covid-19-conflict-and-disasters-evidence-from-afghanistan.

Diwakar, V. and Adedeji, A. (2021) 'Poverty dynamics and social protection in Nigeria'. *CPAN Working Paper.* CPAN.

Diwakar, V. and Brzezinska, I. (2023) 'Poverty dynamics amidst multiple crises in Nigeria'. *DEEP Working Paper 17.* DEEP/Oxford Policy Management.

Diwakar, V., Adedeji, A., Nwosu, E., Obaniyi, F. and Udora, C. (2024) 'Social assistance and coping with crises in Borno, Nigeria'. *BASIC Research Working Paper 31.* Institute of Development Studies. doi:10.19088/BASIC.2024.019.

Diwakar, V., Ghafoori, I. and Nemat, O. (2022) 'Vulnerability in Afghanistan before and during the shift in power'. *CPAN Working Paper.* CPAN.

Diwakar, V., Walker, J.-A., Turnwait, M., Eichsteller, M. and Adeniran, A.P. (2025) 'Poverty dynamics and social assistance amidst intersecting crises in Nigeria'. *BASIC Research Working Paper 35.* Institute of Development Studies. doi:10.19088/BASIC.2025.004.

Ejechi, V. (2024) 'FULL LIST: Kogi, Ekiti, Kwara … states with highest food price inflation'. *The Cable*, 16 June. https://www.thecable.ng/full-list-kogi-ekiti-kwara-states-with-highest-food-price-inflation/.

Eze, P. (2023) '"My friends were amazed": Nigerian women break "male" jobs barrier amid cost-of-living crisis'. *The Guardian*, 2 December. https://www.theguardian.com/global-development/2023/dec/02/my-friends-were-amazed-nigerian-women-break-male-jobs-barrier-amid-cost-of-living-crisis.

FAO and Eni (2021) 'Nigerian water stories'. https://www.eni.com/content/dam/enicom/documents/eng/sustainability/libro-water-stories.pdf.

FAO (2020) 'Adapting targeted support to Kuchi pastoralists in Afghanistan for COVID-19'. https://www.fao.org/3/cb1546en/cb1546en.pdf.

Garba, S. and Dauda, H. (2017) 'With Boko Haram threat receding, Nigeria allows fishing to resume in Lake Chad'. *VOA News.*

Gbahabo, P. and Oduro-Afriyie, E. (2017) 'On the dynamics of the oil resource curse in Nigeria: Theory and implications'. *SSRN.* doi:10.2139/ssrn.2968893.

Hasrat, M.H. (2019) 'Over a century of persecution: Massive human rights violation against Hazaras in Afghanistan'. *OHCR.* https://www.ohchr.org/sites/default/files/Documents/Issues/Racism/SR/Call/mhhasrat.pdf.

HRC (2024) 'A/HRC/55/80: Situation of human rights in Afghanistan – Report of the Special Rapporteur on the situation of human rights in Afghanistan'. https://www.ohchr.org/en/documents/country-reports/ahrc5580-situation-human-rights-afghanistan-report-special-rapporteur.

HRW (2022) 'Afghanistan: Economic roots of the humanitarian crisis'. https://www.hrw.org/news/2022/03/01/afghanistan-economic-roots-humanitarian-crisis.

Humanitarian Coalition (n.d.) 'What is a humanitarian emergency?'https://www.humanitariancoalition.ca/what-is-a-humanitarian-emergency.

Huot, D. and Pain, A. (2017) 'Afghanistan livelihood trajectories: Life on the margins in Sar-i-Pul Province'. *SLRC Working Paper 54*. Secure Livelihoods Research Consortium. https://securelivelihoods.org/wp-content/uploads/14.-Afghanistan-livelihood-trajectories_life-on-the-margins-in-Sar-i-Pul-province.pdf.

IDMC (2020) 'Impacts of displacement: Displaced by violence, Jos, Nigeria'. https://www.internal-displacement.org/publications/impacts-of-displacement-displaced-by-violence-jos-nigeria.

IDMC (2025) 'Nigeria - Floods and conflict combine to trigger displacement in Borno state'. https://www.internal-displacement.org/spotlight/nigeria-floods-and-conflict-combine-to-trigger-displacement-in-borno-state/.

Isah, A. (2020) 'Closed for business: Lessons from Nigeria's border closure'. *Republic*, 4 (2). https://republic.com.ng/february-march-2020/closed-for-business-border-closure.

Kassa, W. and Zeufack, A. (2020) 'Nigeria's border closure: A road block or a speed bump on the road to a successful AfCFTA?' *Africa Can End Poverty*. World Bank. https://blogs.worldbank.org/en/africacan/nigerias-border-closure-road-block-or-speed-bump-road-successful-afcfta.

Musa, M.M. (2025) 'Zulum to resettle over 20,000 IDPs to Borno's liberated communities'. *The Guardian*, 15 February. https://guardian.ng/news/zulum-to-resettle-over-20000-idps-to-bornos-liberated-communities/.

Musa Abdu, A.B., Adamu, I. and Jibir, A. (2018) 'Socio-demographic determinants of poverty in Nigeria and its gender differentials'. *European Scientific Journal*, 14(14). https://core.ac.uk/download/pdf/328026297.pdf.

Nemat, O., Diwakar, V., Ghafoori, I. and Azadmanesh, S. (2022) 'Livelihoods and welfare amidst layered crises in Afghanistan', *IDS Bulletin* 53(3).

OCHA (2024) 'Nigeria: Flood overview, as of 17 September 2024'. https://www.unocha.org/publications/report/nigeria/nigeria-flood-overview-17-september-2024#:~:text=Over%201%2C083%2C141%20individuals%20have%20been,people%20dead%2C%20and%202%2C504%20injured.

OECD (2023) 'SIGI 2023 Global Report'. https://www.oecd.org/en/publications/sigi-2023-global-report_4607b7c7-en.html.

Ojo, O. (2024) 'Tinubu suspends social investment programmes, to review agency's operations'. *Premium Times*, 12 January. https://www.premiumtimesng.com/news/top-news/658379-tinubu-suspends-social-investment-programmes-to-review-agencys-operations.html.

Okon, E.O. (2018) 'Poverty in Nigeria: A social protection framework for the most vulnerable groups of internally displaced persons'. *American International Journal of Social Science Research*, 2(1): 66–80. doi:10.46281/aijssr.v2i1.169.

Omokaro, G.O. (2025) 'Multi-impacts of climate change and mitigation strategies in Nigeria: Agricultural production and food security'. *Science in One Health*, 4. doi:10.1016/j.soh.2025.100113.

People's Gazette (2024) 'Borno spent N40 billion on feeding programme for IDPs: Zulum', *People's Gazette*, 25 February. https://gazettengr.com/borno-spent-n40-billion-on-feeding-programme-for-idps-zulum/.

Policinski, E. and Kuzmanovic, J. (2019) 'Protracted conflicts: The enduring legacy of endless war'. *International Review of the Red Cross*, 101(912): 965–976. doi:10.1017/S1816383120000399.

Sabates-Wheeler, R., Lind, J., Harvey, P. and Slater, R. (2022) 'Strengthening responses at the nexus of social protection, humanitarian aid and climate shocks in protracted crises: BASIC Research framing paper'. *BASIC Research Working Paper 1*. Institute of Development Studies. doi:10.19088/BASIC.2022.001.

Sala-i-Martin, X. and Subramanian, A. (2013) 'Addressing the natural resource curse: An illustration from Nigeria'. *Journal of African Economies*, 22(4): 570–615. doi:10.1093/jae/ejs033.

Salmanu, S. (2024) 'Reopened Nigeria-Niger border promises trade'. *Deutsche Welle*, 4 May. https://www.dw.com/en/reopened-nigeria-niger-border-promises-trade-growth/a-68743397.

SIGAR (2021) 'What we need to learn: Lessons from twenty years of Afghanistan reconstruction'. https://www.sigar.mil/Portals/147/Files/Reports/Lessons-Learned/SIGAR-21-46-LL.pdf.

TOLO news (2016) 'Nearly 99% of Hindus, Sikhs left Afghanistan in last three decades'. *TOLO news*, 20 June. https://tolonews.com/afghanistan/nearly-99-hindus-sikhs-left-afghanistan-last-three-decades.

UNDP (2021) 'Policy brief: The Afghani banking and financial system situation report'. https://www.undp.org/afghanistan/publications/policy-brief-afghan-banking-and-financial-system-situation-report.

UN Women (2022) '"No one is listening": Experiences of women with disabilities in Nigeria during COVID-19'. https://www.unwomen.org/sites/default/files/2022-01/Brief-Experiences-of-women-with-disabilities-in-Nigeria-during-COVID-19-en.pdf.

USAID (2019) 'Country brief: Fragility and climate risks (Nigeria)'. https://www.strausscenter.org/wp-content/uploads/Country-Brief-Fragility-and-Climate-Risks-in-Nigeria-2019.pdf.

WFP (2022) *Pre-Lean Season Assessment Survey Dataset*.

WGI (2025) *Worldwide Governance Indicators, 2024 update*. World Bank. https://www.worldbank.org/en/publication/worldwide-governance-indicators.

World Bank (2022a) *Afghanistan Welfare Monitoring Survey*. https://thedocs.worldbank.org/en/doc/138d0857c9a66e7e2a963a1a6137860e-0310062022/original/Afghanistan-Welfare-Monitoring-Survey.pdf.

World Bank (2022b) 'A better future for all Nigerians: Nigeria poverty assessment 2022'. http://documents.worldbank.org/curated/en/099730003152232753.

World Bank (2023) 'Afghanistan Economic Monitor'. https://thedocs.worldbank.org/en/doc/2ab75317f6e86c9bb6fcf342f72e0b64-0310012023/original/Afghanistan-Economic-Monitor-31-October-2023.pdf.

6 Surviving or thriving? Coping responses and pathways out of poverty amidst polycrisis

Contexts of polycrisis not only affect current poverty dynamics, they also precipitate sustained impoverishment and the intergenerational persistence of poverty. This may emerge through polycrisis driving vulnerable households to sequentially drawdown on and deplete their assets, and with support networks fading without participation as entire communities are affected during challenging times. Short-term coping responses to crises operate along multiple axes, in terms of time (e.g. anticipatory responses ex-ante to ex-post recovery attempts), intensity (low-risk to erosive), sector (economic, social or environmental), scale (individuals up to governments and international institutions), and purpose (survival or growth-oriented), as outlined in the crisis coping wheel presented in Chapter 2.

These responses can be overwhelmed amidst polycrisis, driving a poverty–polycrisis trap. Understanding the ways that coping responses are driven by crises intersections but also drive or amplify crises is important. This bidrectionality can help us understand the ways in which crises evolve, become crises, intersect, and in turn their solutions.

This chapter synthesises existing mixed methods analyses across the 15 focus countries undertaken just prior to and during COVID-19 to understand short-term coping responses and upward mobility amidst polycrisis. Section 6.1 considers how polycrisis may amplify the persistence of poverty amongst future generations, through a focus on increasingly erosive forms of short-term coping with crises, resulting for example in hunger, permanent school dropouts and early marriages. In this process, it draws on individual and household coping responses (the "who"), primarily economic and social responses (the "what"), and disaggregates by intensity (the "how")—again in keeping with the crisis coping wheel presented in Chapter 2.

In Section 6.2, the chapter then considers the opposite extreme by focusing on outliers—individuals and households—managing to sustain poverty escapes amidst polycrisis. The section also considers demographic variations in these pathways out of poverty. Section 6.3 concludes.

DOI: 10.4324/9781003503125-8

6.1 Coping with polycrisis

6.1.1 How do households cope with climate-related disasters, economic crises and low-intensity conflict?

Coping responses (see Figure 2.4 in Chapter 2) to crises can vary considerably depending on the presence and intersections of crises and household demographics and capacities. These responses can depend on the types and intersections of macro-level crises alongside shocks and stressors. Together, they can drive downward mobility and chronic poverty, as well as overwhelm multi-level coping systems that in turn reinforce negative feedback loops. Coping responses are themselves also a function of the poverty experiences of households—shaped by the acuteness (e.g. destitution, extreme or moderate poverty, vulnerable non-poor or resilient non-poor) and temporality of poverty, households' degree of diversification, assets and area of residence, demographic factors (e.g. ethnicity, gender, age), issues of norms, power and agency, as well as access to networks, political connections and institutional support, and the intersections between these factors—which in turn is also deeply affected by crises.

For instance, many households sell assets during crises—but the implications of this differ sharply by wellbeing group. Some better-off households (vulnerable but non-poor, or more resilient households) may sell a few livestock, drawing down on savings in a way that's relatively manageable and even routine. Others, including non-poor households, may reduce food quantity or switch to cheaper staples during a drought. While these can be considered erosive, they often do not carry lasting consequences for income or wellbeing. In contrast, for very poor or socially marginalised households—such as female-headed or ethnically excluded groups— these same actions (like selling livestock or reducing meals) are often taken under conditions of extreme constraint. These become survival or forced responses marked by a lack of alternative options and an inability to access other forms of support (e.g. social networks, government safety nets). Thus, it is important to consider how people's ability to cope are shaped by their economic, gendered and ethnic background, as well as the intersections between these factors. In the crisis coping wheel, this is captured in the "who" part of the wheel as well as the outer circle which influences capabilities indirectly.

The figures below attempt to capture some of these variations for nine of the 15 countries with available data. Figure 6.1 disaggregates coping responses by the presence of climate-related disasters or crises that it intersects with. Figure 6.2 instead summarises household coping responses to shocks and crises (single or intersecting) disaggregated by the poverty trajectory of the household. This is an attempt to better consider gradations of poverty and vulnerability in shaping coping responses. It is worth noting that the varying coping mechanisms options presented in different surveys

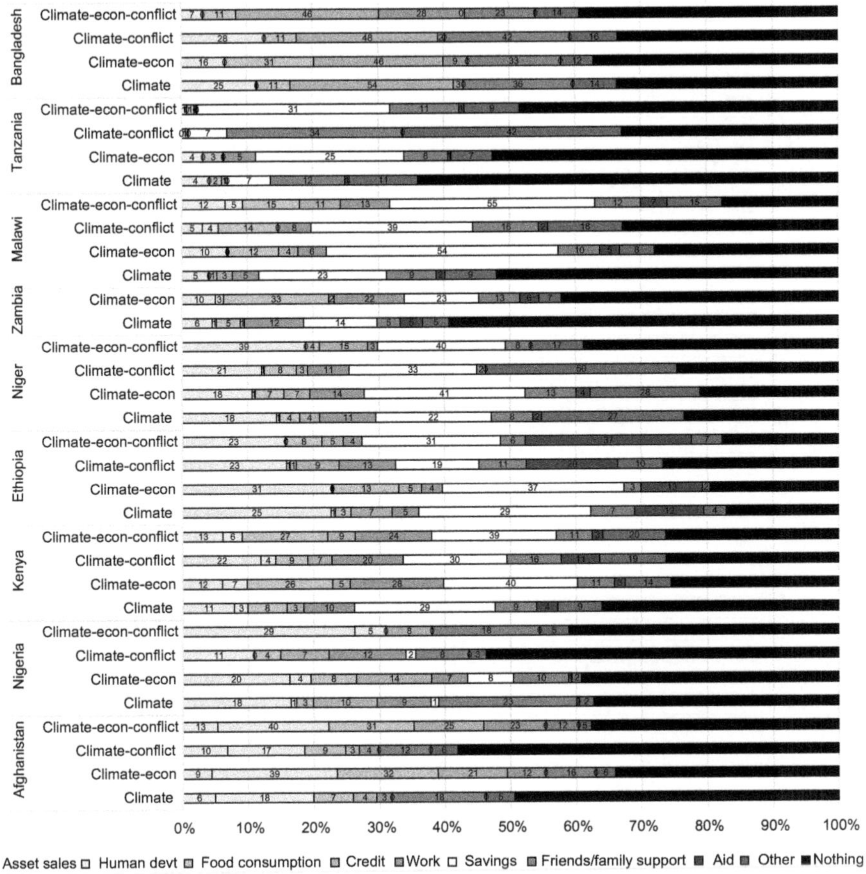

Figure 6.1 Coping responses to crises, disaggregated by crises intersections
Note: sample sizes too small at the triple nexus and conflict–climate nexus in Zambia to disaggregate coping responses. Response shares are indicated per bar, where horizontal bars do not add up to 100 given that in many cases households adopt different coping strategies for different crises. In all countries, coping responses are based on self-reported climate and conflict data. See Annex C for category definitions.
Source: author's analysis of pooled surveys presented in Table 1.1.

and different phrasing of responses even where similar responses are presented limit comparability between countries. This can weaken cross-country comparability.

Despite the challenges noted above, some broad observations can be made when viewing these two figures side by side and complemented with qualitative data, outlined below. This discussion is structured around the intensity of coping responses as a primary entry point—hence largely a framing based on outcomes—while drawing in other elements of the crisis coping wheel including agency-based references into this stratification.

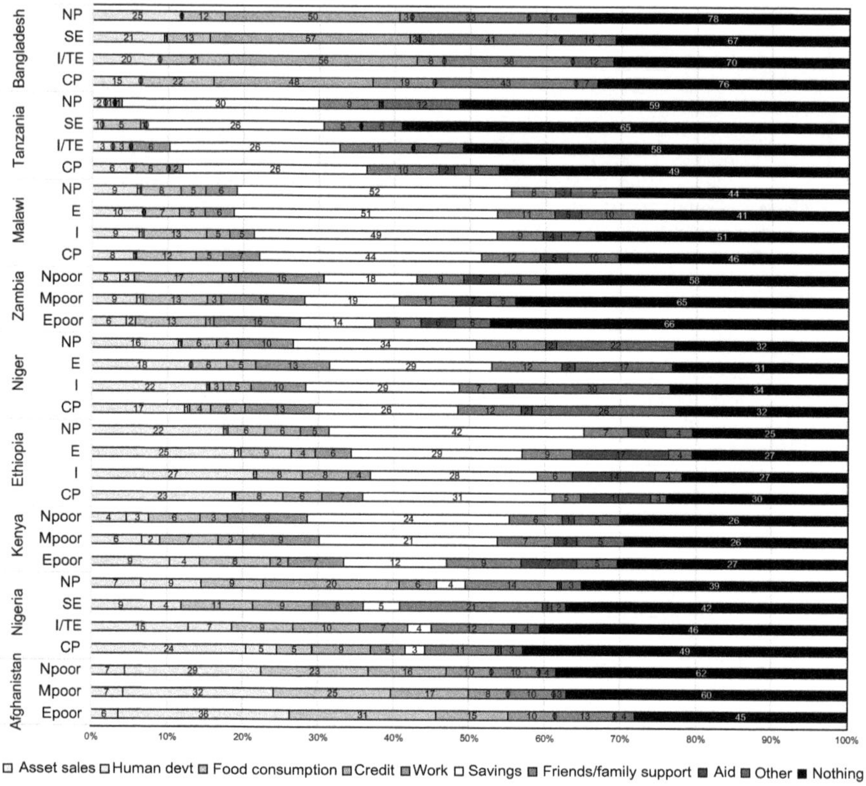

Figure 6.2 Coping responses to crises, disaggregated by poverty trajectory
Note: Epoor = extreme poor; Mpoor = moderate poor; Npoor = nonpoor for cross-section data. CP = chronic poor; I/TE = impoverished or transitory escapers; SE = sustained escapers; NP = never poor for panel data. Response shares are indicated per bar, where horizontal bars do not add up to 100 given that in many cases households adopt different coping strategies for different crises. In all countries, coping responses are based on self-reported climate and conflict data.
Source: author's analysis of pooled surveys presented in Table 1.1.

Low-risk: social support mechanisms

Social protection can be an important entitlement households draw on during crises. However, even its more common instrument—social assistance—remains strikingly limited as a coping response across the low- and lower-middle income countries studied. This may reflect the low value and coverage of social assistance in many countries. A slight exception is in Ethiopia where the Productive Safety Net Program's presence is notable and with some evidence of targeting given lower shares noted amongst non-poor households. Even so, except for Kenya and Tanzania, where rates of social assistance coverage are nevertheless low, households in chronic poverty—typically designed as the primary recipients of such programming—do not appear to be well captured. It is important to caveat that this figure indicates coping responses to shocks, rather than receipt of social assistance regardless of shock prevalence. As such, this result may point to the inadequacy of social assistance alongside potentially inadequate targeting.

Moreover, social assistance has also suffered amidst crises and their intersections. In Tanzania, which has seen substantial progress in the Tanzania Social Action Fund (TASAF), households are still facing challenges due to contexts of heightened precarity. Figure 6.1 taken together with Figure 6.2 suggests that there is some reach of assistance to households experiencing triple crises, but coverage is sparingly low. In addition, as crises continue, recovery is often sidelined and assistance may wane. In 2021 as COVID-19 continued, over half of households that received assistance from the government in Tanzania saw no change or even experienced a decrease in the receipt of assistance compared to 2020, in spite of continued need. Savings during this period diminished as a coping response and loans during the pandemic period also shifted from banks to family and friends. Loans were increasingly used to meet subsistence needs rather than productive purposes (analysis of phone survey data in Diwakar, 2025).

Similarly, during and beyond conflict periods, when disasters strike, relief can be short-lived. This may be because conflict could prevent access to certain communities due to rebel strongholds, recovery pathways may be constrained due to limited investments, or disasters may make it harder to reach remote areas. This means that the poorest populations may suffer in particular without effective government support. In Nepal pre-pandemic, INT25-NP (female, sustained escape, rural Nepal, 2017 LHI) reflected:

> They gave instant noodles, beaten rice, biscuits and so on. It only lasted for two days. Then, we also got about five kilograms of rice, lentils, oil and salt. They also gave us clothes and tarpaulin … Multiple organizations collaborate to provide relief materials to very severely affected areas … they gave materials in this area already, so they will distribute in another area next time.

Similarly, in Bangladesh, based on post-pandemic data analysis, disaster relief often did not reach smallholder farmers: “The Upazila Agriculture Office distributes government-issued incentives to farmers, including seeds, fertilizers, and pesticides … but small farmers often don’t receive them” (KII in rural Bangladesh, 2024). The quotes suggests that flood relief either do not reach poorer households, or where they do such relief may only offset a small portion of immediate losses. Indeed, its small value is unlikely to help households recover over the longer term.

In the absence of adequate social assistance or alongside it, social networks can offer an important protective and promotive function supporting household coping. This can be through family, friends, neighbours or communities providing material support including through remittances or interest-free/low-interest loans, sharing information supporting migration or referrals for job opportunities, acting as a mechanism for collective action, or providing other forms of social and emotional support. These types of social support were consistently observed across countries and poverty trajectories, in some cases more prevalent amongst the upwardly mobile or never poor households (e.g. Nigeria, Ethiopia, Niger). In Niger, social support was in part enabled by NGOs support of informal credit groups or formal tontines for women. For example, INT18-NE (female, never poor, urban Niger, 2018 LHI) started a small business selling maize flour and baobab leaves using proceeds from the women-only savings group that she joined. This enabled her diversification as a risk mitigation strategy. Reciprocal gift exchanges during family celebrations also support these investments. At the same time, norms of seclusion for women in certain communities can limit access to these social networks and reinforce adverse gender norms.

By crises intersection, households experiencing triple crises were often less reliant on these support networks (e.g. in Bangladesh, Niger, Kenya and Afghanistan). This could reflect the macro nature of these crises where entire communities may be affected by disasters, violent conflict or economic crisis and so informal support mechanisms may dry out or fade without participation amidst these sequenced or polycrisis. Indeed, during the COVID-19 pandemic, violent conflict and drought in Ethiopia in 2021, informal or traditional support mechanisms were inadequate:

> People could not support each other because most of the people are poor and many of them are buying food items from the market. So, it is difficult to support poor people as the poverty and food shortage is affecting everyone in the community.
>
> (Female sentinel household interview, Ethiopia, first presented in CPAN PMI, 2022)

Analysis from Ethiopia also points to how social support can be a double-edged sword due to demanding systems of reciprocity that may act to impoverish households (Woldehanna et al., 2022). However, the opposite was true in Nigeria, where friends and family were more prevalent coping mechanisms drawn on for the triple crisis relative to dual crises. Even so, in Nigeria this coexisting with a large reliance on asset sales suggesting erosive coping mechanisms also prevalent for this group experiencing polycrisis.

Stress: savings and the world of work

Relying on savings was the most common response across the largest number of countries where the response option was included in the survey data. This was a response more commonly available to wealthier non-poor or never-poor households. Indeed, the literature also points to reliance on savings as a relatively low-risk strategy (Heltberg et al., 2012). The challenge, however, is when multiple, polycrisis may lead to the rapid erosion of the savings base and thus other stress-based coping responses may complement or substitute these responses. Stress-based coping may emerge from households being under pressure to make decisions urgently, for example following a flood, or stressed by polycrisis that puts stress on their existing resource base. Interestingly, households experiencing triple crises were generally no less able to draw on savings in response to crises compared to households experiencing just climate-related disasters or dual crises. An exception is in Nigeria, where no household experiencing triple crises drew on savings as a primary coping response.

Work-based coping (e.g. selling labour in advance, other household members start working, looking for more employment, working longer hours, or migration) was common in Zambia, Niger, and Kenya, slightly more so typically amongst richer households that had escaped poverty or remained non-poor. By crises intersections, it was a more common response to triple crises in Afghanistan and Bangladesh, but generally less common in the African countries studied. This could reflect common internal migration in South Asia and other research pointing to the uptake of work including by women, bypassing prevailing gender norms during times of heightened precarity (Huot and Pain, 2017). Indeed, there is a well-established, customary nature of internal migration in South Asia, albeit differing from the more recent, crisis-driven internal migration increasingly linked to climate change. Moreover, research in Bangladesh points to work-based coping deepening vulnerability as family labour including of children is engaged in vulnerable and lower-income occupations alongside rising cost of living and limited social support (Rahman et al., 2022; Faruk, 2022). Thus, even where it may help maintain resilience amidst multiple shocks, the degree of resilience may be weak, reflecting the role of work-based coping as a double-edged sword.

The prevalence of economic coping mechanisms in response to triple crises in Afghanistan could also reflect the normalisation of these crises, where people develop forms of coping reflecting longer-term adaptation, for instance through migration, informality, and illicit economies. On the latter, for example, opium production has for decades provided income for rural and conflict affected households in Afghanistan, especially in response to economic shocks, conflict, and climate-related disasters (Fishtein, 2014; Pain, 2011). Its drought-resistant properties and ability to generate profits even from small plots makes it an important source of income for rural households. However, the de-facto authorities banned opium production in 2023, which has led to a dramatic reduction in its cultivation by 95% (UNODC, 2023).

In India, though the survey data does not include coping responses, the qualitative data also points to common work-related responses to crisis. For example, many families in conflict-affected study sites had escaped poverty through on-farm diversification by collecting the Madhuca Longifolia flower from a plant that produced alcohol and then selling this for profit. This was a lucrative livelihood strategy that was possible even during the summer, when heat or drought-like conditions would otherwise prevent crop cultivation. However, once Naxal violence escalated, many families stopped these outdoor activities and thus experienced downward mobility as income from its sales were lost. In its absence, for example, INT10-IN's (male, initial poverty escape, rural India, 2020 LHI) family were driven to sell paddy reserves that led to hunger. It was only since 2018 that the family resumed picking the fruit again as insecurity in their area had diminished. Along with diversified off-farm livelihoods through the interviewee's migration to a nearby town to work in a motorcycle showroom, the household was able to escape poverty.

There is also evidence of a vicious cycle of environmental degradation amidst climate-related disasters and economic crisis. Polycrisis limit economic opportunities and force households into occupations that degrade the land and may reinforce climate change and further downward mobility. For example, amidst climate and economic crises, many households in Zimbabwe increased artisanal mining, which is drudgery intensive and can be dangerous. They were also observed to engage more in gold panning, tree cutting, or overharvesting non-timber forest products that erode natural resources and can drive future impoverishment (Bird et al., 2023a). This work-based response is thus also a form of erosive coping (see discussion below) due to a lack of alternative options often faced by poorer households, reinforcing environmental crises and the bidirectional relationship between negative poverty dynamics and polycrisis.

Adverse: cycles of indebtedness

Adverse coping reflects outcomes that typically stem from distress, survival or forced responses. This is often driven by an inability to access other forms of support noted above, such as savings, social networks or formal finance. In Bangladesh, Afghanistan and Nigeria, credit-based coping mechanisms were common self-reported responses to crises in the survey data, though this was commonly reported in qualitative data across most countries. However, in Bangladesh, while 38% of households were able to take out credit in response to floods, this figure reduced to 33% amongst households additional experiencing floods with economic shocks. This points to a subdued ability to cope while economic crises hit. Indeed, during the COVID-19 pandemic lockdowns, many community savings groups were temporarily or permanently dissolved, limiting the ability of its members to rely on this for longer-term recovery (Diwakar et al., 2022). An interviewee in Nepal reflected that even after lockdown restrictions were eased, recovery was stalled as these groups were sometimes not resuscitated:

> I am involved in an organisation where we collect money every month and provide loans, but we have stopped doing so due to lockdown. Even after the lockdown is lifted, things are still not fully on track. It is the same environment of unemployment and fear.
>
> (KII, male, first presented in CPAN PMI, 2020)

Debt-driven downward mobility was a common result of this confluence of climate-related crises and economic shocks or crises, impacting the ability of households to escape poverty. This was observed commonly in the qualitative data even in countries where credit-related coping responses to crises was less prevalent as the "primary" response in the quantitative data, pointing to the salience of credit as one of many means that households may draw on to guard against crises. In Cambodia, uninsured risks to agriculture due to climate-related disasters and economic crises marked by price variability drove households into arrears, unable to repay seasonal loans, and sometimes prompting destitution where land and homes were sold to help repay these debts (Bird et al., 2023b). Debt was seen as an inescapable consequence of farmers needing to shift agricultural production to rice species due to market pressures, drought and labour shortages, but then becoming over-indebted as harvests failed amidst erratic weather patterns (Guermond et al., 2022). This is contrasted with insights from India during the pandemic, where into the summer of 2021 crops were wasted due to climate variability and lockdowns, but relatively better-off households covered by crop insurance were able to cope without resorting to adverse coping (CPAN PMI, 2022).

In Malawi, volatile agricultural output prices, inability to afford agricultural inputs especially during periods of inflation and high input prices, pests such as fall army worm, and drought and low rainfall or on the other hand floods and heavy rains all have affected crop production. Unusually high costs of agricultural inputs and unusually high prices for food were the most common shocks, reported by 21–25% of all households across the panel waves. Successive climate-related disasters alongside poor prices drive households to fall back into poverty after having escaped it (da Corta et al., 2018). For example, farmers who did not withdraw from tobacco farming before some of the volatile price declines are then forced to take loans to replant for the next agricultural season. This in turn often precipitated defaults and a loss of assets used as collateral. These loans acted to amplify losses that were already stemming from poor prices linked to drought or low rains (Box 6.1).

> If things are not well on the market and you have a loan, it is the person who has a loan that suffers more. Moreover, if you have a bad year and cannot raise money you can't farm without selling assets … And if you have no assets, the following year, you will be grounded.
>
> (INT32-MW, male, sustained escaper, rural Malawi, 2018 LHI, first presented in da Corta et al., 2018)

Box 6.1 A transitory escape from poverty amidst intersecting climatic and economic shocks in Malawi

In 2013 INT32-MW, a cotton farmer, branched out into the selling second-hand clothes. However her business was not yet established when in 2015–16 the district was hit by a drought which severely reduced her maize production. This was further exacerbated by low prices for her cash crops.

> That is the period I can't forget. Of course, we did not produce enough maize due to the drought, but I had a lot of pigeon peas and groundnuts but imagine the vendors buying our pigeon peas at K20 per Kg! (compared to K550 in 2017). This was the beginning of our downfall. We harvested but failed to make profits.

She lost her capital for the second-hand clothes, and she struggled to pay school fees. She then took loans from VSLAs and loan sharks to pay for the school fees and these loans accumulated. But in 2017, she got another poor harvest and so failed to pay all the loans accumulated. As such, she sold her moveable assets (bicycle, sofa set, livestock) and the loan shark came and confiscated her plates and pots. As she reflected: "All the assets are gone, and my house is just like a football pitch". Thus, for INT32-MW, these climatic and price crises not only had knock-on effects for her new non-farm enterprise but also, she took loans which intensified her descent.

Source: INT32-MW, female, sustained escaper, rural Malawi, 2018 LHI, first presented in da Corta et al. (2018).

The examples of debt above also point to a broader insight around moneylenders and others who may be financially "winners" during crisis. These may be individuals and groups that take advantage of situations that negatively affect people in and near poverty and their recovery. Money lenders raising interest rates, traders increasing prices of goods and agricultural inputs, and overall exploitative practices all constitute examples of potential "winners" during polycrisis. This reinforces the need to consider welfare and coping across the distribution including its relational elements.

Erosive and failed coping

Adverse or erosive coping responses (asset sales, human development reduction, and lowering food consumption/quality) were often involuntarily taken under the threat of severe deprivation, reflecting a distinct lack of agency. These were relatively more common across countries for households experiencing negative poverty trajectories, according to the pooled survey data. Amongst these responses that stem from compulsion rather than choice, households in chronic poverty commonly rely on reducing the quantity or quality of food to cope with crises. In Bangladesh and Malawi, these rates were comparable to households experiencing poverty transience or impoverishment, though in Tanzania it was also common amongst households sustaining poverty escapes. Being compelled to reduce food consumption or food quality was often more a more prevalent response amongst crises intersections relative to climate-related disasters alone.

Interestingly, in Zambia and Niger, the share of households coping with crises in this way was instead slightly more pronounced amongst non-poor or never-poor households (alongside households escaping poverty in Niger). However, as noted in the introduction, this likely reflects a more manageable response amongst richer households, rather than having necessarily lasting consequences for wellbeing. The latter would be the case amongst poorer households being driven to involuntarily reduce consumption from an already low base, thus with more severe effects on the intergenerational persistence of poverty.

Distress sales of assets were also highly common, with no clear relationship with triple crises in the quantitative data. However, in Nigeria and Afghanistan it was more common amongst polycrisis relative to climate-related disasters alone. In Bangladesh and Kenya, however, it was at the conflict-climate nexus that asset sales were particularly pronounced, though in both cases this seemed to substitute lowering food consumption. In other words, largely involuntary adverse coping responses linked to food consumption and asset sales were substituting each other. In the qualitative data, urgent livestock sales were a common coping response in many countries including Bangladesh, as the example of INT39-BD in response to ill health and the pandemic highlighted (Figure 6.3). This was also a period marked by Cyclone Amphan.

The lack of a consistent relationship between the triple crises and asset sales likely reflects a reality where coping is shaped not only by the presence of crises. Instead, it is also critically shaped by individual and institutional preparedness—for example through household economic conditions, diversification and safety nets, respectively—alongside access to networks and pre-existing vulnerabilities along demographic markers. This can drive reactive forms of erosive coping, as a sentinel household interviewee in Rwanda noted:

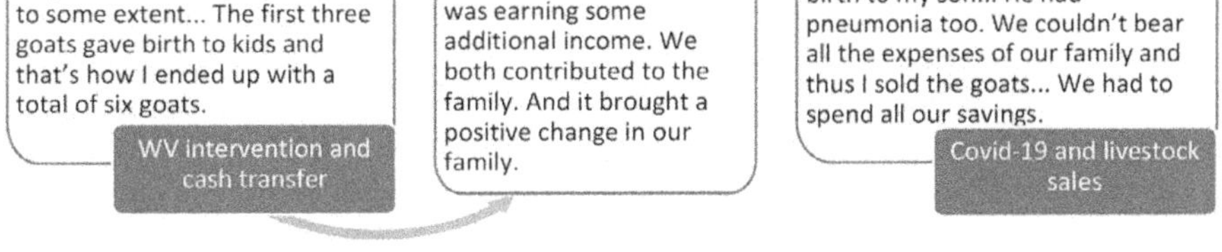

Figure 6.3 Livestock sales to address ill health amid the pandemic
Source: INT39-BD (female, transitory escape, rural Bangladesh, 2021 LHI), first presented in Diwakar et al. (2022).

> The challenge I told you about is to sell the land not because you have planned that but because of the hunger. You sell it at a low price just to prevent kids to die of hunger, not for you to start another project that will bring benefit, but to see children getting what to eat.
>
> (Sentinel household interviewee, rural Rwanda, 2022, first presented in CPAN PMI, 2022)

There is also a temporal dimension to asset sales, where for example this increased during the pandemic months in Nigeria alongside prevalence of hunger, both especially pronounced amongst households in the bottom two quintiles of the welfare distribution based on their pre-pandemic status (Diwakar and Adedeji, 2021). In Zambia, the onset of the pandemic on the back of successive droughts drove households to engage in a distress sale of assets in higher frequency during the pandemic in 2020 relative to just before it (IPA, 2020). In Tanzania, too, asset sales and reducing consumption were common survival responses amongst chronically poor households, more than for other groups (Diwakar, 2025).

There were also a range of adverse gender-differentiated coping responses, again largely observed in conditions of distress. In Ethiopia, child marriage was perceived as an increasingly common response in the absence of alternatives (CPAN PMI, 2021). Increased criminal activity especially in the form of theft was evidenced in Zimbabwe (Bird et al., 2023a). Successive crises marked by hyperinflation, Cyclone Ana, drought and livestock disease in Zimbabwe also drove some women to illegal transactional sex as a survival mechanism (Bird et al., 2023a; Phiri, 2021). Cender norms and abuse is common in this context of heightened economic precarity. Women are often worse affected by these crises, due to lack of resources, skills or access technology. In addition, young women face additional vulnerability to early or forced marriages when climate-related disasters become more intense (Bird et al., 2023a).

Finally, it is striking to note that in the humanitarian contexts identified for this analysis—Nigeria and Afghanistan—human development related coping responses were also highly common, generally more so than other countries studied. This included withdrawing children from school or decreasing expenditures on health or education in both countries, or marrying children off in Afghanistan. In both countries, these largely involuntary survival mechanisms were slightly more common amongst households experiencing triple crises, though in Afghanistan it was also a common response to climate and economic crises. These responses have serious implications for the intergenerational persistence of poverty, not least given the positive relationship between human development and economic growth as well as sustained escapes from poverty (Stewart et al., 2018; Diwakar et al., 2024).

6.1.2 Coping with humanitarian crises

Sequential drawdown on assets in Afghanistan

The high degree of political and economic uncertainty has contributed to households being driven to reactive survival-focused responses and sequential drawdown on assets. For example, during the pandemic, many households reduced their expenditures as well as the quantity or quality of food consumed (Hassen and El Bilali, 2024). Other erosive forms of coping included decreasing expenditures especially on health and education, selling assets and spending savings—all of which could drive the intergenerational persistence of poverty as it reduced the ability of households to respond to future shocks.

Social connections and informal support structures has been a backbone for many families amidst times of crises. However, such informal institutions have been repeatedly devalued in policy and programming responses favour of Western technocratic models that inadequately consider local needs (Gough et al., 2004; Schutte, 2009; Brugh et al., 2019). Moreover, conflict has systematically eroded the ability of households to rely on these informal structures where they do exist (see Box 6.2).

Interestingly, as touched on in the last chapter, analysis of the 2019/20 survey data in Afghanistan also points to a slight increase—albeit from very low levels—of women in poor households who had taken up work in response to the pandemic. This increase was more pronounced amongst households experiencing disasters or insecurity during the pandemic. Instead, men were less likely to enter or in some cases even withdrew from economic activities (Diwakar, 2022). Taken together, these results imply a narrowing gender differential in employment. However, they must be viewed with caution, as the drivers of employment of women in poverty are centred around precarity. Indeed, other analysis from Afghanistan also points to women intensifying income-generating activities as a survival mechanism during a major drought between 2006 and 2008 (Huot and Pain, 2017).

Intergenerational consequences of adverse coping in Nigeria

Coping responses were increasingly overwhelmed amidst intersecting and sequential crises in Nigeria. This meant that they moved towards adverse or erosive forms of coping that reduced household ability to effectively respond to future shocks and remain out of poverty. Taking credit and selling assets were more common, while work or aid from an NGO or the government were less common for households having to cope with insecurity relative to other types of crises and shocks in Nigeria (Diwakar and Brzezinska, 2023). This points to a failure of humanitarian and social protection systems in conflict-affected contexts.

When focusing on the epicentre of violence using survey data from two local government areas (LGAs) in Borno in 2023, some responses were also differences in coping responses based on the household's probability of living in poverty. For example, households with a high probability of poverty (90% or more) were less able to draw on social networks, transfers or assistance in response to violence. They also had less savings and were less likely to migrate. Their weak social and economic support mechanisms meant that they were forced to consume fewer meals, reduce investment in education and engage in a distress sale of assets—all erosive coping responses likely to prolong their state of poverty.

Like in Afghanistan, these involuntary and erosive coping mechanisms are also driving the intergenerational persistence of poverty. Child migration to cities for street hawking or house-help roles was a forced coping response to economic crises for families in the qualitative data. Many households also were unable to afford user costs of education, such as for exams or textbooks, that has driven dropout rates amplified amidst insecurity. Inability to afford medical bills has also further aggravated health conditions according to FGDs.

Another channel through which crises amidst humanitarian contexts are contributing to more chronic forms of poverty is by driving its intergenerational persistence. This emerges due to crises contributing to lower current child wellbeing, and to precarious livelihoods for young men and women. In Nigeria, with inadequate job creation and a large share of government resources directed towards countering insecurity, many young men have

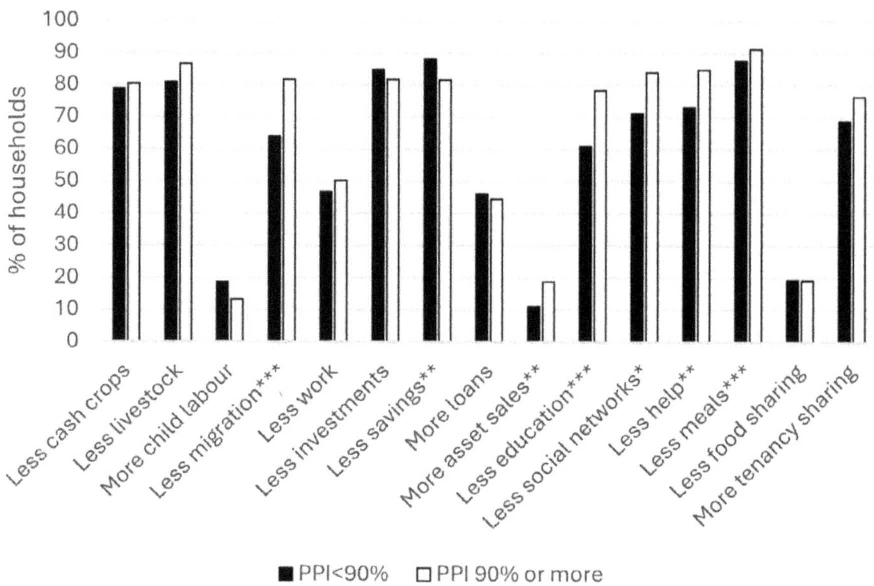

Figure 6.4 Negative coping response to violence, disaggregated by poverty probability [N=1000]

Note: poverty is measured using the Probability of Poverty Index[1]; *** p<0.01, ** p<0.05, * p<0.1.

Source: analysis of Borno survey data (2023), first presented in Diwakar et al. (2024).

instead turned to cybercrime in other parts of the country, while drug abuse was also commonly reported. Several young women instead were driven to early marriages or the sex industry. Child trafficking was another often-irreversible harm raised in FGDs (Diwakar et al., 2025):

> When there is an unfulfilled basic need female community members are tempted to engage in negative coping mechanisms such as survival sex and early marriage. Many families have reported skipping meals because of lack money to buy fuel. firewood or cooking fuel.
>
> (Long-term residents' male group interview in rural northern Nigeria, 2023)

> Another problem in 2022 to 2023 is we are having chronic child trafficking and that has caused chronic poverty in the community.
>
> (Male FGD, rural northern Nigeria, 2023)

Mental health and negative coping responses

These challenges in declining economic and social capital coupled with limited coping capacity has driven a feeling of hopelessness amongst many households in both countries. In Nigeria, trauma was observed amongst IDPs including those who had returned to their homelands, as outlined in the last chapter. In Afghanistan, qualitative insights also pointed to a strong sense of hopelessness given the context of multiple challenges and lack of support: "We don't know what to do. There is no solution, and nothing comes to our mind to do and overcome these challenges. The only thing we can do is to pray and ask Almighty Allah to solve our challenges" (INT2-AF, male, impoverished, rural Afghanistan, 2022 LHI, first presented in Diwakar et al., 2022a).

The wider literature points to a bidirectional relationship between poverty and ill health, including psychosocial illbeing (Lund et al., 2010; Haushofer and Fehr, 2014; Ridley et al., 2020). Mental health challenges permeate amidst violence and polycrisis. In humanitarian contexts, the intensity and scale of loss can lead to heightened anxiety, depression, substance use disorders and trauma, with deeper effects (Kohrt and Kaiser, 2021). Indeed, drug use was prevalent in life histories in both Nigeria and Afghanistan.

Mental ill health can contribute to adverse or erosive coping and long-term poverty trajectories. They can form an invisible barrier to recovery. Even outside of humanitarian contexts, INT10-IN's example in Chapter 4 (Box 4.2) illustrates how conflict and economic crises affected his mental health and education, causing him to fail his class 10 exam and drop out of school. The mental ill health of caregivers can also affect children's educational outcomes (UNICEF, 2021). Outside of education, other pathways through which mental health could affect long-term poverty trajectories is through shaping household decision-making in relation to livelihoods and coping. For example, high anxiety could drive households to engage in a distress sale of assets or risky migration if it impairs proper planning and financial decision-making balancing risks and rewards (Kristoffersen et al., 2024).

Yet mental health is rarely a focus of already burdened healthcare systems in low- and middle-income countries. Weak or broken health systems in humanitarian contexts can amplify poverty, for example through lack of access to maternal and child health services, or through driving out-of-pocket spending or catastrophic health expenditures. Lack of access to treatment can itself increase psychological stress and drive mental health issues. The next two chapters touch on programmatic examples and recommendations for improving psychosocial care amidst crises.

6.2 Sustaining escapes from poverty amidst polycrisis

This section draws on qualitative data to identify strategies that households adopt to sustain poverty escapes amidst polycrisis. It presents these strategies through examples of its application in case study countries.

6.2.1 Education as a critical asset amidst disasters and conflict

Education can act as a portable asset during times of crises (Bird et al., 2010), including during polycrisis. It is portable in the sense of facilitation migration for work, and in the context of displacement due to conflict or disaster. It improves access to better-paid or more secure jobs when people migrate, increases awareness of how to access formal credit, and supports individuals and households in navigating new systems. This adaptation potential coupled with its portable nature as an intangible asset makes education especially valuable in supporting poverty escapes amidst polycrisis. At the same time, certain ideologies of conflict may render education and educated individuals as targets, which may counter the otherwise largely positive role of education as a portable asset (Maynard, 2019).

For the subset of households living in areas affected by climate-related disasters in Malawi, Bangladesh, Tanzania and Zambia, primary and secondary education completion of the household head is associated with a lower probability of chronic poverty and transient poverty and higher probability of resilience amidst economic crises where significant (Figure 6.5, top). Effect sizes are generally larger at secondary levels of education. There are moreover some differences based on education level, where amidst climate-economic crises, completion of lower secondary education is only a significant correlate associated with a lower probability of chronic poverty in Tanzania and Malawi, and a higher probability of resilience in Malawi (Figure 6.5). Results where significant persist across the full sample (Annex Table D6).

The positive relationship between education and resilience more broadly though persists to an extent amidst climate-related disasters and conflict.

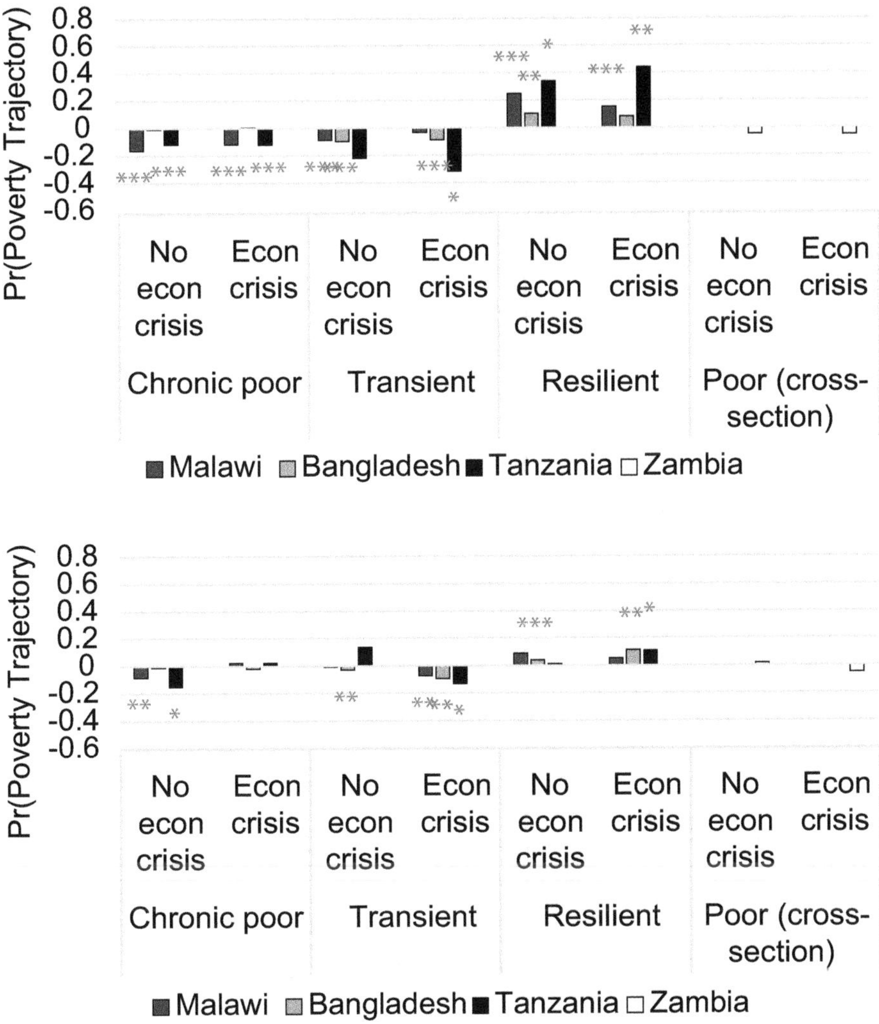

Figure 6.5 Relationship between household head's completion of education (lower secondary levels at top, primary level at bottom) and poverty trajectories, by economic crises, in areas affected by climate-related disasters

Note: average marginal effects are presented. The figures refer to four models (one per country), examining the intersection of education completion of the household head with economic crises, for the subset of households experiencing floods or drought. Asterisks refer to results that are statistically significant at conventional levels (*** p<0.01, ** p<0.05, * p<0.1). All controls are the same as in the main equation presented Section 1.2.1 of Chapter 1.

Source: analysis of datasets referenced in Table 1.1.

Indeed, where significant, the relationship with primary education completion of the head and poverty trajectories is associated with a lower probability of chronic and transient poverty and higher probability of resilience amidst conflict and climate-related disasters (Figure 6.6, bottom). Moreover, lower secondary education completion of the household head is associated with a lower probability of chronic poverty including in the presence of conflict in the subset of areas affected by climate-related disasters. It is also generally associated with a higher probability of resilience for households not affected by conflict (Figure 6.6).

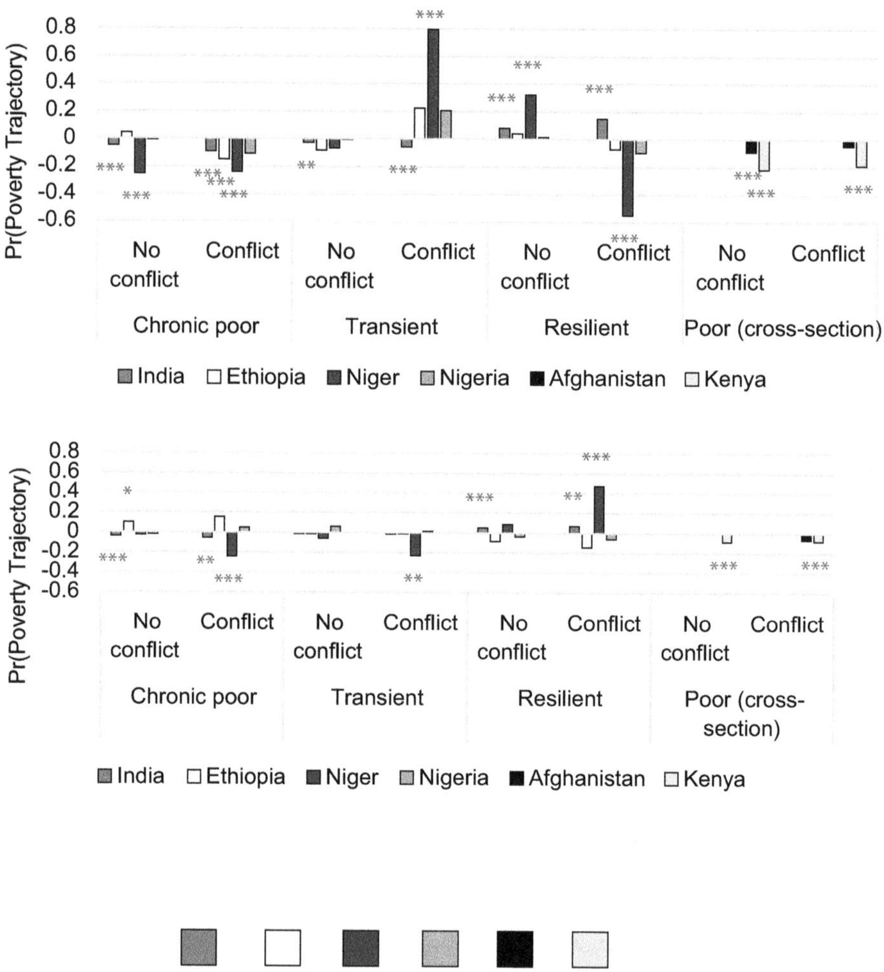

Figure 6.6 Relationship between household head's completion of education (lower secondary levels at top, primary level at bottom) and poverty trajectories, by conflict, in areas affected by climate-related disasters

Note: average marginal effects are presented. The figures refer to six models (one per country), examining the intersection of education completion of the household head with conflict, for the subset of households experiencing floods or drought. Asterisks refer to results that are statistically significant at conventional levels (*** p<0.01, ** p<0.05, * p<0.1). All controls are the same as in the main equation presented in Section 1.2.1 of Chapter 1.

Source: analysis of datasets referenced in Table 1.1.

Again, results persist for the full sample (Annex Table D7). In the qualitative data, education more easily supported individuals to access formal sector jobs, which allowed individuals to invest in livelihood diversification including passive rental income, with this sequence helping provide routes out of poverty.

However, the relationship at secondary levels is reversed and instead associated with a higher probability of transient poverty and lower probability of resilience in Niger amidst conflict and climate-related disasters, suggesting that education as a resilience capacity may be coming under strain. This could be the case depending on conflict ideologies or its dynamics, in areas where educated individuals are targeted (O'Malley, 2010; Novelli and Selenica, 2014). It could also reflect secondary education's link to salaried work—a link which may be broken during times of conflict.

6.2.2 Economic and social drivers of resilience amidst climate-related disasters and economic crises

Climate-smart agricultural diversification: spotlight on Zambia

Investment in climate smart agriculture has the potential to support resilience during climate-related disasters and economic crises. Analysis from rural Zambia pointed to improved maize varieties, practices such as agroforestry, irrigation and ridging strengthened household resilience to flooding and drought. Irrigation has become increasingly important in the context of smaller landholdings and increasing climate-related pressures. However, in many cases climate smart agricultural practices was also associated with transient poverty for households faced with flooding or drought risk (Shepherd et al., 2025). This may reflect the high labour or capital costs of climate smart practices that limit its sustained adoption (Kayula et al., 2022).

Indeed, for these practices to continue to be effective in contexts of economic downturn, broader risk mitigation is essential, often well before crises strike. Some households in Zambia did this through diversification on the farm, for example by cultivating a diversified selection of crops. INT2-ZM (female, sustained escape, rural Zambia, 2024, first presented in da Corta and Bwalya, 2025) in 2020 faced challenges due to border closures that limited her ability to sell onions, which continued amidst low onion prices the following year. However, she planted a variety of rain-fed and irrigated crops, including sunflowers and soybean that were less reliant on expensive fertiliser, which helped offset the losses she experienced through onion sales. INT2-ZM also joined a cooperative in 2021 that later enabled her to gain access to subsidised fertiliser through the Farmer Input Support Programme during the 2023–24 drought. She moreover engaged in value addition, for example by processing and selling cooking oil from sunflowers. To support this, she used her grandmother's social cash transfers, willingly shared, to hire labour to deepen her well—thus restoring water access— and purchase inputs for vegetable cultivation.

The building blocks of INT2-ZM's resilience to climate and economic crises was thus set in place before the 2023–24 drought layered onto the economic downturn. Her adaptation to polycrisis was enabled by on-farm diversification of crops including its value addition, which was in turn supported by cooperative involvement, familial cooperation and social protection (da Corta et al., 2025).

Beyond crop agriculture, the role of larger landholdings and ownership of large livestock are also important in contexts of intersecting economic crises and climate-related disasters. Not only can such forms of within-agriculture diversification help guard against climate-related disasters, but they can also enable households to weather economic crises by spreading risk. As noted in Chapter 3, the cushioning effects of agriculture was noted for the poorest households in a number of countries (e.g. Zambia, Tanzania, Bangladesh), even if it did not consistently enable poverty escapes. However, as noted then, there are also risks to landholdings and livestock that can counteract these processes.

The key is accordingly ensuring multiple income streams. This is because focusing in for example only on livestock or even crop agriculture can still be risky, for example amidst water shortages characterising drought (Shepherd et al., 2025).

> Despite financial difficulties, the household remains resilient due to diverse income streams, including the restaurant, rental earnings, and farming. However, the economic hardship has slowed down their construction efforts, delaying the completion of both their main house and the new rental unit.
>
> (INT6, female, sustained escape, rural Zambia, 2024)

We turn next to a focus on this off-farm diversification to complement farming.

Off-farm diversification: insights from Tanzania and Malawi

Off-farm diversification can be an important way to guard against the negative impact of climate-related disasters on livelihoods (Eshetu and Mekonnen, 2016; Ullah and Shivakoti, 2014). Moreover, in Tanzania, where inflation or other economic shocks had the potential to reduce the demand for outputs or services on top of drought, NFEs were still associated with a lower probability of chronic poverty.

At the same time, NFEs in Tanzania were also associated with a higher probability of transient poverty amidst drought and economic crises, suggesting it can also be risky especially for households closer to the poverty line or just above it. Some of this depends on the size and type of enterprise. For example, in Malawi, farmers who had escaped poverty but subsequently fell back into poverty in the face of climate-related disasters and economic crises typically had smaller non-farm enterprises often in second-hand clothes retail or hardware sales, that were highly elastic to falls in producer incomes. This meant that their diversified portfolio was often inadequate to remain resilient to climate shocks when combined with high prices (da Corta et al., 2018). Instead, households that invested in rental housing, transport, cross-border trade for food crops, or landowners were more easily able to remain resilient to crises that affected farming (da Corta et al., 2018).

More broadly, it is notable that there is a striking dearth of strategies evident to strengthen resilience (i.e. sustained poverty escapes or remaining never poor) amidst climate-related disasters and economic crises across countries investigated (Figures 3.9, 3.10, 3.11 and 4.3 presented in Chapters 3 and 4). For example, the only correlate of resilience that retains significance for households experiencing drought and reporting economic shocks in Tanzania is the household's asset value, even if there are a wider array of correlates associated with a lower probability of poverty (Figure 6.7). This suggests that asset development must remain a central focus in developing sustained pathways out of poverty amidst crises.

Continuous economic and social adaptation: manoeuvring challenges in Zimbabwe

In Zimbabwe, households that remained resilient typically engaged in continuous experimentation which enabled them to prepare for shocks in advance and adapt (Bird et al., 2023a). For example, some households moved into value addition on the farm, collected non-timber forest products for sale or home consumption, began brewing beer or selling cigarettes, or engaging in casual work. This helped them adapt to long-term economic changes like

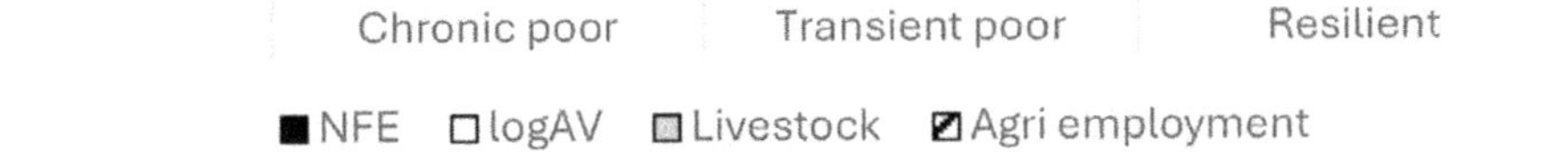

Figure 6.7 Relationship between livelihoods, assets, and poverty trajectories in Tanzania 2008–19, by drought or no drought, among households reporting economic shocks

Note: average marginal effects are presented. The figure refers to four models, examining the intersection of drought with 1) NFEs, 2) log of the number of consumer durable assets, 3) presence of livestock, and 4) head's engagement in agriculture. The first three models rely on relative poverty lines, while the fourth relies on 1.5x the relative poverty line to achieve convergence. Asterisks refer to results that are statistically significant at conventional levels (*** $p<0.01$, ** $p<0.05$, * $p<0.1$).

Source: analysis of TNPS (2008–19), ACLED (2008–19), Global Flood Observatory (2008–18) and CRU-TS (2008–19) data, first presented in Diwakar (2025).

wage stagnation, by increasing the profitability of their economic activities. During the COVID-19 pandemic, initial profits for those who had reoriented their NFEs towards sales of masks and sanitisers was short-lived amidst market saturation. Others instead travelled to South Africa and Botswana to purchase food to sell upon their return for profit.

In many of these cases, barter trade and payment in kind was common as a means of adapting to economic crises, even for those with salaried employment. This is in a context of hyperinflation, where cash withdrawals are restricted and mobile money has taxes (Bird et al., 2023a):

> Some mining families ventured into barter trade. The grocery shop owners would come to the villages with essential commodities and exchange foodstuffs like cooking oil and mealie meal with some grams of gold. This helped most families in coping with the shock.
>
> (KII with traditional leader in rural Zimbabwe, 2021)

Social support was an important part of this response, whether through the community or external provision. For example, in early 2022, humanitarian assistance under the Food Deficit Mitigation Strategy sought to reach 1.5 million people in 26 districts across the country through distribution of grains alongside promoting drought-resistant crops and irrigation, to mitigate the "hungry gap" preceding harvest. This was complemented by targeted support by the government and partners to reach those worst affected by Tropical Storm Ana (FEWS NET, 2022). Rural chiefs also often step in to supplement government support (Bird et al., 2023a). For example, when the COVID-19 food relief funds from the government was identified to be inadequate in 2020, a rural local chief in Bindura noted that his court provided extra grain (KII, rural Zimbabwe, 2021). Similarly, households assisted each other, whether through "Ilima"—a process where community members plough a neighbour's fields in exchange for food—or other forms of food support (Bird et al., 2023a): "Those in need of food were assisted by neighbours. There was a spirit of Ubuntu. Ubuntu is about the essential human virtues such as compassion and togetherness" (male FGD, rural Zimbabwe, 2021).

Women's adaptation responding to patriarchal norms: insights from Niger

In Niger, too, some women continuously adapted to economic crises and climate-related disasters. According to the analysis of qualitative data, they did this by drawing strategically on a small set of networks and time-sensitive opportunities to drive sustained escapes from poverty. For example, as they got older women moved from tala tala (street trading)—which was socially unacceptable for women upon marriage—to seamstressing or engaging in the processing and sale of cooking oil, gradually developing assets through informal savings from tontines or profits. They also relied on targeted social networks, sometimes relying on marriage as a fallback strategy.

Women amidst crises often "played by the rules", manoeuvring and negotiating within patriarchal constraints to forge pathways out of poverty (da Corta et al., 2021). INT4-NE (female, sustained escape, rural Niger, 2020 LHI) was married at the age of 14 as the second wife of her husband, who then left for Libya for extended periods of time without contact or regular remittances, even after she gave birth to their child. She divorced him as a result, remarrying a year after to the son of the former canton chief. However, her husband was not happy because of her child from her first marriage, and so she got divorced again. After this, her first husband sought to re-marry her, agreeing to stop migrating to Libya and help local butchers to sell meat instead. She agreed to his proposal after a year. In 2017, she was part of a social assistance programme where she received cash transfers for nine months that she gave to her husband. In 2019, with the permission of her husband, she enrolled in the local training centre to learn sewing, where she would sell part of the millet rations her husband provided her for food, in order to fund her training costs. She plans to buy a machine if she finishes her training, using profits from her sewing work. INT4-NE's strategy reflects negotiated agency, adapting through remarriage, and investing in off-farm skills development to improve her income-generating potential.

Notably, sustained escapers or those who were never poor either did not speak of climate-related disasters in their life histories or otherwise received support. This is often because the crisis either did not impact their household directly—for example, their home may have been well-built or located in a safer area—or because they had sufficient resources to absorb the shock, whereby the savings they used to respond was relatively minor compared to their total asset or savings base. Support was also sometimes a common part of their experiences. As such, it was not uncommon that sustained escapers did not register these crises as a significant event in their life history narratives.

For example, regarding the role of support in underpinning adaptation, INT6-NE (female, sustained escape, rural Niger, 2020 LHI) experienced a flood in 2015 that affected the whole village, including the collapse of her and her husband's house. However, there was a media broadcast about the flooding. She received two bags of rice, two blankets and a foldable bed, which she attributes to donor support. Though she is unclear who the donors were, she recalls it came from Tahoua, where her husband travels regularly in search of seasonal work. Spousal collaboration through information sharing and network access was an important part of her weathering the flood.

Supportive systems and services: a multi-sectoral intervention in rural Bangladesh

How can asset development be supported? In Bangladesh, when examining a multi-sectoral graduation "plus" intervention, participants who received services related to disaster risk reduction with the ultra-poor graduation (UPG) programme were associated with higher asset ownership and lower poverty likelihood, relative to receiving just the UPG interventions (Diwakar et al.,

2022b). Disaster risk reduction (DRR) can be a critical part of building climate resilience to ensure households do not experience downward mobility during climate-related disasters.

Moreover, the combination of DRR and water, sanitation and hygiene (WASH) interventions with the UPG is associated with a higher probability that households experience an increase in their income (and a lower probability of experiencing declining incomes) in the year preceding the 2021 survey (Diwakar et al., 2022b). This focus on multi-sectoral DRR and WASH interventions to guard against two key sources of downward mobility—climate-related disasters and WASH-related ill health, respectively—is thus an important part of enabling households to weather the intersection of macro-level crises with micro-level shocks such as ill health noted in previous chapters.

Intuitively, DRR could enable assets including livestock and crops to be safeguarded during climate-related disasters, while WASH could help reduce some of the sources of ill health. Indeed, access to WASH and DRR services is also associated with a higher probability that households are able to face a disaster in the future relative to five years preceding the survey, and in turn this preparedness is associated with a higher probability of perceptions of income increase in the years leading up to the survey (Diwakar et al., 2022b). This sequence can thus contribute to sustained escapes from poverty amidst climate-related disasters including during times of economic crises as observed during the intersection of these events during the COVID-19 pandemic period. However, other forms of ill health and livestock death still regularly exerted a downward push on household wellbeing in the qualitative data, suggesting a wider portfolio of responses to ill health and improved veterinary support is still needed to improve the effectiveness of WASH and DRR interventions.

Another way through which these interventions supported pathways out of poverty was through its effect on women's agency. The UPG interventions were delivered primarily to women, while aspects of WASH and DRR were at the household and community levels. This combination meant that women received targeted support alongside support to the wider contexts they drew on in navigating poverty escapes. As a result, the combination of WASH and DRR with UPG, relative to UPG alone, was associated with a higher probability that women participated in making major household decisions. Moreover, this decision-making was associated in turn with a higher probability of increasing income in the years preceding the survey (Diwakar et al., 2022b). The qualitative data reinforced these results, pointing to spousal collaboration and increased confidence in the public sphere stemming from these interventions. In some cases, this was also used to advocate for community-wide improvements to strengthen infrastructure before/after crises:

> We discuss and make decisions mutually. We tell each other that we can do something with our joint income. That's how we manage to make things better for ourselves.
>
> (INT33-BD, female, sustained escape, rural Bangladesh, 2021 LHI)

> Now we can go to the chairman regarding our needs. After joining Nobo Jatra we have this courage. We went to the chairman and told him to repair the road in our village. Also went to collect donations for treatment of a poor person in our village. After joining the village development committee we became independent. Chairman takes us seriously and listens to us … We do a lot for the development of our village.
>
> (Female FGD, rural Bangladesh, 2021)

These examples above speak to the important role of women in livelihood adaptation during crises. Some of this may be supported by NGO-supported collective savings groups or microfinance schemes for women. We also observe women's adaptation regardless of NGO presence, through stronger engagement in agro-processing or contributing to shared irrigation schemes—roles that were previously taken up by men (Diwakar et al., 2024,).

Such examples mirror the book's argument in Chapters 1 and 2 about the impact of polycrisis on downward mobility. The examples here illustrate how multiple intervention programmes—such as the combination of UPG, WASH, and DRR—can collectively address these crises, with positive and mutually reinforcing effects on resilience. These impacts are often bidirectional and synergistic, strengthening outcomes across multiple dimensions and even create new ones. They also drive increased confidence in the public sphere used to advocate for community-wide improvements to strengthen infrastructure before/after crises. This accordingly reinforces the arguments in the book regarding how polycrisis can accelerate downward mobility—and underscores the need for integrated responses to counter these dynamics.

6.2.3 Resilience amidst conflict and humanitarian contexts

Absence of (direct) violence

Most sustained escapers avoided the most severe impacts of conflict, such as displacement, mortality or asset loss. They were often able to maintain stability, for example through secure government employment—despite living in conflict-affected areas. For example, as INT80-NG (male, sustained escape, rural northern Nigeria, 2023 LHI) notes:

> The Boko Haram conflict has not affected my house. I was not displaced … At times I could not go to work due to attacks and explosions. In 2010 I was transferred to Taraba state, I relocated without my family … I was then working with [a government agency]. I was transferred to Yobe state in 2013 where I worked for two years before I was transferred back to Maiduguri again in 2015. I was then earning well and lived a comfortable life in which I can afford the basic necessities of life.

This may reflect insurgencies, banditry and communal conflicts that were instead prevalent in the country with regional variation in intensity. The intensity of conflict was also highest in 2014–15, marked by escalation of Boko Haram violence during those years.

However, people in and near poverty in Nigeria nevertheless did experience different types of economic crises and armed robberies (Figure 6.8). For example, INT46-NG experienced multiple conflict-related events but was able to restart or launch new businesses each time, drawing on support from her husband, a Microfinance Institution (MFI) loan, and access to a bank account and ATM, even during the cashless policy. More broadly, sustained escapers were able to be resilient by adapting to changing circumstances, often involving pursuing different streams of income. Income diversification again was observed across qualitative interviews of sustained escapes. This diversification was both in both farming (e.g. selling maize grits, palm oil, flour) and off-farm (e.g. through petty trading), reflecting the importance of multiple forms of diversification to enable households to better adapt to changing economic conditions.

In Afghanistan, given the wider prevalence of violent conflict and its intensity across much of the country as characterised for example by higher fatality rates, one out of the six sustained escapers interviewed (alongside impoverished and chronically poor respondents) referenced this violent conflict as exerting a downward pressure on his income. INT1-AF (male, sustained escape, rural Afghanistan, 2021 pre-transition interview) noted:

> In the past, we were fully busy and even we were working in two shift days and nights that time the security situation was also good and we could work on the lands during the nights, but now we cannot work during the night to irrigate the lands.

However, he was able to remain out of poverty due to diversified livelihoods: income from his land, his livestock, and from his son who was a newly appointed government employee at the time of interview.

Figure 6.8 Sustaining a poverty escape amidst insecurity and economic crises in Nigeria
Source: INT46-NG, female, sustained escape, peri-urban southern Nigeria, 2023 LHI.

More commonly, sustained escapers also referenced the worsening security situation, though they perceived this to affect the community more broadly rather than directly affecting them. They were in turn often guarded either through diversified livelihoods or through livelihood methods that were less susceptible to external influences. For example, INT17-AF (male, sustained escape, rural Afghanistan, 2021 LHI) observed that no one was willing to invest due to the security condition, as they feared abduction or losing their investment. However, his family had three teachers receiving salaries, while they also raised livestock and sold dairy products, which enabled them to weather the uncertain economic climate. In another example, INT14-AF noted:

> In the last few weeks, the Taliban closed the canal from Dahla dam. Most of the farmers and garden owners were worried that if they did not irrigate their gardens, they may lose them. After a lot of request[s] from the local people, the Taliban released the water … When there was no water in our canal, we used solar energy, but our neighbour was in a horrible situation. They did not have water to irrigate their land, and if in a week or so they did not irrigate their land and garden, most of the grape and pomegranate garden would die.
>
> (Male, sustained escape, urban Afghanistan, 2021 LHI)

For INT14-AF, solar energy that they had pre-violence was instrumental in providing self-sufficiency to irrigate their land during disruptions to the water supply. This is an important buffer in a context where traditional methods may be disrupted due to political or possibly environmental factors. It can support irrigation, also important during drought, as well as provide a supply of electricity including to charge mobile phones and support non-farm enterprises. Reducing dependency on these external systems, enabled in part through solar energy, has thus enabled INT14-AF to be less affected by macro-level crises and ensure stable income from their crops.

Social assistance and other forms of social support

Social support in Afghanistan has historically relied on a mix of formal and informal institutions. INT14-AF reflects on the stability that comes from kinship and community-based informal support structures reflecting a high degree of social cohesion and trust with neighbours that has implicitly offered him a safety net during his sustained escape from poverty:

> We have been living in this place for decades. It gives us a sort of social protection. When we or anyone else faces such a situation, we know better who is rich, who has money, and if we can borrow from them. Therefore, we have a social relationship with people and based on that social relationship, we fulfil our need and reduce our problem. For instance, if a person faces any serious illness, first he goes and borrows

> money from his relatives and friends for the treatment. If the illness is not very serious, he can go and buy medicine on credit and when he finds money will pay back his credit. My family has not faced such a situation. If I face with it, I will utilise my social relationship, as I did for my house construction.
>
> (INT14-AF, male, sustained escape, urban Afghanistan, 2021 LHI)

INT1-AF is a sustained escaper with some downward mobility, albeit not impoverishment—which can be attributed to strong social structures. On the one hand, he notes his wellbeing has deteriorated as his family is unable to irrigate their lands during the night due to petty crime and insecurity. He also reflects that the government did bring seeds in the past but not during cultivation season, and also that NGOs brought rice or other food for poor families including during COVID-19, but he did not benefit. Nevertheless, he has not fallen into poverty due to multiple income streams from irrigated farming and livestock rearing with dairy sold in markets. He positively reflects on the ability of his community to mediate conflicts. This role of strong informal institutions can implicitly be attributed to supporting a degree of social and economic stability:

> Thank God, I have not faced any economic problem, if there was any social issue or concern through consultation with each other we solved it accordingly. If there is any problem, like an argument or a fight between neighbours, or if any one hurt for using unwilling words or speeches, then we have collected the elders and solved the raised issue through gatherings and consultation with both parties.
>
> (INT1-AF, male, sustained escape, rural Afghanistan, 2021 LHI)

Yet with increasing violence pre-transition, much of the informal support structures were weakened. For example, INT16-AF (male, sustained escape, rural Afghanistan, 2021 pre-transition LHI) noted that the Taliban killed the head of their village who was otherwise providing jobs for many in the village and investing in the local economy (Box 6.2). He further noted that on account of other killings in the village, many wealthy families that also performed a social safety net function in the area ended up migrating away. This exodus stemming from violence was a double whammy, insofar as it led to a loss of financial assistance and wage labour in the village, in turn worsening the economic crises and plight of local residents.

Box 6.2 Weakened informal support structures during violence and political crisis in Afghanistan

The security situation has affected the head of the village [Malik]. He had two sons working as security guards with the president of Afghanistan. They had around 50,000 AFN as a salary each. As they had a fixed salary, Malik was working in his garden. Most of the time, he was hiring people for daily wage labour. As the security situation was getting worse, gunmen (Taliban) killed the head of our village and his son. As a result, only their son remained in the village, and the rest migrated to Kabul. The money that was coming to our village and was used as wage for wage labour has stopped ... They had around 17–18 guards; they were local people of this area, and now they are all jobless. They paid salaries, but they actually invested here; they built gardens of grapes and pomegranates and houses with their money. They had a trade of real estate; for instance, they used to buy plain land, build a grape garden or pomegranate, keep it for themselves, or sell to other people.

In the last couple of months, the Taliban has killed five or six people in our village. As a result, approximately ten wealthy people left our village. [A wealthy] family used to help poor people in every Eid and distributed charity both in cash and in-kind; for example, they distributed money equivalent to the price of six cows; to poor people. When there were people in need, the head of the family was supporting them. For example, many people who could not find the money for their wedding ceremonies asked for support from him, and he helped them.

In the same way, his wife was a very generous woman. When a person or a family did not have money for construction, she used to go to his house and pay money to such people. It was typical for them to pay for poor people's weddings and build houses for those in need. Still, when the husband got killed, all of them went to Kabul, and now no one is helping poor people. They were loved by locals.

Source: INT16-AF, male, sustained escape, rural Afghanistan, 2021 pre-transition LHI.

Since the political transition in 2021, formal social assistance in Afghanistan has been further curtailed from an already limited base. At present, most of the support is delivered through humanitarian assistance to food-insecure populations or specific groups—e.g. the UNHCR supporting IDPs, UNICEF focusing on child health, education and protection, the WFP providing food aid and cash-based transfers, and local NGOs also providing support across these areas (Diwakar et al., 2022a).

In contrast, in Nigeria, while government social assistance had limited coverage, it was still useful for those who were able to access it (Figure 6.9). Just one in ten households accessed social assistance in Borno in the leadup with the 2023 survey. There were variations in access according to type of conflict contributing to income loss: 17% of households (71 households) reporting that Boko Haram related violence contributed to asset or income loss received social assistance, compared to just 6% of households (36 households) affected by other types of conflict. Moreover, there was some evidence of social assistance reaching households experiencing both conflict- and

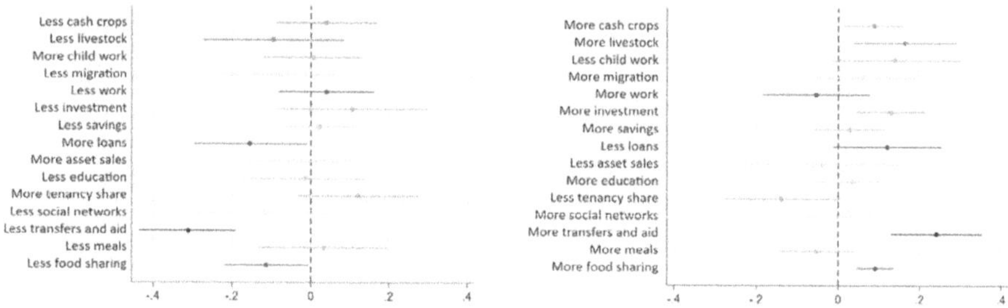

Figure 6.9 AME of social assistance receipt on negative (left) and more positive (right) coping responses to conflict amidst climate-related disasters
Source: analysis of Borno survey data, first presented in Diwakar et al. (2024).

climate-related disruptions, which could reflect the focus of humanitarian actors in country (Diwakar et al., 2024).

This is important because social assistance was associated with a higher probability of positive coping responses to conflict amidst climate-related disasters. For example, social assistance was associated with a lower probability of households relying on loans or sharing food, suggesting it is important in supporting households in meeting basic subsistence needs, even if it is less useful in driving more adaptive or promotive functions. For INT44 (Akwa Ibom, temporary impoverishment), the cash transfer in 2021 enabled her to avoid downward mobility towards destitution (Figure 6.10).

These forms of government or humanitarian assistance though remain scarce, and so are often substituted or complemented by other forms of social support. This includes mutual support from family members or neighbours in providing labour for farming or financial aid. Social norms around these mutual exchanges are important in this process. At the same time, these social support mechanisms may be under pressure when the intersections of crises amplify, which can in turn drive chronic poverty or prevent pathways out of poverty amidst polycrisis.

Moreover, in both countries, role of political favouritism in shaping access to support is strong. In Afghanistan, reports point to humanitarian aid being

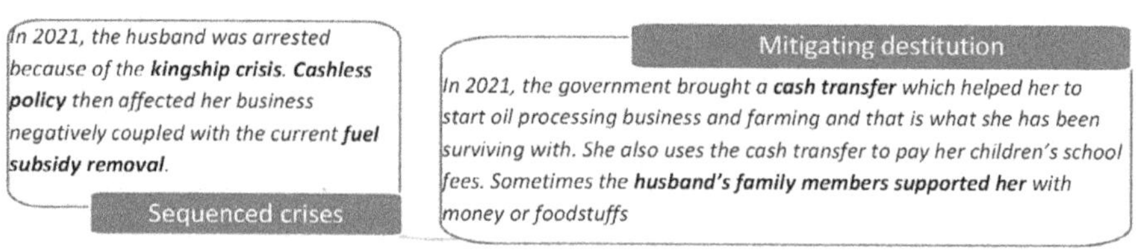

Figure 6.10 The role of cash transfers in mitigating destitution amongst the chronic poor
Source: INT6-NG, female, chronic poor, rural southern Nigeria, 2023 LHI, first presented in Diwakar et al. (2025).

Table 6.1 Summary of key regional differences based on analysis of FGDs and KIIs

Site	*Social assistance and other forms of support*
Borno (North East)	• More targeted support by government and NGOs to IDPs and women (e.g. through Npower). • Urban men and women outside of camps unable to access government support. • Government has strong control over humanitarian donor funding.
Benue (North Central)	• Support from government and private organisations in urban areas—e.g. school feeding, Npower. • Assistance from family in rural areas, no government support there. • Loans, grants, financial credit from government for women in urban areas.
Jigawa (North West)	• State as the darling of ruling federal political parties, urban support (Trader money, Npower, CCT), politicised. • Rural men lack support, rural women rely on associations and cooperatives.
Anambra (South East)	• Men rely on support from peers and family. • Women rely on NGOs (skill acquisition), family, and support from peer groups. • Poor networks hence limited government support.
Akwa Ibom (South South)	• Government aid politicised, diverted from urban areas. • Women support groups help fill the gap in urban areas. • State more adept at mobilising urban women than urban men.
Ekiti (South West)	• Palliative distribution involves preferential treatment. • Women rely on loans, previously used to receive government assistance. • Perception of failed promises by politicians.

Source: Abridged from Diwakar et al. (2025).

Note: M = men, F = women, Y = youth.

diverted to areas and groups seen as loyal to the regime (Elham et al., 2023). In Nigeria, our life history interviews pointed to support in some cases for those relatively better off, such as large commercial farmers rather than smallholder farmers receiving food aid, seeds and fertiliser after floods or drought. Key informant interviews also pointed to strong corruption and patronage networks dictating access to support (Abdulrasaq et al., 2025). This suggests that in Nigeria it may be less about regime loyalty and more around structural or implementer bias in favour of those moderately better off, including chiefs and friends of chiefs. What this means though is that poorer populations are often left out of recovery processes.

6.2.3 Demographic variations in livelihood-based pathways out of poverty

Afghanistan

In Afghanistan, of the six sustained escapers interviewed, two were women. Both were young adults and not the head of the household. Their families had sustained poverty escapes through adapting (proactively and reactively) to contexts of polycrisis. In both cases, like in Nigeria, women whose families had sustained poverty escapes noted the absence of violent conflict, reflecting their residence in a relatively safer part of their districts.

INT18-AF (female, sustained escape, urban Afghanistan, 2021 LHI) was living during a period of heightened insecurity in the country, alongside repeated drought and economic crises. She noted the absence of violent conflict though petty crimes were prevalent. In addition, during the pandemic and a period of heightened economic crises, the respondent noted that she was able to get information about COVID-19 from school. The social networks her family relied on, which previous to the pandemic had supported both asset development and crises response, were not strained due to the lockdown. Instead, neighbours and relatives continued to meet albeit respecting social distancing within the household. The space required for this within the household reflects a position of advantage already, emphasising the role of pre-crises asset development to maintain not only economic but also social resilience during crises.

In response to climate-related disasters overlaid with the pandemic and economic crises, the respondent's family adapted crop cultivation to focus more on wheat and rice after observing poor sales of other crops they had cultivated during the previous year. They also relied on well irrigation. Women's work within the household, in terms of livestock rearing and preparing its milk to sell in the bazaar, helped the family diversify income sources and ensure income during non-harvest times.

Box 6.3 Escaping poverty amidst polycrisis through knowledge-sharing, social networks and adaptation in Afghanistan

Knowledge-sharing during COVID-19 overlaid with economic crises:

> Economic problems have increased since the start of corona. Unemployment has increased, and prices of goods/groceries (food and other daily needs) have increased. We haven't faced any serious difficulty/problem due to corona … [but] it has created a fear in people's minds. People can't live comfortably due to fear of corona like before.
>
> Due to corona some things which were imported from out of the country became expensive as borders were closed, things like chemical fertiliser etc. … Our expenses increased, we have to provide more food, and there is disease and sickness to spend money on for its treatment.

We got most of the information about corona and protection methods through TV channels, and also I got information from school.

I don't know exactly about aid and support. We just heard that any NGO distributed hygienic kits in the community, something like soap etc. Also, I have heard from other areas that some NGO distribute wheat, rice or oil to poor families.

Trust-driven, kinship-based support systems:

[Neighbours and relatives] were coming into our house, but we were sitting far from each other to keep social distances.

My father and uncle built our house; they got a loan because of that. Also, they got a loan to take my father to India for treatment. He had a kind of disease in his chest. My uncles prepared money and took him to a doctor in India. [He] had trust in us that we would return it back.

Diversification and adaptability in response to polycrisis:

As [my parents and relatives] are farmers, their incomes are based on season... When there is not enough water, we can't get better harvests. The river water can't be reached due to drought, so we have to get water from wells. So, it needs electricity to get water for irrigation. So, there would be a big change in harvest and its price due to drought.

My father and uncles were mostly cultivating wheat, rice, tomato, millet, sesame, mung bean, etc. But since the start of corona they haven't cultivated more millet, sesame, and mung beans. As they were not able to sell them last year, it was not a good bazaar. This year they have cultivated more wheat and rice.

We have livestock too (cow), women take care of livestock beside household tasks. We get and make ready the milk to sell. Men have made a contract with a customer in a bazaar (trader who trades milk.).

Violent conflict avoidance, though petty crime prevails:

It is good now; there is no war here. There is robbery in the area. Thieves steal bicycles, motor bikes, or mobile phones.

Source: INT18-AF, female, sustained escape, urban Afghanistan, 2021.

Another interviewee, INT19-AF (female, sustained escape, rural Afghanistan, 2021 LHI), was also able to navigate COVID-19, economic crises and climate-related stressors drawing on a multi-income large household that constituted members with salaried employment and multiple farmers. Her family owns ten jerib (acres) of land and leases an additional ten jerib. On their land they grow wheat, rice, mug beans, tomatoes and sesame, mitigating against risk to certain crop failures. Strong intra-family cooperation—through working on the land together and sharing resources amongst their relatives such as to transport products to the market—coupled with relatively large landholding has enabled them to buffer against crises when they did strike. In many ways, INT19-AF was able to better navigate crises through these strong endowments, observed for example through the absence of crises being explicitly mentioned or reactive strategies drawn on.

Box 6.4 Escaping poverty during crises contexts through pre-existing social capital, multiple stable income streams and land in Afghanistan

Intra-family resource pooling:

> There are 12 people in our family, my father and mother-in-law, my two brothers-in-law, their wives, their children, my husband, me and my son. We all are living in our household ... We are happy that we all are living together happily and healthy.
>
> We have our own farm and men are busy with farming and agricultural activities... They cultivate rice, wheat, mung bean, sesame, tomato, egg-plant, etc. Our own farming land is about ten jerib, but we have taken other people's lands too in rent to work on. Total will be about 20 jerib.
>
> There is no obstacle to [taking harvests to the bazaar]. We have a three-wheel vehicle; they take all kinds of the products to the main bazaar and sell it there as wholesale.

Weathering market risks:

> [The men in the family] cultivated zucchini last year. It did not have a good market last year. So, they were not able to sell it in the market. They distributed unsold zucchini in neighbourhoods for free, because we were not able to keep them.
>
> Those who have their own farm, they are busy on it. They hire people as labour, whenever they need. There are people who are working as daily waged labour in the community or from other areas around here.

Multiple salaried income streams:

> Father-in-law is working as principal, but right now schools are off due to corona... I and my two sisters-in-law are school teachers ... I get my salary, but my sisters-in-law haven't gotten any salary yet, as they are honorary [contractual] teachers. They don't have any fixed salary.

Source: INT19-AF, female, sustained escape, rural Afghanistan, 2021 LHI.

Nigeria

The Nigerian qualitative sample interviewed more households, and at least partly as a result, there was a larger share of sustained escapers in the sample. Table 6.2 summarises variations in pathways out of poverty by gender and age across the six states in Nigeria in which qualitative data was collected by CPAN.

There are notable variations in women's pathways out of poverty in Nigeria, shaped by social norms and legal frameworks, particularly those governing land and asset inheritance. I then discuss why this is important to women's trajectories—e.g. inheritance rights are a critical factor influencing women's economic empowerment within households and can play a key role in accelerating downward mobility, especially following a husband's death or being divorced, or in providing capacity for sustained escape.

There are some notable variations in women's pathways out of poverty in Nigeria, shaped by existing socio-cultural norms and legal frameworks, especially those governing land and asset inheritance. This is important to women's trajectories. For example, inheritance rights governing who owns land or other assets are a critical factor influencing women's economic empowerment within households. These can be daughters inheriting from parents at dowry or parents' death, or women inheriting from husbands after death or divorce—each with quite different implications depending on the legal framework. Such rights can play a key role in supporting sustained escapes but also in accelerating downward mobility, especially following a husband's death or divorce.

On the former, despite the intensity of violence characterising crises intersections in the northeast, women in northern parts of the country under Sharia law have inheritance rights, albeit unequally divided (Oshodi, 2023). Women interviewees in northern states similarly mentioned property inheritance in narratives. Instead, southern Nigeria is governed by customary and statutory law. The former is often patrilineal, and in many communities, women are formally or informally excluded from inheriting land or property, which can amplify gender inequalities. At the same time, early and forced marriages are less common in these areas compared to the north, and education rates are also higher in the south, which together reflects a context of uneven inequalities marked by variations in legal and socio-cultural norms (Azubuike et al., 2024).

The qualitative data furthermore revealed differences in terms of social and economic connections between genders. Women's social networks were more easily mobilised than compared to men and often supported their absorptive capacities. INT65-NG (female, sustained escape, urban northern Nigeria, 2023 LHI) received cooperative loans for her business. This helped maintain her income diversification in times when her government salary (a job she secured through her uncle) was not regularly paid. However, as crises intersected or became prolonged, this reliance on social networks eroded as entire communities became increasingly and more deeply affected. Nevertheless, effect sizes between climate and conflict-related crises and social assistance receipt

Table 6.2 Summary of key regional differences based on analysis of FGDs and KIIs

Site	*Macro crises*	*Livelihood pathways out of poverty*
Borno (North East)	• Boko Haram insurgency • Fuel subsidy removal • Covid-19 • Cashless policy	• M: construction (but lost due to violence), trade, mechanics, cattle fattening • F: farming, livestock, bricklaying, inheritance, restaurants • Y: motorcycle, construction, farm labour, water vending, sewing, car wash
Benue (North Central)	• Floods • Inter-communal conflict • Farmer–herder violence • Kidnapping, drugs, crime • Fuel subsidy removal	• M: civil service especially in urban areas, business, migration • F: community contribution to provide social amenities, cooperatives, rent land, farm • Y: cash transfers, access to capital, urban migration
Jigawa (North West)	• Flooding • Displacement • Border closures • Covid-19 • Cashless policy • Fuel subsidy removal	• M: farming, business, inheritance • F: loans, credit, some support through children begging • Y: tailoring, carpentry, etc, motorcycle, farming, used as political thugs by politicians
Anambra (South East)	• Communal clashes • Farmer–herder violence • Fraud/crime • Urban flooding • Fuel price hikes	• M: Urban transport e.g. motorcycles, roads to market farm produce or sell water, apprenticeship • F: petty trading (state support to access loan facilities), inheritance, farming • Y: yahoo yahoo, government jobs in security, apprentice

Site	*Macro crises*	*Livelihood pathways out of poverty*
Akwa Ibom (South South)	• Fuel subsidy removal • Communal conflicts affecting rural lands	• M: Sell land and start business—constrained with fuel subsidy removal • F: Migration, domestic care • Y: multiple jobs (including crime), domestic work
Ekiti (South West)	• Banditry • Flooding in rural areas • Covid-19 • Fuel subsidy, especially in urban areas • Cashless policy	• M: water and chalk industries, civil service, seasonal jobs and street selling, banditry • F: dependent on loans, trade, labour at construction sites • Y: government jobs, street selling

Source: Abridged from Diwakar et al. (2025).

Note: M = men, F = women, Y = youth.

were higher for women-headed households (Diwakar et al., 2024), which may help somewhat cushion the decline in social support during polycrisis.

Instead, economic connections were often more accessible for men that enabled their adaptation during polycrisis. For example, men more commonly reported receiving information that enabled them to withdraw money prior to the implementation of the cashless policy. Similarly, INT3-NG (female, impoverished, peri-urban southern Nigeria, 2023 LHI) reflected that if her husband were alive, he would have been able to provide her with current information about things.

There are some exceptions to this, albeit rare. INT46-NG (female, sustained escape, peri-urban southern Nigeria, 2023 LHI) experienced a series of conflict and economic crises (Figure 6.11). Her diversified income and spousal collaboration helped prevent impoverishment. She also received early information about the cashless policy, which meant that she was able to withdraw money from the bank in advance of the policy implementation. Her bank account ownership and access to an ATM also helped in this context. However, even here, it may be that the INT46-NG received the information through her husband, where again spousal collaboration in the form of information sharing becomes critical.

Men more generally in the qualitative data though tended to have more diverse livelihood pathways out of poverty, for example through migration to the capital especially with some start-up capital, welding, farming, painting, and employment in NGOs. Young men, in particular, often had various jobs that they combined in pathways out of poverty. In some cases, this included crime ("yahoo yahoo" fraud) alongside farm labour and migration. In most cases, there remained a strong dependence on farming, even amongst those who had migrated to urban areas. Farming on their own land, government-owned land or leased land offered a cushion to economic crises and enabled a degree of subsistence to be achieved in times of distress, as noted in Chapter 3. However, as noted there, there were equally challenges to farming, not least climate-related disasters and common theft and violence occurring often in homes or on farmland.

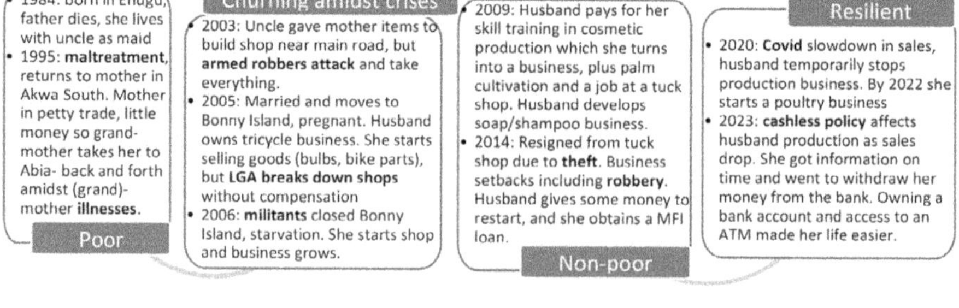

Figure 6.11 Resilience amidst a series of shocks and crises
Source: INT46-NG, female, sustained escape, peri-urban southern Nigeria, 2023 LHI.

6.3 Conclusion

This chapter examined different coping mechanisms adopted by individuals and households in response to crises, disaggregated by the intersections of crises as well as the poverty trajectories of households. It pointed to a range of low-risk to erosive forms of coping, the latter responsible for driving the intergenerational persistence of poverty and reinforcing the poverty–polycrisis trap. In Afghanistan and Nigeria, being compelled to draw down on human development by reducing spending on education and health or withdrawing children from school was relatively more pronounced at the intersection of the triple crises, while they were relatively absent in other countries, indicating that these erosive responses are heightened in the most challenging of humanitarian contexts. At the same time, a degree of normalisation of crises, prompting people to develop long-term coping mechanisms that involves investment in future investment, may undermine the salience and severity of more adverse or erosive coping responses identified in the survey data. There are also examples of economic "winners" during crisis who may take advantage of situations that negatively affect people in and near poverty during times of need.

The chapter then considered pathways out of poverty amidst crises. It identified the critical role of education, especially at lower secondary levels, in supporting sustained poverty escapes in spite of polycrisis. Alongside this, livelihood strategies such as climate-smart agriculture and off-farm diversification, underpinned by regular economic and social adaptation helped navigate rapid change during crises. This type of strategy speaks to ex-ante dimensions of coping responses alongside adaptive strategies that involve continuous experimentation. More broadly, the role of supportive institutions and services of a multi-sectoral nature—such as through DRR and WASH—were also highlighted as strengthening this ex-ante coping drawing on insights from mixed methods evaluation data in Bangladesh.

Women, faced with additional legal and socio-cultural norms that restrict equal access to assets through inheritance or other forms of adverse gender norms oftentimes navigated pathways out of poverty within the parameters of patriarchy. They "played by the rules", and in this process relied on a small select set of trusted networks—including kinship-based support systems—alongside making use of time-sensitive opportunities that could support upward mobility. Spousal collaboration in these contexts alongside wider intra-family resource pooling was also instrumental, as was the role of assets over which this support was structured—especially land, notable for its cushioning effects when other capacities fail.

Interestingly, the chapter also reflects an implicit balance between risk exposure and risk mitigation, reflecting insights from the presence of crises and institutional coping responses outlined in Chapter 2. For example, sustained escapers or those who were never in poverty in Niger either did not speak of climate-related disasters in their life histories or otherwise received support that helped mitigate its effects. Similarly, there was a relative absence of direct violence experienced by interviewees in Nigeria, and households who did experience violence or insecurity in Nigeria and Afghanistan also benefitted from formal or informal support structures. There is however strong heterogeneity to these experiences, with individuals experiencing multiple sources of vulnerability (i.e. intersecting inequalities) often amongst the most affected and with especially constrained means of recovery.

The next chapter builds on this last point, drawing attention to institutional responses to polycrisis to balance the focus up to now largely on individual and household strategies to cope with crises and maintain wellbeing.

Note

1 The PPI, hosted by IPA, estimates the likelihood of a household living in poverty based on a series of ten questions about household assets and characteristics.

References

Abdulrasaq, K., Walker, J.-A., Ukpai, S. and Diwakar, V. (2025) 'Political perspectives of social assistance amidst economic shocks in Nigeria'. *BASIC Research Briefing 7*. Institute of Development Studies. doi:10.19088/IDS.2025.043.

Azubuike, B., Browne, W.J. and Leckie, G. (2024) 'State and wealth inequalities in foundational literacy and numeracy skills of secondary school-aged children in Nigeria: A multilevel analysis'. *International Journal of Educational Development*, 110. doi:10.1016/j.ijedudev.2024.103112.

Baulch, B. (2011) *Why poverty persists: Poverty dynamics in Asia and Africa*. Edward Elgar.

Bird, K., Diwakar, V., Manjengwa, J., Pindiriri, C., Chamunogwa, A., Ndlovu, N. (2023a). 'Understanding poverty dynamics in Zimbabwe in the context of COVID-19'. *CPAN National Report*. CPAN. https://devhubuk.org/zimbabwe/.

Bird, K., Diwakar, V., Roth, V., San, S., Sean, C., Shepherd, A. (2023b) 'Cambodia Poverty Dynamics and Covid-19'. *CPAN National Report*. Institute of Development Studies. doi:10.19088/CPAN.2023.012.

Bird, K., Higgins, K. and McKay, A. (2010) 'Conflict, education and the intergenerational transmission of poverty in Northern Uganda'. *Journal of International Development*, 22(8): 1183–1196.

Brugh., W., Sorokin, G. and Scott, G.R. (2019) 'Combining formal and informal structures in crisis response'. In National Academy of Engineering, *Frontiers of engineering: Reports on leading-edge engineering from the 2018 symposium*. National Academies Press. https://www.ncbi.nlm.nih.gov/books/NBK538717/.

CPAN PMI (2020) 'Nepal Covid-19 Poverty Monitor: December 2020'. *CPAN*. https://www.chronicpovertynetwork.org/covid19-poverty-monitor/nepal-december-2020.

CPAN PMI (2021) 'Ethiopia Covid-19 Poverty Monitor: August 2021'. *CPAN*. https://www.chronicpovertynetwork.org/covid19-poverty-monitor/ethiopia-august.

CPAN PMI (2022) 'India Covid-19 Poverty Monitor: January 2022'. *CPAN*. https://www.chronicpovertynetwork.org/covid19-poverty-monitor/india-january.

da Corta, L. and Bwalya, R. (2025) 'Rural pathways out of poverty'. *CPAN Evidence paper*. Institute of Development Studies. doi:10.19088/CPAN.2025.002.

da Corta, L., Diarra, A., Diwakar, V., Harouna, A. and Poggi, C. (2021) 'Youth inclusion in labour markets in Niger: Gender dynamics and livelihoods'. CPAN. https://www.chronicpovertynetwork.org/resources/2021/6/29/youth-inclusion-in-labour-markets-in-niger-gender-dynamics-and-livelihoods.

da Corta, L., Scott, L., Eichsteller, M. and Gondwe, A. (2018) 'Resilience and sustainable poverty escapes in Malawi'. USAID. https://www.chronicpovertynetwork.org/resources/2019/2/18/resilience-and-sustainable-poverty-escapes-in-malawi-national-report.

Diwakar, V. (2022) 'Welfare of young adults amidst Covid19, conflict, and disasters: Evidence from Afghanistan'. *CPAN working paper*. CPAN.

Diwakar, V. (2025) 'Poverty dynamics amidst intersecting crises in Tanzania'. *DEEP working paper*. DEEP. https://povertyevidence.org/resources/poverty-dynamics-amidst-intersecting-crises-in-tanzania/.

Diwakar, V. and Adedeji, A. (2021) 'Poverty dynamics and social protection in Nigeria'. *CPAN working paper*. CPAN. https://www.chronicpovertynetwork.org/resources/2021/6/28/poverty-dynamics-and-social-protection-in-nigeria.

Diwakar, V. and Brzezinska, I. (2023) 'Poverty dynamics amidst multiple crises in Nigeria'. *DEEP working paper 17*. Oxford Policy Management.

Diwakar, V. and Brzezinska, I. (2024) 'Poverty dynamics amidst multiple crises in rural Bangladesh'. *DEEP working paper 22*. Oxford Policy Management.

Diwakar, V., Adedeji, A., Nwosu, E., Obaniyi, F. and Udora, C. (2024) 'Social assistance and coping with crises in Borno, Nigeria'. *BASIC Research Working Paper 31*. Institute of Development Studies. doi:10.19088/BASIC.2024.019.

Diwakar, V., Ghafoori, I. and Nemat, O. (2022a) 'Vulnerability in Afghanistan before and during the shift in power'. *CPAN working paper*. CPAN.

Diwakar, V., Kamninga, T., Mehzabin, T., Tumusiime, E., Kamal, R. and Pabony, N.A. (2022b) 'Sustaining escapes from ultra-poverty: A mixed methods assessment of layered interventions in coastal Bangladesh'. *CPAN working paper*. CPAN. https://www.chronicpovertynetwork.org/resources/2022/9/7/sustaining-escapes-from-ultra-poverty-a-mixed-methods-assessment-of-layered-interventions-in-coastal-bangladesh.

Diwakar, V., Walker, J.-A., Turnwait, M., Eichsteller, M. and Adeniran, A.P. (2025) 'Poverty dynamics and social assistance amidst intersecting crises in Nigeria'. *BASIC Research Working Paper 35*. Institute of Development Studies. doi:10.19088/BASIC.2025.004.

Elham, M., Atef, S. and Hashemi, S. (2023). 'How the Taliban pilfer humanitarian aid'. *Zan Times*, 24 April. https://zantimes.com/2023/04/24/zan-times-exclusive-how-the-taliban-pilfer-humanitarian-aid/.

Eshetu, F. and Mekonnen, E. (2016) 'Determinants of off farm income diversification and its effect on rural household poverty in Gamo Gofa Zone, Southern Ethiopia'. *Journal of Development and Agricultural Economics*, 8(10): 215–227. doi:10.5897/JDAE2016-0736.

Faruk, A. (2022) 'CLEAR Programme Quarterly Reporting January–March 2022: Covid-19 and Bangladesh: Livelihoods, Coping, and Support. PPRC–BIGD Round 4 Panel Survey'. *CLEAR Programme*.

FEWS NET (2022) 'Zimbabwe food security outlook: February to September 2022'. https://fews.net/sites/default/files/documents/reports/ZW_FSO_Feb2022_Final.pdf.

Fishtein, P. (2014) 'Despair or hope: Rural livelihoods and opium poppy dynamics in Afghanistan'. *EU.* https://opendata.uni-halle.de/bitstream/1981185920/110273/151/820708658.pdf.

Gough, I. and Wood, G. (2004) *Insecurity and welfare regimes in Asia, Africa and Latin America: Social policy in development contexts.* Cambridge University Press.

Guermond, V., Parsons, L., Ly Vouch, L., Brickell, K., Michiels, S., Fay, G. (2022) 'Microfinance, over-indebtedness and climate adaptation: New evidence from rural Cambodia'. https://static1.squarespace.com/static/62f2cf0e5c1d785dc4090f66/t/6327baac4be25f1d0d3ec013/1663548086338/Microfinance-over-indebtedness-and-climate-adaptation_English.pd.

Hassen, T.B. and El Bilali, H. (2024) 'Three years into the pandemic: Insights of the COVID-19 impacts on food security and nutrition in low and middle-income countries'. *Heliyon*, 10(7). doi:10.1016/j.heliyon.2024.e28946.

Haushofer, J. and Fehr, E. (2014) 'On the psychology of poverty'. *Science*, 344(6186): 862–867. doi:10.1126/science.1232491.

Heltberg, R., Hossain, N., Reva, A. and Turk, C. (2012) 'Coping and resilience during the food, fuel, and financial crises'. *The Journal of Development Studies*, 49(5): 705–718. doi:10.1080/00220388.2012.746668.

Huot, D. and Pain, A. (2017) 'Afghanistan livelihood trajectories: Life on the margins in Sar-i-Pul Province'. *SLRC Working Paper 54.* Secure Livelihoods Research Consortium.

IPA (2020) 'Zambia RECOVR survey analysis'. https://poverty-action.org/sites/default/files/Zambia-RECOVR-Survey-Analysis.pdf.

Kayula, M., Odoyo, C.O. and Sichinsambwe, C. (2022) 'Effects of crop insurance and finance on smallscale maize productivity in Zambia'. *International Business Research*, 15(10): 1–48. doi:10.5539/ibr.v15n10p48.

Kohrt, B.A. and Kaiser, B.N. (2021) 'Measuring mental health in humanitarian crises: A practitioner's guide to validity'. *Confl. Health*, 15: 72. doi:10.1186/s13031-021-00408-y.

Kristoffersen, I., Hoang, D. and Li, I.W. (2024) 'Understanding the mental health-based poverty trap: Dynamics in psychological distress and financial precariousness, and the role of self-efficacy'. *Journal of Behavioral and Experimental Economics*, 111. doi:10.1016/j.socec.2024.102219.

Lund, C., Breen, A., Flisher, A.J., Kakuma, R., Corrigall, J., Joska, J.A. (2010) 'Poverty and common mental disorders in low and middle income countries: A systematic review'. *Soc. Sci. Med.*, 71(3): 517–528.

Maynard, J. L. (2019) 'Ideology and armed conflict'. *Journal of Peace Research*, 56(5): 635–649. doi:10.1177/0022343319826629.

Nemat, O., Diwakar, V., Ghafoori, I. and Azadmanesh, S. (2022) 'Livelihoods and welfare amidst layered crises in Afghanistan'. *IDS Bulletin*, 53(3).

Novelli, M. and Selenica, E. (2014) 'Protecting higher education from attack'. UNESCO. https://www.researchgate.net/profile/Ervjola-Selenica/publication/356187892_Protecting_higher_education_from_attack/links/618fc7ae61f09877209070e8/Protecting-higher-education-from-attack.pdf.

O'Malley, B. (2010) 'The longer-term impact of attacks on education on education systems, development and fragility and the implications for policy responses'. Education for All Global Monitoring Report. https://protectingeducation.org/wp-content/uploads/documents/documents_efa_unesco_-_the_longer_term_impact_of_attacks.pdf.

Oshodi, M. (2023) 'The inheritance rights of women in Nigeria'. https://www.iawj.org/content.aspx?page_id=2507&club_id=882224&item_id=4986.

Pain, A. (2011) 'Opium poppy strikes back: The 2011 return of opium in Balkh and Badakhshan Provinces'. Afghanistan Research and Evaluation Unit.

Phiri, M. (2021) 'Zimbabwe's high-risk cross-border trade'. *Inter-Press News Agency*, 4 November. www.ipsnews.net/2021/11/zimbabwes-high-risk-cross-border-trade.

Rahman, H.Z., Rahman, A., Islam, M.S., Faruk, A., Matin, I., Wazed, M.A. (2022) 'Recovery with distress: Unpacking COVID-19 impact on livelihoods and poverty in Bangladesh'. *WIDER Working Paper 2022/13*. UNU-WIDER. doi:10.35188/UNU-WIDER/2022/144-0.

Ridley, M., Rao, G., Schilbach, F. and Patel, V. (2020) 'Poverty, depression, and anxiety: Causal evidence and mechanisms'. *Science*, 370(6522). doi:10.1126/science.aay0214.

Schutte, S. (2009) 'Informal (in)security in urban Afghanistan'. *Iranian Studies*, 42(3): 465–491.

Shepherd, A., Bwalya, R., Chapoto, C., da Corta, L., Eichsteller, M., Diwakar, V. (2025) 'Zambian poverty dynamics and climate resilience: A growing policy agenda through a period of crises'. *CPAN national report*. CPAN.

Stewart, F., Diwakar, V. and Samman, E. (2018) 'The relationship between human development and economic growth'. In F. Stewart, G. Ranis and E. Samman (Eds.), *Advancing human development: Theory and practice*. Oxford University Press.

Ullah, R. and Shivakoti, G.P. (2014) 'Adoption of on-farm and off-farm diversification to manage agricultural risks: Are these decisions correlated?' *Outlook on Agriculture*, 43(4): 265–271. doi:10.5367/oa.2014.0188.

UNICEF (2021) 'The State of the World's Children 2021: On My Mind – Promoting, protecting and caring for children's mental health'. https://www.unicef.org/media/114636/file/SOWC-2021-full-report-English.pdf.

UNODC (2023) 'Afghanistan opium survey 2023'. *UNODC Research brief.* https://www.unodc.org/documents/crop-monitoring/Afghanistan/Afghanistan_opium_survey_2023.pdf.

Woldehanna, T., Tafere, Y. and Yonis, M.B. (2022) 'Social capital as a double-edged sword for sustained poverty escapes in Ethiopia'. *World Development*, 158. doi:10.1016/j.worlddev.2022.105969.

Part III

From evidence to action: policy and programmatic pathways

7 Centring equity and risk in institutional responses to polycrisis

This chapter is a departure from the preceding chapters that were focused on mixed methods research on poverty dynamics amidst polycrisis. The focus of this chapter instead is to identify the extent to which policies and programmes have begun to adopt a framing better suited to those polycrisis in terms of responding to various sources of risk while not compromising equity in this process. In doing so, the intent is to help identify components of a new architecture that helps better account for the complexity and uncertainty of lived experiences in pathways into and out of poverty amidst polycrisis.

To assess the current state of evidence on polycrisis responses, this chapter is organised around a practice-oriented framing relevant to working on poverty eradication amidst crises. Section 7.1 distinguishes policies and programmes that work without considering the presence of polycrisis (i.e. "despite" polycrisis) and may cause harm, those that work "in" polycrisis by doing no harm and being sensitive to contexts of crises, and those that more effectively work "on" polycrisis by tackling root causes and systems that perpetuate poverty amidst crises. In relation to the conceptual model developed in Chapter 2, the focus is especially on institutional strategies to help individuals and households cope before, during and after crises, across socio-economic and environmental entry points. The chapter argues that most examples that work "despite" or "in" polycrisis typically fall under survival or risk-mitigation strategies. Working "on" polycrisis, however, takes us to interventions with more transformative potential.

To operationalise this framing of working "despite", "in" and "on" polycrisis, the chapter presents policy and programme examples of responses to polycrisis in the countries covered in preceding chapters. The relative absence of evaluations of these policies and programmes, many of which are ongoing, means that this analysis is limited to focus on the design rather than implementation and outcomes of interventions. Sections 7.2 and 7.3 examine traditional policy entry points to responding to risks, namely through social protection, disaster risk management, and the humanitarian–development–peace nexus (including links to resilience programming), to consider the extent to which these may be well placed to equitably respond to polycrisis. Section 7.4 then considers the largely

DOI: 10.4324/9781003503125-10

neglected recovery arm of programming, critically important to strengthen in contexts of polycrisis. Finally, Section 7.5 discusses overarching reflections based on these examples and concludes.

7.1 Working "despite", "in" and "on" polycrisis

Figure 7.1 is organised around three categories of poverty reduction strategies: those that work "despite", "in" or "on" polycrisis. It recognises that some poverty eradication policies or programmes implemented in polycrisis may not address crises at all. In other cases, where they do address singular hazards, responses may inadvertently drive the emergence of new crises. For example, during the COVID-19 pandemic, people participating in social protests were arrested in the Philippines and Zimbabwe, with the reason provided being the need to curb the spread of the virus. However, in many cases, "the root causes of social unrest remained unaddressed or even worsened" (Hilhorst and Mena, 2021). Similarly, efforts to move populations to shelters during floods or typhoons had the risk of increasing COVID-19 transmission rates where these were not accompanied by social distancing (Janzwood, 2020). This means that strategies that work "despite" polycrisis can be ineffective or even cause harm, driving further impoverishment and chronic poverty. Recognising accordingly that working "despite" polycrisis is inherently inadequate and moreover often harmful, our focus now turns to working "in" and "on" polycrisis.

Working "in" polycrisis contexts requires aspiring to the basic principle of "do no harm" by developing a deep understanding of intersecting crises, appraising harm including by anticipating potential spillovers, and grounding interventions in strong local knowledge. Most programme designers *intend* to uphold the principle of "do no harm" but often do not fully consider the possible spillover effects—either due to limited understanding of polycrisis dynamics, or simply because they are less familiar with the local context.

The point about understanding and responding to the root causes of social unrest across gradations of vulnerability and poverty is especially important

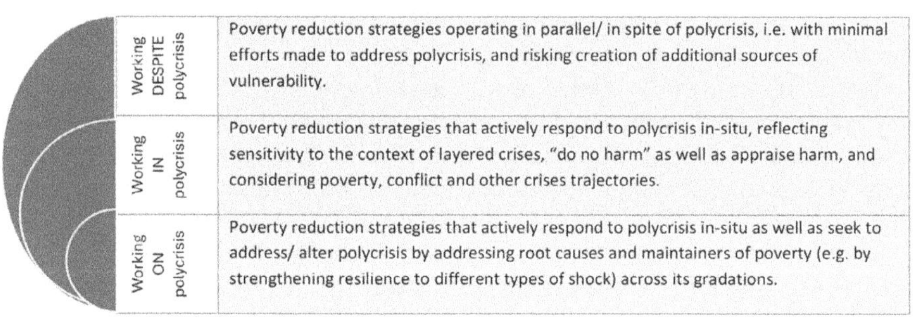

Figure 7.1 Working DESPITE, IN and ON polycrisis
Source: Diwakar (2023).

and moves us towards a focus of working "on" polycrisis, which can help address some of the programmatic and policy gaps noted above. Gradations of poverty and vulnerability place emphasis on the heterogeneity of experiences in and near the poverty line due to multiple, often intersecting sources of disadvantage, rather than homogenising "the poor". Responding to these gradations in turn requires a much deeper reading of local histories, social tensions and different forms of inequalities than is often available to implementers. In its absence, policies may in some cases operate as a band-aid by providing one-size-fits-all short-term relief while neglecting the underlying root causes of poverty and vulnerability. For example, interventions that attempt to mitigate elite capture of food aid in response to climate-related disasters and conflict can have limited long-term sustainability if not accompanied by peacebuilding to help mitigate the sources of violent conflict. Nevertheless, these policy responses are common across the 15 countries studied in this book.

The next section first examines cases of working "in" polycrisis and then differentiates these from projects that more ambitiously work "on" polycrisis to support poverty reduction and break the poverty–polycrisis trap.

7.2 Policy entry points to climate-related disasters and COVID-19 and its legacy effects

7.2.1 Working "in" polycrisis: adapting DRM and COVID-19 programming for agility

DRM holds significant potential for responding to climate and other crises. Indeed, the Sendai Framework for Disaster Risk Reduction 2015–30 recognises threats and hazards including societal threats (ISC and UNDRR, 2020) providing policy backing for this entry point. Some countries reflect this approach in their responses to polycrisis, though these instances are rare. For example, Cambodia's disaster risk response through the National Committee for Disaster Management differentiates by whether the disaster relates to climate or is caused by humans. This committee was operationalised to mobilise a response to the pandemic, facilitated by the leadership of the Prime Minister and including provincial and commune level committees with local leadership (Diwakar et al., 2023).

Even where it was not explicitly set out in mandates of disaster management agencies, some countries starting to more flexibly work "in" climate-related disasters and COVID-19, by integrating COVID-19 considerations into DRM (more frequently) or vice versa (less frequently). Bangladesh adapted the Cyclone Preparedness Programme to include messaging through public announcements and digital platforms, with the dissemination of information combining disaster-related early warning with COVID-19 prevention and protection (Lux, 2020). The country's Disasters Emergencies Committee also focused on WASH-related messaging, which though targeted to the pandemic, can also help reduce the spread of vector-borne diseases during flooding (Diwakar et al., 2023). Nepal similarly relied on DRM funds to respond to the COVID-19 pandemic through distributing face masks and awareness-raising campaigns (Allan et al., 2020), though a challenge is that this may crowd out other disasters where resources are limited or the institutional focus might shift. Finally, in the Philippines, in response to Typhoon Rolly in November 2020 the government instead used the Covid-19 Adjustment Measures Program as a vehicle to deliver support (Farhat and Borja, 2021).

Also, in Bangladesh as well as India, a composite risk matrix was developed as a more ambitious design response considering both COVID-19 and Cyclone Amphan in May 2020. As noted in Box 7.1, this resulted in the development of dispersed evacuation shelters during the cyclone (Potutan and Arakida, 2021). Box 7.1 represents an example of integrating polycrisis responses into the design of interventions. This is likely to become increasingly necessary as the frequency of polycrisis escalates.

Box 7.1 Composite risk matrix to design multi-hazard programming in South Asia

During Cyclone Amphan in 2020, a composite risk matrix approach was developed, which included the impact parameters of the cyclone, as well as those of COVID-19. This helped design a complex system of evacuation shelters for 3 million people, informed by specific vulnerabilities (Srivastava, 2020). Additional support was required because Cyclone Amphan and floods were identified as increasing the risk of COVID-19 transmission (Donoghoe et al., 2022). During the response, the significant advance warning to the cyclone, combined with impact-based forecasts, allowed authorities in India and Bangladesh to repurpose shelters as quarantine facilities in some cases. Where the risk of COVID-19 transmission was high, shelters were half full to facilitate social distancing, whereas shelters in areas with highest exposure to the cyclone operated at full capacity. Ultimately, impact-based, risk-informed early warning systems guided the complex response, including a large-scale evacuation, which saved lives (Srivastava, 2020).

Source: Diwakar et al. (2023).

The composite risk matrix design informed by specific vulnerabilities as highlighted in Box 7.1 requires localised knowledge of population risk profiles as well as access to at-risk groups. This can be supported through interventions that are led by or engage centrally with local actors. In Nepal, community disaster management committees similarly had gender-disaggregated data on groups vulnerable to hazards and at high risk from COVID-19, including older people, pregnant and lactating women, children, and persons with disabilities (Okura et al., 2020). Similarly, women's rights organisations in Bangladesh had access to the Chittagong Hill Tracts area to reach communities otherwise excluded from support on account of the government regulations imposed in terms of accessing these areas (Njeri and Daigle, 2022; Feminist Humanitarian Network and Partners, 2021).

The examples so far are from South and Southeast Asia, where DRM or COVID-19 support was leveraged to respond to polycrisis. In regions of Africa, this similar type of mobilisation through DRM or social protection was relatively rare during the pandemic. For example, though DRM agencies in Kenya were mobilised to deal with the pandemic, this took place much later into the response, with no post-disaster recovery plan (AU and UNDP, 2022).

7.2.2 Working "in" polycrisis through social protection

Alongside DRR, social protection is another entry point sometimes leveraged to respond to climate-related disasters, COVID-19 and their legacy effects of lingering economic crises such as high inflation. In some contexts, social protection is not only a tool for mitigating household-level vulnerability but is also strategically used by governments to reinforce state legitimacy and demonstrate accountability (Ferguson, 2015; Hickey, 2011) at a time where these elements may be stressed.

Cambodia perhaps had one of the clearest responses identified to both flooding and inflation through social protection. The government in late 2022 expanded its cash transfer coverage into a multi-phase programme to target "at-risk" groups near the poverty line with the following criteria:

> [H]ome to a disabled person, [have] one child under 2 years old, elders older than 60 years old, if a woman is the only breadwinner and is living without a husband, and if there are no members between 19 and 59 years old.
>
> (Seavmey, 2022)

Under its flood response, 16 provinces were targeted with households receiving US$20 on three occasions between 2022 and 2023, alongside an additional US$4 per at-risk member. To mitigate rising inflation, at-risk groups were given cash subsidies of US$20–25 per household, and an additional US $5–7 per household member, with slight variation depending on area of residence (Seavmey, 2022).

Evidence from programme outcomes pointed to the transfer being viewed as highly useful, spent most commonly to purchase food, and perhaps as a result levelling off differences in food security between recipients and non-recipients. By the end of the programme, late loan repayments had also decreased for programme participants (General Secretariat for National Social Protection Council, 2024; UNDP, 2024b).

While the example from Cambodia illustrates a direct response to ongoing climate and economic crisis, other countries have also adapted social protection systems to have a "shock-responsive" element that enables scaling vertically and/or horizontally during crises. Some of these also adjust the value of transfers to account for inflation. For example, Malawi's Social Cash Transfer

Program anticipates food inflation during lean seasons and climate shocks, and in response seeks to improve the sensitivity of the programme to unanticipated climate-related and other shocks. It does this by expanding the programme vertically and horizontally during shocks—including top-up transfers paid before and during the lean season—and introducing a mechanism to regularly adjust transfer values to account for inflation (Government of Malawi, 2022).

In other cases, existing programmes may be repurposed for other crises as they emerge. Zambia's COVID-19 Emergency Response and Health Systems Preparedness Project was restructured to address crises relating to cholera and drought as well (World Bank, 2022). This is similar to the example from the Philippines discussed above where COVID-19 mechanisms were reoriented to respond to climate-related disasters. However, a key distinction is that the response in Zambia's case was not purely to reactively address the crisis, but also to more holistically respond to its underlying drivers. Zambia used existing structures in place for WASH support during the COVID-19 period to later address the country's cholera outbreak in 2023 and drought in 2023–24. For example, the project supported WASH in health facilities and drilled boreholes to improve access to water. Project documentation noted the importance of this "as the scarcity of safe water sources during droughts often compels individuals to turn to unsafe alternatives like shallow wells, heightening the risk of waterborne illnesses such as cholera" (World Bank, 2022, 2024b).

All of the examples so far draw attention to working "in" rather than "on" polycrisis. The latter would instead require responding to structural conditions or root causes driving poverty amidst these polycrisis. We now turn to such examples of working "on" polycrisis amidst climate-related disasters and economic crises. Effective responses need to work both *in* (being context-sensitive and doing no harm) and *on* polycrisis (tackling structural drivers) in a more layered approach such that understanding context and addressing root causes go together.

7.2.3 Working "on" polycrisis through multi-sectoral resilience-building interventions

As noted above, working "on" polycrisis represents a higher ambition with more transformative potential as it addresses underlying vulnerabilities that can create crisis-like conditions in the first place. Examples of working "on" polycrisis are often found in programmes that target resilience-building. A multi-sectoral graduation programme in Bangladesh illustrates this (Box 7.2). As another example, India's Resilient Kerala Program (2021–28) seeks to strengthen resilience of the state to disaster and disease outbreaks (World Bank, 2024c). Its activities include fiscal and debt management, disaster risk finance and social protection support (inclusive of risk insurance and adaptive safety net programmes for select vulnerable groups such as fisherfolk), risk-informed urban planning and DRM, and strengthening key economic sectors including public health systems. The project documentation recognises substantial macroeconomic risk due to the COVID-19 crisis, which motivates its macroeconomic management plan within its resilience-building activities. This could be a model to be followed elsewhere and represents an attempt for structurally transformative programming through its whole-of-government approach, reconfiguring planning to deal with future shocks, and its focus on anticipatory action.

Box 7.2 Nobo Jatra's multi-sectoral graduation programme in Bangladesh

Impoverishment in rural Bangladesh over the last decade has been driven by climate-related shocks, ill-health, and more recently COVID-19. Nobo Jatra—a USAID funded activity implemented by World Vision in southwest Bangladesh between 2015 and 2022—combined ultra-poor graduation (UPG) programming with inclusive market systems development, climate-related DRR and WASH interventions. The layering of these interventions was found to improve participants' absorptive and adaptive resilience capacities in ways that helped tackle chronic poverty, including during the period of the pandemic during which the intervention continued to be implemented. DRR training and mobilising and WASH infrastructure also helped improve participants' absorptive and anticipatory resilience capacities and make them less susceptible to income loss and poverty during the pandemic.

Even so, other sources of ill health continued to impoverish. Moreover, "while many respondents were able to escape ultra-poverty through livestock development, there were continued challenges of DRR in the context of flood-related livestock deaths and widely prevalent livestock disease, despite improved veterinary support services." This suggests that there is scope to expand DRM responses to further "focus on livestock amid floods and cyclones ... [through] livestock insurance and access to shelters for livestock during disasters", and to better respond to a wider array of ill health in multi-sectoral graduation programmes.

Source: extracted from Diwakar et al. (2022).

Similarly, Zimbabwe's Resilience Building Fund (Phase 1 from 2017–21, and Phase 2 from 2023–27) was designed as an umbrella programme including interventions to respond to COVID-19, drought and locust outbreaks. It does this through a range of interventions including strengthening WASH services in response to COVID-19, supporting climate-resilient agriculture and introducing a crisis modifier as an early warning action for climate-related disasters. The crisis modifier was activated in 2021 amidst a locust outbreak destroying crops, which involved environmentally friendly chemical spraying and community-based locust management to collect locusts and sell them to bush meal enterprise groups (UNDP, 2023b). However, it doesn't tackle hyperinflation directly, but only acts as a buffer against the impacts of economic crises at the household level through cash transfers, diversification and access to markets. Box 7.3 highlights insights from its evaluation.

Box 7.3 Evaluation outcomes of Zimbabwe's Resilience Building Fund

Evidence from the first phase of the fund found that Zimbabwe Resilience Building Fund (ZRBF) interventions increased the resilience capacity of households and individuals by supporting "asset accumulation, diversification of livelihoods, commercialisation of productivity, market development, improved extension services, and access to early warning information systems—all with the effect of increasing absorptive and adaptive capacities" (UNDP, 2023a). The crisis modifier interventions also helped minimise disruption to the gains accorded through project activities, thus implicitly helping prevent downward mobility.

However, transformative capacities were less evidenced, constrained by currency depreciation and high inflation (UNDP, 2023a). This example thus points to a key limitation of even multi-sectoral resilience programmes that account for some but not all dominant polycrisis—in this case macroeconomic instability. It points to the need for resilience frameworks to more intentionally develop interventions that respond to prevalent systemic risks and crises.

A focus on this type of macroeconomic management was sometimes an important part of the response to COVID-19 (World Bank, 2022). This was also evidenced in some low-income countries. Cambodia "was able to make furlough payments, provide additional social protection coverage and depth, and other public expenditures because of its prudent fiscal management" (Diwakar et al., 2023). At the same time, Cambodia was an exception rather than the norm. Many of the poorest countries were unable to finance similar packages of support. In some cases, there was financial support to formal businesses, but this excluded the many informal sector workers and enterprises where many people in and near poverty worked (Diwakar et al., 2023). Moreover, the economic crises associated with the pandemic drove them to "cut spending in areas critical to the SDGs, including education and infrastructure" and in many cases considerably worsen public debt as a result of having needed to borrow from international financial institutions (UN DESA, 2023).

7.3 Responding to conflict intersections and humanitarian emergencies

7.3.1 Working "on" polycrisis: centring peacebuilding and social cohesion

A noted in Chapter 2, there is a large concentration of people in poverty in countries affected by violent conflict and climate-related disasters. This section continues to explore programmes that work "on" polycrisis to understand interventions that may have more transformative potential in contexts where violent conflict is one of the multiple crises that households experience.

In conflict-affected contexts, there is some recognition of climate concerns typically in programmatic theories of change depending on the type of conflict. This reflects a recognition of climate change not just as an environmental issue but as a conflict instigator or multiplier. In this context, certain projects attempt to pre-empt violence, for example through climate-smart livelihoods to support poverty reduction, early warning action as a risk mitigator and ex-ante peacebuilding interventions.

For example, Nepal's Climate Change and Security Project: Building Resilience to Climate-related Security Risks in West Karnali (2017–22) is a peacebuilding and climate-smart livelihoods project seeking to promote sustainable livelihoods for vulnerable groups, strengthen local governance for natural resource management and dispute resolution, and build social cohesion between communities (UNEP, 2022a, 2022b). Though West Karnali is not currently a conflict-affected region, its ex-ante focus on pre-empting resource-based conflicts draws on observations of climate change-driven water infrastructure deficits during the dry season that has otherwise commonly spurred intercommunal conflicts (Maskey et al., 2023). Its emphasis on governance conditions is moreover an important facet to support transformative change, as it addresses directly some of the structural challenges facing Nepal in its operationalisation of decentralised governance. This shifts resilience from an otherwise overly technical application, as many have criticised (Schulz and Siriwardane, 2015), to instead draw attention to its social and political dimensions. Having a permanent interdisciplinary group of programme and policy thinkers to work together before crises hit would accordingly be essential for anticipating and planning interventions that can effectively address polycrisis.

Results from the project identify that improved water infrastructure management reduced the incentives for conflict over water during the dry season, and improved community relationships thus fostering social cohesion. As a result, at the end of the project, "communities reported the resolution of long-standing natural resource-related disputes and shared examples of successful mediation processes to prevent the escalation of new conflicts", which was further substantiated to conflict resolution identified by the project's conflict tracking tool (UNEP, 2022a, 2022b). This thus reinforces the importance of linking basic service delivery with peacebuilding outcomes through conflict resolution mechanisms as well as conflict sensitivity and monitoring systems built into the project.

In the Philippines, the Conflict Transformation in the Autonomous Region of Muslim Mindanao (ARMM) (2022–23) programme delivers community-driven livelihood and peacebuilding interventions alongside an inclusive governance focus (UNDP Multi-partner Trust Fund Office, 2024; UNFPA, 2022). As part of its activities, it mainstreams early warning systems into municipal plans to address rise in conflict, climate hazards and public health emergencies. It geographically targets communities based on vulnerability to conflict and climate change, and poverty rates (UNDP Multi-partner Trust Fund Office, 2024; FAO, 2023). This integrated risk planning reflects a systems framing, while its community-driven interventions prioritise local ownership and legitimacy important to strengthen in contexts of weak state or local governance capacity. The project's endline assessment found improved livelihood asset base, increased or diversified agricultural production, improved food security, and high levels of trust of government authorities by project participants (UNDP, 2024a).

The examples above point to region-specific interventions, reflecting the subnational dimensions of conflict. As part of these, some interventions bring together various actors, including government at national and subnational levels, alongside NGOs and CSOs. In Kenya, for example, the Ewaso Nyiro camel caravan, established in 2014, passes through arid and semi-arid lands in the northeast of the country. It supports various forms of training, advocacy for ecosystem conservation and social cohesion in relation to water management (Ewaso Ng'iro North Development Authority, n.d.; USAID, 2019). This is an effort to directly respond to recurrent drought and strengthen peacebuilding between pastoralists and farmers. As part of this program, the caravan champions "peace ambassadors" who are trained in conflict monitoring to help complement informal conflict mediation processes that the project also supports (Tafere et al., 2023). This reflects the broader role of public information campaigns and community-led recovery in supporting social cohesion during crises (Jewett et al., 2021). There is also some evidence generated of impact, where in 2019 the caravan helped inform legislation on the sustainable use of natural resources, which led to a process to legislate sand harvesting along the river by two county governments (USAID, 2019).

7.3.2 Working "on" polycrisis: a focus on displaced populations

Programmes that centre on displaced populations or refugees and host communities often have a strong focus on resilience, participatory processes often centred around community-driven development, peacebuilding, and recovery. These form key components within their work "on" polycrisis. In countries affected primarily by climate-related disasters and economic crises, interventions identified recognise displacement as both a humanitarian and development challenge. In this vein, the Socio-Economic Inclusion of Refugees and Host Communities in Rwanda Project (2019–26) supports access to financial services that both refugees and host communities rely on, development of joint refugee-host community enterprises, and infrastructure development which includes rehabilitation of infrastructure affected by environmental damage (World Bank, 2024a). Similarly, the Zambia Refugee and Host Communities Project (2024–28) is a multi-pronged refugee/host community productive inclusion programme that focuses also on climate-resilient infrastructure and supporting livelihood activities for both populations including in climate-smart agriculture. It has a focus on women and youth (World Bank, 2024d).

Instead, interventions that target displaced populations in countries at the climate-conflict nexus often respond to a more complex set of needs with a strong focus on preventing the re-emergence of conflict. For example, the Resilient Livelihoods Development for Women and Youth IDPs in Maguindanao Province (2022–24) in the Philippines targets people displaced by floods and conflict, providing an integrated programme around health, protection and livelihoods. It supports climate-adapted livelihoods for IDPs and their economic inclusion and integration into host communities. Responding to disasters, it supports "gender-responsive, inclusive, and culturally sensitive policies and approaches to community-based disaster risk reduction and management" (UNFPA, 2022). Responding to conflict, it forms solidarity groups of women IDPs and youth and develops women-friendly spaces to enable marginalised groups a forum to support each other during ongoing conflict. This is one of the few programmes that adopt a more agency-focused approach to gender and youth, rather than focusing on them as beneficiaries in need of vulnerability reduction alone.

In Niger and Kenya, livelihood support is also linked with environmental rehabilitation. For example, the Developing the Livelihoods of those Affected by Displacement in Tahoua, Niger (2022–23) project includes cash-for-work tailored around land regeneration projects to combat desertification. It integrates this with protection, community conflict management, social assistance for those affected by wildfires, and service improvements through environmental management (European Commission, n.d.). The Development Response to Displacement Impacts Project (2017–22) in Kenya supports peacebuilding and reduce refugee-host tensions by focusing on improving service delivery and natural resource management amongst communities that have seen a protected presence of refugees (World Bank, 2024e). As part of this, it undertakes integrated natural resource management through public works to counter overexploitation of natural resources and the degradation of grazing lands. This is integrated with a community investment fund for basic services prioritised "especially by girls and women", signalling efforts to support their agency. This operates alongside off-farm livelihood support again with a focus on women, female-headed households, and youth (World Bank, 2024e).

In Afghanistan, the Recovery, Reintegration & Resilience Consortium (R3) Project (2020–23) distributes agricultural inputs, provides training on livestock, supports income generation for women and the socio-economic integration of IDPs, while DRR interventions also strengthen resilience of these populations to natural hazards (UK Government, 2024). An endline evaluation of the programme identified weak resilience-oriented outcomes, with various recommendations (Box 7.4). The last point in Box 7.4 is perhaps an indication that aspirations to operate "on" polycrisis have gone ahead of capacities and knowledge about how to do it. Given that the level of coordinated thinking and management demanded by polycrisis interventions is high, these issues are likely to be common.

Box 7.4 Evaluation recommendations from Afghanistan's Recovery, Reintegration & Resilience Consortium Project

Recommendations to the funder include:

- Developing a more analytical reading of crises, with a real capacity for anticipation, in order to avoid future hotbeds of multidimensional vulnerability.
- Integrating climate change into the analytical and operational grid.
- Adopting a pragmatic approach to governance, according to a decentralised, non-pyramidal, localised model, including all actors and understanding local power dynamics.
- Sanctuarising [protecting/setting aside] funding for resilience programmes to clarify expectations, rationalise decisions and limit uncertainty for implementing partners.
- Imposing a real gender transformative analysis on consortia, especially in contexts like Afghanistan where women play an invisible but essential societal role.
- Defining with implementing partners what value for money can mean in a context like Afghanistan.

Source: Samuel Hall (2023).

7.3.3 Working "on" polycrisis through regional resilience-strengthening

In response to conflict and polycrisis, some programmes adopt a regional (or supra-national) dimension. Regional projects have the benefits of addressing cross-border challenges by supporting coordinated responses for system-level resilience, promoting regional cooperation and knowledge-sharing, and support policy coherence. These can also make use of economies of scale, for example by pooling resources and logistics, to amplify effects and tackle drivers of polycrisis in resource-constrained contexts. The Program to Build Resilience for Food and Nutrition Security in the Horn of Africa (2022–27) covers Ethiopia, Kenya, Djibouti, Somalia and South Sudan. It focuses on strengthening production systems' resilience and the adaptive capacity of pastoral and agropastoral communities to climate change, and in doing so is articulated to also contribute to improving peace and security in the region (MapAfrica, n.d.). Similarly, the Integrated Resilience in the Sahel project phases recognise multifaceted challenges (conflict, climate change and economic effects of the COVID-19 pandemic) and deliver a food systems approach in response (WFP, 2023, 2024), though the specific interventions largely respond to strengthening food security ex-ante to climate shocks.

Cross-border interventions are also sometimes present reflecting the spillover effects or localised regional dimensions of crises. For example, the Integrating Peacebuilding, Development and Humanitarian Efforts on the Kenya and Ethiopia Cross Border (2022–25) project recognises the loss of farming and livestock due to drought and extreme rainfall patterns that drives resource-based conflicts. It thus focuses on improved livelihoods including around hay preservation so that it can be used during drought for livestock or sold in times of need, alongside supporting resource management training including community DRR committees, and peace dialogues in the border region (VSO, n.d.). The focus on cross-border resilience-building highlights the importance of responding to shared risks through coordinated mechanisms that can improve adaptation and social cohesion that could otherwise be undermined due to spillover effects of crises.

In other cases, UN agencies and NGOs may also operate with a global or regional mandate, albeit with country-specific implementation strategies rather than a cross-border focus in implementation. WFP programming is a key example of this (Box 7.5). The agency's focus on food assistance can not only help meet needs in humanitarian emergencies marked by conflict or climate-related disasters, but it can also help mitigate the negative effects of economic crises where for example food price inflation can make access to nutrition out of reach for poorer households. As Box 7.5 suggests, some objectives are better geared towards working "on" polycrisis, such as improving the nutritional status of children and pregnant or lactating women.

Box 7.5 Examples of WFP support to polycrisis during COVID-19

- **Afghanistan:***conflict, extreme climate shocks, severe economic decline, global food and fuel crisis:* scale up food, nutrition, livelihood assistance and cash-based transfers, pre-positioning food in areas inaccessible during winter; new satellite offices to support early warning and anticipatory action.
- **Nigeria:***NE—IDPs, NW—refugees, S—vulnerable populations in urban hotspots affected by Covid-19:* promote access to food, improved nutritional status of children and pregnant or lactating women.
- **Rwanda:***Congolese refugees, Burundian refugees and returnees:* life-saving support, critical food and nutrition assistance. *Covid-19:* technical assistance for expanding social protection.
- **Zambia**: *Covid-19, weak public finances, deteriorating purchasing power, Congolese refugees, political tension ahead of August general elections:* assistance, support of safety net mechanisms and on-demand logistics support.

Source: abridged from Diwakar et al. (2023).

7.3.4 Working "on" polycrisis during humanitarian emergencies and through the humanitarian–development–peace nexus: insights from Afghanistan, Nigeria, Niger and Ethiopia

The humanitarian–development–peace (HDP) nexus is a key entry point that can provide a coordinated response to working "on" polycrisis in humanitarian contexts. Practical implementation of the HDP nexus especially at country and local levels is limited, with the focus remaining largely on international principles (ALNAP, 2022). Even so, there are some examples especially in humanitarian contexts—themselves characterising contexts of protracted polycrisis—that offer learning. This sub-section draws on insights from Afghanistan, Nigeria, Niger and Ethiopia, which form the subset of focus countries identified in the Global Humanitarian Overview 2025 (UN OCHA, 2024) as humanitarian needs contexts.[1]

Responses to polycrisis in Afghanistan typically acknowledge the need for conflict-sensitivity and include provisions for flexibility in approaches. Programmatic responses at the HDP nexus typically align broadly with the Afghanistan Humanitarian Needs Overviews (HNOs). These yearly overviews regularly draw attention to polycrisis that necessitate an inter-sectoral response grounded in flexibility to changing conditions and disaggregation by populations of impact (Box 7.6). The HNO offers a coordinated framework for identifying and targeting humanitarian action based on severity of needs, temporality, and disaggregation by sector, location and socio-demographic characteristics, that can act as an important pre-condition for delivering equitable responses amidst contexts of rapid change. The HNO on its own presents an example of working "in" polycrisis and being sensitive to its conditions, while specific projects within this framing move towards working "on" polycrisis, as discussed below Box 7.6.

Box 7.6 HNO's reflection of ways of working during polycrisis in Afghanistan

- **Changes between years**—The HNO adopted a longitudinal analysis, recognising that intersecting risks were shifting from Covid-19 and conflict in 2021, to drought, climate change and economic shocks in 2022. It accordingly calculated needs with a stronger emphasis on the more recent crises.
- **Seasonality**—Within the year, the HNO also recognised seasonal influences on needs such as 'the onset of winter, rainfall patterns, agricultural planting and harvest seasons, and others' (OCHA, 2023).
- **Inter-sectoral assessment**—It adopted an intersectoral approach based on joint planning assumptions of needs across sectors in response to polycrisis.
- **Horizontal and vertical disaggregation**—The overview estimated needs disaggregated by sector, severity of needs, location, and markers

such as age, sex and disability, thus foregrounding equity considerations in assessing needs.

- **Commitment to flexibility**—Recognising the uncertainty inherent in its assumptions, the HNO committed to updating the needs assessment continuously, as conditions change.

Source: analysis of OCHA data, first presented in Diwakar et al. (2023).

Examples of ongoing projects working "on" polycrisis include:

- Area-Based Approach to Development Emergency Initiatives (ABADEIs) for Local Socio-Economic Recovery and Community Resilience in Afghanistan (2021–25) and the STFA Joint Programme for the Central Highlands Region of Afghanistan: Addressing Basic Human Needs through the ABADEI Strategy (2022–24), which is a localised application of the ABADEI strategy (UNDP Afghanistan, n.d.).
- Afghanistan Community Resilience and Livelihoods Project (2022–25) by World Bank (World Bank, 2024e).

These projects have a common focus on crisis response and resilience and focus on rehabilitation (e.g. of value chains) and reconstruction (of basic services) thus working towards recovery programming. ABEDEIs embed conflict-sensitivity in their design and targeting while relying on DRM and peace committees to respond to climate change and conflict. While the endline evaluation conducted was not found online, a report points to the cash assistance component reducing vulnerability and improving food security "for a significant number of families" (Islamic Relief, 2024). The World Bank project in turn has less of an explicit focus on peacebuilding, but instead recognises the centrality of macroeconomic crisis and so targets its efforts to rebuilding economic infrastructure to create an enabling environment for livelihoods development. All projects focus on marginalised groups, for example IDPS, returnees and minorities under the localised ABADEI project, and women, IDPs and the urban poor under the World Bank project. Flexibility is also built into their ways of working, noting that this is meant to enable them to respond to new opportunities and unforeseen externalities.

In Ethiopia, a set of interventions adopt holistic resilience framings, supporting green diversified livelihoods at the centre of community-driven peacebuilding efforts to work "on" polycrisis. The Lowlands Livelihood Resilience Project (2019–25) includes DRM elements such as through managing water sources, which is informed by conflict analysis, and supports conflict resolution and peacebuilding at multiple scales between communities up to cross-border platforms. It couples this with extension services to support climate-resilient livelihoods through drought-tolerant seeds, irrigation and water conservancy schemes (World Bank, 2019a). The Nature-Based Solutions for Sustainable and Inclusive Development (2023–26) programme similarly focuses on climate-smart agriculture and other means of promoting sustainable food production alongside strengthening local capacity to peacefully resolve resource-based conflicts through dialogue (IWMI, n.d.).

A set of interventions in Niger similarly work "on" polycrisis by supporting resilience for different populations, typically including a dimension around youth and women's empowerment. The Niger Adaptive Safety Net Project (2019–26) frames social assistance as a means to limit impacts of climate shocks and youth exclusion as drivers of conflict (World Bank, 2019b). Other examples incorporate support for diversified economic opportunities, DRM, natural resource management (NRM) including regenerative practices, conflict-management systems and social and ecological risk management. These interventions typically layer on other activities, such as local governance strengthening, empowering communities and civil society organisations and supporting the agency of women and youth. For example, RISE I and II (2014–25) integrate HDP approaches to strengthen governance, economic resilience and NRM (USAID, 2018, 2024; Feed the Future, n.d.). This is slightly different from the resilience interventions in Ethiopia which focus more exclusively on supporting community-driven development. The focus in these projects in Niger instead centres on strengthening localised governance, which is implicitly viewed as a precondition for the local empowerment and NRM strategies it supports.

Box 7.7 RISE 1 evaluation in Niger

The endline evaluation of RISE 1 pointed to its prevention of one in five extremely vulnerable individuals from experiencing severe food insecurity. Households in the programme also reported that they were "more confident in their ability to recover from shocks" because the programme "connected them to different ways to build their resilience, such as accessing loans and insurance; obtaining information about risks and disaster preparedness; benefiting from social cohesion and networks; and learning about ways to diversify their income" relative to the control group who did not participate in the programme (USAID, 2024).

More broadly, the evaluation found that households were able to better manage crises, even during the COVID-19 pandemic period during which endline data was collected. This is precisely the intention behind resilience-building interventions. It suggests that RISE 1 was effective in not only advancing the humanitarian imperative through improving food security outcomes but also in driving more durable resilience-building to absorb and adapt in the face of polycrisis.

Finally, in Nigeria, there are various projects working "on" polycrisis, which together combine elements of shock-responsive social protection, climate resilience and livelihood diversification as household-level interventions delivered as a means of building household resilience. The scale up of the social protection programme is an example of inclusive support in crisis contexts. However, it faces considerable challenges in ensuring wider coverage better aligned to need and overcoming inter-state competition and elite capture that undermines its effectiveness (Abdulrasaq et al., 2025). Its integration with climate adaptation and conflict sensitivity is also limited. The Feed the Future project instead focuses on resilience-building and also has a cash transfer element alongside inclusive livelihoods support. A Feed the Future impact report found that three-quarters of project participants reported that their households were better able to manage and cope with future shocks and stresses (USAID, 2022). The next section elaborates on the last two projects outlined in Table 7.1.

In all of the above cases, addressing the deeper root causes of polycrisis may be essential for real transformation but is often off the table. For example, in contexts like Afghanistan, political change through restoring women's right to work or ensuring an impartial judiciary would be an integral component of this effort. Yet while development and peacebuilding are critical, they sometimes fall short of confronting these foundational social and political exclusions that sustain vulnerability during crises. For example, deeper political and social root causes like gender-based exclusion, elite capture and

Table 7.1 Examples of projects with activities tailored to polycrisis in Nigeria

Project	*Examples of activities tailored to polycrisis*
National Social Safety Net Program-Scale Up, 2022–2025	Shock-responsive time-limited cash transfer, including in response to high inflation of food prices stemming from conflict exacerbated by climate change and COVID-19 supply chain disruptions
Feed the Future Nigeria Rural Resilience Activity, 2019–2025	Cash transfers to support households from secondary stresses (including economic crises) due to COVID-19; climate-smart investments, e.g. drought-resistant seed varieties, and supporting agricultural insurance sign-up; supporting market resilience to shocks including conflict and climate change
Multi-Sectoral Crisis Recovery Project for North Eastern Nigeria, 2017–2025	Supporting productive livelihoods and provision of basic needs to address the macroeconomic crisis and regional disparity; multi-sectoral infrastructure and service provision for immediate recovery from conflict-induced displacement; Contingent Emergency Response Component (including to support climate-related disasters)
RESILAC, 2018–2022	Local natural resource management committees to support social cohesion; diversified livelihoods to combat economic shocks (including through public works, agricultural support and NRM); establishment of Community Development Committees at ward level to bridge communities with administrative/security actors

Source: World Bank, 2023b, 2021a, 2021b; RESILAC, n.d.; Mercy Corps, n.d.; USAID, 2022.

limitations on movement and access to public services are often missing across these programmes, which limit their transformative potential.

7.4 Working "on" polycrisis by promoting recovery programming

7.4.1 Recovering from climate-related disasters and economic crisis

Recovery is a critical component that can enable populations to rebound during and after crises. It can lead to important structural shifts that build resilience to future crises, thus blurring the line with ex-ante interventions aimed at preparing for or preventing crises impacts. The suggestion in this section is not to ignore the centrality of ex-ante resilience-building, but instead to better balance this with ex-post recovery as a largely neglected component.

Indeed, recovery is often underemphasised and with little explicit investment. Indeed, as noted earlier, macroeconomic policy appears to be the main and sometimes sole vehicle for supporting recovery from crises. This was writ large during the pandemic. The problem with this approach is that it largely ignored the many challenges experienced by people in and near poverty, which as a result led to slower recovery, reinforced chronic poverty, or for those who fell into poverty during the pandemic, then drove their sustained impoverishment.

While social protection was meant to help alleviate the pandemic's effects on the global poor, most programmes were short-lived, lasting just three or four months, thus at a considerable divergence with the multiple lockdown waves and COVID-19 legacy effects of continued inflation, let alone other climate, economic or conflict related crises which may have followed. It is then unsurprising that social protection was often inadequate in helping households recover from downward mobility wrought by the pandemic. Aisha's experience is one of many such examples (Figure 7.2).

There is also a need to promote social, economic and environmental recovery during and post-crises, alongside building resilience before crises. This is because people in poverty and women tend to recover more slowly or not at all, as evidence from the COVID-19 pandemic reinforced. Such efforts would need to consider longer-term elements to promote and safeguard sustainability across these three dimensions. A range of programmes in Nepal work "on" polycrisis through supporting recovery. Building Climate Resilience and Reintegrating Economically Displaced Workers Through Climate Smart Agriculture in Terai Flood Plains Nepal (2022–25) recognises the Terai region's climate emergencies and the humanitarian crisis reflected by the migrant returnees. It supports climate-smart livelihood opportunities for economically displaced migrant workers who returned to their communities due to the COVID-19 pandemic, in an effort to concurrently build resilience to climate shocks (GGGI, 2023).

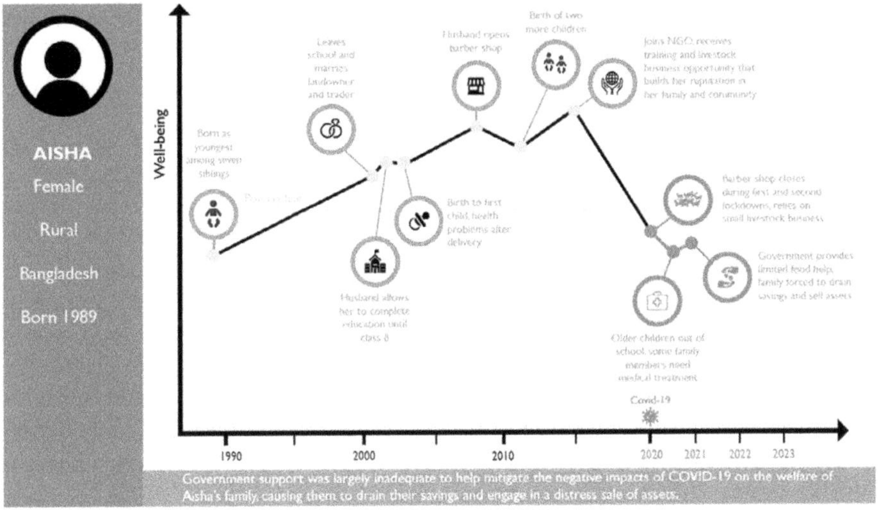

Figure 7.2 Social protection inadequate in improving wellbeing amidst COVID-19 in Bangladesh
Source: Interview with Aisha (Bangladesh, 2022), first presented in Diwakar et al. (2022).

With a broader focus, Nepal's Green, Resilient and Inclusive Development (2022–24) sought to address slow economic recovery from COVID-19, climate change and environmental degradation and persistent poverty amongst women and the most excluded groups recognising they are often disproportionately impacted by climate change. It did this through integrated livelihood solutions (e.g. nature-based solutions, tourism, value chain development, urban resilience, waste management, agroforestry plantations and renewable energy initiatives) (UNDP Nepal, 2023).

The Building Back Better: Organic Agriculture for Smallholder Farmers in Northern Cambodia (2022–26) project, a partnership between the Cambodian Agricultural Cooperative Cooperation Plc and the World Food Programme, is a Public-Private-Producer Partnership that promotes climate-resilient organic agricultural production. Its programme documentation's contextual focus recognises:

> The economic impacts of the COVID-19 pandemic caused many of the most vulnerable Cambodians, often employed in the country's large agricultural sector, to slide back into poverty. The conflict in Ukraine and impacts on fuel and food costs are straining household purchasing power and may lead to a further deterioration in food security and nutrition.
>
> (GASFP, 2024)

As part of its rationale, promoting crop diversification and irrigation is supported, which can reduce climate sensitivity and exposure while improving incomes. The intervention is targeted towards smallholder farmers, especially women and indigenous people, many of whom experienced slower recovery from the pandemic (GASFP, 2024).

7.4.2 Recovery in humanitarian contexts

Recovery in humanitarian contexts is complex not least because of the protracted nature of many crises and crisis intersections. Nigeria's Multi-sectoral Crisis Recovery Project (2017–25) (Table 7.1) focuses on strengthening multi-sectoral infrastructure, climate adaptation, and supporting basic services for IDPs and hosts, thus collectively addressing conflict, climate-related disasters and implicitly macroeconomic crises. An evaluation of its grievance mechanism found it to be effective in rebuilding trust, fostering social cohesion and promoting community resilience, albeit with low public awareness of the existence of the mechanism (Bariki et al., 2024).

The Lake Chad Region Recovery and Development Project (PROLAC) (2020–25) and the RESILAC projects (2018–22) (Table 7.1) are integrated resilience programmes bringing together climate-smart livelihoods support including a public works component, activities to strengthen social cohesion, and building critical infrastructure such as small roads to improve regional market access (World Bank, 2023a; RESILAC, n.d.). The agricultural support under PROLAC is intended to address pandemic-related inflation and staple food price surges, the climate-smart livelihoods support and aspects of infrastructure development is meant to reduce vulnerability to climate shocks and supports households displaced due to violence, while the social cohesion strengthens relationship between IDPs and host communities. Recognising the inherent complexity of working in the context of polycrisis, the project design adopts a modular, iterative and incremental approach that includes crisis monitoring as part of its risk-informed approach, working closely in terms of institutional capacity building and government coordination (World Bank, 2023a).

PROLAC and RESILAC provide an interesting comparative lens of two programmes targeting the same region over similar time periods and goals but with different approaches. PROLAC focuses on institutional strengthening, policy coordination and the development of key infrastructure to reduce drivers of conflict and climate-related fragility. RESILAC has a similar focus to PROLAC on resilience and recovery, though has a relatively stronger focus on bottom-up, localised support facilitated through NGOs. RESILAC also provides psychosocial support as part of its activities, which appear to place a relatively stronger emphasis on conflict rather than climate-related crises. Though no evaluation was found for PROLAC, an evaluation of RESILAC identified some lessons presented in Box 7.8.

Box 7.8 Brief reflections on an evaluation of RESILAC in Nigeria

An evaluation of RESILAC identified better living conditions, in part through the adoption of innovative farming techniques, and strengthened social capital in project areas. On the latter, for example, a community social capital scoring metric identified a 16% improvement in this capital between baseline and endline, "confirming the importance of actions oriented towards living together, inter-religious dialogue and citizenship at the local level" (RESILAC, 2022).

It is important to note that these gains were evidenced in a context of rising tensions around natural resource conflicts. It was also identified during the pandemic period. Taken together, this suggests that resilience programming can play an important role in fostering social cohesion where it intentionally supports relational dynamics. As evidenced in RESILAC, this can be done through actively investing in trust-building through local stewardship of natural resources and more established and accountable local governance structures.

Another example on supporting recovery is provided in Box 7.9 from Ethiopia. While this community-based approach is focused more on short-term rather than medium- or long-term recovery, it helps shift "the paradigm from dependence on external humanitarian aid to community-driven recovery, reconstruction, productivity, and resilience building" (Government of Ethiopia, 2025, p. 41). This may signal an increasing move by national governments to oppose the international aid architecture and external humanitarian financing of polycrisis.

Box 7.9 Managing recurrent crises through a community-based approach in Ethiopia

Buusaa Gonofaa is a programme that mobilises local communities to collect grain and cash reserves and to offer these funds and in-kind support to communities as a means to build resilience in response to recurrent crises including climate-related disasters, displacement and insecurity. It uses these reserves to help reduce international food aid dependency. It has so far mobilised 27 million people in the Oromia region to provide these contributions, covering close to 13,000 tons of grain and ETB 4.2 billion in cash as local reserves. This has been identified to be responsible for graduating 2.4 million people from dependency on external food aid. The programme's local ownership is a key pillar of its sustainability, alongside its cultural grounding.

Source: summarised from Government of Ethiopia (2025); Wako et al. (2023).

7.5 Discussion and conclusion

This chapter highlighted policy and programmatic responses to polycrisis, focusing especially on those that work "in" polycrisis and recognise the need for conflict- or climate-sensitive approaches, and those that more ambitiously work "on" polycrisis by responding to their root causes. The examples show how the world has adjusted quite broadly to operating with a polycrisis perspective. They are embedded in traditional entry points of social protection, DRM and the HDP nexus in responded to crises intersections, alongside the often-neglected arm of recovery programming.

7.5.1 Climate-related disasters and economic crises

From the analysis, it appears that when households experience climate-related disasters that drive or operate concurrently to economic crises, the primary institutional response appears to be focused on the disaster, with little attention placed on mitigating sources of economic precarity. Yet examples are highlighted of ways in which DRM and social protection have been innovatively brought together to support dual crises, such as through trigger designs and strengthening early warning mechanisms for crises. Regionally, most of the examples from DRM—especially supported through government DRM agencies—were identified in South and Southeast Asia, suggesting that governments in these regions have responded more effectively to the polycrisis era. It also in turn points to the potential for considerable strengthening of the DRM sector in regions of Africa. As part of the social protection response, however, there is a strong need for cash transfers across regions of Asia and Africa to go on for longer and be more adequate in value and timeliness across contexts to deal with polycrisis in ways that help safeguard or rebuild resilience.

Macroeconomic management has also been a tool for crisis response, as acknowledged in the chapter. However, as the various examples of maladaptive economic policies highlight (see Chapters 3 and 5), these can end up further reinforcing downward mobility if equity is not centrally considered in the design of these responses. Otherwise, there risks being a double whammy of disrupted government services amidst crises driven by austerity measures, linked to and reinforcing the maladaptive policy responses that together amplify vulnerability and erode coping capacities.

7.5.2 Conflict and humanitarian emergencies

Programming in conflict-affected areas increasingly is attuned to conflict links with climate change, typically responding to these dual challenges through a resilience framework. A range of programmes draw attention to strengthening social cohesion, especially in areas of large displaced populations. This represents a proactive, anticipatory coping response working "on" polycrisis by tackling some of its conflict-related triggers as well as implicitly the thinning of social networks due to intersections of crises. This suggests on the whole that conflict-related programming may be a more common entry point for programming on polycrisis, albeit not universal. Even so, the chapter pointed to an indication that aspirations to operate "on" polycrisis have gone ahead of capacities and knowledge about how to do it. This is not unsurprising given the high level of coordinated thinking and management demanded by polycrisis interventions.

In humanitarian emergencies, the HDP nexus is a common framework though again the operationalisation of this nexus especially at local levels has been criticised (ALNAP, 2022; Peters et al., 2019). This chapter found programmes at the HDP nexus though this was often international donor-funded programmes rather than government national or subnational efforts to operationalise the nexus. The largely donor-funded programmes at this nexus more commonly consider peacebuilding by definition, and as part of this regularly engage with women and youth, though there is still indication that these may be as beneficiaries rather than through more active agency of participants in designing more locally led programmes. Moreover, notable in these programmes is a relative absence on psychosocial support, which reflects the absence of recovery programming more broadly. This is particularly striking given the mental health issues and trauma that can emerge from these contexts. RESILAC is an example of a multi-sectoral programme that did include a focus on psychosocial wellbeing, which other programmes could build on.

Somewhat relatedly, in these contexts of heightened crises' scales and need, there remain programmes that do not adequately reflect on the context of polycrisis or conflict-sensitivity explicitly as noted in Section 7.1. This is unfortunately a common occurrence within government programmes, where coordination between agencies may be a big challenge Yet work by different actors in the same geography can create overlapping programmes of a multisectoral nature; these often unintentional overlaps can also be learned from and more intentionally scaled up as part of a portfolio responses needed given the scale of multidimensional deprivations people face in humanitarian contexts.

Indeed, it is often a combination of responses that can support both equity and risk management in transformational change. Even so, across the few "transformative" programmes identified, there are foundational political or structural factors (e.g. gender-based exclusion, elite capture, and social, political and civic exclusion including in access to public services) that may be inadequately dealt with, pointing to avenues for further strategic and programmatic development.

Having in this chapter overviewed examples of policies and programmes that build resilience and a degree of structural transformation before, during and after polycrisis, the next chapter concludes by setting out recommendations for more transformative programming that can help break the link between polycrisis and poverty.

Note

1 Alongside these primary countries mentioned in the Global Humanitarian Overview 2025 as humanitarian needs contexts, Zambia, Malawi, Zimbabwe, Bangladesh, and the Philippines are referenced under the "flash appeals" category.

References

Abdulrasaq, K., Walker, J.-A., Ukpai, S. and Diwakar, V. (2025) 'Political perspectives of social assistance amidst economic shocks in Nigeria'. *BASIC Research Briefing 7*. Institute of Development Studies. doi:10.19088/IDS.2025.043.

Allan, S.Connolly, D. and Tariq, K. (2020) 'The Opportunity Cost of Covid-19 Emergency Expenditure Reallocation'. *Centre for Disease Protection blog*, 4 December.

ALNAP (2022) *The state of the humanitarian system*. Active Learning Network for Accountability and Performance in Humanitarian Action (ALNAP)/ODI.

AU and UNDP (2022) *Disaster risk reduction in West Africa and the Sahelian region: A review of progress*. African Union (AU)/United Nations Development Programme (UNDP).

Bariki, S., Joel, E., Ribadu, R.B., Shallangwa, S., Hamis, A. and Nwabufo, F.O. (2024) 'Assessment of the Grievances Redress Mechanisms of Multisectoral Crisis Recovery Project in Northeast Nigeria Case Study of Adamawa State, Nigeria'. *International Journal of Research and Innovation in Social Science*, 8(8): 4664–4676. https://ideas.repec.org/a/bcp/journl/v8y2024i8p4664-4676.html.

Diwakar, V. (2023) *'Poverty eradication amidst conflict dynamics and intersecting crises'*. Paper for UN IA-EGM Conference, 10–12 May, Addis Ababa, Chronic Poverty Advisory Network.

Diwakar, V., Kamninga, T., Mehzabin, T., Tumusiime, E., Kamal, R. and Pabony, N.A. (2022) 'Sustaining escapes from ultra-poverty: A mixed methods assessment of layered interventions in coastal Bangladesh'. *CPAN working paper*. CPAN. https://www.chronicpovertynetwork.org/resources/2022/9/7/sustaining-escapes-from-ultra-poverty-a-mixed-methods-assessment-of-layered-interventions-in-coastal-bangladesh.

Diwakar, V., Shepherd, A., Bizoza, A., Lenhardt, A., Shepherd, A., Moonga, A. (2023) 'Equitably responding to and recovering amid polycrisis'. In A. Shepherd *et al.* (Eds.), *Chronic Poverty Report 5 – Pandemic Poverty*. Institute of Development Studies. doi:10.19088/CPAN.2023.021.

Donoghoe, M., Sengupta, S., Costella, C. and Sivanu, S. (2022) 'Climate change, intersecting disasters and social protection: How the Covid-19 experience can prepare us for the future'. *Working Paper*. Red Cross Red Crescent Climate Centre.

European Commission (n.d.) 'Developing the livelihoods of those affected by displacement in Tahoua, Niger'. https://international-partnerships.ec.europa.eu/policies/programming/projects/developing-livelihoods-those-affected-displacement-tahoua-niger_en.

Ewaso Ng'iro North Development Authority (n.d.) 'The Camel Caravan: The Ewaso Ng'iro Camel Caravan: A Journey of Conservation, Coexistence, and Resilience'. https://ennda.go.ke/the-camel-caravan-the-ewaso-ngiro-camel-caravan-a-journey-of-conservation-coexistence-and-resilience/.

FAO (2023) 'Bangsamoro women and youth rising from floods and conflicts'. https://www.fao.org/philippines/news/detail/zh/c/1641682/.

Farhat, M. and Borja, F. (2021) *Regional landscape analysis on disaster risk financing for shock-responsive social protection in Southeast Asia – The Philippines case study.* Oxford Policy Management/United Nations Children's Fund East Asia and Pacific Regional Office.

Feed the Future (n.d.) 'Resilience in the Sahel Enhanced (RISE I)'. https://cg-281711fb-71ea-422c-b02c-ef79f539e9d2.s3.us-gov-west-1.amazonaws.com/uploads/2024/05/USAID2979-RISE-I-Fact-Sheet508c.pdf.

Feminist Humanitarian Network and Partners (2021) *Women's humanitarian voices: Covid-19 through a feminist lens.* Feminist Humanitarian Network.

Ferguson, J. (2015) 'Give a man a fish: Reflections on the new politics of distribution'. *American Anthropologist*, 118(3): 662–663.

GASFP (2024) *Building back better: Organic agriculture for smallholder farmers in Northern Cambodia.* Global Agriculture and Food Security Programme. https://www.gafspfund.org/sites/default/files/2024-05/Building%20Back%20Better.pdf.

General Secretariat for National Social Protection Council (2024) 'Tracking the impacts of the cash transfer program for the poor and vulnerable household during Covid-19 in Cambodia'. *Policy Brief No. 10.* Government of Cambodia. https://www.undp.org/sites/g/files/zskgke326/files/2024-11/final_project_brief_eng.pdf.

GGGI (2023) 'Building climate resilience and reintegrating economically displaced workers through climate smart agriculture in Terai flood plains Nepal'. https://gggi.org/wp-content/uploads/2023/03/Final_E.-KOICA-CSA-Brochure.pdf.

Government of Ethiopia (2025) *Ethiopia: the third voluntary national review 2025.* https://hlpf.un.org/sites/default/files/vnrs/2025/VNR%202025%20Ethiopia%20Report.pdf.

Government of Malawi (2022) *Malawi Social Cash Transfer Programme Strategic Plan 2022–2027.* https://www.unicef.org/malawi/media/8346/file/Malawi%20Social%20Cash%20Transfer%20Programme%20Strategic%20Plan%202022%20-%202027%20.pdf.

Hickey, S. (2011) 'The politics of social protection: What do we get from a "social contract" approach?' *Canadian Journal of Development Studies*, 32(4): 426–438. doi:10.1080/02255189.2011.647447.

Hilhorst, D. and Mena, R. (2021) 'When Covid-19 Meets Conflict: Politics of the Pandemic Response in Fragile and Conflict-affected States'. *Disasters*, 45(Suppl. 1): S174-S194. doi:10.1111/disa.12514.

ISC and UNDRR (2020) *Hazard definition and classification review. Technical Report.* International Science Council (ISC)/United Nations Office for Disaster Risk Reduction (UNDRR).

Islamic Relief (2024) 'A learning review of multi-purpose cash assistance in Afghanistan: Examining reach, inclusion, partnership, and participation'. https://www.calpnetwork.org/wp-content/uploads/2024/04/AfghanistanCashAssistance_Report_080424_v02.pdf.

IWMI (n.d.). *Nature-based solutions for sustainable and inclusive development.* International Water Management Institute. https://www.iwmi.org/projects/nssid/.

Janzwood, S. (2020) 'Evacuating communities affected by disasters during future Covid-19 waves'. *Pandemic Shock: Brief No. 4.* Inter-Systemic Cascade Project, Cascades Institute.

Jewett, R.L., Mah, S.M., Howell, N. and Larsen, M.M. (2021) 'Social cohesion and community resilience during Covid-19 and pandemics: A rapid scoping review to inform the United Nations Research Roadmap for Covid-19 Recovery'. *International Journal of Health Services*, 51(3): 325–336. doi:10.1177/0020731421997.

Lux, S. (2020) *Acting early in times of a pandemic: The challenge of staying ready for extreme-weather events during Covid-19.* German Red Cross.

MapAfrica (n.d.) 'Ethiopia - Program to Build Resilience for Food and Nutrition Security in the Horn of Africa (Djibouti, Ethiopia, Kenya, Somalia, and South Sudan) - Ethiopia Component'. https://mapafrica.afdb.org/en/projects/46002-P-Z1-C00-080.

Maskey, G., Pandey, C.L. and Giri, M. (2023) 'Water scarcity and excess: Water insecurity in cities of Nepal'. *Water Supply*, 23(4): 1544–1556.

Mercy Corps (n.d.) 'Feed the Future Nigeria Rural Resilience Activity'. https://nigeria.mercycorps.org/what-we-do/rural-resilience-activity.

Njeri, S. and Daigle, M. (2022) 'Women leading local humanitarian response during the Covid-19 pandemic: Case studies from South Sudan and Kenya'. *HPG Working Paper*. ODI.

Okura, Y., Neupane, S. and Rana, B. (2020) *Avoiding a perfect storm: Covid-19 and floods in Nepal*. Flood Resilience Alliance.

Peters, K., Peters, L.E.R., Twigg, C. and Walch, C. (2019) *Disaster risk reduction strategies: Navigating conflict contexts*. Overseas Development Institute.

Potutan, G. and Arakida, M. (2021) 'Evolving Disaster Response Practices During Covid-19 Pandemic'. *Int. J. Environ. Res. Public Health*, 18(6): 3137. doi:10.3390/ijerph18063137.

RESILAC (2022) 'Regional report on the results of the Endline survey in the Lake Chad Basin region: Cameroon, Chad, Niger and Nigeria'. https://en.resilac.net/_files/ugd/04c082_8e78e72bc0504ec7b73001fc8b4dd2bd.pdf.

RESILAC (n.d.) *Home page*. https://en.resilac.net/.

Samuel Hall (2023) 'Recovery, reintegration & resilience (R3) consortium Afghanistan: Endline evaluation and learning report'. https://alnap.org/help-library/resources/recovery-reintegration-resilience-r3-consortium-afghanistan/.

Schulz, K., and Siriwardane, R. (2015) 'Depoliticised and technocratic? Normativity and the politics of transformative adaptation'. *Earth System Governance Working Paper No. 33*. Earth System Governance Project.

Seavmey, M. (2022) 'Inflation and floods cash transfers to support over one million people'. *Cambodianess*, 12 December. https://cambodianess.com/article/inflation-and-floods-cash-transfers-to-support-over-one-million-people.

Srivastava, S. (2020) *Protecting the most vulnerable amidst Covid-19 and Cyclone Amphan*. United Nations Economic and Social Commission for Asia and the Pacific.

Tafere, Y., Nashipai, K. and Diwakar, V. (2023) 'Responding to polycrisis in Ethiopia and Kenya'. *CPAN Policy Brief 7*. CPAN/Institute of Development Studies. doi:10.19088/CPAN.2023.007.

UK Government (2024) 'Action Against Hunger UK: Afghanistan Recovery, Reintegration, and Resilience (R3) Programme'. *Development Tracker*. https://devtracker.fcdo.gov.uk/programme/GB-CHC-1047501-Afghanistan%20Recovery,%20Reintegration,%20and%20Resilience%20(R3)%20Programme/transactions.

UN DESA (2023) 'The great finance divide'. *Policy Brief No. 134*. United Nations Department of Economic and Social Affairs (UN DESA).

UNDP (2023a) 'Impact evaluation endline study of UNDP Zimbabwe Resilience Building Fund'. https://www.undp.org/zimbabwe/publications/impact-evaluation-endline-study-undp-zimbabwe-resilience-building-fund.

UNDP (2023b) 'ZRBF Sustainability of Interventions'. https://www.undp.org/zimbabwe/publications/zrbf-sustainability-interventions.

UNDP (2024a) 'Conflict Transformation in Areas Affected by Armed Conflict in BARMM Through Area-based Community Driven Development: Final programme

narrative report'. https://mptf.undp.org/sites/default/files/documents/2024-05/unjp_barmm_ct_final_narrative_report.docx.
UNDP (2024b) 'Impact evaluation of the Cash Transfer Programmes for At-Risk Households Affected by Inflationary Pressure and Severe Floods'. https://www.undp.org/cambodia/publications/impact-evaluation-cash-transfer-programmes-risk-households-affected-inflationary-pressure-and-severe-floods.
UNDP Afghanistan (n.d.) 'Area Based Approach to Development Emergency Initiatives (ABADEI 2.0)'. https://www.undp.org/afghanistan/projects/area-based-approach-development-emergency-initiatives-abadei-20#:~:text=ABADEI%20is%20an%20area%2Dbased,livelihoods%20and%20enhancing%20community%20resilience.
UNDP Multi-partner Trust Fund Office (2024) 'Conflict transformation in BARMM final programme narrative report'. https://mptf.undp.org/fund/jph20.
UNDP Nepal (2023) 'Leaving no one behind in Nepal's green, resilient, and inclusive COVID-19 recovery'. https://cdafn.org.np/wp-content/uploads/2023/04/Project-Completion-Report_LNOB-GRID_Template-1.pdf.
UNEP (2022a) 'Climate Change and Security Partnership Project - Final Report: March 2017 - February 2022'. https://wedocs.unep.org/handle/20.500.11822/40549.
UNEP (2022b) 'EU-UNEP Climate Change and Security Project: Building resilience to climate-related security risks in West Karnali, Nepal'. https://wedocs.unep.org/handle/20.500.11822/40327;jsessionid=39C8EE1F6402FD35FAB3E650ECFD38D4.
UNFPA (2022) 'UNFPA, FAO to jointly implement Australia-supported development initiative for conflict-displaced women and youth in the Bangsamoro region'. https://philippines.unfpa.org/en/news/unfpa-fao-jointly-implement-australia-supported-development-initiative-conflict-displaced-women.
UN OCHA (2024) *Global Humanitarian Overview 2025*. https://www.un-ilibrary.org/content/books/9789211070538.
USAID (2018) 'RISE II Technical Approach: Enhancing resilience in the Sahel, USAID'. https://coilink.org/20.500.12592/5ctpy93.
USAID (2019) *The Caravan*. https://www.partnersforresilience.nl/downloads/files/Camel%20Caravan%202019.pdf.
USAID (2022) 'Rural Resilience Activity: Annual Impact Report Oct 2021 – Sept 2022'. https://dldocs.mercycorps.org/USAID2019NigeriaRuralResilienceRRAimpactOct21Sep22.pdf.
USAID (2024) 'Resilience in the Sahel Enhanced (RISE I)'. https://cg-281711fb-71ea-422c-b02c-ef79f539e9d2.s3.us-gov-west-1.amazonaws.com/uploads/2024/05/USAID2979-RISE-I-Fact-Sheet508c.pdf.
VSO (n.d.) 'Integrating peacebuilding, development and humanitarian efforts on the Kenya/Ethiopia border'. https://www.vsointernational.org/our-work/resilient-livelihoods/idphe.
Wako, W., Chala, D., Gemede, N. and Ero, D. (2023). 'Indigenous social protection mechanism: The practices and challenges of Buusaagonofaa in the Borana Oromo, Southern Ethiopia'. *The Journal of Rural and Community Development*, 18(4): 84–102.
WFP (2023) 'Integrated Resilience in the Sahel'. https://www.wfp.org/publications/integrated-resilience-sahel.
WFP (2024) 'The Sahel Integrated Resilience Programme and Scale-Up 2023–2028'. https://docs.wfp.org/api/documents/WFP-0000157397/download/.
World Bank (2019a) 'Ethiopia – lowlands livelihood resilience project'. World Bank Group. https://documents.worldbank.org/en/publication/documents-reports/documentdetail/631541558922443947/ethiopia-lowlands-livelihood-resilience-project.

World Bank (2019b) 'Niger Adaptive Safety Net Project 2'. https://documents.worldbank.org/en/publication/documents-reports/documentdetail/335281570035902042/niger-africa-p166602-niger-adaptive-safety-net-project-2-procurement-plan.
World Bank (2021a) 'National Social Safety Net Program-Scale Up'. https://documents.worldbank.org/en/publication/documents-reports/documentdetail/182631636126992137/project-information-document-national-social-safety-net-program-scale-up-p176935.
World Bank (2021b) *Project Information Document - National Social Safety Net Program-Scale Up - P176935*. World Bank Group. http://documents.worldbank.org/curated/en/182631636126992137.
World Bank (2022) 'Restructuring paper on a proposed project restructuring of Zambia Covid-19 Emergency Response and Health Systems Preparedness Project'. https://documents1.worldbank.org/curated/en/099062724123518178/pdf/P17418516658d50d4196bc1d217c45471c0.pdf.
World Bank (2023a) 'Lake Chad Region Recovery and Development Project'. https://documents.worldbank.org/en/publication/documents-reports/documentdetail/099042723081016463/p16170601a67b10960ae2309766b0148984.
World Bank (2023b) 'Multi-Sectoral Crisis Recovery Project for North Eastern Nigeria'. https://documents1.worldbank.org/curated/en/099101323111038640/pdf/P1578910287a9c05d09cfe08c8599c27214.pdf.
World Bank (2024a) 'Socio-economic Inclusion of Refugees & Host Communities in Rwanda Project'. https://documents1.worldbank.org/curated/en/099103124043510448/pdf/P164130-e7b96c80-a122-4772-a19b-50a7bce96d21.pdf.
World Bank (2024b) 'Zambia COVID-19 Emergency Response and Health Systems Preparedness Project'. https://projects.worldbank.org/en/projects-operations/project-detail/P174185.
World Bank (2024c) 'The Resilient Kerala Program'. https://projects.worldbank.org/en/projects-operations/project-detail/P174778.
World Bank (2024d). 'Zambia – Refugee and host communities project'. World Bank Group. https://documents.worldbank.org/en/publication/documents-reports/documentdetail/099090924120535793.
World Bank (2024e). 'Eastern and Southern Africa – Development response to displacement impacts project in the Horn of Africa'. https://documents.worldbank.org/en/publication/documents-reports/documentdetail/099102924053511785.

8 Breaking the link between polycrisis and poverty

As the Chapter 7 argued, working *on* polycrisis (i.e. tackling root causes and structural drivers) is more transformative and should be combined with working *in* polycrisis (i.e. context-sensitive programming that avoids harm like social assistance during crisis). Though there is increasing policy and programmatic recognition of the layering of crises, as the preceding chapter highlighted, much of the focus of working "on" polycrisis is through donor-funded programmes, as government responses to the range of crises in low- and middle-income countries remain by and large focused on singular crisis, albeit with some limited engagement with working "in" polycrisis. As a result, piecemeal programmatic and often reactive responses without sufficient attention paid to the root causes that generate and sustain varied crises are likely to be less effective in contributing to poverty reduction over the long term.

This concluding chapter asks what changes require prioritisation in resource-constrained contexts, by who, and "how" in relation to policy implementation to support working "on" polycrisis. It first outlines ways in which governments and international actors can better strengthen risk mitigation before, during and after crises in ways that support people's agency in developing pathways out of poverty. As part of this, Section 8.1 argues for a rebalancing of social, economic and environmental policies. In this process, it situates crisis management within a multi-sectoral approach to understanding and equitably responding to multiple sources of risk and structural disadvantages that generate polycrisis.

Section 8.2 asks how to better balance equity alongside risk mitigation and the systems and actors that can support this rebalance—again focusing on working "on" polycrisis. Two recommendations from this chapter is to appraise and mitigate harm in policy design and implementation (pre, during, post) of polycrisis, and to identify and respond to gradations of vulnerability given the high poverty contexts due to or amplified by polycrisis. Section 8.3 then offers final reflections with a view to developing a forward-looking agenda to motivate a more transformative commitment to poverty eradication in an era of polycrisis.

DOI: 10.4324/9781003503125-11

8.1 Equitably addressing social, economic and environmental risk before, during and after polycrisis

Policies and programmes that promote resilience-building, collective risk management and recovery can help households cope before, during and after crises. Repeated cycles of crises and their intersections make this emphasis across time an increasingly important requirement of programming. In other words, there is an increasing urgency not only to build resilience before crises but to plan for recovery during and after polycrisis. This section explores ways in which social, economic and environmental risk can be mitigated before, during and after polycrisis. As the previous chapters highlighted, these risks and resulting crises are deeply interconnected, and sectoral or joined-up responses need to account for these interconnections. It is in this context that the objective of this chapter is to move the discourse towards a more transformative means of working "on" polycrisis.

The section starts with a recognition of social policy as a key domain through which poverty reduction is often driven. However, while social policy including social assistance is certainly a critical enabler of poverty eradication, it can be inadequate on its own (Vetterlein, 2007; ILO, 2020). Instead, as Table 8.1 presents, social policy should be rebalanced in key ways: 1) with economic and environmental policy, 2) without ignoring consequences of "maladaptive" economic policies, and 3) by focusing on recovery programming alongside ex-ante resilience-building. In all of this, as part of working "in" polycrisis, appraising policies to avoid harm as noted in Chapter 7 is important, especially where there are knock on effects from managing one crisis for others. Responding to root causes alongside this appraisal moves us towards working "on" polycrisis in ways that can help break the poverty–polycrisis trap.

These three dimensions of the proposed social policy reset along with the three examples per dimension that are outlined in Table 8.1 are elaborated in the sub-sections that follow.

8.1.1 Rebalancing social policy from within to strengthen responses to polycrisis

Risk-informed social protection "plus" for equitable crises responses

Social protection, and especially social assistance, has typically been the means through which most governments directly intervene through social policy to support poverty reduction over the last two decades. In high poverty countries grappling with polycrisis, social assistance coverage requires substantial expansion in both coverage and value, especially for informal workers and other groups more commonly out of the purview of traditional programming. This expansion is required alongside other means of improving its effectiveness for example through ensuring adequacy and timeliness.

Table 8.1 A new social policy reset for working "on" polycrisis

Rebalance social policy	*Suggested actions to work towards a rebalance*
WITHIN, through resilience and recovery programming (Section 8.1.1)	• *Advancing social protection*: shock-responsive social protection integrated with livelihood interventions, considering subnational crisis variations. • *Strengthening systems and services*: anti-discrimination and affirmative action interventions; progressive gender equality legislation, pro-poor justice systems not least for people experiencing theft, universal health coverage including trauma-informed psychosocial support. • *Promoting HDP coherence*: operationalisation of the humanitarian–development–peace (HDP) nexus with a stronger focus on peacebuilding; promote recovery programmes to go on for longer than they do during crises.
WITHOUT ignoring harmful consequences of economic policy (Section 8.1.2)	• *Mitigating maladaptive policies*: appraisal of macroeconomic policies and mitigation of negative effects and spillovers on vulnerable groups and specific populations; household debt-management and equitable financial services. • *Risk-proofing growth from below*: sector-specific risk-informed support for affected non-farm MSMEs and urban informal sector (including wage and skill upgrading), strengthened education to labour market links and women's empowerment; weather-based and livestock insurance. • *Rehabilitating infrastructure*: Green rehabilitation of critical infrastructure.
WITH environmental policy (Section 8.1.3)	• *Investing in adaptation*: Increase investment in climate adaptation. • *Supporting climate-smart agriculture*: Remove barriers for women and smallholder farmers to effectively take up climate-smart agriculture, linked to land tenure and peacebuilding interventions where relevant. • *Integration*: conflict management better integrated into disaster risk management; integrate environmental considerations (e.g. through climate-based initiatives, disaster risk management) across economic and social policies; use social assistance/public works as payment for eco-system services (e.g. prevent/reduce deforestation).

Source: built on from Diwakar (2023).

Conflict-affected contexts often have geographic hotspots of violence, in which case a combination of geographic followed by categorical targeting may be an effective means of recognising poverty of "place" and "people". At the same time, going beyond traditional humanitarian hotspots within countries is also important, not least given spillovers of violence and different forms of insecurity that could intersect with other crises to drive chronic poverty or impoverishment. In addition, the greatest numbers of people in poverty may not necessarily be in these hotspots.

A clear example is in Nigeria, where humanitarian attention has focused primarily on the northeast, with limited attention to areas of farmer-herder violence grappling with drought (Diwakar et al., 2025). Community participation as part of this targeting exercise could reduce tensions, thus feeding into an appraisal of harm, and improve the transparency and inclusivity of social assistance programming so that it better accounts for gradations of vulnerability.

There are various examples of where social assistance has adopted a shock-responsive element or been benchmarked to adjust for inflation, as Chapter 7 acknowledged. However, given the increasing frequency of climate and economic crises, all these programmes should have these elements. Moreover, given the range and depth of destructive effects of climate-related disasters, relying on social assistance alone to mitigate socioeconomic impacts is inadequate. During crises, linking social assistance with other food distribution or relief programmes can help fill in the gaps in access or continuity during drought or food shortages stemming from high inflation.

Alongside these measures, resulting gains need to be protected through insurance wherever possible. India's Resilient Kerala programme outlined in Chapter 7 offers an example of where the government has added insurance as a component of investment in polycrisis. Such efforts to appraise and respond to harm for select vulnerable groups—i.e. identifying and responding to gradations of vulnerability—could be learned from and applied to programmes working in conflict-affected areas.

Integrating social assistance (see Table 8.2) with climate-resilient livelihoods and infrastructure programming is also increasingly necessary to support

Table 8.2 A social assistance "plus" framing to promote poverty eradication in Nigeria

Protect (Tackle chronic poverty)	*Prevent (Prevent impoverishment)*	*Promote (Promote sustained poverty escapes)*
• Address multiple and overlapping crises alongside structural challenges (e.g. conflict, climate shocks, limited human development). • Enhance food security (e.g. comprehensive approach to sustainable food systems). • Develop savings and asset base, including through non-contributory social assistance.	• Address ill health and expand free or subsidised universal healthcare for people in and near poverty (including psychosocial services). • Conflict prevention and peacebuilding. • Limit agricultural risk (e.g. scale up irrigation, diversify crops, provide micro-insurance).	• Improve financial inclusion (e.g. ladders from informal groups to formal banking), especially access to capital for non-farm enterprises. • Peace building and livelihood recovery plan in conflict regions. • Ensure safe access (with free/subsidised user fees) for a minimum of three years of secondary school, and strengthen links to employment, including public works.

Source: minor adaptations from Diwakar and Adedeji (2021).

upward income mobility or even maintenance of the status quo amidst crises. Livelihood promotion policies, for example through targeted support, training or access to markets to build productive assets, can help support sustained poverty escapes and building people's agency and resilience before crises hit. These asset-building strategies coupled by strong social and political networks can be supported in advance, rather than only in response to crises such as conflict and climate-related disasters. On the latter, the EU's Solidarity Fund for climate-induced disasters offers an example that includes support for countries to rebuild critical infrastructure following climate-related disasters (EU, n.d.). There is also an instrumental purpose in this: where political actors perceive social protection to be complementary to economic development, this can contribute to the sustainability of social protection interventions.

Supporting basic service delivery and systems strengthening

Basic service delivery under more traditional development assistance—including in humanitarian contexts—is an important part of supporting the agency of individuals and households to build assets and livelihood pathways out of poverty. This includes strengthening education and health systems alongside hygiene, psychosocial support and protection (HRP, 2022). Affirmative action to support equitable access to these services and strengthen decision-making of marginalised groups is an important step.

Social policies addressing risk can also include various factors such as progressive gender equality legislation and anti-discrimination policies to reduce horizontal and intersecting inequalities (across race, ethnicity, religion, age, gender and disability markers alongside economic status). This could help respond to gradations of vulnerability experienced by people living in and near poverty. Alongside this, pro-poor justice systems can help appraise harm and guard against theft and support conflict resolution, universal provision of quality education can act as a portable asset and counter the intergenerational persistence of poverty, and universal health coverage can guard against ill-health driven impoverishment (Diwakar and Shepherd, 2022; Stewart, 2010; Marcus et al., 2017).

In terms of education—an important portable asset—early childhood care and education, school feeding, girls' education, support for labour market or self-employment transitions represent critical demand-side interventions that can support recovery. Improving infrastructure, resources, quality of education and being more intentional to address its distributional effects by accounting for gradations of vulnerability is also important in contexts marked by conflict and other crises (Shepherd et al., 2021; Pereznieto et al., 2017). On the latter, free education including free or subsidised user costs and stipends for poor girls and boys are important. The costs of education are otherwise a significant drain on income and potential savings needed to expand or invest in livelihoods. They are also a key reason for taking out loans—even when education is free.

Addressing ill health is also critical as this is often a key source of impoverishment alongside the macro crises discussed in this book. As part of this, free or subsidised healthcare, as observed in Rwanda's experience, has been instrumental in reducing ill health as a source of impoverishment (Shepherd et al., 2019). It was a critical post-genocide measure to manage risk. The literature on social health insurance in conflict-affected contexts though is limited. Nevertheless, some studies suggest that this can be effective in contexts where insurance systems have been established (Spiegel et al., 2018). Even so, ensuring adequate attention to psychosocial and mental health services remains substantially under-emphasised, yet is a critical aspect of recovery. This is even more important in contexts of polycrisis where for example violent conflict can cause long-lasting trauma or hyperinflation eroding life savings can amplify periods of mental stress and trauma.

HDP coherence through a focus on peacebuilding and recovery

A perennial tension in these measures is that they apply a development-focused agenda to a humanitarian situation. However, humanitarian situations are increasingly protracted crises and so development efforts need to be more substantively incorporated, as work in the HDP nexus argues. Coherence is critical across the HDP nexus and can help support the prioritisation of interventions. These development activities could operate in sequence or combination with humanitarian measures such as to support food security. This can in turn help support people to make certain investments once basic survival needs are met. It can also provide a stronger rationale for recovery-focused interventions to go on for longer than they normally do, alongside those that purely focus on providing immediate relief.

Alongside this, the "peacebuilding" arm of the HDP nexus requires further strengthening, as it can instrumentally help contribute to stability that support more effective crises responses. Indeed, given the impoverishing effects of violent conflict, community-based conflict resolution mechanisms involving diverse stakeholders and peacebuilding remains necessary, especially those that focus on appraising harm ex-ante, developing bottom-up solutions for peace and involving people in and near poverty (across its gradations) in its formulation. Decentralised security functions can support these efforts by empowering local authorities as well as other local actors to be more involved in conflict management (Diwakar et al., 2025). This effort can thus indirectly strengthen social capital to support collective recovery post-crises. It can also contribute to more tailored approaches relevant to the unique characteristics, typologies and ideologies of different conflicts.

8.1.2 Rebalancing economic policy to mitigate harm from polycrisis

Appraising economic policies to mitigate harm

Macroeconomic management is a primary response for governments during economic crises in an attempt to manage its effects. This can be a form of resilience-building where it provides fiscal buffers, reduces government debt and has an insurance element to safeguard consumption of people in and near poverty. Reducing the prices of essential goods and fuel for goods consumed by households in poverty and intervening in key markets are common (if controversial with some economists) means of inflation management, alongside social protection (Blyth and Lonergan, 2014; Shepherd et al., 2023).

In humanitarian contexts, however, macroeconomic management (e.g. through public financial management, business environment reforms or job creation) may be sidelined over a focus on meeting survival needs. Business environment reforms can also be weakened by inadequate institutional capacity or subject to elite capture, reinforcing the need for further research on power dynamics as part of an appraisal of harm when developing suitable economic reforms (Luiz et al., 2019; McKechnie et al., 2018). Job creation interventions to support recovery more broadly need to think and work politically and address structural challenges that constrain women's empowerment, alongside providing financial resources to better link livelihoods with market solutions (Blattman and Ralston, 2015; OECD, 2017; Mallett and Pain, 2017).

This focus points to the centrality of political economy analysis in appraising harm and promoting recovery. This helps highlight who the key stakeholders are and how both formal and informal power structures, elite incentives and institutions shape decision-making including around resource allocations, and accordingly the outcomes observed in terms of poverty dynamics. It can also be a critical tool in helping prevent unintended consequences of policy implementation that may otherwise emerge, for example due to perverse incentives. In the absence of this understanding of the political economy of social assistance, aid allocation and poverty reduction more broadly, governance and finance responses risk reflecting political interests rather than objectives of risk mitigation and recovery.

Lessons from the COVID-19 pandemic also point to the need for complementary interventions to guard against risks stemming from macroeconomic policy: "Household debt-management measures, special measures for returning migrants, measures directly targeting the informal economy, and more equitable financial services could have helped prevent downward mobility by better servicing people experiencing vulnerability or poverty" (Shepherd et al., 2023). Regarding debt management during and beyond the pandemic, a combination of low interest loans for near-poor households and grants for people in poverty can help reverse debt spirals that could otherwise be precipitated amidst intersecting or sequenced crises (Shepherd et al., 2023). Identifying and responding to gradations of poverty and vulnerability can help inform these more tailored responses.

More broadly, the consequences of maladaptive policies should be ex-ante considered in economic policy design. Too often we see crises generating such maladaptive policy responses whether driven by austerity measures or other risk management efforts. In responding to economic risk, however, equity is not adequately considered, as highlighted in Chapters 3 and 5. Recovery programming is also needed to counter adverse effects where they continue to take place. This economic recovery programming should be a key focus of banks, social assistance programmes, NGOs, and local authorities where resources can be directed to supporting these efforts. It should also focus centrally on gender-responsive measures, given the great care responsibilities that women and girls in and near poverty may increasingly be forced to take up when crises emerge and intersect.

Safeguarding "growth from below"

Many people in and near poverty develop pathways out of poverty through "growth from below—that is, through small investments by households in micro-enterprises, smallholder agriculture, the rural non-farm economy, and through the urban informal sector" (Shepherd et al., 2019). These interventions though need adjusting during crises, for example through use of conflict-sensitive targeting, providing mental health and psychological support services, supporting natural resource management, partnering with protection actors, and including activities to foster social cohesion.

Table 8.3 points to examples of more specific economic interventions to guard against key risks to livelihoods that households face, and that could form part of an appraisal of harm in policy and programme design. Table 8.4 instead provides an example of potential interventions that could help guard against risks stemming from polycrisis in Nigeria, as identified from mixed methods research. Evidence-based context-specific research to inform prioritisation of risk mitigation is

Table 8.3 Examples of measures to counter livelihood risks

Risk	*Examples of risk mitigation measures*
Agri-culture	• Predictable, regulated markets, and credit systems enabling on-farm diversification and asset accumulation. • Supportive agricultural advisory services with advice on managing all risks. • Climate-smart solutions including irrigation, with links to high quality, predictable disaster risk management.
Livestock	• Build insurance into dairy enterprises and extend access to veterinary services. • Government support for livestock insurance. • Develop financial institutions to complement reliance on livestock as a risky savings strategy. • Develop emergency feeding and watering preparedness.
Non-farm economy and migration	• Urbanisation and the development of a middle class to expand demand. • Non-farm economy promotion and hard and soft infra-structure to support micro/small businesses, alongside removing regulations which are obstacles to firm progress. • Financial ladders to assist graduation from local savings groups up to formal banks.

Source: Diwakar and Shepherd (2022).

Table 8.4 Livelihood interventions to respond to polycrisis challenges identified in Nigeria

Challenge	*Examples of interventions*
Asset drawdowns amidst sequenced crises	• Graduation-type approach, especially cash-plus interventions which are proven to increase income and food security by more than asset transfers alone. Such interventions could also prevent negative coping strategies in face of shocks—for instance distress asset sales. • Interventions that guard against insecurity and risk related to asset loss, e.g. evidence-based insurance products against loss of assets.
Inadequacy of agriculture amidst climate and conflict shocks	• Further development of climate-smart agricultural (CSA) practices, drawing on examples in place, e.g. Borno implementing conservation agriculture, crop diversification, improved seeds, soil fertility management. • Adoption of technology in agriculture, such as drought-resilient crop varieties or appropriate mechanisation. • CSA as well as technological adoption in agriculture should pay particular attention to the impacts of flooding and drought, insecurities due to violent conflict, and pre-existing vulnerabilities related to poverty and gender.
Volatility of non-farm enterprises amidst conflict and COVID-19	• Reforms of the business environment that take into account the economic, market and political context—as well as potential impact on vulnerable groups. • Use reforms to promote local conflict-resolution and peacebuilding with the aim to foster legitimacy and inclusivity.
Unsustainable debt levels among poorer households following COVID-19	• Debt management interventions to help people struggling with debt, for example through mutual debt support mechanisms, or loan forgiveness or restructuring. • Social protection instruments, for instance COVID-19 cash transfers aimed at reduction of household debt accumulated during the pandemic and promoting financial recovery from crisis. • Expansion of financial inclusion initiatives, for instance widening the coverage of mobile money and micro-finance institutions.

Source: Diwakar and Brzezinska (2023).

important not least to identify more tailored responses but also given the many crises and often limited capacities or political will at hand to more comprehensively support collective risk mitigation. Again, this set of interventions would need additional budgets and other resources amidst polycrisis and a stronger consideration of protection in keeping with "do no harm" principles.

As noted above, asset development can be an important strategy to support poverty escapes. However, women-headed and older heads of households remain particularly vulnerable to asset theft. In situations of violent conflict, the threats to assets can also be greater given its common destruction or theft. As such, insurance of key assets including livestock commonly owned by people in and near poverty would be important. This is not only relevant in conflict-affected contexts but also in areas affected by drought or flooding where these assets can also be destroyed. In Ethiopia, livestock insurance was found to decrease conflict risk while acting as a protective factor for households when rainfall was poor (Sakketa et al., 2025). However, the verification of asset loss may also be challenging in conflict-affected contexts. The relative absence of insurance mechanisms in the institutional responses to polycrisis noted in Chapter 7 point to an important area for programme development that can help mitigate harm.

Rehabilitation of critical infrastructure

A key structural challenge inhibiting recovery especially in humanitarian contexts is of limited infrastructure, which for example may be destroyed during flooding, typhoons or conflict, or its absence may fuel grievances that trigger violence. Yet the recovery of livelihoods during and after crisis through restoring infrastructure is essential. In some cases, the post-conflict period can offer a turning point to refocus attention on recovery. Indeed, the Pretoria Peace Agreement (2022) between the government of Ethiopia and the Tigray People's Liberation Front drove a transition in national priorities from crisis response to peacebuilding and reconstruction (Government of Ethiopia, 2025). Nepal's post-conflict period offers another example of this shift in focus.

In terms of key infrastructure, water, roads for market access, and electricity and connectivity are examples that support agrarian recovery in rural and remote areas where many people in poverty often reside. Infrastructure development or rehabilitation thus underpins an equitable recovery and can make the use of cash transfers or DRM efforts more effective. In CPAN research across countries of engagement, key pieces of infrastructure such as roads, water supply, electricity and connectivity are often raised by people in and near poverty as being important to improve welfare at the household and community level, as these can facilitate businesses and reduce costs of economic activities.

Investments in green infrastructure, for example through mangrove restoration, sustainable urban drainage systems, solar energy or green transport infrastructure, can more be more transformative in responding to both economic and climate-related crises. Such attempts can support economic resilience through their underlying job creation while also supporting climate adaptation (e.g. through carbon sequestration from mangrove restoration) and mitigating environmental harm. Digital infrastructure is also increasingly important when physical infrastructure may be destroyed. However, it remains inaccessible to many people in poverty, especially those facing intersecting inequalities based additionally on rural areas of residence and gender (Faith et al., 2024).

Most government development plans recognise the transformative role of infrastructure in driving economic growth and poverty reduction, though may not adequately deliver these services in hard-to-reach insecure or remote areas where polycrisis effects may be amplified.

> The government made a system for each area and district to receive equal water rights. In some insecure districts and villages, people are taking more water by force. When the water reaches to us, it has a lot of loss along the way … If there is peace, and the government regulates the water supply by providing, canal, streams to everybody … it will have good and positive effect on agriculture. If the government builds a proper canal system, it will improve agriculture product that can improve the economic situation. If water distribution properly takes place, it will create jobs, irrigate more land, and enhance agriculture activities in the province.
>
> (INT17-AF, male, sustained escape, rural Afghanistan, 2021 LHI)

8.1.3 Rebalancing environmental policy to support adaptation to polycrisis

Integration for climate adaptation

Given the foundational crises explored in this book of climate-related disasters and its stressors, it is imperative to integrate environmental considerations into economic and social policies, with a view to driving poverty reduction that is both "sustained" and "sustainable". Yet our understanding of the relationship between environmental sustainability and social inclusion remains weak. What we certainly do know however is that people in and near poverty are amongst those who are disproportionately affected by disasters, in part as they are located in rural areas and working in agriculture where climate-related disasters may have particularly adverse effects that drive impoverishment and poverty persistence (Leichenko and Silva, 2014; Hallegate et al., 2020).

Global climate action centred on mitigation and adaptation thus needs to continue, especially with an equity lens to ensure that their disproportion effects on people in poverty can be mitigated. Considering again gradations of poverty along axes of marginalisation (e.g. due to intersecting inequalities) remains critical to support an equitable response through mitigation- and adaptation-focused action. Within this, there is still much more investment in mitigation than adaptation. People in and near poverty need much more adaptation investment than has been put on the table.

Risk-proofing climate-smart agriculture

Climate-smart agriculture (CSA) offers potential for further development, especially with a view towards integrating equity in its access and uptake, and in this process working towards climate adaptation. This has certainly already had uptake. For example, Borno in Nigeria is implementing conservation agriculture and various practices aligned to CSA (e.g. crop diversification, improved seeds) which have a positive impact on farmer welfare (Ekpa et al., 2018; FAO et al., 2019; Awotide et al., 2015; Olagunju et al., 2020). However, as part of this, responding to gradations of poverty by removing barriers to uptake for the poorest smallholders and women for example needs to be better reflected in programme design. This includes credit constraints, household labour shortages, limited awareness of interventions and structural barriers linked to gender inequality. Climate-smart agriculture moreover requires investment in agricultural research and extension, and in irrigation, mechanisation and livestock development (Kurgat et al. 2020; Jones et al., 2023).

At the same, time, while most CSA interventions represent a strategy to mitigate environmental precarity, their often-technical focus means that they do not include complementary measures to support recovery from economic crises or conflict. This limits their effectiveness given the close relationship between climate and these other crises as highlighted in Chapters 3 and 4. Regarding the climate–conflict nexus, ensuring CSA is supported by strengthened land tenure can mitigate conflict. Examples from Chapter 7 also pointed to the combination of CSA with peacebuilding that can go beyond appraising harm (i.e. working "in" polycrisis) to address root causes of violence (i.e. working "on" polycrisis) while jointly strengthening natural resource management

Strategies that go beyond climate resilience to concurrently address economic crises could have a focus on supporting financial and market inclusion. This can be done for example by carefully combining CSA with access to credit or grants, supporting storage and distribution systems that can help guard against food price inflation during economic crises, and supporting access to CSA inputs for poor households during price shocks. On the former, farmers may already have access to small amounts of credit via savings groups. Credit beyond that needs to be acknowledged to be risky for the farm households as also for the credit provider. This is thus a complex issue, not a magic bullet. Inventory credit schemes seem to work in this context, as do contract farming arrangements. Moreover, for poor smallholders, grants can be better than credit given their situations, as noted above.

Integrating conflict responses with DRR

Interventions are also needed that respond to environmental crises alongside violent conflict. There are some budding recommendations on how to adapt DRR to conflict contexts (Box 8.1), for example by ensuring conflict sensitivity within DRR/DRM programming and adapting its tools. Early warning systems are also important in the context. Though most commonly used to identify triggers for climate-related disasters, some programmes as outlined in Chapter 7 also incorporated triggers for conflict. Yet anticipatory action in relation to violent conflict appears to be a weak focus of programming. Instead, conflict resolution and ex-post peacebuilding interventions tended to dominate responses, suggesting limited focus in policy and programme design on appraising harm before polycrisis.

Box 8.1 Encouraging DRR in, and adapted to, conflict settings

- Integrate conflict considerations into DRR strategies.
- Invest in DRR activities in contexts affected by fragility, conflict and violence.
- Develop an integrated cadre of DRR and conflict specialists.
- Adapt DRR decision-making processes, tools and approaches to include greater consideration of conflict conditions and indicators.
- Harness operational learning to deepen understanding of the benefits and limitations of DRR in contexts of fragility, conflict and violence.
- Learn from affected people's experiences and coping capacities and how they deal with linked disaster and conflict risk.

Source: Peters (2019).

8.2 Cross-cutting principles to rebalance risk and equity

The section above dealt with collective risk mitigation and recovery to better respond to polycrisis. Underpinning this is a need to better balance risk (e.g. by appraising and responding to harm) with equity (e.g. by account for gradations of poverty) in policy design and implementation. This section elaborates on key equity-focused principles of this rebalance to help break the bidirectional relationship between poverty and polycrisis. It first argues that progress towards universalism is needed but equally needs to engage with extra targeting to support the most vulnerable people facing intersecting inequalities due to socioeconomic differences and other factors. This is followed by a discussion of system-level enablers grounded in governance, financing and data architecture to support this drive towards equity amidst polycrisis.

8.2.1 Responding to gradations of vulnerability

Navigating universalism and equity: a focus on axes of marginalisation

There is a question about universalism (e.g. delivering services and strengthening institutions for everyone) and targeting (ensuring those most in need are reached). While service provision and institutional strengthening may be objectives with universalism in mind, equity needs to be a central pillar of this. Indeed, research in conflict-affected contexts points to interventions not reaching those most in need unless these populations are specifically targeted (Mazurana et al., 2014). At the same time, without universalism, in very poor countries with intersecting crises, there may be a large group of households falling into poverty. Taken together, this suggests that a shift towards universalism is important but needs to be complemented by extra targeting to support the most vulnerable.

What can be done specifically when most, if not all, of a country may be living in poverty yet resources are constrained? Some criteria adopted by aid programmes in Afghanistan have been to focus on the worst cases of hunger and populations without labouring capacity (Diwakar et al., 2022). One interviewee (Afghanistan, 2022) suggested the following gradation around which to consider programming, largely aligned with the discussion of gradations of poverty conditioning coping responses in Chapter 6:

1 a few people who are "getting ahead" despite challenges and may even be "winners" amidst the worst crises.
2 people who are "getting by" through effective resilience strategies.
3 the more vulnerable who have ineffective coping responses with limited support and are "going down".
4 the population experiencing the most severe forms of vulnerability who may be "going under" towards destitution due to a catastrophic failure of support for resilience capacities and systems.

A focus on gradations of poverty and vulnerability is particularly relevant in contexts where polycrisis converge with high shares or even the majority of people living in poverty. In these contexts, universalism may either not be possible on account of resource scarcity and political opposition, or even where it is adopted would still require equity considerations to ensure that barriers for the poorest people are effectively removed. Moreover, when it comes to drawing the links to the social contract, these gradations and mobility of wellbeing more generally may be as significant as poverty dynamics.

Other axes of deprivation and marginalisation—in other words, different dimensions of disadvantage, like gender, disability, age, ethnicity, remoteness or displacement, which often overlap and compound people's vulnerability—also need to be considered within these gradations. As the analysis in earlier chapters highlighted, crises do not strike everyone equally, but instead often have a disproportionate impact on already marginalised groups. This includes women in poverty, persons with disabilities, young adults in poverty, and other minorities including indigenous populations and ethnic minorities.

Indeed, individuals experiencing intersecting inequalities are often amongst the most vulnerable populations during polycrisis. Intersecting inequalities may be due to extreme poverty interacting with gender, disability, remote area of residence, age and other minority status. In conflict-affected contexts, IDPs and returnees would also fall within this category, oftentimes also overlapping with poverty status. Such examples reflect structural disadvantages thar marginalised groups experience, so links with the earlier discussion of the need to work more centrally "on" polycrisis. Moreover, as Chapters 3–6 highlighted, in many ways, these intersecting inequalities are a mirror image of polycrisis:

there are multiple crises affecting the context in which people live, and multiple sources of vulnerability and potentially personal crises among those most affected.

What this means for programming is that certain intersections may require prioritisation or complementary interventions in different contexts (Chaplin et al., 2019; Van Ek and Schot, 2017; DFID, 2017). Empowering these groups in poverty may concurrently require strengthening their access to credit or grants, land tenure, and anti-discrimination measures as some of the interventions to strengthen their access to resources and opportunities to build pathways out of poverty. Ensuring these more targeted responses are balanced with macro-level structural solutions is important given the interplay between micro-level intersecting inequalities and macro-level polycrisis.

Addressing wrongful exclusion

Wrongful exclusion refers to eligible individuals being left out of programmes due to elite capture or patronage, as well as due to discriminatory practices or systemic bias. On the latter, for example, people may experience psychosocial or cultural exclusion (e.g. stigma against divorced women, disabled people, youth) that limits their participation in services and supports conducive to improving wellbeing. There is a need to address sources of wrongful exclusion linked to these axes of marginalisation where they do occur in real-time and develop ways to adapt programming to mitigate the drivers of exclusion (Diwakar et al., 2020). This is part of the wider appraisal of policies and programmes to avoid harm, as noted above. In the case of mitigating wrongful exclusion, it necessitates tackling patronage-based practices that could promote elite capture and errors of inclusion, as these may promote exclusion in a resource-constrained context (Zurcher, 2020). This can be supported by using multiple types of data and sources to cross-check eligibility, for example complementing quantitative surveys with transparent and participatory processes and qualitative insights from community elders and others in the programme area.

A bottom-up approach to targeting that considers the institutional requirements of partner institutions is important. This can prevent overloading systems, while supporting local ownership and programme sustainability given local buy-in. In addition, bottom-up approaches can improve the contextual relevance of programme interventions to drive more accurate targeting. It can moreover ensure that programmes do not go beyond the absorptive capacities of implementing partners (Zurcher, 2020). As part of this, recruiting project staff from target groups and the local area can support efforts towards ensuring potentially excluded groups are targeted. However, they may be part of local elites and capture processes, so adequate safeguards (e.g. transparency, accountability, inclusive participation mechanisms) would need to be in place to counter this capture. Adequate data disaggregation can furthermore help identify where there may be gaps in inclusion (Diwakar et al., 2022).

Even with these precautions, in contexts of complex and rapid change wrongful exclusion may still occur, and so strategies need to be developed beforehand and reviewed for its mitigation. Building flexibility and adaptability into programming can enable activities to be modified where needed to overcome exclusion. Grievance redress mechanisms can be an important part of a response strategy, especially where these are easy to get access to, processes are transparent and complaints are addressed quickly. Existing platforms can also be leveraged in this process. For example, youth clubs can be used to support dialogue between different groups and work implicitly to strengthen social cohesion.

Informal and hybrid institutions can also be drawn on to limit wrongful exclusion in targeting. For example, during the pandemic, a system of pre-existing, government-supported village networks were mobilised to reach households in need in Ethiopia. These ad hoc committees collected and redistributed crops from kebele residents who were not covered by the Productive Safety Net Program. It also was a platform through which households pooled food and money redistributed to the most vulnerable groups in the village (Tafere et al., 2023). Such interventions draw on local capacities and knowledge to ensure resources are directed equitably towards poorer people within communities.

However, in Afghanistan, where community development councils have similarly delivered in assistance and development projects, in some areas these have been captured themselves so can perpetuate wrongful exclusion (Allouche et al., 2022). A power and political economy analysis should accordingly underpin efforts to address wrongful exclusion through existing mechanisms.

8.2.2 Supporting system-level enablers

Governance and institutional coordination at the risk-equity intersection

System-level enablers constitute the set of governance arrangements, capacities and coordination that may enable policies and programmes to effectively contribute to their objectives. Strengthened governance is an important foundation for crises response. "Countries with better governance, stronger and well-coordinated institutions—backed by sufficient fiscal space … are better able to muster the multi-sectoral responses needed to mitigate damage" (Lind et al., 2021). How can this governance be supported? This section argues for the need to strengthen government capacity, coordination, trust-building and partnership development before, during and after crises. In this process, it is key to appraise and mitigate harm across government interventions.

Much of the building blocks around partnerships and institution-strengthening need to be in place prior to crisis. An analysis of pandemic responses identified that countries investing in cross-sectoral coordination prior to the pandemic was more successful in their ability to scale-up programming through different policy entry points during the pandemic (Donoghoe et al.,

2022). For example, Ethiopia and Kenya were able to expand support during the COVID-19 pandemic by mobilising pre-existing architecture and systems used to respond to the HIV/AIDS pandemic. Similarly, in many countries, existing social registries were built on and expanded horizontally and vertically, providing a solid foundation from which to create new programmes for at-risk groups (Donoghoe et al., 2022; Gentilini et al., 2020).

The examples above primarily speak to mobilisation of formal institutions. However, existing informal or hybrid institutions can also be particularly valuable as such institutions may hold legitimacy for local populations and be more trusted than externally imposed mechanisms. Indeed, governance capacity as well as legitimacy are important for its ability to manage crises (Christensen et al., 2016). People marginalised along the axes noted earlier—e.g. displaced people, informal workers, women in poverty—tend to be most affected when governance lacks local legitimacy.

Yet too often international actors may sidestep informal institutions in donor programming. For example, in Afghanistan, informal credit institutions have been an important means of ensuring liquidity amongst Afghans experiencing poverty (Kantor, 2012; Pain and Levine, 2022). The financial and social support from community structures and wealthier patrons in Chapter 6 point to other such examples of informal safety nets. Disregarding or failing to support informal safety nets and informal institutions that are widespread can limit the ability to reach the most vulnerable populations and could risk creating parallel systems that are unsustainable over the long term (Allouche et al., 2022; Kantor, 2012; SIGAR, 2021). This may require recognising and identifying the prevalence of existing informal systems, respecting their autonomy, encouraging peer-learning and supporting links between informal and formal services where relevant.

Strengthening these efforts then require in part mitigating sectoral or inter-ministerial competition for funds or political prioritisation. There is scope to do this through multisector frameworks. In Nepal, the ministries of disaster risk reduction and health and population coordinated to "harmonize pandemic response measures with disaster response measures in the three tiers of the government (i.e., at the federal, provincial, and local levels)" (Potutan and Arakida, 2021). At the same time, the resource requirements for coordinated governance can be high. There is a case for reducing the cost of economic and political governance, for example through procurement reforms, administrative consolidation and stricter anti-corruption measures, to support resource distribution (Shepherd et al., 2023). Strong political leadership that supports coordinated institutional strengthening can improve the speed and consistency of crisis management and its resource mobilisation (World Bank, 2024).

Instead, poorly coordinated responses or exclusive reliance on formal institutions could undermine state legitimacy and erode public trust. Trust can be difficult to build and easy to lose, as repeated allegations of ministerial corruption in social assistance fund utilisation in Nigeria has highlighted over the years (Abdulrasaq et al., 2025). Rebuilding this trust can be supported through strengthening transparency, communication and accountability as well as building participatory processes for marginalised groups to meaningfully take part in government initiatives. Alongside this, low corruption and high-quality political leadership can support government resilience during crisis (Brown, 2022). However, this may be rare in conflict situations where governments can be part of the problem, unless conflict is localised and the country's leadership is independent of the conflict. Identifying the most effective routes to pro-poor governance requires a deep understanding of underlying power and patronage systems within countries that may coalesce to undermine equity. As part of this, a much stronger focus on mitigating harm in policies and programming is long overdue and can help strengthen the social contract as a means towards rebuilding trust.

Across the above, a commitment to multilateralism and partnerships can support sustainability of responses (Shepherd et al., 2023; Singh and Bose, 2021). Coordination is needed at multiple scales and both horizontally (e.g. between sectors, local governments or countries) and vertically (from international down to local actors). Vertical coordination as noted above can support more equitable responses, not least given the in-depth knowledge that local actors have in terms of identifying the poorest populations and understanding how contexts of risk and crises might intersect in unique ways to amplify deprivations. While localisation gained strength during the COVID-19 pandemic, in many contexts this reversed as lockdown restrictions were removed (Diwakar et al., 2023).

Moreover, the mentioned projects in the last chapter are mostly donor funded. Less evident are examples of where governments have also adjusted their policies and programming. Governments instead are more siloed typically than international agencies, donor organisations and NGOs. This raises the major question of whether the change which has occurred is a deep one? This is a critical question especially in the light of reduced aid.

Agile financing centred on principles of equity and risk

The interventions above all require an expansion of financial support within countries and internationally, which is no small challenge in a context where global aid and its underlying institutions have been rapidly shrinking. Especially in contexts affected by conflict and humanitarian crises, traditional domestic financing for social assistance and disaster risk management is often inadequate. For example, in 2021, just 12% of ODA went to DRR-related sectors, of which a meagre 3% reached early recovery action (Peters and Weingaertner, 2023). International debt relief can be a transformative action to build fiscal space for governments to better support equity within social, economic and environmental sectors to strengthen crisis preparation and response. In its absence, innovative mechanisms will increasingly need to be pursued as well as external funding, for example by leveraging debt-swap agreements for climate projects to support social assistance and related investments (Diwakar et al., 2025). Transparent and accountable financial management would need to underpin this, reinforcing the need for strong institutions noted above.

Funding mechanisms also need to be agile. This can be supported for example through ex-ante contingency funds incorporated into programmes for deployment when early warning thresholds are reached. Digitalisation can also support quick action as seen during the pandemic (Donoghoe et al., 2022). However, this comes with risks in terms of reducing equity if barriers to access are not removed—access to the internet and connectivity being amongst the constraints limiting the access of people in poverty to these services. More generally, streamlined protocols enabling rapid procurement of support, including recruiting and deploying staff during periods requiring quick action, are essential (de la Poterie et al., 2021). Indeed, as observed in several countries during the pandemic (e.g. Ethiopia, Tanzania, Bangladesh, the Philippines), the length of time of negotiations for scaling-up social assistance, legal contract amendments to disaster protocols, and/or transitions between social assistance phases reduced access during a post-pandemic period where need remained high (Diwakar et al., 2023). This draws attention to the need for expediency supported by the political leadership that can take action quickly and transparently communicate this with the public to maintain trust.

Data and analysis to inform equitable responses

Strengthening data coordination—including in the collection and analysis of data—can help limit wrongful exclusion and duplication. On the one hand, many conflict-affected contexts can be data-poor which can limit our understanding of people's needs and the very impacts of crises that require mitigating action. At the same time, there has been an increase in data collection in conflict-affected and insecure areas over the last two decades through efforts like Households in Conflict Network (HiCN) and other repositories of information on conflict and/or household welfare. Humanitarian actors also routine collect valuable data on needs. In Afghanistan, for example, where polycrisis has long been present, there has been a range of data collection—the Humanitarian Situation Monitoring Pilot (HSMP) and Pre-Lean Season Assessment (PLSA) datasets focus on household and community needs, food insecurity and coping in 2021/22, while the Income and Expenditure and Labor Force Survey presents a nationally representative snapshot of poverty and wellbeing in 2019/20 (Diwakar et al., 2022). These often project-specific datasets could be usefully combined to offer a rich understanding of poverty and wellbeing. This can be aided by strengthen systems of interoperability, including by or in collaboration with national statistics offices, who can play an important role to standardise and integrate data sources in emergency situations.

There is also a range of macro-level data that could be drawn on including by national statistics offices or local universities. Chapters 3–6 illustrate examples of this data to improve our understanding of polycrisis. This includes for example ACLED on violent events and fatalities, the Global Flood Observatory on presence of flooding, precipitation data to derive measures of drought, and local consumer price index data to improve our understanding of inflation. These could be combined with household self-reported data on shocks as earlier chapters convey, to offer multiple perspectives on actual events and perceived negative crises.

The different types of data, units of analysis and objectives offer scope for triangulation that when compared with deeper qualitative insights—on processes, sequences and less tangible drivers of poverty—can furthermore present a nuanced understanding of the needs of people experiencing poverty dynamics amidst polycrisis and the extent to which needs are being met, as Chapter 1 outlines. Mixed-methods triangulation can not only uncover these intangibles but also help validate patterns or catch gaps in coverage and especially interpretation.

As part of this, a longitudinal lens to track data or changes in people's wellbeing over time could help ensure close to real-time targeting where possible. Poverty is a dynamic experience for many, and especially in contexts of polycrisis people can experience dramatic changes in their wellbeing that necessitates regular updating to ensure programmes continue to reach groups in need of support. The results presented in Chapters 3–6 make a strong case for collecting and analysing quantitative and qualitative panel data to understand people's changing welfare and lived experiences in contexts of rapid change, including centrally as part of monitoring, evaluation and learning (MEL) systems (Box 8.2). While the examples pointed to how the world has adjusted quite broadly to operating with a polycrisis perspective, available or accessible evaluations of the programmes were largely limited.

This type of data and analysis moreover needs to increasingly consider the presence of crises, its interactions and probable impacts of different interactions, and how to prevent them (de la Poterie et al., 2021). As part of this, sensitivity to differentiation more broadly is important in crises contexts. A technical focus on crises alone will be inadequate without consideration of the global drivers, the political and economic conditions and structural challenges that generate polycrisis, their long-term effects (Leach et al., 2021; Few et al., 2020), and the heterogeneity of these effects for different populations. The latter would need to consider gradations of vulnerability along intersecting axes of marginalisation. A technocratic solution will only go so far in firefighting crises rather than addressing the root causes necessary in working "on" polycrisis.

Box 8.2 MEL approaches in conflict-affected contexts

An MEL plan should place a strong focus on learning, through establishing learning questions around the intervention, employ feedback loops, and respond to learning for implementors to be able to re-prioritise in real time. DFID suggests five principles for an effective MEL:

- It should be politically aware to priorities, incentives, and contextual reality.
- Conflict and gender sensitivity should be mainstreamed across its focus.
- Resources should be realistic, appropriate, and proportionate.
- The MEL should be innovative, yet also include learning from other contexts.
- In rapidly changing contexts, there is a strong need for adaptability, basing programmes and their MEL in real time, drawing on evidence and learning along the way.

Source: Diwakar et al. (2022).

8.3 Concluding thoughts

Life in an era of polycrisis is likely to continue to be infused with uncertainty and driving "unsustainability". These trends are shaped not least by food and fuel price inflation alongside debt distress, climate-related shocks and stressors, and violent conflict. The long-term effects of these layered crises are largely unknown, but as this book demonstrates, have already been observed to reinforce each other to drive, prolong and deepen poverty across a range of low- and lower-middle income contexts. This operates through a set of direct impacts, macro-level crises intersections with micro-level shocks and stressors, overwhelmed coping systems, and the negative feedback loops these generate between poverty dynamics and polycrisis.

With these challenges come a pressing need to explore pathways and understand how best to respond to polycrisis to ensure that individuals, communities, and systems are able to withstand negative effects and maintain or improve wellbeing. Hence the focus of this book.

The scale of need is great, and only likely to amplify given the increasing intersections of macro-level crises. This book focused especially on violent conflict, economic crises and climate-related disasters, but of course there is a host of other macro-level crises alongside micro-level shocks and stressors that could intersect with and amplify these crises, such as public health emergencies and political instability more broadly. While poverty rates have exhibited a downward trend over the decades, this cannot be taken for granted, as its stagnation prior to and reversal during the COVID-19 pandemic highlighted. Indeed, the poverty–polycrisis trap presented in this book is evidenced to constrain both preventive and recovery-focused solutions.

8.3.1 Poverty as crisis?

So, how then to enable both risk-informed and equitable responses, that respectively work "in" and "on" polycrisis? The earlier parts of this chapter provided some recommendations. A key part of this in resource-constrained contexts is to better consider gradations of people's poverty along intersecting axes of marginalisation amidst complex polycrisis in both research and practice. This would ideally focus on poverty experienced by "people" and related to "place" (Ravallion and Wodon, 1999). Regarding "place" dimensions, these would centre on polycrisis which often have geographic delineations. The focus on poverty experienced by "people" would instead recognise the amplified impacts that crises can have on groups facing intersecting inequalities or those displaced as a result of crises, where the erosion of coping amidst negative feedback loops alongside the direct impacts of polycrisis can otherwise reinforce poverty traps.

Indeed, the structural vulnerabilities that create crises—often embedded in the gradations of vulnerability people experience and their multidimensional deprivations linked to monetary poverty—are too often overlooked. In polycrisis contexts, poverty is both a driver and a consequence of crisis. It moreover has disproportionate and harmful impacts on those already experiencing structural poverty and vulnerability—often groups facing intersecting inequalities due to poverty alongside gender, ethnicity, disability, displacement and/or other factors before and during crises. A response in these conditions thus demands structural change, going beyond even most resilience-building approaches outlined in the preceding chapter. Where universal systems are developed in more transformative approaches, equity-oriented targeting considering gradations of poverty should be embedded within these programmes. An example of this balance between universalism and targeting was presented in Rwanda's health insurance in Section 8.1, which could be learned from and positive practices applied to other sectors and countries.

Finally, given the acute dimensions of poverty in emergency contexts and the polycrisis that permeate within due to these structural conditions, it is time to start treating poverty itself as an emergency. This does not mean responding through largely short-term relief currently characterising the humanitarian system, but endowing poverty programming with the urgency of action and proportionality of responses underlying interventions during times of crises and integrating long-term poverty solutions that appraise and mitigate harm into emergency responses systems. Current systems are not responding with the urgency or integration that is needed. Indeed, the impact of crisis on poverty and vice versa is now so severe that business-as-usual development responses are no longer adequate and could considerably amplify harm.

Treating poverty as an emergency that requires a crisis-level response accordingly leads us instead to a focus on balancing general capacity-strengthening to build resilience with policy responses during and post-crises that can rebuild people's lives and livelihoods. This would necessitate a stronger proportional response to poverty reduction in polycrisis management, in a context where "risk-informed development" (Opitz-Stapleton et al., 2019) has gained some traction but questions of equity remain largely and often intentionally invisibilised. It would also entail fundamentally new ways of responding to poverty through urgent, integrated, multisectoral action that reflects the complexity of polycrisis alongside gradations of people's vulnerability. This requires a Bronfenbrenner-style framing to consider multi-level systems as a way to promote a whole-of-system approach to equitable polycrisis management. Such a framing requires matrix thinking given that we are interested in multiple *levels of actors* across multiple *sectors* to respond to multiple and intersecting *crises* in ways conducive to sustained poverty reduction.

8.3.2 Recasting traditional policy responses

These last two chapters considered practically how existing policy entry points may be strengthened to better support these pillars of equity and collective risk management to break the poverty–polycrisis trap. Table 8.5 summarises some of these actionable takeaways of means to centre on equity to work both "in" (by appraising and mitigating harm) and "on" polycrisis (by addressing root causes across gradations of vulnerability) using conventional policy entry points. The spread of interventions may seem overwhelming for any one ministry, donor or other actor, but can be developed through a portfolio approach to recovery programming, where sequenced or layered projects within portfolios could be "organisation-specific, area-specific, cross-donor, and/or cross-institutional, making efforts where possible to flexibly open up the space for discussion around reforms with the government" (Diwakar et al., 2020).

Two underlying principles referenced throughout this chapter to balance risk and equity are summarised below. These principles cross-cut the examples presented in Table 8.5 and help move us towards considering poverty as an emergency, motivated by increasingly common contexts of polycrisis.

1. *Explicitly appraise and mitigate harm*: there is a strong need to appraise and in turn mitigate harm in the design and implementation of policies across social, economic and environmental sectors. Too often principles of "do no harm" are sidelined in mainstream development programming, yet require reinforcing in contexts of polycrisis given the potential for acute harm that can be created and sustained, including sometimes inadvertently through government policies that seek to reduce risk. The examples of maladaptive economic policies across this book highlight these outcomes. Moreover, doing no harm and appraising harm is just a baseline threshold; more needs to be done to push the pendulum to mitigate harm and support positive transformative change.

2. *Respond to gradations of poverty and vulnerability*: the high rates of poverty and numbers of people in and near poverty in polycrisis reinforces the need to support universal access to key services, coupled with strong targeting to ensure that the poorest individuals are not pushed further behind. When designing targeting, it is important to consider the gradations of poverty (i.e. the different levels of poverty) alongside axes of marginalisation (i.e. the various ways people are marginalised). Accounting for heterogeneity is important is because people living in and near the poverty line often experience multiple, intersecting sources of structural disadvantage and vulnerability that can differentially reinforce root causes and impacts of polycrisis.

Table 8.5 Examples of equitably working “in” and “on” polycrisis from the perspectives of social protection, DRM and the HDP nexus along a resilience–recovery spectrum

Entry point	*Current overview*	*Working “in” polycrisis by appraising and mitigating harm*	*Working “on” polycrisis by responding to gradations of poverty*
Social protect-ion	Strong potential to support equity, but limited coverage, weak use for polycrisis	• Consider whether/how social protection mechanisms may amplify pre-existing inequalities during polycrisis. • Adapt vulnerability definitions to risk factors amplified due to polycrisis. • Develop understanding of impacts of polycrisis to inform real-time updating of social registries.	• **Absorptive:** strengthen shock-responsive social protection through integration with disaster, conflict and social welfare sectors and agencies. • **Adaptive:** expand coverage to vulnerable non-poor. • **Transformative:** investigate scope for universality to respond to polycrisis (e.g. universal basic income, universal coverage during emergencies).
DRM	Locally led anticipatory action critical but underfunded, conflict sensitivity weak, no consideration of economic crises	• Develop (sub)national impact scenarios through a multi-hazard approach (e.g. integrate disaster risk and conflict data platforms). • Consider impacts of non-natural and societal hazards on anticipatory/adaptive capacities of DRM actors. • Establish clear information pathways for responding to intersecting hazards, ensuring these do not destabilise each other.	• **Absorptive:** support community-based disaster preparedness actors (incl. elders, WROs) to consider effects of polycrisis. • **Adaptive:** adapt emergency management systems (incl. local early warning systems) to consider non-natural disasters. • **Transformative:** use DRM as an entry point to address intercommunity conflict and pursue peace, to enable longer-term effective responses to non-natural disasters.

Entry point	*Current overview*	*Working "in" polycrisis by appraising and mitigating harm*	*Working "on" polycrisis by responding to gradations of poverty*
HDP nexus	Helpful strategic framework, but limited operational-isation, potential for embedding resilience	• Collate latest evidence on risk and resilience factors for conflict and violence from (cross-/sub-) national mixed methods research. • Organise periodic multi- stakeholder discussions to understand changing risk and polycrisis trajectories. • Develop a framework on how to incorporate "do no harm" principles.	• **Absorptive:** build networks of trusted relationships, including with community and customary leaders, supporting a plurality of stakeholders. • **Adaptive:** combat wrongful exclusion through a multi-pronged approach, targeting excluded groups, and developing anti-discrimination measures. • **Transformative:** promote peacebuilding activities within or alongside poverty reduction.
Recovery	Often neglected, critical to prevent downward mobility, cross-cutting policy value	• Identify groups at risk of downward mobility (e.g. informal workers, women in poverty, displaced). • Promote matrix design and integrated recovery assessments. • Ensure recovery programming targets groups experiencing intersecting inequalities.	• **Absorptive:** Longer duration of social protection programmes. • **Adaptive:** Livelihood recovery including cash-for-work programmes for groups facing intersecting inequalities but with labouring capacity. • **Transformative:** Climate-resilient infrastructure (e.g. flood-resistant roads/bridges, improved drainage).

Source: built on from Diwakar et al. (2023).

It is critical in these efforts that discourse and policy be reframed away from focusing on the need for people to forge their own paths out of poverty, to instead focus concurrently on the support systems, services, policies, and institutions that can nurture transformative change, and to learn from positive outliers that have emerged in increasingly challenging contexts. It is not "bad luck" that accounts for impoverishment or chronic poverty, but rather systemic failures that reinforce the moral responsibility of key decision-makers to act through integrated crises-informed responses that centre on equity. The time is ripe to stop firefighting polycrisis and build instead a new architecture across the resilience-recovery spectrum that better accounts for the complexity and uncertainty of lived experiences in pathways into and out of poverty.

References

Abdulrasaq, K., Walker, J.-A., Ukpai, S. and Diwakar, V. (2025) 'Political perspectives of social assistance amidst economic shocks in Nigeria'. *BASIC Research Briefing 7*. Institute of Development Studies. doi:10.19088/IDS.2025.043.

Allouche, J., Sida, L., Nelis, T. and Shahab, S. (2022) 'Needs and vulnerability in Afghanistan'. Institute of Development Studies. https://www.ukhih.org/documents/7/needs_and_vulnerability_in_afghanistan.pdf.

Awotide, B.A., Alene, A.D., Abdoulaye, T. and Manyong, V.M. (2015) 'Impact of agricultural technology adoption on asset ownership: The case of improved cassava varieties in Nigeria'. *Food Security*, 7(6): 1239–1258. doi:10.1007/s12571-015-0500-7.

Blattman, C. and Ralston, L. (2015) 'Generating employment in poor and fragile states: Evidence from labor market and entrepreneurship programs'. https://ssrn.com/abstract=2622220.

Blyth, M. and Lonergan, E. (2014) 'Print less but transfer more: Why Central Banks should give money directly to the people'. *Foreign Affairs*, 93(5): 98–109.

Brown, F.Z. (2022) 'Governance for Resilience: How Can States Prepare for the Next Crisis?' *Working Paper*. Carnegie Endowment.

Chaplin, D., Twigg, J. and Lovell, E. (2019) 'Intersectional approaches to vulnerability reduction and resilience building'. BRACED.

Christensen, T., Lægreid, P. and Rykkja, L.H. (2016) 'Organizing for crisis management: Building governance capacity and legitimacy'. *Public Admin. Rev.*, 76: 887–897. doi:10.1111/puar.12558.

de la Poterie, A.T., Clatworthy, Y., Easton-Calabria, E., Coughlan de Perez, E., Lux, S. and van Aalst, M. (2021) 'Managing multiple hazards: Lessons from anticipatory humanitarian action for climate disasters during Covid-19'. *Climate and Development*, 14(4): 374–388. doi:10.1080/17565529.2021.1927659.

DFID (2017) 'Using human-centred design at DFID'. UK Department for International Development. https://diytoolkit.org/tools/personas.

Diwakar, V. (2023) 'Towards a new equilibrium: Why social policies alone will not eliminate poverty'. CPAN/Institute of Development Studies. https://social.desa.un.org/sites/default/files/inline-files/VDiwakar2023-SocPoliciesPovertyEradication.pdf.

Diwakar, V. and Adedeji, A. (2021) 'Poverty dynamics and social protection in Nigeria'. *CPAN Working Paper*. CPAN. https://www.chronicpovertynetwork.org/resources/2021/6/28/poverty-dynamics-and-social-protection-in-nigeria.

Diwakar, V. and Brzezinska, I. (2023) 'Poverty dynamics amidst multiple crises in Nigeria'. *DEEP working paper 17*. Oxford Policy Management.

Diwakar, V. and Shepherd, A. (2022) 'Sustaining escapes from poverty'. *World Development*, 151: 105611. doi:10.1016/j.worlddev.2021.105611.

Diwakar, V., Bizoza, A., Lenhardt, A., Shepherd, A., Moonga, A., Shahan, A. (2023) 'Equitably responding to and recovering amid polycrisis'. In A. Shepherd *et al.* (Eds.), *Chronic Poverty Report 5 – Pandemic Poverty*. CPAN/Institute of Development Studies. doi:10.19088/CPAN.2023.021.

Diwakar, V., Ghafoori, I. and Nemat, O. (2022) 'Vulnerability in Afghanistan before and during the shift in power'. *CPAN working paper*. https://www.chronicpovertynetwork.org/resources/2022/12/16/vulnerability-in-afghanistan-before-and-during-the-shift-in-power.

Diwakar, V., Shepherd, A. and Salomon, H. (2020) *Good practices and strategies to reduce poverty in conflict-affected contexts in Sub-Saharan Africa*. GIZ (Deutsche Gesellschaft für Internationale Zusammenarbeit).

Diwakar, V., Walker, J.-A., Turnwait, M., Eichsteller, M. and Adeniran, A.P. (2025) 'Poverty dynamics and social assistance amidst intersecting crises in Nigeria'. *BASIC Research Working Paper 35*. Institute of Development Studies. doi:10.19088/BASIC.2025.004.

Donoghoe, M., Sengupta, S., Costella, C. and Sivanu, S. (2022) 'Climate change, intersecting disasters and social protection: How the Covid-19 experience can prepare us for the future'. *Working Paper*. Red Cross Red Crescent Climate Centre.

Ekpa, D., Oyekale, A., Yuni, D. and Ibrahim, H. (2018) 'Poverty decomposition for high and low users of climate smart agricultural techniques North-West Nigeria'. *International Journal of Environment and Pollution*, 3: 26–41.

EU (n.d.) 'The Solidarity Fund'. https://www.europarl.europa.eu/factsheets/en/sheet/97/the-solidarity-fund#:~:text=The%20Solidarity%20Fund%20is%20the,an%20expression%20of%20EU%20solidarity.

Faith, B., Roberts, T. and Sesan, G. (2024) '"Those with big phones have the upper hand": Political, gender and digital exclusions in cash and voucher assistance in North East Nigeria'. *BASIC Research Working Paper 25*. Institute of Development Studies. doi:10.19088/BASIC.2024.007.

FAO, ICRISAT and CIAT (2019) 'Climate-smart agriculture in Borno State of Nigeria'. FAO. https://www.fao.org/documents/card/es/c/CA5416EN/.

Few, R., Chhotray, V., Tebboth, M., Forster, J., White, C., Armijos, T. (2020) 'COVID-19 crisis: Lessons for recovery. What can we learn from existing research on the long-term aspects of disaster risk and recovery?'The British Academy. doi:10.5871/bac19stf/9780856726491.001.

Gentilini, U., Almenfi, M., Dale, P., Lopez, A.V., Mujica, I.V., Quintana, R. (2020) 'Social protection and jobs responses to Covid-19: A real-time review of country measures'. *Living Paper (Version 11)*. World Bank.

Government of Ethiopia (2025) *Ethiopia: The third voluntary national review 2025*. https://hlpf.un.org/sites/default/files/vnrs/2025/VNR%202025%20Ethiopia%20Report.pdf.

Hallegate, S., Vogt-Schilb, A., Rozenberg, J., Bangalore, M. and Beaudet, C. (2020). 'From poverty to disaster and back: A review of the literature'. *Economics of Disasters and Climate Change*, 4: 223–247.

HRP (2022) 'Afghanistan humanitarian response plan'. https://reliefweb.int/sites/reliefweb.int/files/resources/afghanistan-humanitarian-response-plan-2022.pdf.

ILO (2020) *ILO monitor: Covid-19 and the world of work* (5th edn.). International Labour Organization.

Jones, K., Nowak, A., Berglund, E., Grinnell, W., Temu, E. and Paul, B. (2023) 'Evidence supports the potential for climate-smart agriculture in Tanzania'. *Global Food Security*, 36. doi:10.1016/j.gfs.2022.100666.

Kantor, P. (2012) 'Understanding informal institutions in Afghanistan'. MEI. https://www.mei.edu/publications/understanding-informal-institutions-afghanistan.

Kurgat, B., Lamanna, C., Kimaro, A., Namoi, N., Manda, L., Rosenstock, T. (2020) 'Adoption of climate-smart agricultural technologies in Tanzania'. *Front. Sustain. Food Syst.*, 4. https://www.frontiersin.org/journals/sustainable-food-systems/articles/10.3389/fsufs.2020.00055/full.

Leach, M., MacGregor, H., Scoones, I. and Wilkinson, A. (2021) 'Post-pandemic transformations: How and why Covid-19 requires us to rethink development'. *World Development*, 138: 105233. doi:10.1016/j.worlddev.2020.105233.

Leichenko, R. and Silva, J. (2014) 'Climate change and poverty: Vulnerability, impacts, and alleviation strategies'. *Wiley Interdisciplinary Reviews: Climate Change*, 5: 539–556.

Lind, J., Roelen, K. and Sabates-Wheeler, R. (2021) 'Social protection, Covid-19, and building back better'. *IDS Bulletin*, 52(1). doi:10.19088/1968-2021.105.

Luiz, J.M., Ganson, B. and Wennmann, A. (2019) 'Business environment reforms in fragile and conflict-affected states: From a transactions towards a systems approach'. *Journal of International Business Policy*, 2(3): 217–236.

Mallett, R. and Pain, A. (2017) *Markets, conflict and recovery: Findings from the Secure Livelihoods Research Consortium*. Secure Livelihoods Research Consortium.

Marcus, R., Mdee, A. and Page, E. (2017) *Do anti-discrimination measures reduce poverty among marginalised social groups?*EBA. https://www.chronicpovertynetwork.org/resources/2017/3/6/do-anti-discrimination-measures-reduce-poverty-among-marginalised-social-groups.

Mazurana, D., Marshak, A.Opio, J.H. and Gordon, R. (2014) 'Surveying livelihoods, service delivery and governance: Baseline evidence from Uganda'. *SLRC Working Paper 12*. Secure Livelihoods Research Consortium.

McKechnie, A., Lightner, A. and te Velde, D.W. (2018) *Economic development in fragile contexts: Learning from success and failure*. ODI.

OECD (2017) 'Gender equality and women's empowerment in fragile and conflict-affected situations: A review of donor support'. *OECD Development Policy Papers No. 8*. OECD.

Olagunju, K.O., Ogunniyi, A.I., Awotide, B.A., Adenuga, A.H. and Ashagidigbi, W. M. (2020) 'Evaluating the distributional impacts of drought-tolerant maize varieties on productivity and welfare outcomes: An instrumental variable quantile treatment effects approach'. *Climate and Development*, 12(10): 865–875. doi:10.1080/17565529.2019.1701401.

Opitz-Stapleton, S., Nadin, R., Kellett, J., Calderone, M., Quevedo, A. and Peters, K. (2019) 'Risk-informed development: From crisis to resilience'. ODI. https://odi.org/en/publications/risk-informed-development-from-crisis-to-resilience/.

Pain, A. and Levine, S. (2022) 'Informal credit briefing note for FCDO'. *Internal briefing note*. FCDO.

Pereznieto, P., Magee, A. and Fyles, N. (2017) 'Mitigating threats to girls' education in conflict-affected contexts: Current practice'. *Evidence Review*. UNGEI/ODI.

Peters, K. (2019) 'Disaster risk reduction in conflict contexts: An agenda for action'. *ODI report*. https://cdn.odi.org/media/documents/12910.pdf.

Peters, K. and Weingaertner, L. (2023) 'Financing disaster risk reduction in humanitarian and crisis settings'. *UNDRR report*.

Potutan, G. and Arakida, M. (2021) 'Evolving disaster response practices during Covid-19 pandemic'. *Int. J. Environ. Res. Public Health*, 18(6): 3137. doi:10.3390/ijerph18063137.

Ravallion, M. and Wodon, Q. (1999), 'Poor areas, or only poor people?' *Journal of Regional Science*, 39(4): 689–711.

Sakketa, T.G., Maggio, D. and McPeak, J. (2025) 'The protective role of index insurance in the experience of violent conflict: Evidence from Ethiopia'. *Journal of Development Economics*, 174. doi:10.1016/j.jdeveco.2024.103445.

Shepherd, A., Bird, K., Dacorta, L., Diwakar, V., Dubey, A., Gelb, S. (2019) 'The Fourth Chronic Poverty Report: Growth'. Overseas Development Institute. https://www.chronicpovertynetwork.org/resources/2019/7/15/the-chronic-poverty-report-on-growth.

Shepherd, A., Nicolai, S. and Diwakar, V. (2021) 'Educating poor and vulnerable children in conflict-affected areas'. *Policy brief.* USAID.

Shepherd, A., Diwakar, V., Bizoza, A., Lenhardt, A., Moonga, A., Shahan, A. (2023) *Chronic Poverty Report 5 – Pandemic poverty.* CPAN/Institute of Development Studies. https://DOI:10.19088/CC.2023.006.

SIGAR (2021) 'What we need to learn: Lessons from twenty years of Afghanistan reconstruction'. https://www.sigar.mil/Portals/147/Files/Reports/Lessons-Learned/SIGAR-21-46-LL.pdf.

Singh, H. and Bose, I. (2021) *Artificial distinction between climate change adaptation and development restricts access to climate finance for developing countries.* Heinrich-Böll-Stiftung. https://eu.boell.org/sites/default/files/2021-07/Shaping%20the%20Future%20of%20Multilateralism%20-%20Singh%20and%20Bose_FINAL_0.pdf.

Spiegel, P., Chanis, R. and Trujillo, A. (2018) 'Innovative health financing for refugees'. *BMC Med.*, 16(90). doi:10.1186/s12916-018-1068-9.

Stewart, F. (2010) 'Horizontal inequalities as a cause of conflict: A review of CRISE findings'. *World Development Report, Background Paper.* World Bank.

Tafere, Y., Shahan, A., Rahem, R. and Diwakar, V. (2023) 'The role of local resources in mitigating the impact of Covid-19'. *CPAN policy brief.* CPAN. https://hdl.handle.net/20.500.12413/18035.

Van Ek, V. and Schot, S. (2017) 'Towards inclusion: A guide for organisations and practitioners'. Light for the World/Mission East/ICCO Cooperation. https://resourcecentre.savethechildren.net/pdf/towards_inclusion_a4_web.pdf/.

Vetterlein, A. (2007) 'Economic growth, poverty reduction, and the role of social policies: The evolution of the World Bank's social development approach'. *Global Governance*, 13(4): 513–533.

World Bank (2024) 'Poverty, Prosperity, and Planet Report 2024: Pathways out of the polycrisis'. doi:10.1596/978-1-4648-2123-3.

Zurcher, C. (2020) 'Meta-review of evaluations of development assistance to Afghanistan, 2008–2018: Chapeau paper'. Federal Ministry for Economic Cooperation and Development (BMZ), Germany, Division for Afghanistan and Pakistan. https://www.sicherheitneudenken.de/media/download/variant/198198.

Annexes

Annex A: Construction of cross-country crises and coping capacity thresholds

Table A1 Definitions and thresholds for cross-country crisis and coping indicators

Dimension	*Indicator/ref. year*	*Definition*	*Threshold*	*Source*
Climate crisis	Natural hazard (2025)	Physical exposure (annual average exposed population) to earthquakes, tsunamis, floods, cyclone winds, storm surges and droughts	Very high: 6.9 or higher High: 5.1 to 6.8 Medium: 3.2 to 5.0 Low/very low: below 3.2	INFORM
	Climate vulnerability (2022)	Vulnerability to climate change impacts and readiness to leverage investments for adaptation in six sectors: food, water, health, ecosystem service, human habitat, infrastructure	Very low: less than 40 Low: 40 to 50 Medium: 50 to 55 High: 55 to 60 Very high: over 60	ND-GAIN
Economic crisis	Growth volatility (2010–23)	Degree of variation or fluctuation in the growth rate of GDP per capita over time, calculated based on standard deviation over the reference period	Very high: standard deviation (SD) over 5 High: between 2 and 5 Medium: between 1 and 2	WDI
	Headline inflation (2020–22)	Raw inflation figure including all items in CPI basket—weighted average of prices for a basket of goods and services typically purchased by households	Very high: double digits High: 5–10% Moderate: 2–5% Low: less than 2%	CPI

Dimension	*Indicator/ref. year*	*Definition*	*Threshold*	*Source*
Social crisis	Global Peace Index (2024)	States ranked according to level of peacefulness, measured by indicators of the absence of violence or fear of violence, categorised by: ongoing domestic and international conflict, social safety and security and militarisation	Very low: 2.91 to 3.40 Low: 2.36 to 2.90 Medium: 1.90 to 2.35	GPI
	Human hazard (2025)	"Human-made hazards include both technological (industrial accidents) and sociological (conflict) events."	Very high: 6.9 or higher High: 5.1 to 6.8 Medium: 3.2 to 5.0 Low/very low: below 3.2	INFORM
Coping capacity	Disaster risk reduction (2014–24)	"Adoption and implementation of national DRR strategies in line with the Sendai Framework for Disaster Risk Reduction 2015–2030 (Sendai target E1 and SDG indicator 13.1.2)"	Very high: 6.9 or higher High: 5.1 to 6.8 Medium: 3.2 to 5.0 Low/very low: below 3.2	INFORM
	Economic management (2023)	Macroeconomic management, fiscal policy, and debt policy performance assessed by World Bank staff based on indicators, observations and judgements.	Very low: below 3.2 threshold Medium: 3.3 to 4 High: more than 4	WB CPIA
	Government effectiveness (2023)	"Perceptions of the quality of public services, the quality of the civil service and the degree of its independence from political pressures, the quality of policy formulation and implementation, and the credibility of the government's commitment to such policies"	Very low: less than -1.0 Medium: -1 to -0.5 High: -0.5 to 0 Very high: above 0	WGI
	Voice and accountability (2023)	"Perceptions of the extent to which a country's citizens are able to participate in selecting their government, as well as freedom of expression, freedom of association, and a free media"	Very low: less than -1.0 Medium: -1 to -0.5 High: -0.5 to 0 Very high: above 0	WGI

Note: underpinning analysis in Chapter 2 (Section 2.2).

Annex B: Poverty definitions and data collection

Poverty lines used in the quantitative household survey analysis is summarised below:

- Afghanistan: national poverty line
- Bangladesh: $1.90 poverty line
- Ethiopia: national poverty line
- India: national (Tendlkar) poverty line
- Kenya: national poverty line
- Malawi: national poverty line
- Niger: national poverty line
- Nigeria: bottom two quintiles (e.g. poorest 40% of households)
- Tanzania: bottom two quintiles (e.g. poorest 40% of households)
- Zambia: national poverty line

Poverty in the qualitative life history data is defined based on a participatory wealth ranking exercise where universal definitions presented below are adapted by study participants to reflect localised definitions.

Table B1 Participatory wealth ranking, starting categories

Levels and name	*Conceptual/Universal Definitions (how we understand these groups from the literature)*
WB 1 Destitute/ ultra poor	WB1 are people who cannot work. So, they depend on others for basic needs (food, housing). However, they often don't have external support (socially excluded). • Food consumption is very low—perhaps 1 meal a day or nothing. • Impaired (e.g. very old, physically or cognitively impaired, severely depressed) or unemployed by circumstance (e.g. remote rural areas after drought) • Tend to be socially, economically and politically excluded from support.

Levels and name	*Conceptual/Universal Definitions (how we understand these groups from the literature)*
	• Homeless or living in leaky un-maintained structure. • In urban areas it may include street children, homeless, or living in extremely poor dwellings (e.g. holes in roofs). Some youth drug addiction. • Begging is common. • Fatalism is common.
WB 2 Extreme poverty	WB 2 are extreme poor and capable of working. They are physically able to work but who have no or few productive assets or capital for trade. • They eat when they work (usually one meal) and go days without food. • They must accept whatever wage is offered (daily wage or piecework) and often desperate for work so tend to accept adverse labour relationships. • Little or no negotiating power with employer so tend to be adversely included in labour markets and other institutions, accept whatever wage/crop price is given. a Petty trading that involves spoiled/fallen fruit/veg/grain and/or extremely small margins (door-to-door traders). b Gleaning in other people's fields after harvest to eat. • Work but earnings are not enough and so are dependent on support from relatives elsewhere (especially in towns) • Difficulty to support children in primary school and so some children may drop out and work/trade. • Vulnerable to shocks which will push them into destitution. • Very poor accommodation; move often (can't afford rent, housing flimsy, very poor access to water and sanitation).
WB 3 Moderate poverty	WB3 are moderately poor, have labouring capacity (not infirm) and some productive assets (land/livestock/bike) or small trade with capital. But in rural areas not enough to escape labouring for wages in order to meet basic needs. • This group also tend to have adverse credit and labour relationships. • May have land/cattle/small business but cannot save enough in good years necessary to withstand shocks (health, drought). • Vulnerable to downward mobility to "very poor" category • Often must sell assets to cope in a crisis and go hungry. • Very limited ability to support education beyond primary. • If have urban employment is often under minimum wage (e.g. guard, domestic worker) • Sometimes depend on remittances from relatives elsewhere (especially in towns)

Levels and name	*Conceptual/Universal Definitions (how we understand these groups from the literature)*
WB 4 Vulnerable but not poor	Vulnerable but not poor: those who have relatively more productive assets (plough, ox cart, oxen, bikes, taxi) and assets made more productive through inputs and which can provide the income necessary to feed the family through the year. • During good times, can save and tendency to diversify assets/ livelihoods. • During bad times, will reduce family consumption in order to meet other regular expenditures (e.g. education, rent, other financial obligations) • Vulnerable to downward mobility with a significant shock, often worse in urban areas • During bad times, reduce family consumption, but not as regular as above. • Ability to meet regular rent and/or own house. • If have formal employment, beyond minimum wage but not high earning • Access to informal credit linked to assets and employment, sometimes struggle to pay back. • Ability to pay some private education for children, e.g. secondary school.
WB 5 Resilient	Resilient in the face of shocks because of substantial assets, social networks and political connections necessary to prevent significant downward mobility relative to overall productive wealth. • It takes several socks or very severe shocks to move this category of people downward into poverty—hence rare. • May employ labour regularly on large farm and have several non-farm businesses or one large enterprise. • Formal employment in higher wage-earning sectors is more secure. This includes civil service. • Access to formal credit and more reliably able to pay back. • Children often finish secondary school.
WB 6 Rich	• Large and several businesses, assets including land if rural, often has well-paid urban employment. Often not resident in rural areas but can be present in peri-urban areas. • Wealth: Often very large, business hiring large amount of local labour. • Non-farm businesses, trade, moneylending and other assets. • Have local political power. • Children often in tertiary education.

Source: co-developed by Lucia da Corta and Flora Kessy and adapted and refined over time through CPAN studies on poverty dynamics for use in a range of rural and urban settings.

Table B2 Qualitative data collection for CPAN poverty dynamics country studies

Country	*Qualitative data collected by a team led by …*
Afghanistan	Orzala Nemat (AREU) with remote support from Lucia da Corta (CPAN)
Bangladesh	Lopita Huq, Salina Aziz (BIGD) and remote support from Lucia da Corta (CPAN)
Cambodia	Theavy Chhom (CDRI) and Kate Bird (CPAN)
Ethiopia	Yisak Tafere (Young Lives, PSI) and Chiara Mariotti (CPAN at time of research)
India	Sonalde Desai, Santanu Pramanik (NCAER) and Vidya Diwakar (CPAN)
Kenya	Elvin Nyukuri (University of Nairobi) and Lucy Scott (CPAN at time of research)
Malawi	Blessings Chinsinga (Chancellor University) and Lucia da Corta (CPAN)
Niger	Aissa Diarra (LASDEL), Aoife McCullough (ODI at time of research) and Lucia da Corta (CPAN)
Nepal	Anita Ghimire (NISER) and Vidya Diwakar (CPAN)
Nigeria	Judith-Ann Walker (dRPC) with support from Lucia da Corta and Vidya Diwakar (CPAN)
Philippines	Manuel de Vera (AIM) and Vidya Diwakar (CPAN)
Rwanda	Roberte Isimbi (Fate Consulting), Lucia da Corta and Kate Bird (CPAN)
Tanzania	Flora Kessy (TTCIH), Kim Kaunde, Judith Kahamba (Sokoine University) and Lucia da Corta (CPAN)
Zambia	Joseph Simbaya (INESOR), Ginny Bond (Zambart) and Lucia da Corta (CPAN)
Zimbabwe	Jeanette Manjengwa (ECSDI) and Kate Bird (CPAN)

Note: all collaborators are CPAN partners or associates. Institutional affiliations part of CPAN are also mentioned in parentheses where relevant.

Annex C: Variable list from panel survey data

The list below provides a non-exhaustive overview of the types of questions and/or response options that constitute each variable. As noted in Chapter 1, there are some variations in the set of response options and wording of questions across countries which limits comparability. Our aim however is not for cross-country comparability of the salience of crises or coping responses, but rather contextually relevant analysis of this when disaggregated by different categories and intersections of crises.

Crises and shocks

- Environmental/agricultural: drought; flood; landslides; heavy rains; unusually high level of crop pests or disease; unusually high level of livestock disease; reduced agricultural water.
- Conflict: insecurity; violence; theft; imprisonment/arrests; political unrest; displacement; assault; ethnic/clan clashes; communal conflict; hijacking; kidnapping; victim of crime.
- Economic: refers to presence of either revenue and/or price shocks.
- Revenue: loss of employment; business bankruptcy; cut-off of remittances; withdrawal of NGO assistance; reduction in earnings of salaried members; departure of income-earning member.
- Price: unusually high increases in food prices; unusual decrease in farm gate prices; food price inflation; unable to sell at fair price; unusual increase in price of inputs; large fall in sale prices.
- Health: serious illness; accident or death of household member; HIV/AIDS; disability of adult worker; illness of earning income member; death of remittance sender.
- Other: divorce; separation; dowry; division of property; court case costs; bribe costs; loss of home for non-disaster reasons; birth in household; eviction; breakup of household; dwelling damaged (without specifying reason); lack of food.

Coping responses

- Asset sales: sold farmland, livestock, assets; rented out or mortgaged assets (productive or consumption assets), sold crop stock.
- Human development: married children; sent children to live elsewhere; sent children to be fostered by relatives; dropped children from school; married girl child/children; transferred children to less expensive schooling; decreased expenditures on health/education.
- Food consumption: reduced quality of diet; skipped meals; ate less food to reduce expenses; changed eating patterns; purchased cheaper food; eating wild foods only.
- Credit: purchased food on credit from traders; took loans from relative or friends; loan from money lender, NGO, institution, non-institutional source; borrowed money; credit purchases; delayed payment obligations.
- Work: sold labour in advance; children/adults who were not working started working; took on more employment; worked longer hours; adult household member took job elsewhere/migrated; sent children into domestic service; forced to change occupation; intensify fishing; started a new business; grow food in contre-saison; sold harvest in advance; piece work on farms belonging to others; food-for-work; petty vending.
- Savings: relied on own savings; spent cash savings.
- Friends/family support: received help from others in the community; emergency receipt of remittance from migrant family member; received unconditional help from relatives/friends; sought refuge with neighbours.
- Aid: received unconditional help from government/NGO; unconditional help from religious institution; used insurance; help from government or NGO cash transfer
- Other: other; sought spiritual help; begging from the streets.
- Nothing: did nothing to compensate.

Other variables

- Log of asset value (LogAV) (typically consumer durables but sometimes mixed with productive assets depending on module question formation) or principle component analysis of wealth score changed to quintiles.
- Cultivable land: own any irrigated or rain/fed farmland/cultivable land.
- Livestock: own any bulls, cows, oxen, yaks, goats, sheeps, camels, horses, donkeys, pigs.
- Electricity: household has electricity (sometimes more detail e.g. whether grid or generator).
- Household size: number of household members.
- Age/age-squared: age and age-squared of household head.
- Female: female household head.
- Primary education: head completed primary education but not lower secondary education.

- Secondary education: head completed lower secondary education or higher.
- Agricultural employment: head engaged in agricultural employment (7 days pre-survey, or main employment in 12 months pre-survey, depending on question formation).
- Non-farm enterprise: household owns a non-farm enterprise.
- Remittances: household received remittances (typically 12 months pre-survey).
- Urban: household resides in an urban area.
- Region: region of household residence (e.g. zone, province, or county).

Annex D: Regression results

The models below present full regression results for:

1 the full baseline model without interaction terms (Tables D1 and D2). Multinomial logistic regressions are specified in countries with panel data (Ethiopia, Niger, Nigeria, Malawi, Bangladesh, Tanzania), and logistic regressions otherwise (Afghanistan, Kenya, Zambia).
2 the full baseline model with three-way interaction terms (Tables D3 to D7). In this specification, given non-convergence issues, we collapse the outcome to a binary across the panel datasets and hence adopt logistic regressions (rather than multinomial logistic regressions for countries with panel data). In these tables, the outcomes are instead =1 if the household experienced chronic poverty or poverty transience (including impoverishment or churning), and =0 otherwise (i.e. if the household was resilient or remained non-poor).
3 the two-way intersection of crises with lower secondary education completion as an example, conditional on climate-related disasters (Tables D8 and D9). Results for controls are similar across other two-way intersections presented in the book. Multinomial logistic regressions are specified in countries with panel data (Ethiopia, Niger, Nigeria, Malawi, Bangladesh, Tanzania), and logistic regressions otherwise (Afghanistan, Kenya, Zambia).

AMEs are presented across models. Further model details are outlined in Chapter 1.

Table D1 Correlates of poverty (dynamics), (multinomial) logistic regression conducted on full sample of households in economic crisis-affected countries

	Zambia	*Malawi*		*Bangladesh*		*Tanzania*	
VARIABLES	Poor	Chronic poor	Transient poor	Chronic poor	Transient poor	Chronic poor	Transient poor
Cultivable land	N/A	0.195	0.116	-0.578*	-0.467***	N/A	N/A
	N/A	(0.227)	(0.202)	(0.297)	(0.115)	N/A	N/A
Livestock	-0.246**	-0.410***	-0.135	-0.365	0.0773	-0.931	-0.0922
	(0.110)	(0.141)	(0.150)	(0.246)	(0.109)	(0.639)	(0.328)
Non-farm enterprise	-0.247***	-0.0479	0.0446	-0.116	-0.0772	0.239	0.142
	(0.0953)	(0.379)	(0.268)	(0.277)	(0.103)	(0.565)	(0.424)
Violent conflict	-0.777*	-0.468**	-0.0555	0.871**	0.00314	-2.316***	-1.073***
	(0.447)	(0.227)	(0.223)	(0.391)	(0.190)	(0.849)	(0.398)
Economic shocks	-0.138	0.0912	0.0864	0.810**	-0.0931	0.810	0.654*
	(0.0918)	(0.115)	(0.123)	(0.378)	(0.182)	(0.523)	(0.347)
Climate-related disasters	0.294**	0.304**	0.0560	1.054	0.521*	-0.382	-0.0664
	(0.120)	(0.139)	(0.149)	(0.866)	(0.273)	(0.627)	(0.560)
Household size	0.440***	0.437***	0.222***	0.651***	0.239***	0.278***	0.138***
	(0.0243)	(0.0318)	(0.0359)	(0.0672)	(0.0310)	(0.0913)	(0.0469)
Primary education	0.00882	-0.462***	-0.250	-0.621*	-0.376***	-0.537	-0.762**
	(0.113)	(0.179)	(0.180)	(0.376)	(0.128)	(0.438)	(0.342)
Lower secondary education	-0.473***	-1.276***	-0.678***	-0.616	-0.988***	-23.58***	-2.601***

	Zambia	*Malawi*		*Bangladesh*		*Tanzania*	
	(0.116)	(0.200)	(0.160)	(0.455)	(0.166)	(1.295)	(0.872)
Head in agriculture	0.0257	-0.109	0.0847	0.724**	-0.0498	0.298	0.669*
	(0.133)	(0.139)	(0.140)	(0.295)	(0.113)	(0.982)	(0.360)
Remittances	-0.0369	-0.254**	-0.0543	0.168	-0.164	0.0407	0.271
	(0.128)	(0.125)	(0.120)	(0.426)	(0.141)	(0.568)	(0.267)
Electricity	-1.444***	-22.70***	-0.858***	-1.197***	-0.709***	-23.86***	-0.485
	(0.136)	(0.341)	(0.295)	(0.352)	(0.119)	(1.253)	(0.522)
Assets	-0.403***	-0.169***	-0.00521	-0.966***	-0.510***	-0.0416***	-0.00541
	(0.0278)	(0.0196)	(0.0201)	(0.110)	(0.0453)	(0.0155)	(0.00339)
Urban residence	-0.671***	0.241	0.365*	N/A	N/A	-2.508**	-0.485
	(0.124)	(0.468)	(0.196)	N/A	N/A	(1.037)	(0.426)
Constant	2.846***	-1.106*	-0.981*	5.135***	5.230***	0.302	-0.0576
	(0.416)	(0.568)	(0.519)	(1.579)	(0.662)	(3.205)	(1.981)
Region controls	Yes	Yes		Yes		Yes	
Head demographic controls	Yes	Yes		Yes		Yes	
Pseudo R2	0.396	0.127		0.200		0.262	
Observations	8307	3078		5018		771	

Note: reference group = non-poor for Zambia cross-section data, and resilient for Malawi, Bangladesh and Tanzania panel data; robust standard errors in parentheses; *** $p<0.01$, ** $p<0.05$, * $p<0.1$.

Table D2 Correlates of poverty (dynamics), (multinomial) logistic regressions conducted on full sample of households in conflict-affected countries

	Afghanistan	*Kenya*	*India*		*Ethiopia*		*Niger*		*Nigeria*	
VARIABLES	*Poor*	*Poor*	*Chronic poor*	*Transient poor*	*Chronic poor*	*Transient poor*	*Chronic poor*	*Transient poor*	*Chronic poor*	*Transient poor*
Cultivable land	0.00876	-0.169***	-0.0844	0.112	-0.321	-0.222	-0.297*	-0.377**	0.971***	0.397
	(0.0689)	(0.0637)	(0.0835)	(0.115)	(0.316)	(0.279)	(0.180)	(0.192)	(0.323)	(0.249)
Livestock	-0.0733	-0.498***	-0.101	0.160*	-0.189	-0.283	-0.214	0.0780	0.648**	0.331
	(0.0678)	(0.0580)	(0.0645)	(0.0900)	(0.254)	(0.240)	(0.178)	(0.215)	(0.319)	(0.236)
Non-farm enterprise	-0.172**	-0.681***	0.00468	0.155**	0.383	0.322*	-0.124	0.122	-0.435	0.468**
	(0.0849)	(0.0646)	(0.0849)	(0.0774)	(0.264)	(0.165)	(0.182)	(0.197)	(0.270)	(0.186)
Violent conflict	-0.0439	-0.0754	0.491**	0.155	0.361	0.0149	-0.336	0.112	0.620	0.188
	(0.0813)	(0.0717)	(0.194)	(0.191)	(0.317)	(0.249)	(0.573)	(0.577)	(0.581)	(0.449)
Economic shocks	0.319***	-0.0498	0.188	0.00909	-0.00580	0.258	-0.302**	0.00593	0.544**	0.578***
	(0.0659)	(0.0789)	(0.240)	(0.227)	(0.289)	(0.231)	(0.150)	(0.213)	(0.241)	(0.193)
Climate-related disasters	-0.134**	0.0594	-0.223**	-0.415***	-0.401	0.103	0.243	0.0672	0.0963	0.256
	(0.0608)	(0.0628)	(0.0875)	(0.109)	(0.281)	(0.260)	(0.156)	(0.189)	(0.292)	(0.187)
Household size	0.287***	0.324***	0.131***	-0.0372***	0.374***	0.171***	0.235***	0.0398	0.728***	0.340***
	(0.0153)	(0.0123)	(0.0101)	(0.0131)	(0.0411)	(0.0384)	(0.0239)	(0.0265)	(0.0691)	(0.0539)
Primary education	-0.248***	-0.563***	-0.291***	-0.291***	-0.0930	-0.186	-0.520	-0.550*	-0.398	-0.325
	(0.0831)	(0.0727)	(0.0707)	(0.0758)	(0.312)	(0.203)	(0.320)	(0.312)	(0.297)	(0.285)

	Afghani-stan	*Kenya*	*India*		*Ethiopia*		*Niger*		*Nigeria*	
Lower secondary educ.	-0.707***	-1.584***	-0.594***	-0.748***	-0.973**	-1.067***	-2.008*	-2.367***	-1.120***	-0.541**
	(0.0724)	(0.0849)	(0.149)	(0.119)	(0.459)	(0.268)	(1.062)	(0.839)	(0.374)	(0.273)
Head in agriculture	0.275***	0.0428	0.0822	0.167**	-0.116	-0.301	0.508**	0.320	0.519	0.264
	(0.0670)	(0.0545)	(0.0720)	(0.0826)	(0.249)	(0.190)	(0.242)	(0.323)	(0.395)	(0.203)
Remittances	0.0173	-0.0466	-0.387***	0.0627	-0.212	0.318*	-0.00371	-0.0702	-24.28***	-1.251**
	(0.0852)	(0.0615)	(0.149)	(0.143)	(0.377)	(0.180)	(0.120)	(0.148)	(0.622)	(0.609)
Electricity	-0.282***	-0.208	0.217**	-0.00692	-0.828	0.178	-1.098	-0.189	-0.755**	-0.257
	(0.0797)	(0.145)	(0.0934)	(0.108)	(0.584)	(0.280)	(0.685)	(0.405)	(0.330)	(0.222)
Assets	-0.774***	N/A	-7.514***	-2.089***	-0.599***	-0.274***	-0.131***	0.0373	-0.386***	-0.165***
	(0.0887)	N/A	(0.338)	(0.295)	(0.129)	(0.0811)	(0.0263)	(0.0402)	(0.0787)	(0.0580)
Urban residence	0.470***	0.171**	0.591***	-0.0205	-1.552***	-0.919**	-1.642***	-1.912***	-0.685	-0.273
	(0.110)	(0.0732)	(0.128)	(0.122)	(0.578)	(0.372)	(0.431)	(0.418)	(0.480)	(0.234)
Constant	6.164***	-1.947***	-0.0238	-0.707**	-2.844**	-0.657	-2.573***	-2.137**	2.305	2.075*
	(0.859)	(0.215)	(0.252)	(0.313)	(1.397)	(0.702)	(0.996)	(0.873)	(1.554)	(1.099)
Region controls	Yes	Yes	Yes		Yes		Yes		Yes	
Head demo-graphic controls	Yes	Yes	Yes		Yes		Yes		Yes	
Pseudo R2	0.225	0.198	0.128		0.145		0.178		0.317	
Observations	18116	21773	40018		4875		3436		1326	

Note: reference group = non-poor for Afghanistan and Kenya cross-section data, and resilient for Ethiopia, Niger and Nigeria panel data; robust standard errors in parentheses; *** p<0.01, ** p<0.05, * p<0.1.

Table D3 Relationship between economic crises, climate-related disasters, and livelihood moderators [outcome = chronic or transient poverty], logistic regressions conducted on full sample of economic crisis-affected countries

Interactions	*Cultivable land*		*Livestock*				*Non-farm enterprise*			
	Malawi	*Bangladesh*	*Malawi*	*Bangladesh*	*Tanzania*	*Zambia*	*Malawi*	*Bangladesh*	*Tanzania*	*Zambia*
No climate disaster	0.0950*	-0.0250	-0.0388	0.0207	N/E	-0.00650	-0.0651	-0.0273	N/E	-0.0272*
# No conflict	(0.0520)	(0.0420)	(0.0403)	(0.0435)	N/E	(0.0171)	(0.0894)	(0.0567)	N/E	(0.0142)
No climate disaster	-0.0100	N/E	-0.0970**	N/E	0.00683	-0.00693	-0.00883	N/E	-0.0342	-0.0282*
# Conflict	(0.0526)	N/E	(0.0398)	N/E	(0.124)	(0.0178)	(0.113)	N/E	(0.172)	(0.0148)
Climate disaster#	-0.0111	-0.0506***	-0.0501	-0.00442	0.117	-0.0809***	-0.0225	-0.0114	0.0541	-0.0581**
No conflict	(0.0509)	(0.0123)	(0.0419)	(0.0123)	(0.141)	(0.0248)	(0.0881)	(0.0123)	(0.105)	(0.0264)
Climate disaster#	0.0148	-0.0724***	-0.0451	0.0737**	-0.0498	-0.0871***	0.0714	0.0148	0.0248	-0.0622**
Conflict	(0.0624)	(0.0270)	(0.0407)	(0.0355)	(0.0585)	(0.0263)	(0.0782)	(0.0314)	(0.0759)	(0.0282)
Other controls	Yes	Yes	Yes	Yes	Yes	Yes	Yes	Yes	Yes	Yes
Observations	3,078	4,999	3,078	4,993	750	8,307	3,078	4,988	750	8,307

Note: reference group = non-poor for Zambia cross-section data, and resilient for Malawi, Bangladesh and Tanzania panel data; N/E = not estimable due to small cell sizes for interacted variables; robust standard errors in parentheses; *** $p<0.01$, ** $p<0.05$, * $p<0.1$.

Table D4 Relationship between economic crises, climate-related disasters and livelihood moderators [outcome = chronic or transient poverty], logistic regressions conducted on full sample of households in conflict-affected countries

Interactions	*Cultivable land*				*Livestock*				*Non-farm enterprise*			
	India	*Ethiopia*	*Niger*	*Kenya*	*India*	*Ethiopia*	*Niger*	*Kenya*	*India*	*Ethiopia*	*Niger*	*Kenya*
No climate disaster # No conflict	0.00383	-0.0219	-0.0595	-0.0318***	0.000826	-0.0332	-0.0286	-0.0735***	-4.37e-05	0.0664**	-0.0679*	-0.0941***
	(0.0109)	(0.0433)	(0.0448)	(0.0117)	(0.00874)	(0.0378)	(0.0379)	(0.0113)	(0.0108)	(0.0313)	(0.0391)	(0.0109)
No climate disaster # Conflict	0.0317	0.102	0.113	0.0312	0.0520**	-0.121	N/E	-0.0432	0.0328*	0.159*	0.0105	-0.128***
	(0.0345)	(0.0969)	(0.144)	(0.0325)	(0.0264)	(0.114)	N/E	(0.0319)	(0.0175)	(0.0943)	(0.176)	(0.0299)
Climate disaster # No conflict	-0.0392***	-0.122**	-0.0675**	-0.0350**	-0.0447***	-0.128*	-0.0124	-0.0767***	0.0246	0.0239	0.0416	-0.100***
	(0.0140)	(0.0546)	(0.0324)	(0.0148)	(0.0134)	(0.0705)	(0.0380)	(0.0131)	(0.0157)	(0.0558)	(0.0325)	(0.0157)
Climate disaster # Conflict	0.0528**	0.0476	0.159	0.00706	0.0761***	0.0561	-0.179	-0.0886***	0.0217	-0.0749	0.0488	-0.0956***
	(0.0270)	(0.113)	(0.194)	(0.0284)	(0.0179)	(0.114)	(0.184)	(0.0261)	(0.0304)	(0.0976)	(0.211)	(0.0282)
Other controls	Yes	Yes	Yes	Yes	Yes	Yes	Yes	Yes	Yes	Yes	Yes	Yes
Observations	40,018	4,873	3,436	21,773	40,018	4,873	3,419	21,773	40,018	4,873	3,436	21,773

Note: reference group = non-poor for Afghanistan and Kenya cross-section data, and resilient for Ethiopia, Niger and Nigeria panel data; N/E = not estimable due to small cell sizes for interacted variables; Robust standard errors in parentheses; *** p<0.01, ** p<0.05, * p<0.1.

Table D5 Relationship between economic crises, climate-related disasters and livelihood moderators [outcome = chronic or transient poverty], logistic regressions conducted on full sample of households in humanitarian context countries

	Afghanistan			*Nigeria*		
	Land	*Livestock*	*NFE*	*Land*	*Livestock*	*NFE*
No climate disaster # No conflict # No econ. crisis	-0.00353	0.00779	0.0107	0.135***	0.0884*	0.0150
	(0.0178)	(0.0192)	(0.0279)	(0.0469)	(0.0537)	(0.0395)
No climate disaster # No conflict # Econ. Crisis	-0.00123	-0.0172	-0.0576**	0.0208	0.00122	0.0643
	(0.0218)	(0.0196)	(0.0288)	(0.0607)	(0.0547)	(0.0406)
No climate disaster # Conflict # No econ. Crisis	0.000181	0.00192	0.0391	0.308**	0.377***	-0.0165
	(0.0410)	(0.0425)	(0.0559)	(0.150)	(0.138)	(0.112)
No climate disaster # Conflict # Econ. crisis	0.0473	0.0347	-0.0538	N/E	N/E	N/E
	(0.0395)	(0.0413)	(0.0461)	N/E	N/E	N/E
Climate disaster # No conflict # No econ. crisis	0.00139	-0.00643	-0.0833**	0.0623	0.0886	0.0646
	(0.0308)	(0.0326)	(0.0369)	(0.0893)	(0.0700)	(0.0695)
Climate disaster # No conflict # Econ. crisis	-0.0105	-0.0657***	-0.0685**	-0.0674	0.0795	0.0639
	(0.0213)	(0.0203)	(0.0269)	(0.114)	(0.105)	(0.0830)
Climate disaster # Conflict # No econ. crisis	-0.0697	0.0549	0.0305	0.00517	-0.0932	0.224
	(0.0775)	(0.0774)	(0.0725)	(0.114)	(0.114)	(0.167)
Climate disaster # Conflict # Econ. crisis	0.0451	0.0113	0.0584	0.00736	-0.122	0.0629
	(0.0379)	(0.0400)	(0.0508)	(0.202)	(0.159)	(0.141)
Other controls	Yes	Yes	Yes	Yes	Yes	Yes
Observations	18,116	18,116	18,116	1,322	1,322	1,322

Note: reference group = non-poor for Afghanistan cross-section data, and resilient for Nigeria panel data; robust standard errors in parentheses; N/E = not estimable due to small cell sizes for interacted variables; *** $p<0.01$, ** $p<0.05$, * $p<0.1$.

Table D6 Relationship between economic crises, climate-related disasters and education moderators [outcome = chronic or transient poverty], logistic regressions conducted on full sample of households in economic crisis-affected countries

Interactions	*Lower Sec. educ. completion of head*				*Pri. educ. completion of head*			
	Malawi	*Bangladesh*	*Tanzania*	*Zambia*	*Malawi*	*Bangladesh*	*Tanzania*	*Zambia*
No climate disaster # No economic crisis	-0.139***	-0.0476	N/E	-0.0707***	-0.0390	-0.0332	N/E	0.00541
	(0.0363)	(0.0498)	N/E	(0.0176)	(0.0417)	(0.0396)	N/E	(0.0163)
No climate disaster # Economic crisis	-0.159***	N/E	-0.444**	-0.0725***	-0.105*	N/E	-0.216***	0.00543
	(0.0475)	N/E	(0.219)	(0.0179)	(0.0588)	N/E	(0.0811)	(0.0171)
Climate disaster # No economic crisis	-0.221***	-0.0948***	-0.197	-0.0521*	-0.0849*	-0.0352**	0.00642	-0.00957
	(0.0457)	(0.0133)	(0.235)	(0.0301)	(0.0507)	(0.0141)	(0.135)	(0.0299)
Climate disaster # Economic crisis	-0.134***	-0.0676	-0.225	-0.0553*	-0.0555	-0.0999**	-0.104*	-0.00923
	(0.0514)	(0.0542)	(0.191)	(0.0319)	(0.0510)	(0.0423)	(0.0615)	(0.0321)
Other controls	Yes	Yes	Yes	Yes	Yes	Yes	Yes	Yes
Observations	3,078	5,004	750	8,307	3,078	4,972	749	8,307

Note: reference group = non-poor for Zambia cross-section data, and resilient for Malawi, Bangladesh and Tanzania panel data; N/E = not estimable due to small cell sizes for interacted variables; Robust standard errors in parentheses; *** $p<0.01$, ** $p<0.05$, * $p<0.1$.

Table D7 Relationship between economic crises, climate-related disasters and education moderators [outcome = chronic or transient poverty], logistic regressions conducted on full sample of households in conflict-affected countries

Interactions	*Lower Sec. educ. completion of head*						*Pri. educ. completion of head*					
	India	*Ethiopia*	*Niger*	*Kenya*	*Afghanistan*	*Nigeria*	*India*	*Ethiopia*	*Niger*	*Kenya*	*Afghanistan*	*Nigeria*
No climate disaster # No conflict	-0.0700***	-0.176***	N/E	-0.250***	-0.132***	-0.121**	-0.0315***	-0.0626*	-0.0822	-0.0734***	-0.0512***	-0.0739
	(0.0121)	(0.0330)	N/E	(0.0142)	(0.0157)	(0.0490)	(0.00871)	(0.0366)	(0.0564)	(0.0137)	(0.0187)	(0.0455)
No climate disaster # Conflict	-0.0871***	N/E	0.274	-0.221***	-0.112***	-0.184*	-0.0376*	-0.201**	N/E	-0.0606*	-0.0908**	-0.00591
	(0.0279)	N/E	(0.187)	(0.0309)	(0.0429)	(0.108)	(0.0206)	(0.0980)	N/E	(0.0330)	(0.0451)	(0.0661)
Climate disaster # No conflict	-0.0677***	-0.0374	-0.290***	-0.227***	-0.122***	-0.0685	-0.0454***	0.0931*	-0.0855	-0.103***	-0.0162	0.0110
	(0.0148)	(0.0585)	(0.0907)	(0.0165)	(0.0207)	(0.0684)	(0.0101)	(0.0549)	(0.0652)	(0.0146)	(0.0230)	(0.0815)
Climate disaster # Conflict	-0.144***	-0.00605	N/E	-0.194***	-0.0927**	0.0424	-0.0638**	0.0260	N/E	-0.102***	-0.0693	0.0379
	(0.0290)	(0.104)	N/E	(0.0270)	(0.0461)	(0.127)	(0.0256)	(0.169)	N/E	(0.0245)	(0.0537)	(0.193)
Other controls	Yes	Yes	Yes	Yes	Yes	Yes	Yes	Yes	Yes	Yes	Yes	Yes
Observations	40,018	4,832	3,217	21,773	18,116	1,322	40,018	4,873	3,429	21,773	18,116	1,322

Note: reference group = non-poor for Afghanistan and Kenya cross-section data, and resilient for Ethiopia, Niger and Nigeria panel data; N/E= not estimable due to small cell sizes for interacted variables; robust standard errors in parentheses; *** p<0.01, ** p<0.05, * p<0.1.

Table D8 Correlates of poverty (dynamics), (multinomial) logistic regressions conducted on subset of households experiencing climate-related disasters in conflict-affected countries

	Afghanistan	*Kenya*	*India*		*Ethiopia*		*Niger*		*Nigeria*	
VARIABLES	Poor	Poor	Chronic poor	Transient poor	Chronic poor	Transient poor	Chronic poor	Transient poor	Chronic poor	Transient poor
Cultivable land	0.150	-0.123	-0.0528	0.151	-0.968	-0.525	-0.288	-0.455**	0.426	-0.463
	(0.106)	(0.0998)	(0.154)	(0.149)	(0.702)	(0.453)	(0.231)	(0.208)	(0.946)	(0.527)
Livestock	-0.185	-0.554***	-0.138	0.0427	0.993	-0.674	-0.237	-0.0967	1.303**	0.379
	(0.113)	(0.0802)	(0.132)	(0.162)	(0.875)	(0.519)	(0.264)	(0.278)	(0.613)	(0.518)
Non-farm enterprise	-0.216*	-0.590***	0.212	0.303*	-1.056**	0.260	0.0594	0.278	-0.218	0.572
	(0.128)	(0.100)	(0.151)	(0.179)	(0.492)	(0.299)	(0.188)	(0.225)	(0.543)	(0.371)
Violent conflict	-0.0418	-0.104	0.457	0.00573	0.622	-0.0178	0.0206	0.365	-0.808	-1.315**
	(0.128)	(0.0967)	(0.297)	(0.323)	(0.403)	(0.382)	(0.695)	(0.759)	(0.949)	(0.619)
Conflict # Lower Secondary Education	0.277	0.210	-0.404	-1.467**	-19.40***	1.417*	19.25***	28.84***	-0.276	0.975
	(0.303)	(0.208)	(0.523)	(0.617)	(1.246)	(0.737)	(1.190)	(1.846)	(1.129)	(0.892)
Economic shocks	0.205*	-0.0551	0.390	0.189	0.553	0.495	-0.434**	0.000138	-0.0396	0.615*
	(0.119)	(0.0880)	(0.290)	(0.337)	(0.380)	(0.362)	(0.196)	(0.291)	(0.416)	(0.346)
Household size	0.328***	0.284***	0.0881***	-0.0608**	0.302***	0.237***	0.269***	0.0313	0.730***	0.379***
	(0.0226)	(0.0169)	(0.0162)	(0.0245)	(0.0651)	(0.0783)	(0.0353)	(0.0411)	(0.120)	(0.0981)
Primary education	-0.106	-0.494***	-0.513***	-0.319**	1.129***	0.146	-0.337	-0.697	0.0804	0.308
	(0.149)	(0.103)	(0.136)	(0.157)	(0.404)	(0.359)	(0.397)	(0.681)	(0.568)	(0.674)
Lower secondary educ.	-0.530***	-1.347***	-0.777***	-0.646**	0.362	-0.516	-20.25***	-1.253	-0.237	-0.0861
	(0.127)	(0.136)	(0.253)	(0.268)	(0.560)	(0.473)	(0.589)	(1.090)	(0.586)	(0.588)

	Afghanistan	Kenya	India		Ethiopia		Niger		Nigeria	
Head in agriculture	0.236**	0.103	-0.0226	-0.227	-0.0521	-0.326	0.602*	0.122	1.211*	0.496
	(0.103)	(0.0747)	(0.140)	(0.143)	(0.371)	(0.415)	(0.365)	(0.503)	(0.679)	(0.385)
Remittances	-0.0801	-0.0118	-0.863**	-0.193	-1.804**	0.201	0.132	0.267	-22.85***	0.100
	(0.136)	(0.0843)	(0.355)	(0.280)	(0.768)	(0.293)	(0.164)	(0.222)	(1.221)	(1.038)
Electricity	-0.426***	-0.365*	0.191	0.0417	-1.580	0.315	-1.564**	-0.258	-1.198*	-0.749*
	(0.139)	(0.197)	(0.164)	(0.182)	(1.255)	(0.533)	(0.765)	(0.528)	(0.655)	(0.399)
Assets	-1.241***	N/A	-8.734***	-3.168***	-0.425**	-0.559***	-0.155***	0.0666	-0.350***	-0.119**
	(0.0870)	N/A	(0.781)	(0.659)	(0.175)	(0.153)	(0.0388)	(0.0623)	(0.0850)	(0.0601)
Urban residence	0.717***	0.0793	0.783**	0.226	-1.411*	-0.921*	-0.811	-1.918***	-0.571	-0.678
	(0.195)	(0.132)	(0.320)	(0.288)	(0.775)	(0.556)	(0.546)	(0.663)	(1.286)	(0.633)
Constant	10.47***	-3.331**	1.085**	-0.968*	-2.897	0.906	-3.502***	-3.138**	1.007	1.344
	(0.935)	(1.352)	(0.524)	(0.560)	(2.071)	(1.414)	(1.257)	(1.446)	(2.279)	(1.657)
Region controls	Yes	Yes	Yes		Yes		Yes		Yes	
Head demographic controls	Yes	Yes	Yes		Yes		Yes		Yes	
Pseudo R2	0.261	0.189	0.128		0.167		0.168		0.315	
Observations	6,628	8,078	7,872		1,117		1,359		415	

Note: reference group = non-poor for Afghanistan and Kenya cross-section data, and resilient for Ethiopia, Niger and Nigeria panel data; robust standard errors in parentheses; *** p<0.01, ** p<0.05, * p<0.1.

Table D9 Correlates of poverty (dynamics), (multinomial) logistic regressions conducted on subset of households experiencing climate-related disasters in economic crisis-affected countries

	Zambia	*Malawi*		*Bangladesh*		*Tanzania*	
VARIABLES	*Poor*	*Chronic poor*	*Transient poor*	*Chronic poor*	*Transient poor*	*Chronic poor*	*Transient poor*
Cultivable land	N/A	-0.0917	-0.0663	-0.525*	-0.456***	N/A	N/A
	N/A	(0.264)	(0.275)	(0.300)	(0.118)	N/A	N/A
Livestock	-0.618***	-0.442**	0.0670	-0.441*	0.0858	-0.978	-0.0958
	(0.223)	(0.186)	(0.188)	(0.248)	(0.112)	(0.807)	(0.364)
Non-farm enterprise	-0.460**	0.410	0.207	-0.0991	-0.0588	0.460	0.222
	(0.188)	(0.397)	(0.361)	(0.287)	(0.104)	(0.585)	(0.453)
Violent conflict	-1.541*	-0.518**	-0.194	0.915**	0.0767	-2.406**	-1.014**
	(0.871)	(0.261)	(0.298)	(0.395)	(0.185)	(1.219)	(0.448)
Economic shocks	-0.0673	0.0653	-0.0892	0.873**	-0.0290	0.615	0.791**
	(0.218)	(0.153)	(0.180)	(0.415)	(0.201)	(0.506)	(0.350)
Economic # Lower Secondary Education	-0.0298	0.664	0.637	0.434	0.109	1.484	-0.530
	(0.421)	(0.610)	(0.497)	(1.161)	(0.638)	(2.581)	(2.039)
Household size	0.293***	0.473***	0.132**	0.646***	0.215***	0.283***	0.138***
	(0.0450)	(0.0430)	(0.0520)	(0.0696)	(0.0301)	(0.0904)	(0.0506)
Primary education	-0.0193	-0.316	-0.441	-0.681*	-0.383***	-0.371	-0.585
	(0.253)	(0.248)	(0.274)	(0.388)	(0.134)	(0.463)	(0.376)
Lower secondary education	-0.337	-1.658***	-1.123***	-0.659	-1.036***	-21.76***	-1.706
	(0.280)	(0.465)	(0.390)	(0.496)	(0.178)	(2.157)	(1.338)

	Zambia	Malawi		Bangladesh		Tanzania	
Head in agriculture	0.388*	-0.00132	-0.188	0.773***	-0.0884	0.238	0.597
	(0.213)	(0.158)	(0.185)	(0.297)	(0.113)	(1.025)	(0.398)
Remittances	0.335	-0.210	-0.0563	0.267	-0.146	-0.0402	0.491*
	(0.242)	(0.159)	(0.156)	(0.426)	(0.145)	(0.651)	(0.272)
Electricity	-1.288***	-22.00***	-2.213***	-1.253***	-0.678***	-23.16***	-0.546
	(0.343)	(0.599)	(0.576)	(0.369)	(0.122)	(1.684)	(0.591)
Assets	-0.425***	-0.170***	0.0165	-0.998***	-0.519***	-0.0535***	-0.00582
	(0.0584)	(0.0232)	(0.0246)	(0.114)	(0.0467)	(0.0196)	(0.00400)
Urban residence	-1.164***	-0.136	0.260	N/A	N/A	-2.791**	-0.459
	(0.276)	(0.628)	(0.376)	N/A	N/A	(1.261)	(0.516)
Constant	2.729***	-0.756	-0.213	6.689***	5.902***	0.345	-0.219
	(0.941)	(0.697)	(0.742)	(1.431)	(0.601)	(3.752)	(1.980)
Region controls	Yes	Yes		Yes		Yes	
Head demographic controls	Yes	Yes		Yes		Yes	
Pseudo R2	0.244	0.126		0.201		0.265	
Observations	1,609	1,548		4,634		651	

Note: reference group = non-poor for Zambia cross-section data, and resilient for Malawi, Bangladesh and Tanzania panel data; robust standard errors in parentheses; *** p<0.01, ** p<0.05, * p<0.1.

Index

Note: *Italic* page number refer to *figures* and **Bold** page number refer to **tables**.

For Product Safety Concerns and Information please contact our EU
representative GPSR@taylorandfrancis.com
Taylor & Francis Verlag GmbH, Kaufingerstraße 24, 80331 München, Germany

www.ingramcontent.com/pod-product-compliance
Ingram Content Group UK Ltd.
Pitfield, Milton Keynes, MK11 3LW, UK
UKHW020152200926
475702UK00016B/2667
9781032821344